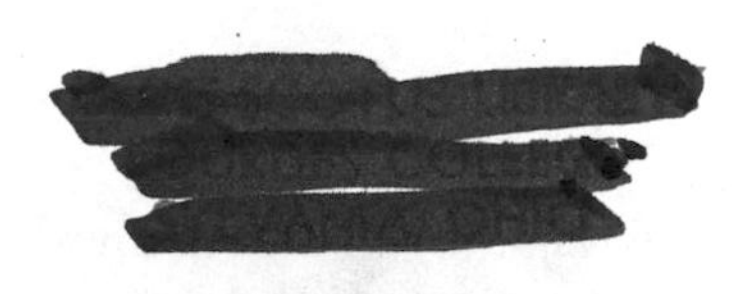

EMORY UNIVERSITY STUDIES IN LAW AND RELIGION

John Witte Jr., General Editor

BOOKS IN THE SERIES

Faith and Order: The Reconciliation of Law and Religion
Harold J. Berman

Rediscovering the Natural Law in Reformed Theological Ethics
Stephen J. Grabill

Lex Charitatis: A Juristic Disquisition on Law in the Theology of Martin Luther
Johannes Heckel

The Best Love of the Child: Being Loved and Being Taught to Love as the First Human Right
Timothy P. Jackson, ed.

The Ten Commandments in History: Mosaic Paradigms for a Well-Ordered Society
Paul Grimley Kuntz

Religious Liberty, Volume 1: Overviews and History
Douglas Laycock

Religious Liberty, Volume 2:
Douglas

Building Cult
Martin E.

Suing for America's Soul: John Whitehead, The Rutherford Institute, and Conservative Christians in the Courts
R. Jonathan Moore

Theology of Law and Authority in the English Reformation
Joan Lockwood O'Donovan

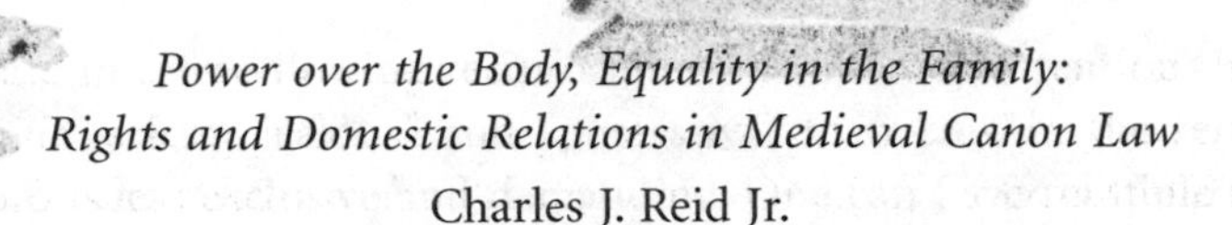

Power over the Body, Equality in the Family: Rights and Domestic Relations in Medieval Canon Law
Charles J. Reid Jr.

Religious Liberty in Western Thought
Noel B. Reynolds and W. Cole Durham Jr., eds.

Political Order and the Plural Structure of Society
James W. Skillen and Rockne M. McCarthy, eds.

The Idea of Natural Rights: Studies on Natural Rights, Natural Law, and Church Law, 1150-1625
Brian Tierney

The Fabric of Hope: An Essay
Glenn Tinder

Liberty: Rethinking an Imperiled Ideal
Glenn Tinder

Religious Human Rights in Global Perspective: Legal Perspectives
Johan D. van der Vyver and John Witte Jr., eds.

Natural Law and the Two Kingdoms: A Study in the Development of Reformed Social Thought
David VanDrunen

Early New England: A Covenanted Society
David A. Weir

God's Joust, God's Justice: Law and Religion in the Western Tradition
John Witte Jr.

Religious Human Rights in Global Perspective: Religious Perspectives
John Witte Jr. and Johan D. van der Vyver, eds.

Justice in Love
Nicholas Wolterstorff

The Best Love of the Child

Being Loved and Being Taught to Love as the First Human Right

Edited by

Timothy P. Jackson

William B. Eerdmans Publishing Company
Grand Rapids, Michigan / Cambridge, U.K.

Published 2011 by
Wm. B. Eerdmans Publishing Co.
2140 Oak Industrial Drive N.E., Grand Rapids, Michigan 49505 /
P.O. Box 163, Cambridge CB3 9PU U.K.

Printed in the United States of America

17 16 15 14 13 12 11 7 6 5 4 3 2 1

Library of Congress Cataloging-in-Publication Data

The best love of the child: being loved and being taught
to love as the first human right / edited by Timothy P. Jackson.
p. cm. — (Emory University studies in law and religion)
Includes bibliographical references.
ISBN 978-0-8028-6539-7 (pbk.: alk. paper)
1. Child rearing — Religious aspects — Christianity.
2. Love — Religious aspects — Christianity.
I. Jackson, Timothy P. (Timothy Patrick)

BV4529.B48 2011
248.8′45 — dc22

2010041743

www.eerdmans.com

This volume is dedicated to

Don S. Browning

(1934-2010)

sage scholar, beloved friend,
and the intellectual father
of many of us concerned with
children and the family

Contents

Foreword x
John Witte Jr.

Preface: Love Begets Love xiii
Stephen G. Post

Editor's Acknowledgments xxv

General Introduction 1
Timothy P. Jackson

Part I: Social-Psychological Perspectives

1. When "Good Enough" Isn't Really Good Enough: Aiming for the "Best" for All Young People 19
Peter L. Benson and Eugene C. Roehlkepartain

2. Does Best Love of the Child Mean Parents Should Facilitate a Love of the Sacred? 47
Annette Mahoney and Ken I. Pargament

3. Parent-Child Reminiscing: Creating Best Love through Sharing Stories 71
Robyn Fivush

Part II: Historical Perspectives

4. Raising a Loving Child in Late Medieval and Early Modern Europe (1400-1700) 93
Steven Ozment

5. The Duties of Love: The Vocation of the Child in the Household Manual Tradition 113
John Witte Jr. and Heather M. Johnson

6. The Right to Life and Its Application to the Welfare of Children in the Canon Law and the Magisterium of the Catholic Church: 1878 to the Present 142
Charles J. Reid Jr.

Part III: Philosophical and Theological Perspectives

7. Collective Responsibility for Children in an Age of Orphans 179
Cynthia Willett

8. Original Sin and Christian Parenting: A Constructive Proposal 197
Richard R. Osmer

9. "Best Practices" for Nurturing the Best Love of and by Children: A Protestant Theological Perspective on the Vocations of Children and Parents 226
Marcia J. Bunge

Part IV: Legal Perspectives

10. What's Love Got to Do with It? (Part I): Loving Children in Cases of Divorce or Death in the Jewish Tradition 253
Michael J. Broyde

11. What's Love Got to Do with It? (Part II): The Best Interests of the Child in International and Comparative Law 277
Rana Lehr-Lehnardt and T. Jeremy Gunn

12. Can Law Shape the Development of Unconditional Love in Children? 317
Margaret F. Brinig and Steven L. Nock†

13. The Best Love of the Child? An Integrational View 347
Don S. Browning†

Contributors 373

Index 379

Foreword

The goal of this volume is to offer a complement, if not corrective, to the "best interest of the child" logic that still dominates modern legal and social science discussions of children. The twenty contributors herein argue that talk of children's rights needs to be balanced by talk of children's duties, and that calculations of a child's legal entitlements need to be based on the child's natural needs and stage of development. The premise of their argument is that the most important right of the child is the right to be loved and the right to learn to love others. This insight can be traced to some of the earliest philosophers, theologians, and jurists in the West, and it is being rediscovered anew in the latest social science and humanities literature on healthy child development. The pages that follow make out that case.

None of the contributors herein denies the enormous benefit brought to children by the rise of "children's rights" in the past century. One would be hard-pressed today to defend some traditional legal structures that rendered children the exclusive property and prerogative of the *paterfamilias,* and left states and private parties with little recourse in the event of parental abuse or neglect. One would also be hard-pressed today to deny that a child has inherent rights to life, to a name, home, and family, to food, shelter, education, healthcare, and vocational opportunity, to freedom from abuse, cruelty, neglect, or abandonment, to protection from enslavement, exploitation, or trafficking, and more. Children are the most voiceless, voteless, and vulnerable among us, rendering protection of their rights indispensable both domestically and internationally. How, why, when, by whom, and against whom these children's rights are vindicated are questions that merit the kind of reasonable discussion found in these pages. But no one herein disputes the fact that all children have basic rights.

The issue is how best to vindicate these rights for children in different cultures and societies, and at different stages of their physical, emotional, sexual, moral, and religious development. Here rights talk alone provides an insufficient guide to discuss the special needs and concerns, interests and aspirations, callings and duties of children. The authors thus summon the wisdom and methods of various disciplines — theology, philosophy, ethics, history, psychology, anthropology, law, and education theory — to propose a more nuanced guide of what's best for the children we love and who love us. Particularly critical for the development and protection of children, a number of contributors argue, is the place of religious instruction and participation, of family cohesion and narratives, of communal commitment and investment.

This volume is part and product of a major project on the "The Child in Law, Religion, and Society," undertaken by our Center for the Study of Law and Religion at Emory University. Our project as a whole is focused on children *qua* children — in their being and becoming, in their birth and growth. As a team of twenty scholars, directed by Professor Martin E. Marty, we are studying the rites and rights attached to birthing and naming, baptism and circumcision, education and discipline. We are examining the steps and stages in a child's physical, emotional, sexual, moral, and spiritual formation, as well as the rituals and ordeals, and the rights and responsibilities, attached to each. We are examining the pathos of child abuse and rape, child poverty and homelessness, juvenile delinquency and violence, and illegitimacy and infanticide. And, we are probing the mystery of the child — that combination of innocence and imagination, acuity and candor, empathy and healing, sharing and caring that uniquely become a child.

On behalf of my Center colleagues, I wish to express our deep gratitude to The Pew Charitable Trusts and The John Templeton Foundation for their generous funding, and to the contributors to this volume for lending their time and talents so generously. I express our deep gratitude to Professor Stephen Post, President of the Institute for Research on Unlimited Love, for his astute advice on the development of this project and his generous efforts to secure ample funding. Special thanks as well to our Emory Center colleagues, April Bogle, Eliza Ellison, Anita Mann, Linda King, and Amy Wheeler for their excellence in staffing this project on children, which is scheduled to yield a score of other volumes besides this one. Readers who are particularly taken with this volume might wish to read two complementary volumes that have also emerged from this child project — a legal symposium titled "What's Wrong with Rights for Children?" (*Emory International Law Review* 20 [2006]: 1-239) and an anthology edited by the distinguished Catholic jurist, Patrick M. Brennan, *The Vocation of the Child* (Eerdmans, 2008).

This volume on "the best love of the child," owes much to the inspiration and insight of its editor Professor Timothy P. Jackson. One of the nation's leading Christian ethicists, Professor Jackson has devoted a good deal of his career to mapping the intellectual architecture and practical ethics of the virtue of love. His twin volumes, *Love Disconsoled* (Cambridge University Press, 1999) and *The Priority of Love* (Princeton University Press, 2003), will long endure as classic treatments of the complex commandments and counsels of love. His interdisciplinary insights into love are on full display in this volume. Like his earlier interdisciplinary anthology, *The Morality of Adoption* (Eerdmans, 2005), this volume draws judiciously and expertly from a variety of disciplines to provide a kaleidoscopic tour of what truly is the best love of the child.

JOHN WITTE JR.
Director, Center for the Study of Law and Religion
Emory University

Preface: Love Begets Love

Stephen G. Post

A common aspiration is to raise a child who will do "unto others" through a readiness to help the poor, treat the ill with compassion, volunteer after a catastrophe, or perhaps rescue the innocent from annihilation. This book is titled *The Best Love of the Child.* It should be read as a challenge not just to Christians, but to people of all faiths, for the "best love" of the child is one that begets love in the child over the course of a lifetime.

We need the concerted effort of our best minds to better understand and implement the power of love in the lives that we parents bring into the world. This is the great revolution that has not yet quite happened, and it is just as much a part of "pro-creation" as is producing a biological being. We can design a better human future though parental love at its best. This is an infinitely more plausible vision than all the misplaced aspirations to create human "perfection" though the power of biological science to tinker with our bodies. There is a passage in 1 John: "God is love, and those who abide in love abide in God and God abides in them." The best we can do for our children is to give them every opportunity to discover the joy and nobility that love brings to a life.

It Begins with Parents

This best love of the child begins with the dynamic of love in our marriages. The great Harvard sociologist Pitirim Sorokin, writing in 1954, pointed out how unless husband and wife have a flow of love between them, they cannot model or transmit it to their children. In a passage that is of perennial significance, Sorokin wrote:

> As a general rule the families with prevalent discordant relationships among their members, especially between husband and wife, where a newly born baby is unwelcomed, where it is deprived of the grace of love and from its early days breathes the poisonous air of discord and enmity in the relationship of the members of the family to itself and to one another; where there is neither a set of high values preached and practiced, nor wise and loving discipline combined with creative freedom; such families tend to produce morally erratic persons, little capable of self-control, selfishly irresponsible, careless of the interests and well-being of others, and frequently criminal or delinquent. (2002, pp. 194-95)

Conversely, where marriages are characterized by the vision of love, harmonious relationships, and wisdom, their children are more likely to be caring, compassionate, and morally creative. The love of a harmonious couple is a foundation for the development of a loving child. This is why so many parents determine not to fight in front of their kids in those inevitable moments of conflict.

Sorokin's words are based in good science. Researchers, for example, have probed the lives of people who rescued Jewish children during the Holocaust. It turns out that so much goes back to how they were raised. Rescuers had one or more of the following assets as children: tender loving care in their homes, discipline with explanations and discussion around such ideals as the Golden Rule, an emphasis on independence of mind, an altruistic model in a parent or a non-parent mentor, a respect for people who are different, and a childhood illness or loss that tested them and gave them courage. Studies show that about half of the rescuers acted because they could not live with the guilt of doing otherwise, another 10 percent because they adhered to ethical principle, and the rest because they were moved by compassion. As parents we want to raise the kind of children who care not just for the nearest and dearest, but who lean outward to the neediest and a shared humanity. Research shows us that such children do not emerge from a vacuum, but from families that shape them into being people of deep concern. Clearly rescuing behaviors grew out of patterns of relating to others that were established early in life (Oliner & Oliner, 1988).

Sorokin's famous studies of "good neighbors" in the United States date back to the 1950s. He looked at large numbers of people who were identified by their peers as generous, kind, and helpful people. When asked to state the factors that contributed to their good neighborliness, 21 percent indicated religion, 29 percent parental and family training, 8 percent education and schooling, 11 percent personal experience, 28 percent universal life experience, and less than one percent mentioned books. He concluded from these data, and other similar findings, that the single most important factor in the "altruization" of humanity is the family and parents, followed by general life experience (minus family and religion), and then by religion, the second most important single factor involved in creating goodness. The role of educational institutions is modest, by which he meant efforts to "teach" goodness didactically in a classroom (Sorokin, 1950, p. 57).

The bottom line is that loved people love people, while hurt people hurt people, and this is all set in motion in the early years. This dynamic begins even at birth. Developmental psychologist Mary Ainsworth of Johns Hopkins University found that the kind of mother a baby has predicts emotional traits later in life (1978), though much the same can surely be said for the kind of father a baby has. She observed interactions between mothers and infants and divided the mothering styles into three categories. Then a year later she tested the emotional qualities of the toddlers by observing their responses to brief separations. Mothers who had been warm, tender, and consistently responsive raised "secure" toddlers who used their mother as a safe haven from which to explore the environment. Such toddlers were fussy and upset when their mothers left the room, but reached out to them in smiles when they returned. When their mothers picked them up they were easy to console. These toddlers were "secure." By contrast, a cold, resentful mother produced an "insecure-avoidant" toddler who was indifferent to the mother's departures and ignored her return, focusing instead on such items as a toy object in a corner. Another group of toddlers were clingy with their mothers, refused to explore the room independently, and became anxious and agitated when their mothers left the room. They also cried frequently. When the mothers returned the toddlers reached out, but arched away and resisted the mother's attempts to console them. These toddlers had experienced inconsistent and erratic emotional interactions during their first year of life. Ainsworth called them "insecure-ambivalent" toddlers.

What happened to these toddlers as they grew older? The securely attached developed into empathic, caring, happy, resilient, likable grade-schoolers with more friends and a tendency to seek out help when needed. The infants of cold mothers became distant, hostile to authority, and difficult-to-reach grade-schoolers. In addition, they would not ask for comfort even if hurt, and they had a mean streak that included a tendency to provoke and upset other kids. These adolescents, poorly loved in infancy and childhood, were aggressive and hurtful. The infants of inconsistent and erratic mothers were timid, lacking in confidence, easily frustrated, and asked for help even when they could do things for themselves. Followed into their twenties, the insecurely attached showed susceptibility in adolescence to delinquency, substance abuse, pregnancy, and other problems, and they were less popular.

So what goes on in that dynamic between a mother and an infant matters a lot. Tender loving care leads to emotional health and fosters empathy and caring in those of us who are fortunate enough to have experienced it as infants. The key is an infant's experiencing consistent, empathic, soothing interactions with the caregiver. It is also important that the caregiver's facial expressions mirror the baby's sadness or joy, creating comfort and trust. When the baby experiences no response, or harsh and hostile responses, the baby feels distrust and fear. So when a caregiver interacts in a dance of joyful empathy with an infant, a whole emotional soul is being created bit by bit. There are innumerable small acts done with great love, from the humming of a soothing melody to a deep mutual gaze. Under conditions of secure attachment, even more neuronal synapses are created than would be the case were the baby in a state of isolation and fear.

While these early years are not fully determinative, and while deficits can be overcome with counseling, later relationships, and the right community, psychologists recognize that these early years dispose us toward love, or toward its many opposites such as fear, hostility, hatred, and indifference, all of which are rooted in the neural circuits of "fight-flight" rather than "care-connection." We all have both kinds of neural circuits, but these early relationships in the family push one or the other into dominance.

Love deprivation in the first several years of life, when the foundations of empathy, trust, and conscience are established, has devastating consequences. In monkeys that have access only to a wire mother-like entity with a milk bottle, the result is high anxiety, avoidant behavior, a failure to express empathy, and a failure to thrive physically (Harlow, 1951). Yes, we can place our trust in the work of Godly love in the lives of our children later in life, but such sudden transformations might not be necessary were we as parents better able to model and sustain love. *It is much easier to nurture creative givers in the garden of the family and faith community from infancy and childhood than it is to transform a selfish adult into a generous person with a kind heart. Transformations happen, certainly, but are usually difficult for the indi-*

vidual, who must look upon early life as an obstacle to be overcome rather than a time of growth.

Only a certain minority of what William James referred to as "sick souls" find a rebirth into compassion, and usually through reintegration with non-family groups. It is more likely that those deprived of good parental love will live unfortunate lives, harmful to self and others, cynical, and conflicted. They are broken reeds who suffer through life, unless born anew through some powerful emotional dynamic, sometimes in the form of an unexpected and unmerited love from a spouse, a non-parent mentor, or some spiritual source. Why not take the easier path of raising children of love in a gradual and deliberate manner? Easier said than done, of course, and so many of us do our best but fall short. From our knees we pray to a God who is Father to us all that an Unlimited Love might do what we could not. This brings us to faith, and so many parents of newborns who have not been active in a faith community for years join one because they know that they are going to need such cultural support if goodness is to hold sway in their child's life.

It Takes a Faith Community

As Friedrich Nietzsche predicted, the family has to some degree been slowly ground down into a collection of random individuals pursuing selfish ends. The idea that marriage is a sacred institution in part because spouses are entrusted to raise children who can do good in the world is admittedly a way of thinking that flies in the face of the greed and materialism that permeate society. But I have only rarely met parents who do bring children into the world in the hope that they will be adults who live unselfish and good lives through developing their talents to contribute meaningfully to the lives around them. A community of faith that shares this vantage point is most helpful in transforming love as aspiration into reality.

Parents face a desperate challenge as they struggle against a culture that so often works against this noble aspiration. Christian parents of any denomination or tradition are in a constant battle to nurture their children in faith, hope, and love despite a world of shocking crudeness, hostility, and violence. Violent videogames and websites, bullying in schools, and the lyrics of some genres of music all pull our minds and emotions downward. The faith community is the only cultural institution that can provide an alternative, so parents need to partner with it.

Parents become saddened when their adolescent children are lost along the way, and they are in great need of a spiritual life to cope with this in patience, hope, and wisdom. The faith community provides a perspective on staying true to our children, no matter how wayward they become. The Parable of the Prodigal Son is so central for the parents of adolescents. It is about forgiving and embracing a young man, presumably a teen, who has squandered every asset his father provided. It is, in essence, the Parable of the Forgiving Father. It is important to remember, as Karl Barth stressed, that in the final analysis we are all adoptive parents, for God is the real parent who has an authority that we, as temporal parents, do not. There will be many deserts, many times when parents feel that only Godly love can plant a rose of joy in their hearts, for the difficult dynamics of adolescence and the desperate detours in growing up require a love that is unconditional, wise, and profoundly loyal. The allusion here is to Isaiah 35, to the desert and the rose. Sometimes parents grow weary and can only find tender loving care through the grace of God.

In the New Testament it is written, "We love because he first loved us" (1 John 4:19). How can the primary hope for Christian parents be other than raising a child who practices *agape* love, a love that is more enduring, efficient, and universal than our human nature alone can produce? It is a love inspired by the example of Jesus, and formed in the power of the Holy Spirit and a faith community that elevates us beyond the limits of human compassion alone.

From the Christian perspective, Jesus adored children and modeled love for them in remarkable ways. He saw a purity and love in their hearts that set the paradigm for those who would enter the kingdom of heaven. Jesus compared the essential love of God to the love of human parents: "If you then, who are evil, know how to give good gifts to your children, how much more will your Father in heaven give good gifts to those who ask him?" (Matt. 7:9-11). The nurture of the Christian child in a life of love has a central place in every faith community. They are exhorted to love, but much more important, they also see love in action and participate in it as they go beyond the doors to help in a nursing home or in the construction of a house for Habitat. Love is primarily transmitted from person to person, and our families and churches are meant to provide the context for this passing of the torch. We want children who bring a tender love to the world, for "God loves a cheerful giver" (2 Cor. 9:7). We want children who refuse to hate, and who love others not just "because of" their gifts and attributes, but "in spite of" their flaws and imperfections. We want children who know the love, joy, peace, patience, kindness, generosity, faithfulness, gentleness, and self-control that constitute the fruits of the Spirit (Gal. 5:22). We want them to feel the spiritual strength or "locus of control" over their external environment so that they can move forward in life and bring love and justice to those around them, regardless of circumstances.

Most of us can look back on our lives in faith communities and identify non-parents who loved us in those active and deeply emotional ways that sparked the same dynamic in our lives of giving. This may not have been "soft love." I do not like the language of "tough love" because it invites excess. But faith communities are good at *carefrontation* — at the art of speaking the truth to youth with love in a manner that builds up rather than tears down. We need to create a culture in which concern for others is discussed, and where the principle of the Golden Rule is established.

On the home front, a small suggestion is to keep posters and dictums around the home as wall hangings. In our home, we have a framed picture by Norman Rockwell titled *The Golden Rule* over the fireplace, and a poster that includes a dozen or more versions of the Rule from different religious traditions. When there are issues with our children or their friends, I ask them to tell me how what they are doing or saying lives up to the Rule. This is actually quite effective in raising a caring child, as researcher Nancy Eisenberg has shown (1992). A wise parent knows how to confront destructive and self-destructive behaviors with effective love that educates morally and builds character. If and when things get out of control and tensions mount, good family counseling is absolutely essential.

A Consistent Aspiration across Society

The African American poet Elizabeth Alexander wrote a poem titled "Praise Song for the Day," which she read at Barack Obama's Presidential Inauguration, one stanza of which is this:

> Some live by *love thy neighbor as thyself,*
> others by *first do no harm* or *take no more*
> *than you need.* What if the mightiest word is love?

It is the mightiest word. Families, schools, neighborhoods, businesses, health care settings, religions, politics, athletic teams, and media all can contribute to a seamless web in which love is encouraged, modeled, and rewarded with immensely positive outcomes. This is the way forward for our children, and there is no other way that will allow them to thrive and be free of a myriad of destructive and self-destructive attitudes and antisocial activities.

Ideally, all the institutional settings in which the child spends significant time can expect, model, organize, recognize, and celebrate loving behaviors. Communities can organize to bring schools, workplaces, sports teams, healthcare, and neighborhood associations into a seamless pattern of love. There are examples of this now around some areas of the United States.

Schools matter. As a boy in an Episcopal school in New Hampshire, I began to study *agape* love with the Reverend John Walker, who later became dean of the National Cathedral, and I tended to take more seriously than some the school prayer, which I repeated each morning in chapel:

> Grant, O Lord,
> That in all the joys of life we may never forget to be kind.
> Help us to be unselfish in friendship,
> Thoughtful of those less happy than ourselves,
> And eager to bear the burdens of others;
> Through Jesus Christ our Savior. *Amen.*

Good Christian parents spend their good money even in hard times to keep their children in Christian schools in the young and impressionable years, before it is too late. This is often a very wise investment. Families, churches, and schools all have to work together in the early formative years. The Montessori schools are useful because the older children, who are seventh- and eighth-graders, actively tutor and help the younger ones. Thus, helping behaviors are built into school life, and most children find that this inspires them to learn.

Boy Scouts and Girl Scouts provide children with opportunities to learn the value of service. Longitudinal studies highlight that participation in Scouts does in fact make a difference in many lives, encouraging a pro-social service approach over the years.

We need cultural systems — and media especially — that support love rather than selfishness, hate, conflict, rudeness, and other negative energies, systems that support the power of love in friendship, cooperation, and the pursuit of knowledge. With regard to maladaptive social behaviors, it is well documented that volunteering in adolescence helps prevent teen pregnancy and academic failure, enhances social competence and self-esteem, and protects against antisocial behaviors and substance abuse (Allen et al., 1997).

There is a health aspect to raising a caring child. Paul Wink and Michele

Dillon, in their research on generative adolescents becoming healthier adults (2007), present novel findings based on longitudinal data. Do generative qualities in adolescents predict better mental and physical health in adulthood? The authors address this question by examining data gathered from two adolescent research cohorts first interviewed in California in the 1930s and subsequently interviewed every ten years until the late 1990s. Generativity, defined as behavior indicative of intense positive emotion extending to all humanity, was measured in three dimensions: givingness; prosocial competence; social perspective. Using this multidimensional measure of generative behavior, the authors were able to isolate a potential mechanism underlying the generativity-health connection. The results of the study indicated that generative adolescents indeed do become both psychologically and physically healthier adults, and that this health effect is more pronounced in the psychological realm. They found that positive intrafamilial relationships strongly predicted generativity. The physical health effect appears to be the result of the prosocial competence dimension of generativity. Wink and Dillon's study lends crucial support to the notion that it is good to be good, and that the benefits of altruism accrue across the entire lifespan.

We need to recognize that colleges and universities have tremendous power to inhibit or encourage the power of love. One major survey suggests that college students are becoming more narcissistic. Sociologist Jean Twenge (2006) and colleagues examined the responses of 16,475 college students nationwide who completed an evaluation called the Narcissistic Personality Inventory (NPI) between 1982 and 2006. In 2006, two-thirds of students had above-average scores, 30 percent more than in 1982. Narcissists are more likely to have short-lived romantic relationships, to lack emotional warmth, and to exhibit dishonesty and over-controlling or violent behaviors. The authors trace this trend back to the self-esteem movement that began in the early 1980s and has simply gone too far with regard to permissiveness, overindulgence, and other cultural factors. Easy characterizations are rightly met with skepticism, but to the extent that this report is accurate, it is cause for concern. We must recognize this problem as a failure in college and university leadership and pedagogy. Colleges should take their mission to shape character more seriously, and many are doing so with success.

One of the healthiest things we can do for young people is to help them cultivate sincere giving activities in their lives. As a by-product, they can and will discover a set of emotions that are antithetical to hostility and self-preoccupation. This transformation of being and of doing seems to promote

tion and the Institute for Research on Unlimited Love (www.unlimited loveinstitute.com).

References

Ainsworth, M. M., M. Blehar, E. Waters, and S. Wall. (1978). *Patterns of attachment: A psychological study of the strange situation.* Mahwah, NJ: Erlbaum.

Allen, J. P., S. Philliber, S. Herrling, and G. P. Kuperminc. (1997). Preventing teen pregnancy and academic failure: Experimental evaluation of a developmentally based approach, *Child Development* 68: 729-42.

Eisenberg, N. (1992). *The caring child.* Cambridge, MA: Harvard University Press.

Harlow, H. F. (1951). The nature of love, *The American Psychologist* 13: 673-85.

Oliner, S. P., and P. Oliner. (1988). *The altruistic personality.* New York: Free Press.

Post, S. G., ed. (2007). *Altruism and health: Perspectives from empirical research.* New York: Oxford University Press.

Sorokin, P. A. (1950). *Altruistic love.* Boston: Beacon Press.

Sorokin, P. A. (2002). [1954 original]. *The ways and power of love: Types, factors, and techniques of moral transformation,* with an "Introduction" by S. G. Post. Philadelphia, PA: Templeton Press.

Twenge, J. (2006). *Generation me: Why today's young Americans are more confident, assertive, entitled — and more miserable than ever before.* New York: Free Press.

Wink, P., and M. Dillon. (2007). Do generative adolescents become healthy older adults? In S. G. Post, ed., *Altruism and health: Perspectives from empirical research.* New York: Oxford University Press, pp. 43-54.

Editor's Acknowledgments

The editor would like to express his immense gratitude to John Witte Jr. and Stephen Post for their invaluable assistance in inspiring and organizing this project. I would also like to thank The Pew Charitable Trusts, The John Templeton Foundation, The Institute for Research on Unlimited Love, and Emory's Center for the Study of Law and Religion for their generous financial support. A special word of appreciation is due to the contributors for their splendid essays in this volume, as well as to Kathryn Bryan for her expert transcription of our roundtable conversations and her copyediting of the manuscript. Without these sources of aid and insight, *The Best Love of the Child* would never have been conceived or delivered. Any remaining birthmarks are my own responsibility, of course.

ple. Adding to the challenge, only 37 percent of parents know and actively nourish teenagers' sparks. This is true across all demographic and socioeconomic groups. A result is that too many young people go through life with too little direction and purpose [illegible] Benson & Scales, 2009).

Integrating Spiritual Development into Understanding of Optimal Development

Noticeably absent from the rapidly expanding field in theory, research, and practice in child and adolescent development is the domain of spiritual development. A content analysis of Social Science Abstracts and PsycINFO [illegible] found that less than 1 percent of the articles and [illegible] of children and adolescents [illegible] addressed spirituality or religion (Benson, [illegible]). A parallel [illegible] religious studies, which have provided some suggestive explorations of children and childhood [illegible] have [illegible] and then [illegible] as an important theme (Benson, [illegible]).

[illegible] is [illegible] and important [illegible] people. UCLA's Higher Education Research Institute recently [illegible] the spiritual lives and interests of [illegible] colleges and universities. Three [illegible] of the students say they believe "we are all spiritual beings." The researchers also found that [illegible] college freshmen [illegible] interest in spirituality" and "believing in the sacredness of life," and nearly two thirds say that "my spirituality is a source of joy." [illegible] say it is "very important" to seek spiritual growth opportunities (Astin et al., [illegible]).

[illegible] growing [illegible] the academic and in practice [illegible] spiritual [illegible] into [illegible] developmental [illegible] Through its [illegible] Spiritual Development in Childhood and Adolescence [illegible] Search Institute has [illegible] building a broad consensus around [illegible] of spiritual development. Our core hypothesis is that every person develops spiritually, just as every person develops cognitively, emotionally, or socially. And [illegible] development, some young people [illegible]

General Introduction

TIMOTHY P. JACKSON

The Right to Be Loved and the Duty to Become Loving

Jesus Christ associated the kingdom of God with the humility of children (Matt. 18:3-4), while La Rochefoucauld called youth "a continual drunkenness," "the delirium of reason."[1] William Wordsworth recollected his childhood as bearing "the glory and freshness of a dream,"[2] while William Golding saw his as "a sickness that you grow out of."[3] Medieval Japanese Buddhists saw birth as "being induced into what is profane and bit by bit leaving a sacred dimension" and thus saw children as possessing "a positive kind of unworldliness."[4] In contrast, some Puritan clerics saw children as willful and fallen creatures who need to be disciplined, even "broken," by their parents and/or the church.[5] Thus has "the child" oscillated as a cultural icon, representing innocence and opportunity, something to be venerated and/or recaptured, but also embodying neediness and instability, something

1. François de La Rochefoucauld, *Collected Maxims and Other Reflections,* trans. E. H. Blackmore, A. M. Blackmore, and Francine Giguere (Oxford: Oxford University Press, 2008), p. 77.

2. Wordsworth, "Intimations of Immortality from Recollections of Early Childhood" (henceforth IOI).

3. Golding, quoted in the *Guardian,* June 22, 1990.

4. William R. LaFleur, *Liquid Life: Abortion and Buddhism in Japan* (Princeton: Princeton University Press, 1992), pp. 35 and 37.

5. See Marcia Bunge, ed., *The Child in Christian Thought* (Grand Rapids: Eerdmans, 2001).

to be lamented and/or overcome. This ambivalence is as old as Herod's paranoia and Joseph's magnanimity before the Christ Child; it finds modern expression in extremes ranging from predation on anonymous children (Andrei Chikatilo, Wayne Williams), to murdering one's own offspring (Joseph Goebbels, Susan Smith), to caring for the offspring of others (Father Flanagan, Angelina Jolie), to risking one's life to save children unknown to you (Irena Sendler, Sir Nicholas Winton). Double-mindedness about the young has taken an especially telling (and troubling) form in recent American jurisprudence. Between 1976 and 2005, twenty-two juveniles who killed were tried as adults and executed in the United States; in 2005, the Supreme Court ruled that offenders under the age of eighteen are different and that capital punishment is "cruel and unusual" in their cases and thus unconstitutional.[6] Such is the depth and complexity of youth and our attitudes toward it.

One can only marvel at a phase of human life that is so protean and elusive and that calls up such different reactions. The assumption of this collection is that it is precisely because the child is simultaneously strong and weak, wise and foolish, beautiful yet unfinished that he or she *is* our best and *deserves* our best. But what constitutes optimal treatment for the young? One popular way to approach children and their welfare is in terms of "rights." The United Nations' "Convention on the Rights of the Child" (1989), for example, recognizes "the inherent dignity and . . . the equal and inalienable rights of all members of the human family," including children.[7] Those under the age of eighteen should not be denied basic human entitlements and freedoms. Indeed, "childhood is entitled to special care and assistance," according to the Convention.[8] And to what do children have a right? Commonsensical items include food, shelter, clothing, safety, education, health insurance, and medical treatment, even adoption if necessary. A unifying thesis of the present volume, however, is that the *first* right of the child is *the right to be loved,* even as the first *duty* of parents and the surrounding society is *to give such love wisely and effectively.* Every child, to live a fulfilling life, needs loving care. Secure attachments with empathic parents or other consistent caregivers, the emotional security of an environment where love is given and received — these are crucial for lifelong flourishing.

6. U.S. Supreme Court, *Roper v. Simmons,* No. 03-633.

7. United Nations High Commission for Human Rights, "Convention on the Rights of the Child," November 20, 1989, Preamble.

8. "Convention on the Rights of the Child," Preamble.

How, more specifically, ought we to love our children? What styles of parental love, what cultural ideals and aspirations, are truly salutary? What do our faith traditions — Judaism and Christianity in particular — offer us as guiding principles? Is there room for a new and refreshing dialogue between faith, history, philosophy, and law on how best to love the child? And where do mediating institutions fit in — local governments, churches, synagogues, schools, clubs, etc.? These are some of the key questions addressed in these pages.

Beyond the usual focus on *rights* of and love *for* the child, we also examine the *duties* of and love *from* the child. What is to be expected from children as bearers of sanctity, and what do and should they cherish? How can we create familial and institutional contexts that nurture love for and from our children so that they (and we) might thrive? How do we cultivate a next generation that will appreciate our common humanity, the kind of children who will live lives of generosity and compassion for all people? These questions are not so commonly asked or answered, for three main reasons. First, talk about the "rights" of children usually dwells on their dignity and what they are owed in justice, rather than on their sanctity and what they can be asked for in and through love. Second, "love" itself is a much-sentimentalized notion in our culture and often lacks substantive moral meaning; it can connote anything from narcissistic desire to self-sacrificial service. Third, worry about the perils of intrusive or tyrannical government makes the robust language of empowering people for goodness, rather than merely restraining them from evil, seem unwise to many. Frequently, the negative right of parents to raise their offspring as they see fit, without major interference by the state, or of children not to be neglected or exploited, with minor oversight by the state, is the keynote of public discourse about families. The positive right of progeny to acquire a certain character is typically either denied in the name of pluralism or privatized in the name of liberalism. We can talk about the *basic interests* of children, especially as *self-interested* individuals, but to aspire to an interpersonal and intrapersonal account of their *best love* is utopian. Or so the contemporary story often goes.

A second unifying thesis of this book, nevertheless, is that the right of a child *to be loved* is best fulfilled by teaching him or her, in turn, how *to love others*. Ideally, the virtue of love (a.k.a. charity) propagates itself, and one is best loved when one is helped publicly and privately to become loving oneself. Equally important, such moral pedagogy is not optional "philanthropy" but a concrete duty, to be exercised by civil and ecclesial figures responsible for the common good, as well as by parents and other parties responsible for individual children. A plausible pluralism about the forms of the good life must not drive us to relativism about fundamental virtue, and a prudent liberalism about the limits of the nation-state should not blind us to governmental and nongovernmental means of communicating excellence. A society that fails to equip its children to become lovers — "philanthropists" in a literal and binding sense — is self-defeating. It *ipso facto* fails to realize the goods that depend on love of humanity, including personal autonomy and social justice. If infants do not receive broad and unconditional care from adults, before the infants can actively merit it, they will never reach the maturity that allows them to make choices, calculate deserts, and raise their own families. A crucial burden of this book, then, is to show how negative rights and justice for the young are not enough, even as positive rights and love from the young are not too much.

In sum, affirming "the best love of the child" means attending to both the objective and the subjective genitive in that phrase — i.e., both the love that the world should have for children and the love that children should have for the world. In the balance of this Introduction, I set the stage for what follows by clarifying the relation of rights to justice, defining the types of love and how they bear on children, and briefly recounting the specific contents of the thirteen chapters. Some of the chapters are religious, others secular; some are retrospective, others prospective; some descriptive, others prescriptive; but all are concerned with who is a child, what is best for him or her, and how love mediates the two.

Justice and Rights

Concern over the legal and social protections and provisions due to and from the child raises the question of the relation between love and justice. In American and European societies, the conventional wisdom is that justice is the first political virtue (John Rawls) and that "rights" is the fundamental political language (Ronald Dworkin). Justice is typically defined in terms of "giving each his or her due" *(suum cuique),* which in turn is a matter of keeping contracts, rewarding merit, and punishing demerit. Keeping contracts (procedural justice), rewarding merit (distributive justice), and punishing demerit (retributive justice) exhaust the legal field, moreover. Rights, in turn, may be positive or negative, and first, second, or third generation, but the paradigmatic subjects of rights are autonomous persons and their self-conscious interests.

First-generation rights are civil and political and are usually formulated in terms of liberty or noninterference (freedom of speech, freedom of religion, freedom of assembly, etc.); second-generation rights are economic and cultural and are usually formulated in terms of equality or social support (the right to subsistence wages, the right to housing, the right to healthcare, etc.); third-generation rights are more elusive and controversial but are usually formulated in terms of fraternity or collective thriving (the right to a sustainable environment, the right to participate in a cultural heritage, the right to intergenerational equity). So defined, justice and rights are interrelated: to satisfy the interest-based rights of persons is to do justice.

There is no denying the crucial importance and intimate connection of justice and rights, but, as defined above, they immediately make problematic the lot of children. Young children have recognizable needs and potentials, but they are not "persons" in the technical sense of autonomous agents, self-aware across time. In addition, most children cannot form valid contracts and are not capable of achieved merit or demerit; thus they stand in an ambiguous relation to traditional procedural, distributive, and retributive justice. It isn't merely fetuses that are commonly denied the right to life, for instance; early infanticide is defended by some as compatible with both human rights and social justice (Michael Tooley and Peter Singer).

To be sure, children's "rights" have been repeatedly endorsed in the West over several decades — the Geneva "Declarations of the Rights of the Child" (1923) and the United Nations "Convention on the Rights of the Child" being cases in point. There are also a number of national and international organizations, political and ecclesial, with "Justice for Children" in their titles. Nonetheless, these endorsements and organizations are often theoretically confused and practically unstable, as this volume will show. Parents have nurtured their offspring for millennia, and politicians have kissed babies for centuries. But a central contention of this book is that proper care for the world's children requires us to move beyond concentration on justice- and interest-based rights to embrace love- and need-based rights. Interest-based rights are those founded on the capacity of autonomous agents to make self-conscious decisions — what Kant called "dignity" — and these have a central place in a good society. But an alternative vocabulary of "needs and potentials," based on sanctity and dependency, is also indispensable, especially when the subject is children. For Jews and Christians, sanctity is a holiness and inviolability that stems from being made in God's image; for many secular philosophers, sanctity can be uncoupled from the Deity and identified with supreme noninstrumental worth. Dignity, in contrast, no matter who construes it, is an achievement that admits of degrees and so is not universal among human beings.

The Six Loves

What kind of love has been and ought to be shown to children, and what kind of love do and should children themselves manifest? Is the example of children itself a partial model for adults? Some argue that there is ultimately only one kind of "love," frequently construed as "mutuality," but I assume here basic distinctions between types. In fact, I affirm the four traditional Greek loves — *eros, philia, storge,* and *agape* — as well as the distinctively Roman (not to say American) virtue of self-love *(amor sui).* I spend a good deal of this Introduction discussing how the best love of the child (objective genitive) relates to these five loves. In addition, however, and equally important, I propose a sixth type of love not often considered at length and, to my knowledge, seldom formally named. It is the best love of the child (subjective genitive), and I shall call it, following Wordsworth, "primal sympathy."[9]

Let me now define the six loves in turn and note how they interrelate.

In Plato's *Symposium,* Diotima defines *eros* as "desire for the perpetual possession of the good."[10] Following her lead, I understand *eros* as any discriminating urge to possess or join with a person or thing because of its per-

9. See IOI, ll. 180-91:

> What though the radiance which was once so bright
> Be now for ever taken from my sight,
>   Though nothing can bring back the hour
> Of splendour in the grass, of glory in the flower;
>   We will grieve not, rather find
>   Strength in what remains behind;
>   In the primal sympathy
>   Which having been must ever be;
>   In the soothing thoughts that spring
>   Out of human suffering;
>   In the faith that looks through death,
> In years that bring the philosophic mind.

I considered *philapedia* as a possible name for the love children commonly have for the world, but there seems to be no way to keep even this neologism from calling up associations with pederasty.

10. Plato, *The Symposium,* trans. Walter Hamilton (Middlesex, UK: Penguin Books, 1951), 205e, p. 86.

ceived excellence. As such, *eros* is broader than sexual appetite. One may be erotically attracted to a work of art or a powerful idea, for instance. As C. S. Lewis observes in *The Four Loves,* sexual passion (Venus) is technically a subset of *eros.*[11] For my purposes, nevertheless, it is normally sufficient to stick with common usage and treat *eros* and "sexual desire" or "romantic love" as simple synonyms. The key point is that *eros* is acquisitive and self-interested: it looks at the positive qualities of the other and how these can benefit me. This attitude need not be "selfish" or otherwise morally suspect, but it is self-referential, and it is contingent on the merit of the object. If the object of erotic love ceases to be beautiful or pleasurable or at least useful, then the love ceases.[12] This love *does* alter "when it alteration finds."[13]

Philia is the ancient Greek word usually translated "friendship." From Aristotle and Thomas Aquinas to Lawrence Blum and Gilbert Meilaender, this notion is much analyzed, but I take two features to be basic. Friendship presupposes significant *equality* between the parties and significant *mutuality* among the parties. There need not be perfect equality across the whole range of human predicates — intelligence, social status, moral virtue, physical strength, etc. — but there does have to be a substantive enough parity of interests, aims, opinions, and aptitudes for genuine communion to be possible. Friends do not "keep score," calculating what is owed to each other based on past performance — that is the province of justice — but they do

11. Lewis, *The Four Loves* (New York and London: Harcourt Brace Jovanovich, 1960), pp. 131-32.

12. I am aware of the neo-Platonic tradition of "non-acquisitive *eros,*" but this phrase seems to me self-contradictory.

13. Cf. Shakespeare, Sonnet 116:

> Let me not to the marriage of true minds
> Admit impediments; love is not love
> Which alters when it alteration finds,
> Or bends with the remover to remove:
> O, no, it is an ever-fixèd mark,
> That looks on tempests and is never shaken;
> It is the star to every wand'ring bark,
> Whose worth's unknown, although his height be taken.
> Love's not Time's fool, though rosy lips and cheeks
> Within his bending sickle's compass come;
> Love alters not with his brief hours and weeks,
> But bears it out even to the edge of doom.
> If this be error and upon me proved,
> I never writ, nor no man ever loved.

participate in a free-flowing reciprocation of time and attention. In addition, *philia* is less "jealous" and "possessive" than *eros*, in the sense that friendship is less exclusive and demanding. One can have multiple friends, but, as is often observed, for *eros* "three's a crowd." C. S. Lewis nicely captures the difference here by noting that the orientation of romantic lovers is face-to-face, gazing into each other's eyes, while that of friends is side-by-side, concentrating on some common enterprise.[14]

Storge is the third classic Greek love, usually glossed as "parental love." I think of it as special affection for the less than fully personal; thus it includes on my definition not only the natural love of a father and a mother for their child but also the fondness of a pet-owner for his or her pet. Unlike with friendship, the dynamic in this case is one of profound in-equality and dependency. The parental figure in a storgic relation cares for and nurtures a being who is not yet (and may never be) a "person" — in the technical sense of a self-conscious rational agent, capable of autonomous choices. Moreover, there is (and can be) no reciprocity or repayment in kind from the weaker to the stronger. To be sure, parents receive pleasure from their children, even when very young, and they may eventually come to be their children's friends. But a mother's joy in nursing her son and a father's gratification in teaching his daughter how to walk are not the mutuality between peers that characterizes *philia*.

In my lexicon, *agape* is an indiscriminate love that affirms the well-being of every human life. *Agape* is the type of love that God has *for* humanity and which God mandates *from* humanity in the two great love commands summarized by Jesus: "'You shall love the Lord your God with all your heart, and with all your soul, and with all your mind.' This is the greatest and first commandment. And a second is like it: 'You shall love your neighbor as yourself.' On these two commandments hang all the law and the prophets" (Matt. 22:38-40). Whereas *eros* is appraisive in nature and therefore variable, *agape* fundamentally bestows worth and so is (ideally) constant.[15] While the unconditional and nurturing character of *agape* suggests affinities with *storge*, *agape* differs from parental love in being more inclusive, less tied to genetic kinship or emotional bonding, even as it differs from friendship in being less appraisive. Putting the point another way, *eros* and *philia* look to the individual's achieved merit (a.k.a. dignity); *storge* looks to

14. *The Four Loves*, p. 91.

15. I take the "appraisal/bestowal" terminology from Irving Singer, *The Nature of Love*, vols. 1-3 (Chicago: University of Chicago Press, 1984-1987).

his or her biological affinity (a.k.a. heredity); but *agape* looks to the loved one's human needs and shared potentials (a.k.a. sanctity). Elsewhere, I have elaborated on these New Testament themes by identifying three features of *agape* that are embodied by Christ and manifest in his interpersonal relations: (1) unconditional commitment to the good of the other, (2) equal regard for the well-being of the other, and (3) passionate service, open to self-sacrifice, for the sake of the other.[16]

Amor sui, the fifth species, might be paraphrased as self-respect or even prudence, and its importance is often emphasized by feminists and other champions of the oppressed. Some fans of self-love even extol it as the most crucial love, the *sine qua non* of all the others. I myself consider it a central human good, and imparting the capacity for it is surely part of the best (objective) love of the child, but for three reasons I won't dwell on it here. First, in not having an object other than self, self-love is not, strictly speaking, an interpersonal habit or attitude. Second, however instinctive the disposition to self-love might be, I take Jesus to have shown that we do not naturally know how to love ourselves. Christians look first to God and Christ for examples of proper self-love: "Love one another *as I have loved you.*" Third, self-love is more of an ancillary effect of virtue than its substance or cause. Paradoxically, it is best achieved by self-forgetfulness rather than self-absorption. This is not to say that *amor sui* is an inappropriate end, but it is to say that it is an impossible beginning. We cannot achieve self-love by starting with it or by aiming at it directly. Relatedly, helping to make others capable of self-love is itself an act of *agape* rather than *amor sui.*

The five loves adumbrated above are normally thought to exhaust the field, but, as noted, I want to isolate a sixth. (It is indeed a kind of sixth sense.) The love of the child (subjective genitive) is a primal sympathy that is spontaneous and ecstatic. It is without the self-consciousness and voluntariness of *agape,* and it need not be explicitly open to self-sacrifice, but it resonates well with the broad gratitude and deep wonder associated with charity. A child's primal sympathy affirms the world as a good gift, without questioning its whence or whither. I do not mean to say, of course, that all children lead happy lives or that they all have cheerful dispositions. The grim statistics on child abuse and teenage suicide rule out such Pollyannaism. I am willing to say, however, that, barring abuse or chemical imbalance, many

16. See Jackson, *Love Disconsoled: Meditations on Christian Charity* (Cambridge: Cambridge University Press, 1999) and *The Priority of Love: Christian Charity and Social Justice* (Princeton: Princeton University Press, 2003).

children are natural mystics, innocent seers into innocence. Hence we must not lose sight of the blessings, as well as the burdens, of childhood. Growth to maturity is a great benefit, but childhood is not simply a liability to be overcome. The child is not merely an adult waiting to happen, the sooner the better; he or she has distinctive powers and insights that moved Wordsworth to hail it as "trailing clouds of glory." Wordsworth dramatically lamented the loss of "the glory and the dream" of youth, but he saw both the limits of wistful retrospection and the distinctive "visionary gleam" of childhood.[17] We should do likewise, not romanticizing the child but allowing its best love of the world — playful and unconditional — to inform our own.

Some Common "Amorous" Mistakes and Their Impact on Children

Anders Nygren caused immense conflict and confusion when he put *agape* and *eros* at odds, not just distinguishing them but opposing them.[18] In (at least sometimes) vilifying preferential desire as incompatible with Chris-

17. See IOI, ll. 57-77:

> Whither is fled the visionary gleam?
> Where is it now, the glory and the dream?
>
> Our birth is but a sleep and a forgetting:
> The Soul that rises with us, our life's Star,
> Hath had elsewhere its setting,
> And cometh from afar:
> Not in entire forgetfulness,
> And not in utter nakedness,
> But trailing clouds of glory do we come
> From God, who is our home:
> Heaven lies about us in our infancy!
> Shades of the prison-house begin to close
> Upon the growing Boy,
> But he beholds the light, and whence it flows,
> He sees it in his joy;
> The Youth, who daily farther from the east
> Must travel, still is Nature's priest,
> And by the vision splendid
> Is on his way attended;
> At length the Man perceives it die away,
> And fade into the light of common day.

18. Anders Nygren, *Agape and Eros*, trans. P. S. Watson (New York: Harper & Row, 1969).

tian charity, he tragically denied the meaning of human finitude and thereby the incarnational significance of Jesus' life and our own. As psychosomatic beings, we all live in part by *eros,* and to deny this is cruel to creatures and unfair to the Creator. It is also to saddle children with an entirely disembodied picture of virtue. A God who would make us needy of material and other aesthetic supports and then permanently deprive us of these is not worthy of worship. As Jesus says, "Is there anyone among you who, if your child asks for bread, will give a stone? Or if the child asks for a fish, will give a snake? If you then, who are evil, know how to give good gifts to your children, how much more will your Father in heaven give good things to those who ask him!" (Matt. 7:9-11). *Eros* is not merely to be tolerated as unavoidable, moreover; wisely conceived, it is the font of some of our greatest satisfactions and achievements. To leave the impression that agapic love rejects venereal instincts in particular is to burden children with a lifetime of shame and self-loathing.

Bishop Nygren is not unique in misconstruing the loves, and juveniles are not the only victims. To this day, prudery treats *eros* as nonexistent or illegitimate, while hedonism sees it as the prime or even the sole good, and young and old alike suffer as a result. Men and women do not live by bread alone, but neither do they commune with God alone. The Trappist Abbey of Gethsemane in central Kentucky inscribes "God alone" over one of its main arches, but this seems at best a pious hyperbole. (Traditionally, God is the *Summum Bonum* and the exclusive object of worship, but God is not the *solum bonum* or the only object of love.) A more democratic spirit harkens back to Aristotle and tries to make friendship the source and end of the other affinities, thus failing to see that philial relations are themselves dependent on other sustaining loves. The challenge for a proper understanding of the six loves is to give each its due without either conflating them or condemning some in favor of others. This can best be done, I believe, by lexically ordering them. Sexual desire, friendship, parental affection, and self-love are not to be denigrated, but they are to be dethroned.[19] Even primal sympathy must be schooled by and into a mature and willing benevolence.

As the New Testament suggests in several places (e.g., 1 Cor. 13), all human actions and principles are to be put under the governance of *agape.* Christianly understood, it is only when they are directed by the proper love of God and neighbor that the other five loves come into their own. Again quot-

19. Søren Kierkegaard, *Works of Love,* trans. Howard V. Hong and Edna H. Hong (Princeton: Princeton University Press, 1995), pp. 140-50.

ing Jesus, "As the Father has loved me, so I have loved you; abide in my love. If you keep my commandments, you will abide in my love, just as I have kept my Father's commandments and abide in his love. I have said these things to you so that my joy may be in you, and that your joy may be complete. 'This is my commandment, that you love one another as I have loved you. No one has greater love than this, to lay down one's life for one's friends'" (John 15:9-13).[20] *Agape,* at least as biblically conceived, has priority over the other loves — it is their source and measure — but only a Gnostic asceticism despises matter and its laws and flesh and its longings. True love delights in the real world of embodied life, being, as the saying goes, in that world but not of it. Thus our first obligation to our children is to teach them charity; the second is to assist them in realizing other goods (including other loves) in their proper places. Securing our children's future romantic happiness, friendly fellowship, material wealth, personal pride, and so on is not the (main) *motive* for teaching them charity — the latter is valuable for its own sake — so away with "the gospel of prosperity." Genuine charity can be as costly as the cross. Paradoxically, however, important benefits do (sometimes) follow as *consequences* of *agape.* "Those who want to save their life will lose it, and those who lose their life for my sake will find it" (Matt. 16:25). The trick is not to let the left hand know what the right hand is doing (Matt. 6:3).

The Individual Chapters

The issues outlined above are explored herein from a range of scholarly disciplines: sociology, psychology, history, biology, neurophysiology, philosophy, theology, and law. Hence our title, *The Best Love of the Child: Being Loved and Being Taught to Love as the First Human Right.* Among the social-psychological essays, Peter Benson and Eugene Roehlkepartain argue that we have settled for a too-negative ideal for our children, that of keeping them out of trouble rather than preparing them for thriving. Citing a wealth of recent research, they advocate an emphasis on "optimal development," instead of pathology avoidance. Annette Mahoney and Ken Pargament explore whether optimal development should include parents fostering their children's spiritual formation. What was once a commonplace of life, the family as school of

20. In this passage from John, the original word translated as a form of "love" is, in every case, a variant of *agapao.* Note in particular that, though friends are the *recipients* of the greatest love, that love itself is not *philia* but *agape.*

religious education, has increasingly been challenged in the name of social tolerance and juvenile rights of self-determination. Mahoney and Pargament are aware of the hazards of religious parochialism, but they nevertheless highlight the potential benefits of teaching the young "to love the sacred."

Robyn Fivush documents the myriad ways in which childhood identity and solidarity with others are produced by storytelling. At least as important as principles and rules, rewards and punishments, laid out by parents are the family narratives that parents, often mothers, relate to their offspring. Narratives, like anything else, can be falsified or abused, but they typically provide children with a sense of place and worth in the wider world.

In our first historical perspective, Steven Ozment looks at the norms and practices of parental love in late medieval and early modern Europe. Through a detailed examination of texts and art from the period, he helps to settle the long-running debate over whether the medievals fully recognized the distinctiveness of childhood or cared deeply for their young as such. Yes, they did, Ozment argues emphatically. Indeed, as he observes, child abuse was evidently less common than it now is, and "parents and children in the past have something to teach the modern family today." John Witte Jr. and Heather Johnson look at the theological and legal precepts on the duties of children, found in the English-language household manual tradition of the fourteenth to the nineteenth centuries. These household manuals were "the spiritual 'Dr. Spocks' of their day," as Witte puts it, and they contain fascinating interpretations of "the vocation of the child" to love and be loved. Charles Reid Jr. treats the emerging meanings of "the right to life" in Roman Catholic canon law and magisterial instruction, from 1878 to the present. The issue of to whom the right to life applies — when do we have "a child" before us? — challenges us to this day, and Reid provides an invaluable historical background to the contemporary discussion.

Cynthia Willett leads off the philosophical and theological section by raising the crucial question of collective responsibility for children. The challenge of inducing fathers to commit to caregiving for their progeny is given much attention today, and rightly so, but equally important are the extrafamilial sources of support, not just for children but also for adults. An over-accent on individual autonomy can make "orphans" of us all, Willett points out, by leading us to neglect the communal wellsprings of human selfhood. True freedom, in contrast, can be found, paradoxically, in recognizing and empowering social relations of interdependence. Richard Osmer is concerned with a theological "orphan" of another sort: the much-abused concept of sin, including original sin. Christianity is so often equated with a cruel judgmentalism, it is understandable that contemporary Christian authors tend to deny or ignore sin's biblical lineage. Osmer helps us acknowledge the dangers of the rhetoric of sin, especially when it is used to justify "breaking the will" of children, but he also makes the case for a sense of sin's being indispensable for sound moral pedagogy. Responsible Christian parenting must still communicate to children the universality of sin and the ambiguity of all human efforts to respond to evil.

Marcia Bunge elaborates a distinctively Protestant understanding of "vocation" or "calling" and how this relates to both parents and children. She describes the latest developments in "theologies of childhood" and "child theologies," two disciplines with similar names but different methods and aims. Theologies of childhood attend to scripture and tradition to determine what is owed to the young by adults and to adults by the young, while child theologies emphasize how focusing on young children and childhood can help reshape Christian theology and practice as a whole. Both approaches accent the agency of children — how they are frequently marginalized but also how they shape and challenge adults, morally and spiritually.

Michael Broyde launches the legal perspectives with characteristic bravado by declaring that "there is no obligation found in Jewish law to love one's children." Indeed, Broyde avers, the Jewish law discussion of the rights and duties of children leaves love "essentially unmentioned." This somewhat shocking thesis is mitigated, however, when we realize that what Broyde calls "love" is not Old Testament *hesed* or New Testament *agape,* but rather *eros* or perhaps *storge* (see above). Emotional attraction cannot be commanded, he notes, but there is a forceful mandate in the Jewish tradition for parents to care for and support their children, even when the children are "unwanted" or "unloved." The Hebraic accent on duties rather than rights, and on actions rather than emotions, makes the responsibility of fathers, mothers, and relevant third parties especially stringent in divorce and custody cases. Rana Lehr-Lehnardt and T. Jeremy Gunn ask, like Broyde, "What's love got to do with it?" Rather than halakhic rules, they examine international law and how "the best interest of the child" has emerged as a dominant norm, including in the United Nations Convention on the Rights of the Child. Despite criticisms, Lehr-Lehnardt and Gunn maintain that "love and affection" can and should be considered in resolving family-law disputes. Making love a broader legal standard, however, they deem an "impossibility."

It is important to recognize here that, again like Broyde, Lehr-Lehnardt and Gunn construe "love" as contingent emotion or attraction. Margaret Brinig and Steven Nock take a different tack. They argue that a central end of the law is to foster "unconditional love" in children, but unlike the other contributors they have in mind love-as-active-altruism instead of love-as-emotive-affection. God's love for the world and parents' love for their offspring provide models of "unconditional love," but such love is fundamentally agapic rather than erotic. More specifically, the authors find that unconditional love is best inspired and sustained in "recognized, legal, stable relationships." This means, for them, "marriage (as opposed to informal cohabitation), childbirth to married as opposed to single parents, and adoption as opposed to foster care or kin care (except in some ethnic subgroups with traditions of large roles played by extended families)." Finally, Don Browning formulates "an integrational view" of the best love of the child, one that draws on legal discussions of "best interests" and "best care" standards — including the work of Margaret Brinig — as well as on philosophy, theology, and evolutionary psychology. Browning offers a synthetic vision that would do justice to both love-as-affection and love-as-commitment, to both children-as-receivers and children-as-givers of love, and to both fathers and mothers as partners in a familial covenant of care. His defense of a stable marriage between husband and wife as the optimal environment in which to foster the best love of the child is sure to be provocative.

This volume draws on a range of resources to suggest a significant redirection of the theory and practice of childrearing. It puts the child's positive right to be loved and duty to become loving ahead of traditional considerations of negative rights and justice. Given the polymorphous yet supremely valuable nature of childhood, such a paradigm shift will inevitably cast up both heat and light. I trust that all of the essays thus show the way to a warmer and brighter vision of childcare. Few things are more important, since the best love of the child is nothing less than the best love of us all.

PART I

Social-Psychological Perspectives

CHAPTER 1

When "Good Enough" Isn't Really Good Enough: Aiming for the "Best" for All Young People

Peter L. Benson and Eugene C. Roehlkepartain

Introduction

When it comes to our children, we live in a society that seems satisfied just to keep them out of trouble. As evidence, review the vast majority of indicators of "child well-being" that, with few exceptions, only name the things we want our children and youth to avoid: poverty, disease, drugs, alcohol, experiencing or perpetrating violence, dropping out of school, getting pregnant (or getting someone pregnant), and others in the same ilk.

To be clear: Those *are* things we want our children to avoid or never experience. Each of these "bad things" can have long-term negative, even deadly, consequences for young people's development. We must, as a society, do much better at meeting basic human needs, ensuring food, shelter, quality healthcare, and safety for all children and youth. We must also target and reduce — if not eliminate — the risks and deficits that diminish or thwart healthy development, including guns, unsafe streets, predator adults, abuse, family violence, exclusion, alcohol and other drugs, racism, sexism, and other forms of prejudice and discrimination.

But even if we do all those things, we haven't reached the "best" for children or their communities. As Karen Pittman eloquently articulated, "Problem free is not fully prepared" (Pittman & Fleming, 1991). And, paradoxically, we cannot make great strides in eliminating or reducing these problems if we only focus on eliminating the problems. It's not that we're not trying, often heroically. Dedicated, effective parents, educators, youth workers, social workers, and others are pouring their energy, passion, and time into the lives of children and adolescents. The evidence of their investments are the millions of young people who find their way to successful adulthood, guided by caring and responsible adults, peers, and institutions.

But despite all the efforts, programs, investments, and innovations, far too many young people experience inadequate support, encouragement, boundary-setting, and the other experiences and relationships that guide them to adulthood. The reality is that these dedicated teachers, child advocates, family members, and other allies are swimming upstream. Our best chance for reducing these challenges lies in identifying and nurturing the core elements of optimal development. In the process, we build strengths within young people, their families, and their communities that greatly increase the odds that they'll either avoid the challenges or overcome them.

This essay seeks to articulate the importance of focusing on optimal development (as opposed to pathology) as a foundation for nurturing the best love of, for, and from children. The challenge is to become intentional in identifying, measuring, and organizing community life to nurture the kinds of outcomes that represent "the best" for and from our young people — or, in the words of Christian scriptures, to "have life, and have it in its fullest" (John 10:10, CEV).

A History, and Consequences, of a Negative Focus

For decades, research, policy, and public conversation about young people have focused primarily on naming, then overcoming, their problems or risk factors (Benson, Leffert, Scales, & Blyth, 1998; Furstenberg, 2000). Far more attention has been paid to developmental dangers than developmental opportunities, more attention to obstacles to well-being than to well-being itself. Even the vast amount of research that has been done on resilience can be viewed as being primarily about how people attain adequate functioning in the face of serious developmental threats, not how they overcome those challenges to thrive (Masten, 2001). As Seligman and Csikszentmihalyi (2000) write about the field of psychology:

> Psychologists have scant knowledge of what makes life worth living. They have come to understand quite a bit about how people survive and endure under conditions of adversity. . . . However, psychologists know very little about how normal people flourish under more benign conditions. Psychology has, since World War II, become a science largely about healing. It

> concentrates on repairing damage within a disease model of human functioning. This almost exclusive attention to pathology neglects the fulfilled individual and the thriving community. (p. 5)

At the root of our dilemma is the lack of vision. We simply do not have a frame of reference, a shared understanding, a common dream, for growing great kids. Without a shared vision rooted on promoting the potential of each and every child, we create, at best, national and community initiatives designed to put out fires. We fear drug and alcohol use by our young, so we invest heavily in prevention programs. We fear violence in communities and schools, so we aspire to rules and weapon detectors that are meant to curb it. We fear losing our top-dog role in the global economy, so we create big initiatives to drill science and math skills into our young.

In many ways, we have adopted a conventional medical model in caring for young people. Unless they are "sick," we don't treat them. The result is that too many are showing up needing urgent or emergency care — at a high cost to society and the young people themselves. And, as Lerner (2007) notes, "If we view teens as 'broken,' then our responsibility is to 'fix' them" (p. 9), which has led to a plethora of programs that have had little impact on changing the life trajectories for young people.

Over time, there has been a growing sense that an exclusive focus on deficits and risks is inadequate, both theoretically and strategically. Models driven by risk, deficit, and pathology may unintentionally become part of the problem in that they label youth and/or fuel negative stereotypes of youth. They tend to focus on single negative behaviors (be it problematic alcohol consumption, premature sexual activity, violence, or something else), and rarely attend to children and youth as whole persons embedded in communities and social networks. Furstenberg (2000) described the implications of these social and scientific trends for the broader public perception of youth:

> Such an approach inevitably treats successful adolescents and young adults as escape artists who manage to dodge the hazards of growing up, rather than focusing on the ways that young people acquire and master skills, construct positive identities, and learn how to negotiate social roles simultaneously in the youth culture and adult world. (p. 900)

Finally, and most problematically, the collective focus in our culture on young people's problems also results in feelings of hopelessness and powerlessness among adults and would-be advocates. Adults too often avoid young people rather than getting involved in their lives in a positive way. For example, focus groups by Public Agenda found that a major reason people do not take action for children is that they have little to offer. "The public's definition of the problem — which focuses on broad moral and economic problems — makes them feel that there is very little that can be done to help children," researchers summarized. "Their tolerance for the problems of children stems, in other words, not from indifference but from a feeling of helplessness" (Immerwahr, 1995).

The result is greater isolation of young people — whom Patricia Hersch poignantly described as *A Tribe Apart* (1998). When adults become suspicious and fearful of teenagers, we deprive our young of the allies and guides they so desperately need. When we segregate adults and youth into different living and learning spaces, we deprive our young of the sustained connections they need to flourish.

The Introduction of Strength-Based Approaches

Since the late 1980s, scholars and practitioners have begun looking more at positive developmental trajectories, a focus that uses such language as positive youth development, healthy development, or "asset building." Positive youth development has been approached and framed in many different ways (Benson, Scales, Hamilton, & Sesma, 2006), and the field encompasses a vast territory of disciplines, concepts, and strategies. One review of positive youth development (Benson & Pittman, 2001) suggests four distinguishing features of this field:

1. It is *comprehensive* in its scope, linking a variety of: (a) ecological contexts (e.g., relationships, programs, families, schools, neighborhoods, congregations, communities) to (b) the production of experiences, supports, and opportunities known to (c) enhance positive developmental outcomes.
2. Its primary organizing principle is *promotion* (of youth access to positive experiences, resources, and opportunities and of developmental outcomes useful to both self and society).
3. It is, as the term implies, *developmental*, with emphasis on growth and an increasing recognition that youth can (and should be) deliberate actors in the production of positive development.
4. And it is *symbiotic*, drawing into its orbit ideas, strategies, and practices

from many lines of inquiry (e.g., resiliency, prevention, public health, community organizing, developmental psychology).

Damon (2004; Damon & Gregory, 2003) first argues that positive youth development represents a sea change in psychological theory and research, with observable consequences for a variety of fields including education and social policy. In Damon's view, positive youth development takes a strength-based approach to defining and understanding the developmental process. More precisely, it "emphasizes the manifest potentialities rather than the supposed incapacities of young people" (2004, p. 15).

There is more to this statement than initially meets the eye. In actuality, it connotes a significant critique of mainstream psychological inquiry that is quite ubiquitous in the positive youth development literature. This critique is that understandings of child and adolescent development have been so dominated by the exploration and remediation of pathology and deficit that we have an incomplete — if not distorted — view of how organisms develop.

Second, Damon, like many other positive youth development advocates, holds up the *centrality of community* as both an incubator of positive development as well as a multifaceted setting in which young people can exercise agency and inform the settings, places, people, and policies that in turn impact their development.

Finally, Damon notes that positive youth development, in its efforts to identify the positive attitudes and competencies that energize healthy developmental trajectories, is not afraid to *identify values, moral perspectives, and religious worldviews* as constructive developmental resources, even though this "flies in the face of our predominantly secular social-science traditions" (2004, p. 21).

Several attempts have been made to articulate the core concepts and principles in positive youth development (Benson & Pittman, 2001; Benson, Scales, Sesma, & Hamilton, 2006; Catalano et al., 1999; Hamilton, Hamilton, & Pittman, 2004; Eccles & Gootman, 2002). A synthesis of these reviews suggests considerable consensus on these six principles:

1. All youth have the inherent capacity for positive growth and development;
2. A positive developmental trajectory is enabled when youth are embedded in relationships, contexts, and ecologies that nurture their development;
3. The promotion of positive development is further enabled when youth

participate in multiple, nutrient-rich relationships, contexts, and ecologies;

4. All youth benefit from these relationships, contexts, and ecologies. Support, empowerment, and engagement are, for example, important developmental assets for all youth, generalizing across race, ethnicity, gender, and family income. However, the strategies and tactics for promoting these developmental assets can vary considerably as a function of social location;
5. Community is a viable and critical "delivery system" for positive youth development; and
6. Youth are major actors in their own development and are significant (and underutilized) resources for creating the kinds of relationships, contexts, ecologies, and communities that facilitate positive youth development.

One youth development approach that has both a robust research base and a strong network of community action is the framework of Developmental Assets, created by Search Institute. Grounded in extensive research in resiliency, prevention, and youth development (Benson, 2006; Lerner & Benson, 2003; Scales & Leffert, 2004), these building blocks of development (shown in Table 1 on p. 25) identify the ways families, schools, congregations, and communities need to provide support, empowerment, boundaries and expectations, and constructive ways for young people to spend their time. They also name the inner strengths young people need, such as commitment to learning, positive values, social competencies, and a positive identity. In light of the backlash against empty praise and vacuous self-esteem-boosting programs (Bronson, 2007; Damon, 1995), it merits noting that asset building balances positive reinforcement with high expectations and boundaries as well as other dynamics that point toward a best, not shallow, love of the child. The research is clear that (a) each asset contributes to health; (b) the assets are synergistic and symbiotic; and (c) they are additive or cumulative.

The theory of Developmental Assets draws heavily on developmental systems theory and other core principles of regulation and plasticity (Lerner, 2007). The twenty external assets and the twenty internal assets are hypothesized to co-relate in dynamic interaction: Ecologies rich in external assets generate internal assets, and internal assets propel active human agents to find and/or create ecologies that are life supporting.

The research literature on assets is quite extensive (Benson, 2006; Benson, Scales, Hamilton, & Sesma, 2006; Scales & Leffert, 2004). A number

Table 1

Search Institute's 40 Developmental Assets

EXTERNAL ASSETS

Support

1. Family support
2. Positive family communication
3. Other adult relationships
4. Caring neighborhood
5. Caring school climate
6. Parent involvement in schooling

Empowerment

7. Community values youth
8. Youth as resources
9. Service to others
10. Safety

Boundaries and expectations

11. Family boundaries
12. School boundaries
13. Neighborhood boundaries
14. Adult role models
15. Positive peer influence
16. High expectations

Constructive use of time

17. Creative activities
18. Youth programs
19. Religious community
20. Time at home

INTERNAL ASSETS

Commitment to learning

21. Achievement motivation
22. School engagement
23. Homework
24. Bonding to school
25. Reading for pleasure

Positive values

26. Caring
27. Equality and social justice
28. Integrity
29. Honesty
30. Responsibility
31. Restraint

Social competencies

32. Planning and decision making
33. Interpersonal competence
34. Cultural competence
35. Resistance skills
36. Peaceful conflict resolution

Positive identity

37. Personal power
38. Self-esteem
39. Sense of purpose
40. Positive view of personal future

Complete asset frameworks and definitions for different ages are available at www.search-institute.org/assets.

of studies, for example, are designed to identify which subset of the forty assets best explains behaviors or sets of behaviors. These include a number of studies examining the relationship of assets and high-risk behaviors (e.g., Leffert et al., 1998). Concurrently, there is a wave of studies showing how assets predict prosocial outcomes, such as compassion, service, and generosity (Benson, Clary, & Scales, 2007; Roehlkepartain & Scales, 2007).

Two themes emerge from this research. First, a subset of the assets — usually in the range of six to ten assets — accounts for most of the explained variance in a particular phenomenon (e.g., alcohol use, violence, school success). Second, when looking at the multiple phenomena in a comprehensive understanding of health and well-being, each asset adds value to the explanation of one or more of the measures included in a reasonable approximation of human well-being.

More specifically, the importance of the Developmental Assets becomes evident when we see how the levels of assets young people experience are strongly associated with the choices young people make. Since 1990, Search Institute has studied assets in about 3 million young people across the United States. The more assets young people experience, the better their outcomes, including much lower levels of engagement in high-risk behaviors and much higher levels of thriving behaviors, such as serving others, valuing diversity, and caring for their own health.

Table 2 (on p. 27) illustrates the power of Developmental Assets, based on a sample of 150,000 sixth- to twelfth-grade youth in twenty-seven states surveyed by Search Institute in 2003. Across a range of risk behaviors, we see that the more assets young people have, the less likely they are to engage in high-risk behaviors. At the same time (and key for our discussion), we see that the more assets they have, the more likely they are to engage in thriving behaviors. Indeed, levels of assets are better predictors of high-risk involvement and thriving than poverty or being from a single-parent family (Benson, 2006).

The framework of Developmental Assets was specifically developed to suggest a language of the common good for children in a pluralistic society. It seeks to create space for all aspects of community life to engage with and invest in young people. Thus the framework is not religious in its focus (though it includes faith communities as a resource for development). However, several recent studies have documented the role of Developmental Assets in enriching a religious or spiritual life (Benson, Scales, Sesma, & Roehlkepartain, 2005; King & Benson, 2006; Scales, 2007). Furthermore, levels of Developmental Assets have been found to moderate the impact of religious participation and commitment on adolescent risk and thriving behav-

Table 2

The Power of Assets to Prevent and Promote

Selected Behavior Patterns	Percentage of 6th- to 12th-Grade Youth Reporting Behavior Pattern, by Number of Assets			
	0-11 Assets	11-20 Assets	21-30 Assets	31-40 Assets
Selected High-Risk Behavior Patterns				
Problem alcohol use — Has used alcohol three or more times in the past month or got drunk once in the past two weeks.	45	26	11	3
Illicit drug use — Used illicit drugs (cocaine, LSD, PCP or angel dust, heroin, marijuana, and amphetamines) three or more times in the past year.	38	18	6	1
Sexual intercourse — Has had sexual intercourse three or more times in lifetime.	34	23	11	3
Depression/attempted suicide — Is frequently depressed and/or has attempted suicide.	44	29	15	5
Violence — Has engaged in three or more acts of fighting, hitting, injuring a person, carrying or using a weapon, or threatening physical harm in the past year.	62	38	18	6
Selected Thriving Behaviors				
School success — Student's grades are A- or higher.	9	19	34	54
Helping others — Student helps others one hour or more per week.	62	79	89	96
Valuing diversity — Student places high value on interacting with people of other racial and ethnic backgrounds.	39	60	76	89
Leadership — Student reports being a leader in a group or organization in the last 12 months.	27	48	69	88
Maintains good health — Student reports an active interest in nutrition and exercise.	9	19	31	44

SOURCE: Benson, 2006. Based on aggregate Search Institute sample of 148,189 students surveyed in 2003.

iors (King & Furrow, 2004; Roehlkepartain & Patel, 2006; Wagener et al., 2003), thus reinforcing a dynamic interplay between multiple ecologies and domains of development.

The challenge is that the average young person we've surveyed experiences only about nineteen of the forty assets. In addition, a majority (59%) of young people in the United States may well be "at risk" or "vulnerable," from a youth-development perspective (Table 3 on p. 29). Hence, the normative developmental trajectory in the United States, from a Developmental Assets perspective, is at best mediocre. Overall, only 8 percent of young people reach the threshold of optimal development, which this research sets at experiencing at least thirty-one of the forty Developmental Assets. Though there is some variability in the specific numbers by gender, race-ethnicity, and socioeconomic status, no group of young people is, on average, flourishing with a strong foundation of assets in their families, in their communities, and within themselves.

In short, we as a society are failing to provide young people with even the basic foundation needed to make responsible choices and grow up to be healthy, caring, responsible, and generous. It is worth noting here that the societal capacity for promoting optimal (or asset-rich) development is largely a citizen and community capacity that can be triggered when social norms and shared vision are developed and activated (Benson, 2006).

Emerging Attention to Optimal Development

The focus on healthy development balanced with risk reduction has been an important rebalancing of the equation. However, because we have not yet developed a clear vision of what is best for young people, we continue to focus on adequate or "good enough" development. When adolescents function adequately, in the sense of avoiding serious problems, this may be a source of relief, but it seems hardly to be the sine qua non of adolescent development.

Since the turn of the millennium, a new emphasis has emerged that goes another step to focus on optimally successful development, which is alternately called thriving (Benson, 2008; Scales & Benson, 2005; Theokas et al., 2005) or flourishing (Keyes, 2003). Instead of focusing on reducing risks and getting by, this emphasis on thriving shifts attention to concepts such as life satisfaction, hope, generosity, spirituality, connectedness, self-regulation, and prosocial orientation (Moore & Lippman, 2005). The focus on positive youth development and asset building opened the door to this emphasis.

Table 3

Levels of Developmental Assets Among U.S. Youth, Grades 6 to 12

	0-10 Assets	11-20 Assets	21-30 Assets	31-40 Assets
	At-Risk	Vulnerable	Adequate	Optimal
Total	17%	42%	32%	8%
Male	22%	45%	28%	6%
Female	13%	40%	36%	11%
Grades 6-8	15%	38%	36%	12%
Grades 9-12	19%	45%	30%	6%
American Indian	23%	42%	27%	8%
Asian/Pacific Islander	15%	46%	31%	8%
Black/African American	13%	47%	34%	6%
Hispanic	23%	45%	27%	5%
White	17%	40%	33%	10%
Multiracial	18%	46%	30%	7%
Low Family Income	22%	45%	28%	5%
Moderate or High Family Income	14%	40%	35%	11%

SOURCE: Benson, 2006. Based on aggregate Search Institute sample of 148,189 students surveyed in 2003. The sample included 202 cities in 27 states.

One approach to this emerging focus on optimal development flies under the banner of thriving. Thriving suggests not only internal satisfaction and competence, but also demonstrable excellence *or* substantive positive growth. It is more than capacities or potentialities, such as the capacity to love. It suggests actualities — capacities translated into actions.

For the last several years, Search Institute and colleagues from Tufts University, Fuller Theological Seminary, Stanford University, and the Thrive Foundation for Youth have collaborated to build theories and frameworks for thriving. What has emerged is a core question: How do young people become the kind of persons who embrace life and make full use of their special gifts (which we call "sparks") in ways that benefit themselves and others?

Thus, we conceptualize the thriving process as animated by a passion for, and the exercise of action to nurture, a self-identified interest, skill, or capacity. It could be anything from the love of writing poetry to disassembling and rebuilding car engines. We refer to this self-identified core passion — a central component of thriving — as a person's "spark." The pursuit and exercise of this interest is done for its own sake. The motivation is intrinsic, not extrinsic. Time engaged in pursuing this passionate interest often generates a kind of affect akin to joy. The identification and nurturing of one's core passions is a critical component of thriving, and indeed, is a principal source of the energy that drives a person's development over time.

This emerging understanding of thriving has links to the field of positive psychology (Seligman & Csikszentmihalyi, 2000) and grows out of an applied developmental systems theory that emphasizes the bi-directional interaction between the person and his or her environment (Bronfenbrenner & Morris, 1998; Lerner et al., 2002). Our definition of "thriving," then, has three key, interconnected parts (Benson & Scales, 2008):

- Thriving represents a dynamic, bi-directional interplay over time between a young person who is intrinsically animated and energized by discovering his or her specialness or sparks, and the developmental contexts (people, places) that know, affirm, celebrate, encourage, and guide its expression;
- Thriving involves a balance between continuity and discontinuity of development over time that is optimal for a given individual's interactions with his or her contexts; and
- Thriving reflects both where a young person is currently in his or her journey as well as whether he or she is on a path of exemplary adaptive developmental regulation.

Undergirding a theory of thriving is a generous view of human capacity and potential. This vision of human nature identifies the possibility of youth making active and constructive contributions to the development of self, community, and society. This view brings to the fore the notion that the individual — and not just the environment — is a prime actor in the shaping of his or her own positive developmental trajectories.

In this approach, the capacity to love is certainly a necessary ingredient for optimal development, but is it sufficient? Perhaps one with the capacity to love could be said to then have the potential to thrive in this dimension, but is that person really thriving without actually loving and being loved? Lerner (2004) further argues that young people who are thriving develop an "orientation to transcend self-interest and place value on, and commitments to, actions supportive of a social system promoting equity, democracy, social justice, and personal freedoms" (p. 24).

Thus, thriving is an active word — a dynamic concept, not an endpoint. Though the status question "How are young people doing?" (which lies at the heart of positive youth development) is important, a thriving perspective presses us to ask the process question about the path they are on. Are they headed to hopeful futures, irrespective of their present conditions? The process is animated by a passion for and the exercise of action to nurture, a self-identified interest, skill, or capacity — one's "spark." The motivation is intrinsic, not extrinsic. Time engaged in pursuing "the spark" often generates a kind of affect akin to joy. The process also bears similarity to "flow" (Csikszentmihalyi, 1990).

We contend that every young person has a spark — something inside that is good, beautiful, and useful to the world. These sparks come in many forms. Recent interviews with thousands of American teenagers tell us they include writing poetry, making music, helping people, leading, being a peacemaker among friends and peers in one's high school, making one's community better, or taking care of the earth. When sparks glow, we feel whole. We feel useful. Life has meaning. It feels good to get up in the morning (Benson, 2008).

Through a variety of major studies of youth and families all across America, we've learned a great deal about sparks, their role in helping youth navigate through adolescence, and their impact on the health and well-being of teenagers. Search Institute sponsored or commissioned three national studies that engaged more than 3,500 adolescents and 2,000 parents of teenagers in talking about sparks in adolescence.

We learned that young people can be very articulate about the characteristics of kids with sparks versus those without sparks. When describing their own sparks, they frequently use words like "relish," "love," "reason to smile," "passion," "sacrifice," "emotion," "commitment," "focus," "lights my fire," the kind of vocabulary one might expect to hear from someone describing a love interest and/or an important relationship. Their enthusiasm and passion are almost infectious.

We also found that 69 percent of adolescents say they have sparks, and 62 percent can actually describe their sparks. The challenge, of course, is that 31 percent don't think they have a spark — about 12 million young peo-

events, experiences, and changes. Furthermore, consistent with current developmental theories, the use of the term "development" emphasizes the reality of change across time within the domain. It does not imply a linear, invariant, or orderly progression of universal stages, but a set of interactive and dynamic processes and paths that vary widely in how they are accomplished. These tasks may be worked on multiple times, in any order and/or simultaneously, in cycles, throughout one's life, in response to aging, life events, and/or other stimuli, and with potentially deeper, richer, and/or different results in subsequent cycles.

This framework suggests that spiritual development is a core developmental process that occurs for all persons, regardless of their religious or philosophical beliefs or worldview. Young people engage in theses processes in many different ways with different emphases and levels of intensity (from highly engaged to passive). And many young people tap their own culture or religious tradition's belief systems, narratives, and community to give form to this process.

It is important to note, too, that these tasks do, in fact, overlap with other conceptions of thriving and youth development. For example, "connecting and belonging" overlaps with the Developmental Assets focused on support. And the task of "becoming aware" overlaps with the core concepts of spark. This overlap may be sorted out as the theories mature. Or, just as likely, we will see that these overlapping concepts reinforce our understanding of the dynamic interplay and interconnections across multiple areas of development, each with "fuzzy" edges that are integrated in a dynamic interplay of holistic development within a person and between the person and his or her environment.

Expecting the Best Love *from* the Child

An important underlying theme in positive youth development that is amplified as we focus on optimal development is the role of a young person's own agency in shaping one's own development and in contributing to the greater good. Thus, optimal development is not a one-way process of society "molding" the child; rather, optimal development is the dynamic interplay of the child's identity, spark, and/or spirit as it finds its own place in and contributions to the world. Or, we might say, optimal development must include a clear sense of not only expecting the best love *for* the child, but also expecting the best love *from* the child.

In fact, the two go hand in hand. Though one might presume that a focus on nurturing one's own passion, joy, and gift is a path to hedonism or self-centeredness, the opposite is true. Young people who grow up in developmentally rich environments and embedded in a web of loving, healthy relationships are themselves more likely to be generous and engaged in social justice, to form positive relationships with others, and to be civically engaged (Benson, Clary, & Scales, 2006; Roehlkepartain, Naftali, & Musegades, 2000; Scales & Benson, 2003; Schervish, Hodgkinson, & Gates, 1995). It's as though the process of being grounded in one's true essence opens a life to the world. As Marian Wright Edelman (1993) eloquently puts it:

> I have always believed that I could help change the world because I have been lucky to have adults around me who did — in small and large ways. Most were people of simple grace who understood what Walker Percy wrote: "You can get all A's and still flunk life." . . . I and my brothers and sister might have lost hope — as so many young people today have lost hope — except for the stable, caring, attentive adults in our family, school, congregation, civic and political life who struggled with and for us against the obstacles we faced and provided us positive alternatives and the sense of possibility we needed. (p. 7)

Expecting the best from the child does not mean that they need to have more programs that seek to "fix" young people. Rather, it calls for engaging them in relationships and opportunities that cultivate those commitments within them. "Children do not learn morality by learning maxims or clarifying values," writes James Q. Wilson (1993). "They enhance their natural sentiments by being regularly induced by families, friends, and institutions to behave in accord with the most obvious standards of right conduct — fair dealing, reasonable self-control, and personal honesty. A moral life is perfected by practice more than by precept; children are not taught so much as habituated" (p. 249).

Young people are too often viewed primarily as consumers or recipients of services, not as resources to their families, their schools, their congregations, their communities, and society. Institutions focus on how they can "serve" youth, "meet young people's needs," "attract young people" — all of which can assume that young people are the receivers, not the givers. "Political science, anthropology, sociology, and education have all been influenced by the notion that children are not full-fledged individuals," Silvia Blitzer Golombek writes. "These fields often reflect the belief that children are empty vessels into

Mobilizing a "Best" Society

Best love requires major transformations in society — in our understanding of the place of young people in bringing their "best love" to society as well as the transformation of contexts (schools, neighborhoods, congregations, communities) and relationships to attend to the developmental paths of all young people. "Best love" emerges as a life orientation when contexts and communities and young people work in concert, each cultivating, expecting, and bringing out the strengths of the others. So, best love for the child requires:

- Young people who are engaged and active in shaping their own lives and contributing to society;
- Contexts that are developmentally rich, aligned, and connected; and
- Young people who are embedded in a web of life-giving relationships at home, with peers, with many caring adults, and throughout community life.

These themes present both a vision for and a challenge to society. Within this vision is an optimistic sense of what communities and institutions are capable of — being transformed into more developmentally attentive contexts that attend to the interplay of context and person (Benson, Scales, & Mannes, 2003).

There is enormous developmental power embedded in community and society. But this capacity to connect with young people as a natural part of what it means to be a citizen or as a natural way of being a school, neighborhood, congregation, or family has somehow gone underground. We expect programs to fill the void. Moving young people to the center of community life (not as passive recipients, but as contributing actors and resources) requires altering how citizens and their leaders see and value our young, and it makes responsibility and accountability for kids a personal issue.

At a recent conference, youth-development leaders Cindy Carlson and Richard Goll of Hampton, Virginia, posted this slogan on the wall: "This is not about changing youth; it's about changing community." We would ratchet this up to a higher level: It's not about changing youth; it's about transforming society.

The best love of our children requires deep transformation at every level, from individual relationships in families, neighborhoods, and communities; to schools, congregations, and other places young people spend time; to our broader society and the policies that shape their economic and developmental fortunes.

A helpful first step would be to create a national report that shifts the focus from indicators about "fixing kids" to one that focuses on contexts. Here are some candidates for indicators that place accountability where it belongs:

- The percentage of the federal budget spent on children and youth.
- The number of times children and youth are mentioned in the President's State of the Union address.
- The percentage of news media stories that cast youth in a favorable light.
- The percentage of neighborhoods that have created a sense of trust across multiple households.
- The percentage of public schools with funding adequate for meeting their educational and human development objectives.
- The average starting salary for public school teachers and for youth workers.
- The percentage of communities that have articulated a community-wide vision for child and adolescent development.
- The percentage of children and youth who have access to high-quality daycare, after-school, and other youth-development programs.
- The number of politicians who run for election on a pro-child, pro-youth agenda.

A report card on these kinds of commitments would be disturbing. And it could be getting worse. For example, the share of the federal domestic budget in the United States fell by 23 percent from 1960 to 2006 (from 20.1% in 1960 to 15.4%). Furthermore, in 2000, the U.S. federal government spent $2,106 per child and $21,122 per adult over 65 (Isaacs & Lovell, 2007; also see Carasso, Steuerle, & Reynolds, 2007). Add to this discrepancy that 78 million baby boomers are moving into retirement. Educated, active, and mobilized, this is a voting bloc that will place high demand on budget decisions. Unless we find a way for our nation to fall in love with its kids, to invest in creating healthy communities and nurturing healthy youth, the dollar ratio will only worsen.

A political strategy, by itself, will not turn the tide. Social will leads to political will. The challenge for society is for millions of adults to recognize that they have an opportunity and obligation as part of citizenship and civic life to engage with, support, and encourage young people. Though adults seem to recognize that it is important for young people to form positive relationships with adults, there remain significant gaps between what adults say is important and what they actually do. One national study of adults' engagement with young people outside their own family estimated that fewer than 10 percent of American adults can be said consistently to experience both strongly favorable attitudes (a component of personal motivation to engage) and a perception of collective permission (social motivation) for engaging with young people in these ways (Scales, 2003).

Changing these norms and expectations for adults and investing in transforming the contexts in which young people are nurtured must become urgent priorities for society and its institutions, not just for parents, teachers, and youth workers. Without such transformation, we will continue to see too many young people fall through the cracks. Furthermore, we will never be able to move beyond an implicit acceptance of mediocre or adequate development, not the best love for and from our children.

The Right to Thrive

A focus on optimal development begins with seeing each life as precious and filled with potential. It recognizes that all citizens have responsibility and capacity to nurture this potential. It calls for schools and communities to know each of its young so well that it can nurture and benefit from each child's spark. It recognizes that governmental policy requires deep transformation, moving from a preoccupation with preventing problems to a proactive investment in promoting human potential.

As more and more people come to understand and focus on what it means to nurture the best love of, for, and from the child, we will find a shared voice, a shared vocabulary, and a shared concern for how well our neighborhoods and schools and communities find their own place in not only overcoming challenges and building strengths, but also in cultivating what is best in, for, and from all of our children. As this effort grows, perhaps we will reach a tipping point where our nations commit to ensuring that all young people are on the path to a hopeful future.

The continued refinement of these approaches, priorities, and strategies can bring new energy to realizing our greatest visions for young people's positive development. The United Nations Rights of the Child document, ratified by all members (except by the U.S. and Somalia), states that children have the right to survive, to be protected, and to participate. To these, we would add a fourth right: to thrive.

For many, this right may not seem to meet the criteria of a "basic human right." Some argue for a more linear progression in which communities and nations must first overcome vexing challenges such as disease, hunger, war, hatred, and ethnic cleansing. Then they must create functioning political, economic, service, and civic infrastructures. Only when all those things are taken care of can society address "higher-order" "privileges" or "wants." In fact, in our work with asset building, we hear people working in juvenile justice or foster care systems say that they will not provide asset-rich experiences (such as leadership, service activities, or cultural enrichment) to all the youth in their systems unless they "earn the privilege."

Yet, if we seek to nurture the best love of, for, and from the child, we must not fall into the trap of assuming that this is only possible for the privileged. There are other ways to view the progression. Rather than seeing human, community, and societal development as a hierarchy of needs to be met, it's probably more realistic to understand that all these dynamics interact with each other simultaneously. Thus, having a deep sense of purpose, hope, and connection may be key to surviving and overcoming poverty or victimization, as may be attested by the high levels of religious, civic, and moral commitment in developing countries (Inglehart et al., 2004).

It is time to embed thriving or optimal development in our expectations for our children and for ourselves. To expect the best is one important step in moving toward the best for the future of our children and our societies.

References

Astin, A. W., H. S. Astin, J. A. Lindholm, A. N. Bryant, K. Szelényi, and S. Calderone. (2005). *The spiritual life of college students: A national study of college students' search for meaning and purpose.* Los Angeles: Higher Education Research Institute, UCLA.

Benson, P. L. (2008). *Sparks: How parents can ignite the hidden strengths of teenagers.* San Francisco: Jossey-Bass.

Benson, P. L. (2006). *All kids are our kids: What communities must do to raise caring and responsible children and adolescents,* 2nd ed. San Francisco: Jossey-Bass.

Benson, P. L. (2003). Developmental assets and asset-building community: Conceptual and empirical foundations. In *Developmental assets and asset-building communities: Implications for research, policy, and practice,* ed. R. M. Lerner and P. L. Benson, pp. 19-43. New York: Kluwer Academic/Plenum.

Benson, P. L., E. G. Clary, and P. C. Scales. (2007). Altruism and health: Is there a link during adolescence? In *Altruism and health: Perspectives from empirical research,* ed. S. G. Post, pp. 97-115. New York: Oxford University Press.

Benson, P. L., and N. Leffert. (2001). Childhood and adolescence: Developmental Assets. In *International encyclopedia of the social and behavioral sciences,* ed. N. J. Smelser and P. G. Baltes, pp. 1690-1697. Oxford: Pergamon.

Benson, P. L., N. Leffert, P. C. Scales, and D. A. Blyth. (1998). Beyond the "village" rhetoric: Creating healthy communities for children and adolescents, *Applied Developmental Science* 2, no. 3: 138-59.

Benson, P. L., M. Mannes, K. Pittman, and T. Ferber. (2004). Youth development, developmental assets and public policy. In *Handbook of adolescent psychology,* 2nd ed., ed. R. M. Lerner and L. Steinberg, pp. 781-814. New York: John Wiley.

Benson, P. L., and K. Pittman. (2001). *Trends in youth development: Visions, realities, and challenges.* Norwell, MA: Kluwer Academic Publishers.

Benson, P. L., and E. C. Roehlkepartain. (2008). Spiritual development: A missing priority in youth development. In *New Directions for Youth Development* 118: 13-28.

Benson, P. L., E. C. Roehlkepartain, and S. Rude. (2003). Spiritual development in childhood and adolescence: Toward a field of inquiry, *Applied Developmental Science* 7, no. 3: 205-13.

Benson, P. L., and P. C. Scales. (2009). The definition and measurement of thriving in adolescence, *Journal of Positive Psychology* 4, no. 1: 85-104.

Benson, P. L., P. C. Scales, S. F. Hamilton, and A. Sesma Jr. (2006). Positive youth development: Theory, research and applications. In *Handbook of child psychology, Vol. 1: Theoretical models of human development,* 6th ed., ed. W. Damon and R. M. Lerner, pp. 894-941. New York: John Wiley.

Benson, P. L., P. C. Scales, and M. Mannes. (2003). Developmental strengths and their sources: Implications for the study and practice of community building. In *Handbook of applied developmental science: Promoting positive child, adolescent, and family development through research, policies and programs, Vol. 1: Applying developmental science for youth and families: Historical and theoretical foundations,* ed. R. M. Lerner, F. Jacobs, and D. Wertlieb, pp. 369-406. Newbury Park, CA: Sage Publications.

Benson, P. L., P. C. Scales, A. Sesma Jr., and E. C. Roehlkepartain. (2005). Adolescent spirituality. In *What do children need to flourish? Conceptualizing and measuring indicators of positive development,* ed. K. A. Moore and L. H. Lippman, pp. 25-40. New York: Kluwer Academic/Plenum.

Bronfenbrenner, U., and P. Morris. (1998). The ecology of developmental processes. In *Handbook of child psychology. Vol. 1: Theoretical models of human development,* 5th ed., ed. R. M. Lerner, pp. 993-1028. New York: Wiley.

Bronson, P. (2007). How not to talk to kids: The inverse power of praise. *New York.* Downloaded on August 14, 2007, from http://nymag.com/news/features/27840/.

Bunge, M. J. (2001). *The child in Christian thought.* Grand Rapids: Eerdmans.

Carasso, A., C. E. Steuerle, and G. Reynolds. (2007). *Kids' share 2007: How children fare in the federal budget.* Washington, DC: Urban Institute.

Catalano, R. F., M. L. Berglund, J. A. Ryan, H. S. Lonczak, and J. D. Hawkins. (1999).

Positive youth development in the United States: Research findings on evaluations of positive youth development programs. Seattle: Social Development Research Group.

Csikszentmihalyi, M. (1990). *Flow: The psychology of optimal experience.* New York: Harper & Row.

Damon, W. (2004). What is positive youth development? *The Annals of the American Academy of Political and Social Science* 591, no. 1: 13-24.

Damon, W. (1997). *The youth charter: How communities can work together to raise standards for all our children.* New York: Free Press.

Damon, W. (1995). *Greater expectations: Overcoming the culture of indulgence in America's homes and schools.* New York: Free Press.

Damon, W., and A. Gregory. (2003). Bringing in a new era in the field of youth development. In *Developmental assets and asset-building communities: Implications for research, policy, and practice,* ed. R. M. Lerner and P. L. Benson, pp. 47-64. New York: Kluwer Academic/Plenum.

Eccles, J. S., and J. A. Gootman. (2002). *Community programs to promote youth development.* Washington, DC: National Academy Press.

Edelman, M. W. (1993). *The measure of our success: A letter to my children and yours.* New York: Harper Perennial.

Furstenberg, F. F. (2000). The sociology of adolescence and youth in the 1990s: A critical commentary, *Journal of Marriage and the Family* 62: 896-910.

Golombek, S. B. (1995). Children as philanthropists: The younger, the better. In *Care and community in modern society: Passing on the tradition of service to future generations,* ed. P. G. Schervish, V. A. Hodgkinson, and M. Gates, pp. 139-59. San Francisco: Jossey-Bass.

Hamilton, S. F., M. A. Hamilton, and K. Pittman. (2004). Principles for youth development. In *The youth development handbook: Coming of age in American communities,* ed. S. F. Hamilton and M. A. Hamilton, pp. 3-22. Thousand Oaks, CA: Sage.

Hein, K. (2003). Enhancing the assets for positive youth development: The vision, values, and action agenda of the W. T. Grant Foundation. In *Developmental assets and asset-building communities: Implications for research, policy, and practice,* ed. R. M. Lerner and P. L. Benson, pp. 97-117. New York: Kluwer Academic/Plenum.

Hersch, P. (1998). *A tribe apart: A journey into the heart of American adolescence.* New York: Ballantine.

Immerwahr, J. (1995). *Talking about children: A focus group report from Public Agenda.* Washington, DC: Public Agenda.

Inglehart, R., M. Basañez, J. Díez-Medrano, L. Halman, and R. Luijkx. (2004). *Human beliefs and values: A cross-cultural sourcebook based upon the 1999-2002 values surveys.* Mexico City: Siglo Veintiuno Editores.

Isaacs, J., and P. Lovell. (2007). *Priority or afterthought? Children and the federal budget.* Alexandria, VA: First Focus.

Keyes, C. L. M. (2003). Complete mental health: An agenda for the 21st century. In *Flourishing: Positive psychology and the life well-lived,* ed. C. L. M. Keyes and J. Haidt, pp. 293-312. Washington, DC: American Psychological Association.

Keyes, C. L. M., and J. Haidt. (2002). *Flourishing: Positive psychology and the life well-lived.* Washington, DC: American Psychological Association.

King, P. E., and P. L. Benson. (2006). Spiritual development and adolescent well-being and thriving. In *The handbook of spiritual development in childhood and adolescence,* ed. E. C. Roehlkepartain, P. E. King, L. M. Wagener, and P. L. Benson, pp. 384-98. Thousand Oaks, CA: Sage.

King, P. E., and J. L. Furrow. (2004). Religion as a resource for positive youth development: Religion, social capital, and moral outcomes, *Developmental Psychology* 40: 703-13.

Larson, R. W. (2000). Toward a psychology of positive youth development, *American Psychologist* 55, no. 1: 170-83.

Leffert, N., P. L. Benson, P. C. Scales, A. Sharma, D. Drake, and D. A. Blyth. (1998). Developmental assets: Measurement and prediction of risk behaviors among adolescents, *Applied Developmental Science* 2, no. 4: 209-30.

Lerner, R. M. (2007). *The good teen: Rescuing adolescence from the myths of the storm and stress years.* New York: Crown Publishers.

Lerner, R. M. (2004). *Liberty: Thriving and civic engagement among America's youth.* Thousand Oaks, CA: Sage.

Lerner, R. M., and P. L. Benson. (2003). *Developmental Assets and asset-building communities: Implications for research, policy, and practice.* New York: Kluwer Academic/Plenum.

Lerner, R. M., C. Brentano, E. M. Dowling, and P. M. Anderson. (2002). Positive youth development: Thriving as the basis of personhood and civil society, *New Directions for Youth Development: Pathways to Positive Development Among Diverse Youth* 95: 11-33.

Marty, M. E. (2007). *The mystery of the child.* Grand Rapids: Eerdmans.

Masten, A. S. (2001). Ordinary magic: Resilience processes in development, *American Psychologist* 56: 227-38.

Moore, K. A. (1997). Criteria for indicators of child well-being. In *Indicators of children's well-being,* ed. R. M. Hauser, B. V. Brown, and W. R. Prosser, pp. 36-44. New York: Russell Sage Foundation.

Moore, K. A., and L. Lippman. (2005). *What do children need to flourish? Conceptualizing and measuring indicators of positive development.* New York: Kluwer Academic/Plenum.

Moore, K. A., L. Lippman, and B. Brown. (2004). Indicators of child well-being: The promise for positive youth development, *The Annals of the American Academy of Political and Social Science* 591: 125-47.

Palmer, P. J. (1999). *Let your life speak: Listening for the voice of vocation.* San Francisco: Jossey-Bass.

Pittman, K. J., and W. P. Fleming. (1991). *A new vision: Promoting youth development.* Written transcript of live testimony by Karen J. Pittman given before the House Select Committee on Children, Youth, and Families. Washington, DC: Center for Youth Development and Policy Research.

Roehlkepartain, E. C. (2008). Seeking common ground in understanding spiritual development: A preliminary theoretical framework. Minneapolis: Search Institute. Available at: www.search-institute.org/csd/major-projects/definition-update.

Roehlkepartain, E. C., P. E. King, L. M. Wagener, and P. L. Benson. (2006). *The handbook of spiritual development in childhood and adolescence.* Thousand Oaks, CA: Sage.

Roehlkepartain, E. C., E. D. Naftali, and L. Musegades. (2000). *Growing up generous: Engaging youth in giving and serving.* Bethesda, MD: Alban Institute.

Roehlkepartain, E. C., and E. Patel. (2006). Congregations: Unexamined crucibles of spiritual development. In *The handbook of spiritual development in childhood and adolescence,* ed. E. C. Roehlkepartain, P. E. King, L. M. Wagener, and P. L. Benson, pp. 324-36. Thousand Oaks, CA: Sage Publications.

Roehlkepartain, E. C., and P. C. Scales. (2007). Developmental assets: A framework for enriching service-learning (fact sheet). Scotts Valley, CA: National Service-Learning Clearinghouse (www.servicelearning.org).

Scales, P. C. (2007). Spirituality and adolescent well-being: Selected new statistics. Downloaded December 29, 2007, from www.search-institute.org/csd/articles/fast-facts/selected-statistics

Scales, P. C. (2003). *Other people's kids: Social expectations and American adults' involvement with children and adolescents.* New York: Kluwer Academic/Plenum.

Scales, P. C., and P. L. Benson. (2005). Adolescence and thriving. In *Encyclopedia of applied developmental science,* ed. Celia B. Fisher and Richard M. Lerner, pp. 15-19. Thousand Oaks, CA: Sage.

Scales, P. C., and P. L. Benson. (2004). Prosocial orientation and community service. In *What do children need to flourish?* ed. K. A. Moore and L. Lippman, pp. 339-56. New York: Kluwer Academic/Plenum.

Scales, P. C., and P. L. Benson. (2003). Prosocial orientation and community service. In *What do children need to flourish? Conceptualizing and measuring indicators of positive development,* ed. K. A. Moore and L. Lippman, pp. 339-56. New York: Kluwer Academic/Plenum.

Scales, P. C., and N. Leffert. (2004). *Developmental assets: A synthesis of the scientific research on adolescent development,* 2nd ed. Minneapolis: Search Institute.

Schervish, P. G., V. A. Hodgkinson, and M. Gates. (1995). *Care and community in modern society: Passing on the tradition of service to future generations.* San Francisco: Jossey-Bass.

Seligman, M. E. P., and M. Csikszentmihalyi. (2000). Positive psychology: An introduction, *American Psychologist* 55, no. 1: 5-14.

Takanishi, R. (1993). An agenda for the integration of research and policy during early adolescence. In *Early adolescence: Perspectives on research, policy, and intervention,* ed. R. M. Lerner. Hillsdale, NJ: Erlbaum.

Theokas, C., J. B. Almerigi, R. M. Lerner, E. M. Dowling, P. L. Benson, P. C. Scales, and A. von Eye. (2005). Conceptualizing and modeling individual components of thriving in early adolescence, *Journal of Early Adolescence* 25, no. 1: 113-43.

Wagener, L. M., J. L. Furrow, P. E. King, N. Leffert, and P. L. Benson. (2003). Religious involvement and developmental resources in youth, *Review of Religious Research* 44, no. 3: 271-84.

Wilson, J. Q. (1993). *The moral sense.* New York: Free Press.
Yust, K. M., A. N. Johnson, S. E. Sasso, and E. C. Roehlkepartain. (2006). *Nurturing child and adolescent spirituality: Perspectives from the world's religious traditions.* Lanham, MD: Rowman & Littlefield.

CHAPTER 2

Does Best Love of the Child Mean Parents Should Facilitate a Love of the Sacred?

Annette Mahoney and Kenneth I. Pargament

Introduction

This essay explores what the social sciences have to say about whether "best love of the child" necessarily involves parental efforts to facilitate children's spirituality. Prior to the twentieth century, this issue was largely moot as societies across the globe concurred that spiritual formation of youth was a major priority, and religious institutions were deeply embedded within cultures to promote this goal regardless of variations in their theological teachings. However, spirituality is becoming increasingly privatized in postmodern societies where people decreasingly participate in particular religious communities. Even in the U.S. where 84 percent of adolescents believe in God (12% are not sure and 3% do not believe in God; Smith, 2005), national surveys imply that at least half of the youth receive minimal formal religious education to help them form a spiritual identity. For example, around 48-50 percent of U.S. adolescents and parents of young children say they attend religious services monthly or less (Smith, 2005). Thus, even counting participation in religious classes or service groups outside of weekend services, many youth experience very little religious training under the auspices of a religious organization. Further, even the most devout adolescents spend far less time engaged in institutionally based religious activities than other pursuits (e.g., school, sports, Internet/media consumption; Smith, 2005). This situation raises fundamental questions about parents' responsibility to facilitate their children's spirituality.

In this essay, we explore the challenging questions that parents face in deciding whether and how to help their children to develop a well-formed spiritual identity or, stated differently, to come to "love" the sacred. We approach these questions from the perspective of social science theory and research. Our focus here is on U.S. families with adolescents because they comprise the samples used in the majority of scientific studies on religion, and on youth and family. It should be kept in mind that this research primarily pertains to Christianity, not "religion" globally speaking. Contrary to the notion that the U.S. is highly religiously diverse, U.S. families are overwhelmingly Christian. For example, the recent National Study of Youth and Religion (NSYR) involving a large representative sample of adolescents found that 75 percent endorse a Christian affiliation (52% Protestant, 23% Catholic), 16 percent report no religious affiliation, 7 percent affiliate with one of the many minority U.S. religions, particularly Latter Day Saints (LDS, 2.5%) and Judaism (1.5%), and nearly 2 percent do not know or disclose an affiliation (Smith, 2005).

At the outset, we want to acknowledge that we intend to be provocative. Namely, we hope to prompt scholars as well as parents to make the spiritual formation of youth a priority. However, our goal is not to persuade the minority of parents in the U.S. who strongly hold worldviews that are antithetical to religion or spirituality to join the ranks of believers for the sake of their children. We refer such parents to an excellent book, *Parenting Beyond Belief*, as a resource to help them pass along a sense of ethics and morality to their children as they embrace secularism (McGowan, 2007). Rather, our intention is to address the larger audience of those who are not self-avowed secularists (notably, 94% of U.S. parents of adolescents do not describe themselves as atheists or agnostics; Smith, 2005). This audience includes the disengaged but vaguely religious or spiritual, the ambivalent or confused, the lightly churched, the nontraditional serious seekers, and the devout traditionalists.

Remarkably, up to 90 percent of U.S. parents say they desire religious training for their children (Gallup & Castelli, 1989). The motives underlying this desire are not well researched, but probably reflect the following idealistic belief: Making children aware of the sacred is an act of love by adults that will, in turn, facilitate a child's motivation and ability to be loving toward others. This essay takes a closer look at the two-sided assumption that "best love of child" entails a responsibility by parents to facilitate a love of the sacred by youth, which then promotes the child's love of others. Further, we offer a theoretical model regarding "the best love of the sacred" to optimize these hoped-for benefits. To set the stage for this discussion, we start with a review of studies, most of which are sociological, about links between global markers of youth's religious involvement (e.g., church attendance rates) and better psychosocial adjustment. We then review sociological studies indicating that parents play the most significant role in their offspring's spiritual development. Next, we move the discussion of spirituality beyond global sociological indicators of religious involvement. We first summarize Pargament's empirically informed, psychological model of a well-integrated spiritual orienting system, the hallmarks of which are complexity and flexibility in both the pathways and destinations of an individual's search for the sacred (Pargament, 2007). We use this model to highlight the psychological and social dangers of the remarkably simplistic and self-centered view of spirituality that most U.S. adolescents seem to have. We then discuss dilemmas that parents face in fostering their children's deep spiritual commitment for their own and others' benefit, without promoting intolerance. We close with suggestions for how parents might facilitate a spirituality on the part of their children that balances deep commitment with compassionate love for others.

Definitional Issues

Prior to proceeding, we want to explain our view of the terms "religion" and "spirituality." We rely on Pargament's definition that religion is "a search for significance in ways related to the sacred" (Pargament, 1997). Each element of this formulation merits elaboration. The "significance" component refers to whatever people construe as most important in their lives, whether it is psychological, social, physical, or spiritual in nature. The "search" refers to the means or pathways that individuals use to achieve their chosen destinations. Of course, not every search for a desired destination is religious in nature. In fact, the sphere of religion is unique because it incorporates perceptions of the sacred into either the desired destinations or pathways of a person's life journey. In our view, the core of "the sacred" involves perceptions of God, higher powers, divinity, and/or transcendent reality, but extends to any aspect of life that takes on spiritual character and significance by virtue of its association with the core (Pargament & Mahoney, 2005). This tripartite definition encompasses both the substantive and functional dimensions of religion. The substantive dimension of religion refers to beliefs, practices, and feelings rooted in theological understandings of reality (i.e., ideas about the sacred), regardless of whether based on personal or institutional thinking. The functional dimension of religion refers to the multitude of psychological (e.g., sense of security or meaning) and social (e.g., communal cohesion or control) purposes that religion may serve. Although some have begun to divorce spirituality from religion, we hold that the most central function of religion is to facilitate spirituality, which we define as "the search for the sacred" (Pargament & Mahoney, 2002). Spirituality thus forms the "heart and soul" of both private and institutional forms of religion because it centers on how people integrate the sacred into their lives. While other legitimate scholarly conceptions of spirituality exist, it is useful to keep in mind that religion and spirituality are not mutually exclusive for most U.S. adults. Moreover, compelling empirical evidence indicates that only 2 to 3 percent of adolescents in the U.S. can be accurately depicted as "spiritual but not religious" (Smith, 2005). With this in mind, we assume that standard measures of religiousness reflect spirituality, although the search for the sacred (i.e., spirituality) occurs both within and outside the context of traditional religious organizations (Pargament & Mahoney, 2002).

Benefits to Youth of Facilitating a Love of the Sacred

Like social scientists, perhaps the first question many parents ask about their children's spirituality is pragmatic, something along the lines of: "Will my child benefit by being spiritual?" The basic answer seems to be yes from a scientific point of view. To elaborate, we feature findings from the NSYR because this is by far the most comprehensive examination of religion and adolescents to date (Smith, 2005; Smith & Faris, 2002a, 2002b). Briefly, this project involved the telephone survey of a nationally representative sample of 3,270 adolescents (ages 13-17) as well as detailed qualitative interviews with 327 adolescents.

Adolescents and outcomes. Ample social science research indicates that the odds adolescents will experience desirable psychological and social outcomes improve as their self-reported levels of religiousness increase (Regnerus, Smith, & Fritsch, 2003; Smith, 2005; Smith & Faris, 2002a, 2002b; Wagener, Furrow, King, Leffert, & Benson, 2003). More specifically, higher adolescent religiousness has been consistently linked to less maladjustment, including drug, alcohol, and tobacco use, delinquency, suicide, depression, and risky sexual behaviors. Further, greater adolescent religiousness has been tied to numerous prosocial outcomes (Donahue & Benson, 1995; Regnerus, 2003; Smith, 2005; Wagener et al., 2003). These include greater hopefulness, life satisfaction, involvement with families, skills in solving health-related problems, emotional coping, academic achievement, political and civic involvement, and participation in community service. Such evidence primarily comes from large national surveys that correlate single-item indices, such as frequency of religious attendance and prayer, with outcomes. In addition, these findings emerge after controlling for multiple demographic factors, such as age, gender, race, region of residence, parental marital status, parental education, and family income. Moreover, these links cannot be fully attributed to certain genetically grounded personality traits of teens. Thus, religion matters even after taking into account seemingly "hard-wired" personality tendencies, such as risk aversion or conformity, that may steer teens toward both religious commitment and positive psychosocial outcomes (Smith, 2005). Furthermore, research does not suggest that the links between religion and desirable outcomes are merely due to reverse-causation, whereby youth self-select out of religion the more they engage in negative behaviors (e.g., alcohol use) or experience negative life events (e.g., family problems; Smith, 2005).

Children and outcomes. Because pre-adolescents presumably are unable to provide reliable reports on their own religiousness, studies on the benefits of religion for this age-group focus on parental religiousness. Indirect evidence in favor of positive outcomes of religion rests on a few studies that suggest that more religiously committed parents tend to be warmer and more engaged with their young children (Mahoney, Pargament, Swank, & Tarakeshwar, 2001). Remarkably, only two published studies have directly examined links between parental religiousness and child development. One study found null results using a convenience sample of predominantly black, low-income mothers of Head Start enrollees (Strayhorn, Weidman, & Larson, 1990). The other is a recent, methodologically rigorous, longitudinal study using a large, nationally representative sample, and it offers compelling evidence about the benefits of parental religious attendance (Bartkowski, Xu, & Levin, 2008). Namely, greater religious attendance by parents, individually and together as a couple, is tied to better child functioning in multiple domains: behaviorally (e.g., better self-control and less impulse control or disruptive behavior problems), socially (e.g., better interpersonal skills), emotionally (e.g., less internalizing symptoms), and cognitively (e.g., more advanced approaches to learning), as reported by teachers and parents, and after controlling for a wide range of demographic factors.

Dosage makes a difference and no guarantees. While the basic conclusion is "yes" to the question of whether religion is beneficial to youth, two critical qualifications exist. First, studies imply that the most religiously committed reap most of the benefits. This can be described as a "dosing effect." For example, the benefits of religion for adolescents seem to be largely attributable to differences between the most religiously involved teens compared to those who are disengaged from religion. Smith's (2005) analysis of four religious types within the NSYR sample sheds light on this fact. Specifically, 63 percent of U.S. teens were categorized into one of four distinct religious types: the Devoted (8% of American youth), the Regulars (27%), the Sporadic (17%), and the Disengaged (12%). Notably, the other 37 percent did not fit neatly into one of these four types due to inconsistency in their religious attitudes and behaviors. The Devoted attended religious services weekly or more and rated faith as very or extremely important to daily life; the Regulars attended two to three times monthly, and rated faith from very to not very important in daily life; the Sporadic attended a few times a year to monthly and rated faith as somewhat to not very important; and the Disengaged never attended (or attended often but self-identified as nonreligious) and rated faith as somewhat to not very important. Other criteria for the four groupings were a felt closeness to God, involvement in religious youth groups, and prayer and scripture reading, with the Devoted reporting highest levels and Disengaged reporting the lowest levels. Almost all of the desirable outcomes emerged only for the Devoted and Regular groups, contrasted with the Disengaged. The benefits for the Devoted and Regular groups were clear across multiple behavioral, emotional, and relational domains: substance abuse (e.g., drink alcohol weekly or more often, or use marijuana), academic functioning (e.g., earning poor grades, cutting classes, being expelled), sexual activity and attitudes, (e.g., opposing premarital sex, likelihood and frequency of sexual intercourse), emotional well-being (e.g., subjective happiness, satisfaction with physical appearance), depressive symptoms (e.g., feeling sad and depressed, alone and misunderstood), parent-child relationships (e.g., perceived feelings of being cared for, close, and understood, more dinners per week with parents), moral reasoning and honesty behaviors (e.g., less likely to believe that morals are relative, less lying), moral compassion (e.g., caring about poor and elderly) and more civil involvement and nonreligious volunteer activities. In short, the roughly 35 percent of teens who are clearly committed to religion enjoy psychosocial benefits from religion compared to those 12 percent who are disengaged. These findings also suggest that religion is not especially helpful for the roughly 53 percent of U.S. adolescents whose faith is sporadic or poorly integrated.

The second major qualification is that not all youth without a strong faith suffer, nor do all highly religious youth benefit from their faith. This reality can be easily obscured when probabilistic findings are simplified into black-and-white distinctions in the media as well as in scholarly discourse. Two examples about the parent-child relationship based on NSYR data illustrate these issues. Teens who fall into the Disengaged religious type are three times more likely to disagree with the statement "my parents love and accept me a lot for who I am" compared to teens who fall into the Devoted group (26% versus 7%). It does not follow, however, that most religiously Disengaged teens feel unloved by their parents. In fact, the majority of the religiously Disengaged, specifically 74 percent, feel that their parents love and accept them, compared to 83 percent of the Regulars and 93 percent of the Devoted. A different example brings home the fact that religion does not guarantee desired outcomes. Specifically, teens classified as Devoted and Regulars are more likely than the Disengaged (57% and 48% versus 40%) to say that they "have fun hanging out with and doing things with their father very or fairly often." Thus, greater religious involvement by teens is tied to more frequent father-child interactions. Nevertheless, many of the Devoted (43%) and Regular (52%) teens still do not enjoy much day-to-day interaction with their fathers. A careful look at nearly every group contrast between the most and least religious youth makes it clear that social science research always deals with relative odds, not guarantees. An incomplete understanding of real differences found at a group level can obscure the fact there are many cases that don't fit the general rule. Sensitivity to the underlying nature of scientific evidence allows a balanced appreciation of the benefits of religion, one that avoids exaggerated positive claims by those who are personally committed to a faith life and dismissive skepticism by those who are not personally religious or spiritually inclined.

Parents' Role in Helping Youth Discover the Sacred

In light of the many psychosocial benefits associated with religion, even more secularly oriented, "lightly churched" parents may hope that their child will discover the sacred. For instance, in our own research, we are finding that first-time parents of infants, who are both high and low in self-reported spirituality, often say something to the effect, "I want my child to know about God and religion, but to decide for himself or herself what to believe." Taking a hands-off approach to children's spiritual formation seems commonplace, based on the frequency of family discussions about sacred matters reported by nationally representative samples. For instance, only one-third of families with adolescents talk about God, the scriptures, prayer, or other religious or spiritual topics more than once a week (Smith, 2005; Smith & Kim, 2003). Similarly, in families with children, the mean frequency of a family member talking to a given child about the family's religious beliefs or traditions falls between several times a month to several times a year (Bartkowski et al., 2008). Presumably, many parents think their child can discover the sacred on his or her own, and they avoid strongly influencing their child's search via a great deal of discussion or teaching about spiritual issues.

Apparently, parents are also unaware of or unmoved by studies demonstrating that youth are strongly influenced by their parents' stance toward religion, with or without much direct discussion. For example, about three in four U.S. teens consider their own religious beliefs to be somewhat or very similar to their parents. Only 6 percent consider their beliefs to be very different from their mother and 11 percent very different from their father (Smith, 2005). A closer look at responses to the question of how important religion is to daily life helps to illuminate the well-established and powerful "transmission effect" from parents to offspring for variables such as religious affiliation, frequency of attendance, prayer, etc. The NSYR revealed that 67 percent of U.S. teens who report their faith is extremely or very important in their daily lives have parents who also say that their faith is extremely important; but only 8 percent of devout teens have parents who view their faith as not very or not at all important. At the other end of the continuum, 61 percent of teens who say their faith is somewhat or not very important in their daily lives also have parents who say the same thing; only 8 percent of the less engaged teens have parents who say their faith is extremely important. Finally, when parents say faith is not at all important in their daily lives, 47 percent of their teens also say this. So, contrary to the notion that children spontaneously discover the sacred when left to their own devices, most youth become deeply engaged in a faith life when their parents are. Conversely, most youth who are minimally engaged in either private or public spheres of faith have parents with lukewarm feelings about religion and low levels of religious activity (e.g., attendance, prayer). The take-home message is that parents nearly always shape the spiritual identities of their children one way or the other.

Social scientists have posited a variety of explanations as to why parents play a critical role in shaping their children's religious attitudes and practices. Transmission models highlight that parents pass along faith by modeling religious practices, values, and beliefs (e.g., showing faith by word and deed, consistency in how they live out their faith; Boyatzis, Dollahite, & Marks, 2006; Regnerus, Smith, & Smith, 2004). Such carry-over seems particularly potent when parents are intentional about conveying their faith (Okagaki & Bevis, 1999). Other research based on transactional models of religion highlight that youth are not merely passive recipients of parental values (Boyatzis et al., 2006; Boyatzis & Janicki, 2003). Rather dyadic parent-child discussions of faith predict greater religious involvement by youth, and such belief and commitment seems best nurtured by both fathers and mothers who allow their children to observe, discuss, and take an active role in developing their own faith (e.g., Flor & Knapp, 2001; Myers, 1996). Parents are also theorized to promote their children's religiousness by channeling them into social groups that reinforce and help maintain the child's religious beliefs and commitment to religious norms (Regnerus et al., 2004). But while religious peer and congregational influences are salient in shaping youth religiousness, these forces overlap with parental influences, and together create synergistic effects (Regnerus et al., 2004; Schwartz, 2006; Smith, 2005). Overall, it seems that if spirituality is not valued or lived by parents, if it is relegated to a separate, less important sphere outside the family, most children will reject it, even if they are exposed to it outside of the family during childhood.

Given that parents wittingly or unwittingly facilitate or inhibit their children's love for the sacred, questions arise why parents would be reluctant to invest in this role. We are unaware of social science research that speaks directly to the thinking of parents who endorse a belief in God and have generally favorable attitudes toward religion or spirituality, but do little to encourage or guide their children's spiritual lives. By contrast, it is widely accepted that parents have a major responsibility, and often try, to influence their pre-teens' and teens' academic, artistic, athletic, recreational, and social lives. Why the difference when it comes to spirituality? Perhaps parental reluctance in the spiritual sphere reflects notions about children's autonomy and need for individuality; some parents may understand separation of church and state as separation of church and family. Or perhaps parents assume that youth will discover the sacred through mystical, personal experiences best left untouched by adults. Many parents also may suffer from a lack of confidence and knowledge about how to guide children along a spiritual path because their own journeys left them unprepared for the task. Thus, they may relegate the job to congregations and religious leaders. Finally, many parents may be immobilized and fail to take action due to their own personal ambivalence and minimal commitment to spirituality.

What Kind of Love of the Sacred Is Optimal?

The nature of an optimal spiritual orientation system. "So, can you tell me what kind of love of the sacred is best?" This is a key question parents may have who want their children to experience the psychosocial benefits associated with a strong love of the sacred. Currently, most studies that deal directly with adolescents' religiousness and outcomes assess religion via global items. These include single questions about religious affiliation, frequency of religious service attendance, overall importance of religion or spirituality in daily life or in shaping major life decisions, thoughts about God (e.g., felt closeness, doubts, nature of God), subjective religious experiences (e.g., making a personal commitment to God, conversion experiences), religious practices (e.g., prayer, meditation, scripture reading), and involvement in religious youth groups (Regnerus et al., 2003; Smith, 2005). Such data beg the question of exactly what kind of "love of the sacred" helps versus hinders a child's love of others. We now summarize key elements of Pargament's (2007) integrative model of spirituality as one way to gain insight into the nature of a spiritual system that may be optimal, particularly during developmental transitions and times of stress. Because very few studies on youth and religion directly examine the interplay of specific spiritual resources or struggles in specific situations (e.g., religious coping; Mahoney, Pendleton, & Ihrke, 2005), this model is based largely on research with adults. Nevertheless, it provides a picture of what kind of spirituality parents might ideally hope their children possess when they are grown for psychological and social purposes.

As discussed earlier, we define spirituality as the search for the sacred. This search is dynamic rather than static, evolving rather than fixed. The search begins with the individual's discovery of the sacred. Once found, the individual takes one or more spiritual paths to nurture his or her connection to the sacred. Changes from within or outside of the individual's world, however, can violate, threaten, harm, or point to the limits of the individual's understanding of the sacred. The individual must then cope to preserve and protect a bond with the sacred as best he or she can. At times, though, in spite of the person's best efforts to sustain the sacred in the coping process, internal or external pressures can throw the individual's spiritual world into turmoil. Spiritual struggles can be short-lived experiences, followed by a return to established spiritual pathways. But struggles can also represent a fork in the road that leads to permanent disengagement from the search for the sacred, temporary disengagement from the search followed by rediscovery of the sacred, or fundamental transformations in the perceived character of the sacred. Following a transformation, the individual shifts again to efforts to hold on to the sacred. The search proceeds across the lifespan and unfolds in a larger field of situational, social, cultural, and psychological forces that both shape and are shaped by the nature of the search.

There is, of course, tremendous diversity in the ways in which the sacred is perceived and understood (i.e., discovery) and in the paths that people take to conserve or transform their relationship with the sacred (i.e., conservation or transformation). Over time, however, most people develop specific preferences about the particular pathways and destinations they choose to follow. Based on personal, situational, and social forces, individuals find some pathways and destinations more compelling than others. One person strives to make the world a sacred place by acts of kindness to others and efforts to bring about a more equitable society. Another seeks a personal relationship with Jesus largely through scriptural study, prayer, and devotion. One person tries to experience the sense of transcendence in daily life through meditative practices and outdoor experiences. Yet another attempts to discover ultimate truths about the origins of the universe through scientific study. These preferred configurations of pathways and destinations come together to form highly individualized spiritual orienting systems — frameworks of spiritual beliefs, practices, relations, experiences, and values that consistently guide and direct the search for the sacred (Pargament, 2007).

Given the many manifestations of spirituality, what might be the characteristics of a well-functioning spiritual system from a scientific perspective? Although theologians can argue for the ontological "Truth" of a spiritual system, scientists must remain neutral about such claims. Instead, scientists judge the merits of spirituality based on the pragmatic benefits it yields. Our earlier discussion about links between global measures of religiousness and desirable psychosocial outcomes for youth and families illustrates this point. But an emphasis on static outcomes can obscure the multilayered, dynamic process embedded within spirituality. By contrast, process criteria of spirituality refer to concepts of balance, dynamism, comprehensiveness, flexibility, and interconnectedness. Along these lines, we argue that the most effective spirituality lies not within or outside a particular tradition nor within the individual, but is a dynamic integration of individuals in interaction with situations and their larger context.

What then are the hallmarks of a well-integrated spirituality? We suggest that it is not defined by a spiritual trait, belief, practice, emotion, or relationship, but by the degree to which the individual's spiritual pathways and destinations fluidly work together. At its best, spirituality is defined by pathways that are broad and deep, responsive to life's situations, nurtured by the larger social context, capable of flexibility and continuity, and oriented toward a sacred destination that is large enough to encompass the full range of human potential and luminous enough to provide the individual with a powerful guiding vision. This kind of spirituality depends fundamentally on an individual's ability to reflect upon and articulate his or her dynamic spiritual journey in a sophisticated manner so that healthy adaptations can be made across the lifespan. At its worst, spirituality is dis-integrated, defined by pathways that lack scope and depth, fail to meet the challenges and demands of live events, destructively clash and collide with the surrounding social system, change and shift too easily or not at all, and misdirect the individual. Such systems tend to reflect a minimal knowledge or awareness by individuals of their own spiritual pathways or destinations, which can break down easily under stress or are not sufficiently complex to allow for a transformation when necessary. It is beyond the scope of this chapter to illustrate concretely all of the possible problematic spiritual pathways and destinations associated with a dis-integrated spiritual system (see Pargament, 2007). However, with the basic features of a well-integrated spiritual system in mind, we now turn to evaluate recent empirical discoveries about the substance of many adolescents' love of the sacred.

The Nature of U.S. Youths' Spiritual Orienting System

Moralistic Therapeutic Deism (MTD). As part of the NSYR, in-depth qualitative interviews were conducted with a nationally representative sample of 327 adolescents. This fascinating work greatly illuminates the substance of U.S. teens' spiritual orienting systems. By analyzing teens' interview responses, especially in light of their responses to structured survey items, Smith (the lead researcher) concluded that the majority of teens across all denominations hold a remarkably simplistic and self-serving understanding of religion. He coined this spiritual orientating system Moralistic Therapeutic Deism (MTD), which consists of five core elements:

1. A God exists who created and orders the world and watches over human life on earth.
2. God wants people to be good, nice, and fair to each other, as taught in the Bible and by most world religions.

3. The central goal of life is to be happy and to feel good about oneself.
4. God does not need to be particularly involved in one's life except when God is needed to resolve a problem.
5. Good people go to heaven when they die.

Another major observation was that almost all teens seemed only vaguely conscious of the nature of their spirituality, despite most (82%) saying religion was at least somewhat important to their daily lives. As a group, they were tongue-tied and inarticulate when asked to elaborate about their faith, their religious beliefs and practices, and its meaning or place in their lives. Although most could readily discuss a wide range of sensitive, highly personal topics, such as premarital sex, sexually transmitted diseases, alcohol and drug use, money, peer pressure, or romantic, academic, athletic, and career endeavors, even most of the devout teens had trouble finding words to explain their views about their faith. In fact, many teens gave the impression the interview itself was the first time an adult had asked them to share their thoughts about their own religion and spirituality. Thus, the contours of MTD were derived by extracting major themes from the disparate, halting utterances of the teens.

While it is beyond the scope of this essay to review the many possible psychosocial (or theological) roots of MTD, we would like to address a central question parents may have, especially since many of them presumably also endorse aspects of MTD. That is, if MTD is "working" for many teens to accomplish so many desirable outcomes, what could be wrong from a psychosocial perspective with this spiritual approach to life? Based on thematic coding of transcriptions of interviews, teens themselves indicated that religion is important for many of the same scientifically documented benefits cited earlier:

a) gives guidance in how to be a good person
b) helps to cope with problems and troubles
c) creates feelings of mental and psychological security
d) helps to keep a positive attitude about life
e) yields general mental and emotional benefits that sustain a good perspective on life
f) builds personal confidence and sense of purpose and motivation
g) contributes to maturity
h) helps one to be successful, socially involved, healthier
i) most important, helps a person to feel good and to be happy

With regard to the second issue of responding to life challenges, people who see the sacred as purely loving and protective are vulnerable to disappointment or disillusionment, for they may be unable to reconcile their narrow, albeit positive, representation of the sacred with exposure to pain, suffering, and evil in the world. This can trigger painful spiritual struggles with the divine, such as doubting or questioning God's power or feeling angry and abandoned by God. Such spiritual struggles are robustly tied to poorer psychological and medical functioning cross-sectionally and longitudinally (Pargament et al., 2005). In fact, the consistency and magnitude of links between spiritual struggles and negative psychological outcomes outweigh the benefits associated with global religiousness and positive religious coping methods, such as interpreting a negative event as being part of God's will. Furthermore, an inability to resolve spiritual struggles is tied to increasing psychological maladjustment over time. Fortunately, greater religious involvement appears to help individuals come to terms with spiritual struggles that a "small god" view of the sacred can trigger in the times of stress. But limited access to religious resources can leave people mired in debilitating spiritual struggles.

Problematic pathways. Other problems can involve the spiritual pathways people select to reach their destinations (Pargament, 2007). We consider two of these problematic pathways as revealed in MTD. The first problem concerns an insufficient depth and/or breadth of spiritual pathways. Ideally, spirituality is a way of being that is broad and deep, touching on virtually every dimension of life. Of course, real people often fall short of such an ideal. But a lack of breadth or depth in the routes by which one establishes and sustains a connection to the sacred increases the risk of spiritual struggles, which as noted above, can elicit serious psychological distress. The MTD model of spirituality suggests that most teens believe that being a moral person is the primary means by which to be a spiritual person. A core belief is that God wants people to be good, nice, and fair to each other, as taught in the Bible and by most world religions. The problem, of course, lies not with this attitude per se. Rather, the problem has to do with the teens' shallow understanding of this pathway and the fact that many other options exist. Most seemed to have a relatively simple reward-punishment understanding of the "whys" that underlie ethical behavior. This is consistent with their generally limited or misguided knowledge of their own religious traditions. For example, many Christian teens were comfortable talking about God in general, but not specifically about Jesus, and few mentioned key concepts like "sin," "salvation," or "grace." Of course, many adults also show a fragmented spirituality, marked by limited depth in spiritual knowledge. For example, though nine out of ten adults have a copy of the Bible in their homes, only 35 percent know who delivered the Sermon on the Mount (Gallup & Lindsay, 1999).

What are the psychosocial risks of a spirituality marked by a restricted depth or breadth in routes to search for the sacred? At some point, most people encounter strong evidence that being a good, moral person fails to address fully disturbing questions about suffering, meaning, personal responsibility, and God. In contrast, a well-integrated spirituality comes with a deep, rich set of spiritual pathways to help one wrestle with ultimate spiritual questions. This includes an extensive store of sacred concepts and stories, a variety of spiritual rituals and practices, and connections with a community of fellow-believers to help handle the complexities and paradoxes of human wrongdoing and suffering (Pargament, 2007). But a scattered or simplistic grasp of religion, particularly with regard to morality, can trigger the kinds of spiritual struggles discussed earlier, which are linked to added psychological pain. Moreover, if morality is the sole pathway connected to the sacred, blockage of this route can easily end the journey altogether.

A second set of problems in a dis-integrated spiritual system have to do with a poor fit between pathways and destinations. MTD also illustrates these dangers. According to MTD, the central goal of life is to be happy and to feel good about oneself. The main pathway to achieve this goal is to be a good, moral person, which also leads to the ultimate destination of going to heaven in the afterlife. Morality in MTD means to be nice, kind, pleasant, respectful, responsible; to work on self-improvement and taking care of one's health; and to do one's best to be successful by society's standards (e.g., educational and financial accomplishments). It also means not being socially disruptive or interpersonally obnoxious. Essentially, many teens appear to subliminally operate under a sacred contract that states: If I am a nice, pleasant, and good person (sacred pathway) then God will ensure that good things happen to me on earth and later in heaven (sacred destinations). Such a system can degenerate into spiritual hypocrisy where the person goes down a spiritual path, such as attending church, merely for nonspiritual reasons. Especially in extreme forms, this approach to spirituality turns the fundamental precepts of the most prevalent world religions in the U.S. (i.e., Christianity, Judaism, LDS, and Islam) on their head. Rather than pursuing a connection to the sacred as the ultimate destination regardless of the personal costs, a connection to the sacred becomes a means to the end goal of attaining personal gratification. Thus, one values religion, not for a love of the sacred per se, but for the instrumental good the sacred does for the self.

Beyond theological concerns, these assumptions are psychologically and socially risky. For one thing, teens who encounter serious stress or trauma may be unable to reconcile their expectation that if they were good and loving then they should not experience suffering. Subsequent doubts and anger toward God are likely to occur that exacerbate psychological distress. Such spiritual struggles are fairly common as initial reactions to trauma, but may be especially difficult to resolve for those who have relied only on morality as a sacred pathway and have limited awareness or practice with more adaptive spiritual pathways for such situations. In addition, the sacred contract reflected by the MTD's poor match between a given spiritual pathway (morality) and destination (personal happiness) can lead to undesirable outcomes for others. Teens who believe that good things happen to good people may reason that those who suffer misfortune deserve these consequences because they obviously did not deserve God's protection. This may foster condemnation or apathetic disinterest to the plights of others, rather than proactive compassion and love for others.

An overly simplistic understanding of the MTD pathway of morality can go awry in a different way in traumatic situations. Here an individual may sincerely elevate pleasing God to the ultimate spiritual destination and then infer that misfortune happened because he or she failed to follow the sacred pathway of morality adequately. The individual may react by doubling or tripling investment in some spiritual activities, but forgo other more sensible spiritual or psychosocial solutions to the situation. For instance, a teen may reason that contracting a sexually transmitted disease or being emotionally abused by a parent represents a punishment from God because of the teen's moral failures. This kind of thinking could lead the individual to spiritual activities designed to hide the perceived moral transgressions (e.g., private ritual purification, prayer for God to take away the problem) rather than to seek more useful solutions, such as intervention from medical or mental health professionals.

Here we have highlighted a few examples, along with illustrative empirical research, that suggests that a simplistic and poorly integrated spiritual orienting system, like MTD, has risks. It neither encourages individuals to develop a sufficiently complex view of the sacred nor fosters a flexible range of pathways to deal with the diverse situations that challenge one's spirituality. This sets the stage for painful spiritual struggles that exacerbate psychological distress. Thus, parents who want to ensure that their child reaps the benefits of religion are advised to help their child move toward a well-integrated spiritual orienting system. We suggest that such complexity comes about by fostering a child's deep commitment to a particular spiritual identity. This entails being an involved guide on this journey so the child develops a sufficiently rich set of spiritual resources to foster faith over time, and grow through rather than become mired in spiritual struggles. High levels of commitment are most likely to yield benefits — psychologically, socially, and ultimately spiritually. In a paradoxical way, facilitating a search for the sacred that goes beyond ensuring one's own well-being, as is the case with MTD, enhances the chances that spirituality will be a sustaining force across all of one's life. But this process of fostering complexity raises yet another set of dilemmas.

Spiritual Commitment: Compassion and Love, or Intolerance and Hatred?

Is it possible to foster commitment to a particular spiritual identity and, at the same time, encourage tolerance of others' spirituality? This is a key question for many parents, one that boils down to a question of how to balance a serious love of the sacred with love for others. Open any newspaper and it will be hard to avoid the reality of religiously justified conflicts and the major problems they create. Parents may wonder, "How can I or others be a model of commitment without being fanatical and thereby breeding intolerance, prejudice, even hatred on the part of youth?" Such fears may be immobilizing to parents and lead them to giving up entirely on the task of spiritual socialization.

Perhaps the findings from NSYR are reassuring. Specifically, Smith (2005, p. 115) concluded: "When it comes to their [teens'] thinking about what is legitimate for other people, most affirm pluralism, religious inclusivity, and individual authority. This is true for notable percentages of teens even in America's more conservative and strict religious traditions." Despite media stereotypes about conservative Christians, this observation meshes with the fairly weak links found between global markers of religious conservatism (e.g., single items about affiliation, fundamentalist reading of Bible) and prejudice and intolerance toward others (Pargament, McConnell, Mahoney, & Silberman, 2007). Nevertheless, high levels of commitment to particular sacred destinations and pathways could create serious interpersonal conflict. Three problematic scenarios come to mind.

First, a deeper commitment to a particular set of religious beliefs and practices could increase a child's awareness of differences across religious and secular groups about the nature of the sacred. While such knowledge could merely foster a deeper appreciation of the unique features of one's own faith, a hypersensitivity to others' quite different views could trigger insecurity. This could escalate to perceiving other groups as a threat to one's own faith. And, perceiving a different religious group as a direct spiritual threat, or desecration, of one's own religious group has been robustly tied to higher levels of prejudice, perceived conflict, and hostility toward the "outsiders," even after taking into account general levels of religiousness and other attitudes tied to these outcomes (e.g., particularism, authoritarianism). Such studies have dealt with Christians perceiving Jews (Pargament et al., 2007) and Muslims (Raiya, Pargament, Mahoney, & Trevino, 2008) as desecrators of Christianity, but the theoretical model in these studies used can just as easily be applied to other groups, such as Jewish or Muslim believers' views of Christians, or liberal and conservative Christians' views of each other.

Second, deeper commitment to an exclusivist view about spiritual pathways could foster youths' hostility toward others. Exclusivism refers to perceiving one's own religion as the only true faith or pathway that leads to the sacred. Such beliefs have been tied to greater intolerance and hostility to others (Pargament, 2007; Pargament et al., 2007). In our view, an important part of a well-integrated spiritual system is the humble recognition that any one approach to the sacred is limited, and that tolerance for multiple pathways to the sacred is needed. Thus, all children, including those who grow up to be spiritually informed secularists or those who become devout believers within a given tradition, should strive toward the spiritual virtue of humility. Spiritual humility refers to the recognition that any approach to the sacred is limited by human frailty and fallibility. Children who are raised within a family or community that takes a dogmatic approach toward religion, be it religious belief or nonbelief, may be unable to develop a respect for the community of all children and families.

Third, coming closer to home, some may fear that urging a child's spiritual commitment could backfire and lead to family conflict because the child might embrace the faith more fervently than others in the family. Some may want their children to be "spiritual" but not "too spiritual." Such fears are not entirely unfounded based on research showing that conflict between family members over certain religious issues, in fact, creates more family distress (Mahoney, 2005). On the other hand, one study shows that the more college students and their mothers share their respective views about spirituality, the more they resolve any kind of conflict via collaborative discussion; this is true for pairs who are similar or dissimilar in overall level of religious commitment (Brelsford & Mahoney, 2008).

What to Do: Foster Deep Commitment Balanced by Deep Compassion

Parents who want their child to develop a sophisticated spiritual orientation that is truly useful are likely to wonder exactly how, practically speaking, to go about doing this. Unfortunately, as far as we know, social science research is essentially silent on this question. The majority of empirical research on religion is aimed at establishing that religion matters psychologically and socially, and that religious beliefs and behaviors cannot be reduced to other seemingly more basic psychological or biological processes. Little well-controlled research has treated spiritual formation as important and worthy of serious investigation in and of itself. Thus, we know little empirically about what specific kinds of religious socialization processes within the home facilitate a sophisticated understanding of the sacred (Boyatzis et al., 2006). We therefore offer a few ideas, noting the lack of strong empirical footing.

First, parents can foster commitment by being role models of commitment. This will probably require strengthening one's own religious and spiritual life. The deeper and more explicit parents' own faith lives are to their children, the more likely youth are to adopt and incorporate a well-developed faith system into their own lives. Second, parents can help youth be articulate by being articulate themselves. As Smith (2005, p. 267) notes, "Philosophers like Charles Taylor argue that inarticulacy undermines the possibilities of reality. So, for instance, religious faith, practice, and commitment can be no more than vaguely real when people cannot talk much about them. Articulacy fosters reality." This means helping youth to practice talking about their faith by dialoguing with youth, using spiritual vocabularies, grammars, stories, and key messages about faith. Especially to the extent that faith in American culture is becoming a foreign language, parents need to be bilingual in their own homes, being fluent in both secular and spiritual language systems. Third, seek resources to learn about developmental issues related to the evolution of a spiritual identity and what kinds of information children most seem to need at different stages. Numerous websites and thoughtful books are available about how to facilitate children's spirituality, written by theologically diverse religious scholars (Yust, Johnson, Sasso, &

Religion, Number 3. Chapel Hill, NC: The National Study of Youth and Religion, www.youthandreligion.org.

Regnerus, M., C. Smith, and B. Smith. (2004). Social context in the development of adolescent religiousness, *Applied Developmental Science* 8: 27-38.

Schwartz, K. D. (2006). Transformations in parent and friend faith support predicting adolescents' religious faith, *The International Journal of the Psychology of Religion* 16: 311-26.

Smith, C. (with M. L. Denton). (2005). *Soul searching: The religious and spiritual lives of American teenagers.* New York: Oxford University Press.

Smith, C., and R. Faris. (2002a). *Religion and American adolescent delinquency, risk behaviors and constructive social activities: A research report of the National Study of Youth and Religion, Number 1*. Chapel Hill, NC: The National Study of Youth and Religion, www.youthandreligion.org.

Smith, C., and R. Faris. (2002b). *Religion and the life attitudes and self-images of American adolescents: A research report of the National Study of Youth and Religion, Number 2*. Chapel Hill, NC: The National Study of Youth and Religion, www.youthandreligion.org.

Smith, C., and P. Kim (2003). *Family religious involvement and the quality of parental relationships for families with early adolescents: A research report of the National Study of Youth and Religion, Number 5*. Chapel Hill, NC: The National Study of Youth and Religion, www.youthandreligion.org.

Strayhorn, J. M., C. S. Weidman, and D. Larson. (1990). A measure of religiousness, and its relation to parent and child mental health variables, *Journal of Community Psychology* 18: 34-43.

Wagener, L. M., J. L. Furrow, P. E. King, N. Leffert, and P. Benson. (2003). Religious involvement and developmental resources in youth, *Review of Religious Research* 44: 271-84.

Yust, K. M. (2004) *Real kids, real faith: Practices for nurturing children's spiritual lives.* San Francisco: Wiley & Sons.

Yust, K. M., A. N. Johnson, S. E. Sasso, and E. C. Roehlkepartain. (2006). *Nurturing child and adolescent spirituality: Perspectives from the world's religious traditions.* Lanham, MD: Rowman & Littlefield.

CHAPTER 3

Parent-Child Reminiscing: Creating Best Love through Sharing Stories

Robyn Fivush

There were many such stories, and he understood just how important they were, and listened with patience and respect. A life without stories would be no life at all. And stories bound us, did they not, one to another, the living to the dead, people to animals, people to the land?

Smith, 2004, p. 189

Introduction

Human beings tell stories; we tell stories about ourselves, our adventures, and our relationships (Bruner, 1987). We tell stories to strangers to help them understand who we are, we tell stories to our friends to share the events of our lives, and we tell stories with our families to create shared histories that bond us together through time. Stories are the glue that holds us together through tough times, and helps us celebrate the joys. Stories commemorate, evaluate, and interpret the past, and with each telling, stories help us create a sense of our selves in the present, connected to our past and to others. Essentially, stories are the way we understand our selves, our emotions, and our relationships, and these stories are created and re-created in countless daily social interactions throughout our lives.

The kinds of stories that individuals tell about themselves are shaped by larger social, cultural, and historical contexts (Bernsten & Rubin, 2004; Fivush, 2007; McAdams, 2001, Nelson, 2003; Ozment, this volume). Cultures define the shape of a life, the stages of development (e.g., infancy, adolescence, old age), and the related canonical events (e.g., school graduation, wedding, retirement). Individuals within a culture define themselves in relation to this "life script," whether in conformity to or deviance from the expected events and relationships. Thus individual stories link us to the larger social community, its history and values. Indeed, from the moment of birth, infants are surrounded by stories, stories of their parents and their parents before them, of family and friends, and of how this new life will unfold and enrich the ongoing narrative (Fiese, Hooker, Kotary, Schwagler, & Rimmer, 1995). Through stories, we come to understand our emotional and moral place in the world (Sclater, 2003), who we are, how we relate to others, and why this matters. By sharing our stories with others we share ourselves and our commitments.

It is in this sense that stories express "best love." As parents and children together co-construct the stories of their lives, they are creating and sustaining emotional bonds. Moreover, by helping children create richly textured stories of the past, stories that are emotionally expressive and coherent, parents are helping their children create a more coherent and emotionally regulated sense of self, in which the child feels both loved and loving. Thus parental love is both expressed and sustained through parent-child co-constructed stories, and becomes internalized in the child as a positive sense of self as a loving and giving individual. In this chapter, I review the research on parent-child reminiscing, the ways that parents and children together co-construct stories about their past, and show how this process is related to children's developing sense of self and emotional well-being. I then turn to a discussion of how this process is gendered, for both parents and children, and discuss the role of mothers, fathers, daughters, and sons. Finally, I return to the issue of "best love" and discuss how the research on parent-child co-constructed stories informs our understanding of how love is created and expressed through interactive stories that validate the child, regulate aversive affect, and create a positive sense of self.

Before delving into the specifics of these arguments, I present an illustrative excerpt from a conversation between a mother and her 6-year-old daughter about a bike trip during a family vacation the previous summer:

Mother: And we were all goin' on a bike and you didn't wanna go on a bike and so you were just going to jog but you got so tired —

Child: NOT TIRED! (very loud)

Mother: (Laughing) You didn't get tired. OK. You didn't get tired —
Child: (giggles)
Mother: — but you wanted to sit on the bike seat I was peddling. What do you remember about that?
Child: Wanting you to go really really slow. My legs were hurting.
Mother: (laughs) Why were your legs hurting?
Child: Cuz I was like this (spreads legs wide) all the time.
Mother: Cuz your legs were spread apart like that.
Child: Yeah, but if you went slowly I could relax.
Mother: Uh huh.
Child: And you went too fast.
Mother: But you had fun, though, didn't you?
Child: It was great!
Mother: What was that, a half-mile or something?
Child: I was afraid I might, uh, you might go flying off the edge (both laughing), edge of the bridge and, umm, I just wanted to jog.
Mother: And you were afraid of riding on the bike with me across the bridge, huh?
Child: Uh huh uh huh uh huh.

As can be seen in this example, both mother and daughter are actively engaged in telling this story, clearly enjoying both the story and the current interaction. Importantly, they discuss not just what happened but how they felt about it; thoughts and emotions are seamlessly integrated into the story and provide the rich tapestry of a shared event in which each individual has her own perspective yet shares the experience with the other. Note that mother and child negotiate each other's interpretations, evaluations, and emotions about the event. In this small example of everyday reminiscing we see the building blocks of children's developing understanding of self and other, and how emotional relationships are to be understood and evaluated. Each individual is her own person with her own interpretation and perspective on what happened, and each works to understand and value the perspective of the other. The story is clearly co-constructed, yet deeply individual. In this way, this mother is helping her child to understand her emotions, to value her own perspective, and to share who she is with others. Intriguingly, there are clear and enduring individual differences in the extent to which families engage in this kind of elaborated reminiscing.

Maternal Reminiscing Style

Over the past two decades, research has amply demonstrated individual differences in maternal reminiscing that fall along a dimension of elaboration (see Fivush et al., 2006, and Nelson & Fivush, 2004, for reviews). (I focus first on mothers, because much less research has been conducted with fathers, but I return to the issue of gender later in the chapter.) Some mothers engage in richly detailed, highly embellished reminiscing, whereas other mothers engage in more skeletal and less detailed reminiscing (Engel, 1986; Fivush & Fromhoff, 1988; Hudson, 1990; Peterson & McCabe, 1992, 1994). To provide a flavor of this difference, here are two short excerpts from longer conversations between two mothers and their 40-month-old children. The first is a highly elaborative mother, discussing going to the aquarium with her son:

Mother: Remember when we first came in the aquarium? And we looked down and there were a whole bunch of birdies . . . in the water? Remember the name of the birdies?
Child: Ducks!
Mother: Nooo! They weren't ducks. They had on little suits. (pause) Penguins. Remember what did the penguins do?
Child: I don't know.
Mother: You don't remember?
Child: No.
Mother: Remember them jumping off the rocks and swimming in the water?
Child: Yeah.
Mother: Real fast. You were watching them jump in the water, hmm?
Child: Yeah.

Here we see that the child is engaged in the conversation although not recalling any accurate information. With each additional question, the mother provides additional information such that by the end of this excerpt, there is a sense of story, a coherent account of seeing the penguins at the aquarium. Even though children in the early preschool years contribute little to these conversations, highly elaborative mothers continue the conversation, adding more and more detail with each additional question, inviting their children to share this past experience with them. In essence, highly elaborative mothers create rich coherent stories of the shared past with their children. Contrast this with the next example, of a low elaborative mother and her 40-month-old child:

> Mother: What kind of animals did you see, do you remember?
> Child: Lollipops.
> Mother: Lollipops aren't animals, are they? Who, what kind of animals did you see?
> Child: Giraffe.
> Mother: You saw giraffes? And what else?
> Child: RRROAR!
> Mother: What's roar?
> Child: Lion.
> Mother: What else did you see?
> Child: ROAR!
> Mother: What else did you see?

As can be seen, this mother does not seem interested in creating a rich story of what she and her child experienced together. Even when the child recalls some information, the mother does not follow in and elaborate on this; she does not discuss what the lion sounded like or looked like. Rather she seems focused on having her child recall specific pieces of information about the event. There is no sense of story here, only attention to isolated details. Thus, highly elaborative mothers work to weave a coherent narrative of the shared past to a greater extent than do low elaborative mothers.

Importantly, mothers are consistent over time in their elaborative style. Mothers who are highly elaborative with their young preschool children remain more highly elaborative than less elaborative mothers throughout the preschool years and into middle childhood (Harley & Reese, 1999; Reese, 2002; Reese, Haden & Fivush, 1993). Moreover, highly elaborative reminiscing is not simply a matter of being more talkative. Mothers who are highly elaborative during reminiscing are not necessarily talking more in other conversational contexts, including book reading, playtime, or during everyday caring routines such as eating and bathing (Hoff-Ginsburg, 1991; Haden & Fivush, 1996). The fact that highly elaborative reminiscing is not a general conversational style indicates that reminiscing is a unique context in which mothers have particular goals for sharing the past. In contrast to talking about the here-and-now, reminiscing allows the participants to create a shared history over time that reinforces connections in the present, thus creating and maintaining enduring emotional bonds.

Not surprisingly, maternal reminiscing style is related to children's developing autobiographical memory skills (Bauer & Burch, 2004; Farrant & Reese, 2000; Fivush & Vasudeva, 2002; Flannagan, Baker-Ward, & Graham, 1995; Haden, 1998; Harley & Reese, 1999; Hudson, 1990; Peterson, Jesso, & McCabe, 1999; Peterson & McCabe, 1992; Welch-Ross, 1997). By the end of the preschool years, children of more highly elaborative mothers come to tell more coherent and more detailed narratives of their own past experiences than do children of less elaborative mothers. The research indicates that children are learning the forms and functions of recalling the past through participating in mother-guided reminiscing. Children who engage in more elaborated maternally guided reminiscing come to value and to excel at sharing their past with others. But importantly, elaborated reminiscing is not only related to developing autobiography; children of mothers who engage in more highly elaborative reminiscing also develop better emotional understanding and emotional regulation skills.

Reminiscing and Emotion

Highly elaborative mothers not only reminisce about the facts of what happened, they focus on emotions, evaluations, and interpretation of events to a greater extent than do less elaborative mothers. By including more of this kind of information, highly elaborative mothers are imbuing the past with a sense of meaning; these more subjective aspects of past events highlight the subjective nature of our memories, how we thought and felt about the past, and how this may be the same or different than how others thought and felt (Fivush, 2001; Fivush & Nelson, 2006). The discussion and negotiation of emotions and interpretations provide a sense of self in the past as connected both to others through shared meaning and to the present through ongoing evaluation. And, again, children of more elaborative mothers include more information about their own and others' emotions in their own autobiographical narratives than children of less elaborative mothers (Adams, Kuebli, Boyle, & Fivush, 1995; Fivush & Haden, 2005). Thus highly elaborative mothers help their children to understand their own and others' emotional lives and, through this understanding, how to understand self and other.

Thus far, I have not made a distinction between reminiscing about emotionally positive events and reminiscing about more stressful and negative events. Unfortunately, stressful events befall us all, including children, and recalling and reminiscing about these kinds of events serve different functions and have different consequences than reminiscing about positive events. Whereas sharing the positive events of our lives together helps to create emotional bonds and define affirmative relationships through time, reminiscing about stressful events may serve a more didactic function, helping children to understand how and why this event occurred, how negative emotion can be resolved, and how to prevent or cope with similar events in the future. Essentially, parent-guided reminiscing about stressful events may help children learn to regulate their emotions.

Emotional regulation involves a set of skills that help alleviate aversive affect and prepare individuals for action to change the situation. Lazarus and Folkman (1984) describe two broad classes of coping skills, emotion-based coping and problem-based coping. Emotion-based coping includes such activities as expressing and understanding the emotional impact, and strategies for decreasing the emotional intensity, including relaxation and distraction. Problem-based coping includes such activities as reframing the event from multiple perspectives, creating a more coherent understanding of the causal framework to understand how and why the event occurred, and planning for future occurrences when appropriate.

Many coping activities occur through disclosing the event to others. In fact, a substantial body of research has demonstrated that individuals who write about the stressful events of their lives, sharing their deepest thoughts and feelings about the events, subsequently show better psychological (i.e., less depression, less anxiety, higher sense of well-being) and physical health (i.e., fewer doctor visits, better immune-system functioning) than individuals who do not write about these events, or even those who simply recount the event but do not include thoughts and emotions (see Pennebaker, 1997, for an overview). More specifically, the inclusion of emotion words and cognitive processing words (words such as "think," "understand," "realize," which indicate thinking through and reformulating the event) as well as words that help create a more coherent narrative (words that express temporal and causal structure, such as "and then," "because," and "if/then" constructions) are related to subsequent well-being. These patterns suggest that creating more emotionally expressive and causally coherent narratives of stressful events help individuals to engage in the "language of coping."

Young children do not yet have the cognitive or emotional skills to create expressive, coherent narratives on their own, but are dependent on a more competent adult to help structure the narrative through joint reminiscing. Thus, through highly elaborated mother-guided reminiscing, in which children are learning to create more emotionally expressive and detailed narratives of past experiences, children may also be learning critical emotion regulation skills. Reminiscing may be a particularly important context for children's developing emotional regulation skills because in recalling their own experiences, children are able to draw on lived experiences and thus may be better able to re-create the emotion under discussion. Yet at the same time, children are not in the heat of the moment, where the emotion may be overwhelming and disorganizing. Thus in reminiscing, mother and child can reflect on and evaluate the experience from multiple perspectives, and mothers can help children understand how and why these events occurred in a real-world context that is safe (Dunn, Brown, & Beardsall, 1991; Fivush, 1998).

Indeed, mothers focus on different aspects of negative and positive events when reminiscing. Not surprisingly, mothers and children discuss more negative emotion when reminiscing about negative than positive events, but they also focus more on creating a causal explanatory framework for the event, discussing causes and consequences, and especially providing resolutions (Ackil, Van Abbema, & Bauer, 2003; Fivush, Berlin, Sales, Mennuti-Washburn, & Cassidy, 2003; Sales, Fivush, & Peterson, 2003). Essentially, mothers use the "language of coping" when discussing negative experiences. As might be expected given the robust individual differences in maternal reminiscing style already described, mothers also differ in the extent to which they engage in the language of coping. For example, here are two mothers, each with their 4-year-old child discussing a thunderstorm. While thunder and lightning may not be stressful for adults, they often are for young children, and discussing these kinds of common childhood fears may provide a forum for children to learn how to understand and cope with more realistic fears as they grow older. The first mother engages in an elaborative, emotionally expressive, and causally coherent discussion with her young daughter:

Mother: And what happens when there's a big thunder and lightning storm?
Child: I'd want to be with my mom and dad (whispering).
Mother: Yes, you want to be with your mom and dad. And what happens if you're sleeping and there's a big bunch of thunder in the middle of the night? What happens sometimes?
Child: Scared.
Mother: Scared. Do you tremble like that? (Child nods head "yes.") Do you shake? Huh? (Child nods head "yes.") Then what do you do?

Child: I get up and go to my mom and dad (whispering).
Mother: You get up and go to your mom and dad. And what do we do?
Child: Say don't worry.
Mother: Say don't worry. Do we hold you? (Child nods head "yes.") Yes, does holding help when you're scared? (Child nods head "yes.") Yes.

The very fact that this child whispers in response to her mother's questions indicates that she finds this situation and this conversation stressful. As can be seen, this mother not only helps her daughter to understand and express her emotional reaction, she makes sure to end the conversation with a reassuring resolution, reinforcing her daughter's knowledge that someone will be there to take care of her. Note also that this is likely not the first time that this pair has discussed this event; the mother is helping the child to learn a "script" for what happens in this stressful situation, and helps the child to articulate for herself how to resolve this event through internalizing the parental soothing ("Say don't worry") while still providing the physical comfort needed. Contrast this with a second mother reminiscing with her 4-year-old son. The conversations are remarkably similar in that both children are scared of the storm and both come into their parents' bed, but this mother does little to help her son to understand or resolve his emotional reaction; nor does she provide any memory of physical comfort to alleviate his fear:

Mother: . . . why did you come in bed with Mommy and Daddy? 'Cause how did you feel, how did that storm make you feel?
Child: Umm, I feel really scared.
Mother: A little bit scared?
Child: Really scared.
Mother: You were really scared. What scares you about the thunderstorm, honey?
Child: (It) broke the TV.
Mother: Yeah, that scared you because the TV went off. (Changes topic.)

Here we see that this mother also confirms her son's emotion, but after confirming that he was very scared, she does not follow with a way to alleviate this aversive emotional experience. Instead, she focuses her son again on what scared him, and then drops the conversation without providing any emotional resolution.

Mothers who are more elaborative during emotional reminiscing facilitate the development of emotional understanding and regulation in their children (Laible, 2004a, 2004b). Children of more elaborative mothers are better able to recognize their own emotions and those of others, they are better able to describe why they and others might feel certain emotions, and they are better able to describe possible resolutions to aversive emotions. Most important, reminiscing plays a unique role in preschool children's developing understanding of emotion. Laible (2004a) directly compared maternal elaborations in the context of reminiscing and storybook reading, and found that only maternal elaborative reminiscing predicted children's later emotional understanding. Thus it seems that the context of reminiscing about one's own personal stressful experiences is critical in developing emotion regulation skills.

As children grow older, and begin to participate more fully in reminiscing, maternal elaboration may help children learn more sophisticated coping skills and may facilitate higher levels of psychological well-being, even for chronically stressed children. We studied mothers and their 8- to 12-year-old children coping with chronic asthma (Fivush & Sales, 2006; Sales & Fivush, 2005). Asthma involves multiple kinds of stressors, ranging from everyday parent-child conflicts involving something that the child wanted to do but could not because of her asthma (e.g., staying overnight at a friend's house, playing soccer), to traumatic, life-threatening asthma attacks involving hospitalization. We asked mothers and children to discuss both a conflict and an emergency room event. We also assessed both mothers' and children's coping skills and children's emotional well-being using standardized clinical inventories.

Mothers who had better coping skills engaged in more elaborative, emotionally expressive reminiscing, and their co-constructed narratives were more explanatory and coherent. To illustrate, here is a mother and her son discussing why the child cannot spend the night at a friend's:

> Mother: I was just thinking that maybe we should talk about some of those times um. . . . When you want to go and spend the night with one of your friends at the last minute and you don't have your medicine, and I have to tell you not to. I want a chance to talk about that.
>
> Child: Okay.
>
> Mother: So, do you understand why when I say no that you can't go over there and spend the night if you don't have medicine?
>
> Child: Yes.
>
> Mother: Why do you think I say that?
>
> Child: Because I might have like an asthma attack or something.

Mother: Um hum. And I think that it's real important because medication is a really preventative type of thing and it's important for you to have it every single day. You know . . . I know sometimes things come up, you fall asleep or whatever and you can't take the medicine but for the most part you should have it every single day to help you keep well. Ok, so you understand that but I know you still feel bad about it when I have to say no. How does that make you feel?

Child: Bad, I feel mad that I can't go.

Mother: But I'm saying no for your own good, because I want you to be healthy, and I worry about, I don't want you to have an asthma attack.

In this conversation, the mother structures the narrative in such a way that she draws out the child's own understanding of why he cannot engage in this desired behavior, and then goes on to elaborately explain her thinking. Even so, she allows that this is still emotionally difficult and validates her son's emotional reaction, and ends the conversation with an explanation that reifies the emotional relationship between the two of them. Children of mothers who engaged in this kind of coherent, explanatory, and emotionally expressive reminiscing themselves displayed better coping skills. Moreover, it was what mothers were doing in these conversations that predicted children's coping more than what children were doing, suggesting that children are still dependent on adults' structuring of the experience in ways that help the child to understand and cope. Support for this interpretation is that mothers and children who co-constructed more emotional expressive and explanatory narratives had children who displayed fewer internalizing behaviors (e.g., depression, anxiety) and fewer externalizing behavior problems (e.g., acting out, aggression). Children's own coping skills (which were not particularly sophisticated yet) were unrelated to the narratives or to their own emotional well-being. Thus the overall pattern suggests that mothers who help their children to create more coherent explanatory narratives of stressful events are helping their children learn to regulate aversive affect and to cope with life's difficult experiences.

Family Reminiscing as a Gendered Activity

The focus on mothers in developmental research is embedded in a larger theoretical and historical context. Historically, mothers have been (and continue to be) the primary caregivers, and this is true across cultures (see Lamb, 1981). Theoretically, due partly to historical gender roles and partly to the biological necessity that breastfeeding leads to mothers spending more time and being in closer proximity to infants and young children than are fathers (Chodorow, 1978), mothers have been studied as the primary socialization agent within the family. With changing gender roles over the last four decades, there has been a growing interest in the role of fathers as well (Lamb, 1981).

In conceptualizing parent-child reminiscing, gender becomes a critical variable. As adults, females tell longer and more detailed stories about their personal experiences, and focus more on emotions and social relationships, than do males (see Fivush & Buckner, 2004, for a review). These differences in autobiographical narratives are related to gender identity, in that females report valuing emotional experience and emotional expression more than do males (see Fischer, 2000, for a review) as well as valuing interpersonal relationships more than do males (Gilligan, 1982). Several theorists have argued that differences in gender identity are linked to socialization experiences, in which females are socialized to express more emotions and to value emotional experience more than males (Brody & Hall, 1993), as well as to privilege social relationships over autonomous experiences (Gilligan, 1982). As argued here, parent-child co-constructed stories about the past are a critical site for the socialization of self and emotion. And, indeed, we see gender differences in this activity.

Although only a few studies on parent-child reminiscing have included fathers, the results suggest that gender of both parent and child is important. Mothers are generally more elaborative and more emotionally expressive than fathers when reminiscing with their children (Bohanek, Fivush, Zaman, Thomas-Lepore, Merchant, & Duke, under review; Fivush, Brotman, Buckner, & Goodman, 2000; Kuebli & Fivush, 1992), in line with the general findings on gender differences in adults. Intriguingly, however, gender of child also matters. Both mothers and fathers are more elaborative and more emotionally expressive when reminiscing with daughters than with sons (Fivush, Berlin, Sales, Mennuti-Washburn, & Cassidy, 2003; Reese & Fivush, 1992). Even when discussing their own childhood experiences, parents tell more elaborated and more emotionally expressive stories to daughters than to sons (Buckner & Fivush, 2000). Thus both in terms of a gendered model of storytelling and in terms of how stories are co-constructed with them, daughters are the recipients of more elaborated and more emotional reminiscing than are sons. Interestingly, although there are few gender differences in how boys and girls themselves tell stories of their past early in development, by the end of the preschool years, girls are telling more elaborated and more emotionally expressive stories than are boys (Buckner & Fivush, 1998), and this difference is consistent across adolescence (Zaman & Fivush, in prep). Thus the overall pattern suggests gender differences from the time children first begin to engage in parent-guided reminiscing, differences that continue to be expressed throughout development in both personally told stories and stories shared within the family.

It is also the case that gendered family reminiscing has differential consequences for daughters and sons. In a longitudinal study of families with children just entering adolescence, we examined the way in which families told stories about their past in relation to children's developing sense of self (Bohanek, Marin, Fivush, & Duke, 2006; Bohanek, Marin, & Fivush, in press; Marin, Bohanek, & Fivush, in press). Families were asked to discuss stressful events that they had experienced together as a family; the majority of events families chose to talk about included the death of a family member (mostly grandparents), the death of a beloved pet, and a serious illness (mostly of parents or children). We examined how the family as a whole reminisced about these experiences, and we assessed children's self-concept and well-being two years later as they entered adolescence. The gendered patterns are a bit complicated, but essentially, mothers who facilitate more elaborated, causally coherent, and emotionally explanatory narratives about stressful events have children, both boys and girls, who show higher levels of self-esteem, higher levels of self-efficacy (the idea that the self is an active agent that can make things happen in the world), and lower levels of internalizing and externalizing behaviors. Fathers who engage in more elaborated, causally coherent, and emotionally explanatory narratives about stressful events have sons who also show these positive outcomes, but, provocatively, their daughters are showing poor outcome, especially more internalizing behaviors (e.g., depression, anxiety). It is simply not clear why we are seeing the detrimental effect of parental elaborative reminiscing on daughters, but one possibility focuses on the developmental tasks girls are facing as they enter adolescence and their own sexual identity. In this situation, girls may be looking to their father for strength and protection, rather then emotional sharing, and so at this particular developmental point there is an inverse relation between paternal emotional expression and daughters' well-being, but that this would reverse as daughters get older. This is obviously a highly speculative interpretation and additional research is needed to follow up on this finding. We do know, as discussed by Brinig (this volume), that fathers play an important role in child outcome more generally, so this anomaly is in need of additional research to place it in context.

Regardless of the ultimate interpretation, what is clear across the research is that mothers who engage in more elaborative reminiscing, creating more causally coherent and emotionally expressive narratives with their children, have children who are themselves creating more elaborated stories of their personal past, are better able to regulate aversive emotion, and have higher levels of self-esteem and self-efficacy. Fathers' role is more complex and more speculative. These findings bring us back to the issues raised at the beginning of this chapter: What does this kind of family storytelling tell us about the best love of the child?

Reminiscing, Emotional Bonds, and Best Love

An underlying assumption in the family reminiscing literature is that sharing stories together helps to create and maintain strong emotional bonds over time. A critical way to assess emotional bonds within families is through attachment. Attachment is a core construct in developmental psychology, and refers to the emotional bond between individuals, especially between mothers and children (Bowlby, 1969, 1988; see Cassidy & Shaver, 1999, for an overview). Essentially, infants who receive sensitive and responsive caregiving will develop expectations that their needs will be met; they develop a sense of themselves as worthy of care, of others as trustworthy, and of the world as safe and secure. In contrast, infants who do not receive optimal sensitive caregiving will develop a more ambivalent emotional bond; they will be unsure of themselves as worthy of care, unsure others will be there to meet their needs, and come to see the world as unsafe and unpredictable.

Attachment relationships formed in infancy are carried through childhood and into adulthood, as internal working models, or representations, of self, others, and the world (Thompson, 2000). Securely attached infants develop into children and adults who feel good about themselves and care about other people. As securely attached infants develop into childhood, they show better emotional understanding, more prosocial skills, such as empathy and conscience development, and have more rewarding social relationships. Insecurely attached infants do not develop into trusting individuals, they feel unsure of themselves and their place in the world, and because they remain concerned about whether their own needs will or will not be met, they find it more difficult to engage in rewarding social interactions (Thompson, 2000).

Perhaps not surprisingly, attachment and reminiscing are dialectically related. Several theorists have postulated that, as children's language skills develop, attachment relationships will be expressed in mother-child communication (Bowlby, 1988; Bretherton & Mulholland, 1999; Thompson, 2000). More specifically, if mothers and children are secure in their love for each other, they will be better able to engage in fluent, open expression of thoughts and feelings than insecurely attached mothers and children. Thus, attachment status should predict reminiscing style. In turn, more elaborated and emotionally expressive reminiscing will facilitate the maintenance and extension of secure attachment bonds (Fivush & Reese, 2002). Through more elaborated expressive reminiscing, especially about emotionally difficult experiences, mothers and children build more coherent narratives about their shared past, which provides an evolving base for maintaining and elaborating the internal working model of attachment (Main, Kaplan, & Cassidy, 1985).

By having clear, coherent, and elaborated representations of past shared experiences, children of highly elaborative mothers will be able to build and maintain coherent representations of self and others in interaction. Thus, secure attachment facilitates elaborated reminiscing, and elaborated reminiscing facilitates secure attachment. Multiple studies have now confirmed that secure attachment is related to more highly elaborative reminiscing (Fivush & Vasudeva, 2002; Laible, 2004a; Reese & Farrant, 2003). Specifically, more securely attached children and their mothers are more elaborative about the emotional and evaluative aspects of past events, particularly for negative emotions (Farrar, Fasig, & Welch-Ross, 1997; Laible, 2004a; Laible & Thompson, 2000; Newcombe & Reese, 2004; Oppenheim, Nir, Warren, & Emde, 1997).

As we have seen throughout this chapter, more elaborated and emotionally expressive and explanatory narratives are also highly beneficial for children in helping them to regulate aversive affect, create a sense of self as worthy (self-esteem), as capable of acting on the world (self-efficacy), and as having a higher sense of well-being (fewer internalizing and externalizing behavior problems). The emerging pattern is one in which responsive parenting creates secure attachment bonds, in which the infant feels loved and safe, and leads to a greater ability to share oneself with others through stories. In turn, more securely attached mothers and children engage in more elaborated and emotionally expressive and explanatory stories that both build the emotional bond between parent and child and help the child develop critical skills such as emotional regulation and self-esteem.

Moreover, more coherent and emotionally expressive and explanatory stories are related to moral understanding and generativity. Mothers who are more elaborative when reminiscing have preschoolers who develop higher levels of conscience and engage in more conscientious behaviors, including helping others, as they grow older (Laible, 2004a, 2004b; Laible & Thompson, 2000). Through elaborated emotionally regulated stories children learn to value the experiences of self and others, and this provides a basis for children's understanding of others' perspectives and needs, leading to a moral stance (Fivush, 2001; Sclater, 2003). Pratt and his colleagues (Arnold, Pratt, & Hicks, 2004; Frensch, Pratt, & Norris, 2007) have demonstrated that adolescents who know family stories, and that take on the voice of their parents in these stories, show higher levels of moral reasoning and also engage in more prosocial community activities. And in emerging adulthood, these kinds of family stories are related to generativity, the belief that caring and nurturing others is a positive goal and brings satisfaction to the self.

Other chapters in this volume have shown how helping others creates a sense of well-being for self (Post, this volume), and that intervention programs for youth at risk are effective when they involve these youths in projects to help others (Benson, this volume). The link between this research and the work presented in this chapter is that parents who co-construct rich elaborative stories with their children facilitate loving relations and emotional bonds built on a sense of trust and value that the child can both internalize in creating a sense of a worthy and valuable self, and turn outward, as a sense of valuing and caring for others. Thus parent-child co-constructed stories both create more emotionally attuned relationships and help the child become a more resilient individual, capable of loving oneself and others. Through stories we express and create love; when parents help children tell their own stories, they are both demonstrating and expressing their love for their child and helping their child become a loving individual.

References

Ackil, J. K., D. L. Van Abbema, and P. J. Bauer. (2003). After the storm: Enduring differences in mother-child recollections of traumatic and nontraumatic events, *Journal of Experimental Child Psychology* 84: 286-309.

Adams, S., J. Kuebli, P. Boyle, and R. Fivus. (1995). Gender differences in parent-child conversations about past emotions: A longitudinal investigation, *Sex Roles* 33: 309-23.

Arnold, M. L., M. W. Pratt, and C. Hicks. (2004). Adolescents' representations of parents' voices in family stories: Value lessons, personal adjustment, and identity development. In M. W. Pratt and B. H. Fiese, eds., *Family stories and the life course: Across time and generations*, pp. 163-86. Mahwah, NJ: Erlbaum.

Bauer, P. J., and M. M. Burch. (2004). Developments in early memory: Multiple mediators of foundational processes. In J. M. Lucariello, J. A. Hudson, R. Fivush, and P. J. Bauer, eds., *The development of the mediated mind*, pp. 101-25. Mahwah, NJ: Erlbaum.

Bernsten, D., and D. C. Rubin. (2004). Cultural life scripts structure recall from autobiographical memory, *Memory & Cognition* 32: 427-42.

Bohanek, J., K. Marin, R. Fivush, and M. Duke. (2006). Family narrative interaction and adolescent sense of self, *Family Processes* 45: 39-54.

Bohanek, J. G., K. Marin, and R. Fivush. (in press). Family narratives and adolescents' self-esteem and adjustment, *Journal of Early Adolescence.*

Bowlby, J. (1988). *A secure base: Clinical applications of attachment theory.* London: Routledge.

Bowlby, J. (1969). *Attachment and loss: Vol. 1. Attachment.* New York: Basic Books.

Bretherton, I., and K. A. Mulholland. (1999). Internal working models in attachment relations: A construct revisited. In J. Cassidy and P. R. Shaver, eds., *Handbook of attachment: Theory, research, and clinical applications*, pp. 89-111. New York: Guilford Press.

Brody, L. R., and J. A. Hall. (1993). Gender and emotion. In M. Lewis and J. M. Haviland, eds., *Handbook of emotions*, pp. 447-60. New York: Guilford Press.

Bruner, J. (1987). Life as narrative, *Social Research* 54: 11-32.

Buckner, J. P., and R. Fivush. (2000). Gendered themes in family reminiscing, *Memory* 8, no. 6: 401-12.

Buckner, J. P., and R. Fivush. (1998). Gender and self in children's autobiographical narratives, *Applied Cognitive Psychology* 12: 407-29.

Cassidy, J., and P. R. Shaver, eds. (1999). *Handbook of attachment: Theory, research, and clinical applications.* New York: Guilford Press.

Chodorow, N. J. (1978). *The reproduction of mothering: Psychoanalysis and the socialization of gender.* Berkeley: University of California Press.

Dunn, J., J. Brown, and L. Beardsall. (1991). Family talk about feeling states and children's later understanding of others' emotions, *Developmental Psychology* 27: 448-55.

Engel, S. (1986). *Learning to reminisce: A developmental study of how young children talk about the past.* Unpublished doctoral dissertation, City University of New York.

Farrant, K., and E. Reese. (2000). Maternal style and children's participation in reminiscing: Stepping stones in children's autobiographical memory development, *Journal of Cognition and Development* 1: 193-225.

Farrar, M. J., L. G. Fasig, and M. K. Welch-Ross. (1997). Attachment and emotion in autobiographical memory development, *Journal of Experimental Child Psychology* 67: 389-408.

Fiese, B. H., K. A. Hooker, L. Kotary, J. Scwagler, and M. Rimmer. (1995). Family stories in the early stages of parenthood. *Journal of Marriage and the Family* 57: 763-70.

Fischer, A. H. (2000). *Gender and emotion: Social psychological perspectives.* New York: Cambridge University Press.

Fivush, R. (2008). Remembering and reminiscing: How individual lives are constructed in family narratives, *Memory Studies* 1: 45-54.

Fivush, R. (2001). Owning experience: The development of subjective perspective in autobiographical memory. In C. Moore and K. Lemmon, eds., *The self in time: Developmental perspectives,* pp. 35-52. Mahwah, NJ: Erlbaum.

Fivush, R. (1998). Gendered narratives: Elaboration, structure and emotion in parent-child reminiscing across the preschool years. In C. P. Thompson, D. J. Herrmann, D. Bruce, J. D. Read, D. G. Payne, and M. P. Toglia, eds., *Autobiographical memory: Theoretical and applied perspectives,* pp. 79-104. Mahwah, NJ: Erlbaum.

Fivush, R. (1991). The social construction of personal narratives, *Merrill-Palmer Quarterly* 37: 59-82.

Fivush, R., L. Berlin, J. M. Sales, J. Mennuti-Washburn, and J. Cassidy. (2003). Functions of parent-child reminiscing about emotionally negative events, *Memory* 11: 179-92.

Fivush, R., M. Brotman, J. P. Buckner, and S. Goodman. (2000). Gender differences in parent-child emotion narratives, *Sex Roles* 42: 233-54.

Fivush, R., and J. Buckner. (2003). Constructing gender and identity through autobiographical narratives. In R. Fivush and C. Haden, eds., *Autobiographical memory and the construction of a narrative self: Developmental and cultural perspectives,* pp. 149-67. Hillsdale, NJ: Erlbaum.

Fivush, R., and F. Fromhoff. (1988). Style and structure in mother-child conversations about the past, *Discourse Processes* 11: 337-55.

Fivush, R., and C. A. Haden. (2005). Parent-child reminiscing and the construction of a subjective self. In B. D. Homer and C. S. Tamis-LeMonda, eds., *The development of social cognition and communication,* pp. 315-35. Mahwah, NJ: Erlbaum.

Fivush, R., C. A. Haden, and E. Reese. (2006). Elaborating on elaborations: Maternal reminiscing style and children's socioemotional outcome, *Child Development* 77: 1568-88.

Fivush, R., C. Haden, and E. Reese. (1996). Remembering, recounting and reminiscing: The development of autobiographical memory in social context. In D. Rubin, ed., *Reconstructing our past: An overview of autobiographical memory,* pp. 341-59. New York: Cambridge University Press.

Fivush, R., and K. Nelson. (2006). Mother-child talk about the past locates the self in time, *British Journal of Developmental Psychology.*

Fivush, R., and E. Reese. (2002). Origins of reminiscing. In J. Webster and B. Haight, eds., *Critical advances in reminiscence work,* pp. 109-22. New York: Springer.

Fivush, R., and J. M. Sales. (2006). Coping, attachment, and mother-child reminiscing about stressful events, *Merrill-Palmer Quarterly* 52: 125-50.

Fivush, R., and A. Vasudeva. (2002). Remembering to relate: Socioemotional correlates of mother-child reminiscing, *Journal of Cognition and Development* 3: 73-90.

Flannagan, D., L. Baker-Ward, and L. Graham. (1995). Talk about preschool: Patterns of topic discussion and elaboration related to gender and ethnicity, *Sex Roles* 32: 1-15.

Frensch, K. M., M. W. Pratt, and J. E. Norris. (2007) Foundations of generativity: Personal and family correlates of emerging adults' generative life-story themes, *Journal of Research in Personality* 41: 45-62.

Gilligan, C. (1982). *In a different voice: Psychological theory and women's development.* Cambridge, MA: Harvard University Press.

Haden, C. (1998). Reminiscing with different children: Relating maternal stylistic consistency and sibling similarity in talk about the past, *Developmental Psychology* 34: 99-114.

Haden, C. A., and R. Fivush. (1996). Contextual variation in maternal conversational styles, *Merrill-Palmer Quarterly* 42: 200-227.

Haden, C., R. Haine, and R. Fivush. (1997). Developing narrative structure in parent-child conversations about the past, *Developmental Psychology* 33: 295-307.

Harley, K., and E. Reese. (1999). Origins of autobiographical memory, *Developmental Psychology* 35: 1338-48.

Hoff-Ginsburg, E. (1991). Mother-child conversations in different social classes and communicative settings, *Child Development* 62: 782-96.

Hudson, J. A. (1990). The emergence of autobiographic memory in mother-child conversation. In R. Fivush and J. A. Hudson, eds., *Knowing and remembering in young children,* pp. 166-96. New York: Cambridge University Press.

Kuebli, J., and R. Fivush. (1992). Gender differences in parent-child conversations about past emotions, *Sex Roles* 27: 683-98.

Laible, D. (2004a). Mother-child discourse in two contexts: Links with child temperament, attachment security, and socioemotional competence, *Developmental Psychology* 40: 979-92.

Laible, D. (2004b). Mother-child discourse about a child's past behavior at 30-months and early socioemotional development at age 3, *Merrill-Palmer Quarterly* 50: 159-80.

Laible, D., and R. Thompson. (2000). Mother-child discourse, attachment security, shared positive affect, and early conscience development, *Child Development* 71: 1424-40.

Lamb, M. E. (1981). Fathers and child development: An integrative overview. In M. E. Lamb, ed., *The role of the father in child development,* 2nd ed., pp. 1-71. New York: Wiley.

Lazarus, R. S., and S. Folkman. (1984). *Stress, appraisal, and coping.* New York: Springer.

Main, M., K. Kaplan, and J. Cassidy. (1985). Security in infancy, childhood and adulthood: A move to the level of representation. In I. Bretherton and E. Waters, eds., Growing points of attachment theory and research, *Monographs of the Society for Research in Child Development* 50 (1-2, Serial No. 209): 66-104.

Marin, K. A., J. G. Bohanek, R. Fivush. (in press). Positive effects of talking about the negative: Family narratives of negative experiences and preadolescents' perceived competence, *Journal of Research on Adolescence.*

McAdams, D. P. (2001). The psychology of life stories, *Review of General Psychology* 5: 100-122.

McCabe, A., and C. Peterson. (1991). Getting the story: A longitudinal study of parental styles in eliciting narratives and developing narrative skill. In A. McCabe and C. Peterson, eds., *Developing narrative structure,* pp. 217-53. Hillsdale, NJ: Erlbaum.

Miller, P. J. (1994). Narrative practices: Their role in socialization and self-construction. In U. Neisser and R. Fivush, eds., *The remembering self: Construction and accuracy in the life narrative,* pp. 158-79. New York: Cambridge University Press.

Nelson, K. (2003). Self and social functions: Individual autobiographical memory and collective narrative, *Memory* 11: 125-36.

Nelson, K., and R. Fivush. (2004). The emergence of autobiographical memory: A social cultural developmental theory, *Psychological Review* 111: 486-511.

Newcombe, R., and E. Reese. (2004). Evaluations and orientations in mother-child narratives as a function of attachment security: A longitudinal investigation, *International Journal of Behavioral Development* 28: 230-45.

Oppenheim, D., A. Nir, S. Warren, and R. N. Emde. (1997). Emotion regulation in mother-child narrative co-construction: Associations with children's narrative and adaptation, *Developmental Psychology* 33: 284-94.

Pennebaker, J. W. (1997). *Opening up.* New York: Guilford Press.

Peterson, C., B. Jesso, and A. McCabe. (1999). Encouraging narratives in preschoolers: An intervention study, *Journal of Child Language* 26: 49-67.

Peterson, C., and A. McCabe. (1994). A social interactionist account of developing decontextualized narrative skill, *Developmental Psychology* 30: 937-48.

Peterson, C., and A. McCabe. (1992). Parental styles of narrative elicitation: Effect on children's narrative structure and content, *First Language* 12: 299-321.

Reese, E. (2002a). A model of the origins of autobiographical memory. In J. W. Fagen and H. Hayne, eds., *Progress in Infancy Research,* vol. 2, pp. 215-60. Mahwah, NJ: Erlbaum.

Reese, E., and K. Farrant. (2003). Origins of reminiscing in parent-child relationships. In R. Fivush and C. A. Haden, eds., *Autobiographical memory and the construction of a narrative self: Developmental and cultural perspectives,* pp. 29-48. Mahwah, NJ: Erlbaum.

Reese, E., C. Haden, and R. Fivush. (1996). Mothers, fathers, daughters, sons: Gender differences in reminiscing, *Research on Language and Social Interaction* 29: 27-56.

Reese, E., C. A. Haden, and R. Fivush. (1993). Mother-child conversations about the past: Relationships of style and memory over time, *Cognitive Development* 8: 403-30.

Sales, J. M., and R. Fivush. (2005). Social and emotional functions of mother-child reminiscing about stressful events. *Social Cognition* 23: 70-90.

Sales, J. M., R. Fivush, and C. Peterson. (2003). Parental reminiscing about positive and negative events. *Journal of Cognition and Development* 4: 185-209.

Sclater, S. D. (2003). What is the subject? *Narrative Inquiry* 13: 317-30.

Smith, A. M. (2004). *In the company of cheerful ladies.* New York: Anchor Books.

Thompson, R. (2000). The legacy of early attachments, *Child Development* 71: 145-52.

Welch-Ross, M. K. (1997). Mother-child participation in conversation about the past: Relationship to preschoolers' theory of mind, *Developmental Psychology* 33: 618-29.

Zaman, W., and R. Fivush. (in prep). Gender differences in adolescent narratives.

PART II

Historical Perspectives

CHAPTER 4

Raising a Loving Child in Late Medieval and Early Modern Europe (1400-1700)

Steven Ozment

There is no more precious, friendly, lovable thing on earth than a pious, disciplined, obedient, and teachable child.

Viet Dietrich, 1546[1]

The Changing Field of Family History

Refocusing Family History

Faced with the challenge of modern childrearing, modern parents and educators have understandingly looked to the past for insight and guidance. What they have found there recently is a furious debate over parental love in centuries past: whether such love existed, effectively prepared a child for adult life, and can offer modern parents and educators a worthy model of childrearing.

Not a few scholars still doubt premodern parents' ability to recognize the world of a child, maneuver effectively within it when they do, and give a child the proper upbringing he or she requires. On the other hand, scholars

1. "Von der Kinderzucht," in Oskar Reichmann, ed., *Etliche Schrifften für den gemeinen man/von unterricht Christlicher lehr und leben und zum trost der engstigen gewissen* (Assen, 1872), p. 121. Cf. Steven Ozment, *When Fathers Ruled: Family Life in Reformation Europe* (New Haven: Yale University Press, 1983), pp. 132ff.

who see only abuse and neglect in the history of childhood are today losing credibility. Although a consensus still awaits us, sympathy for parents in the past is replacing blanket indictments of traditional parent-child relations.

From my own forays into the family life in late medieval and early modern Europe, I believe the following conclusions may be drawn:

1. Wherever one visits the civilized Western world in centuries past, surviving records make it clear that parents viewed the bearing and rearing of children to be society's "job one." And when time, place, and resources are taken into account, those parents also give every appearance of having addressed their task conscientiously to the best of their ability. For all the bad parents one may discover, it is impossible to find a culture or a civilization that has only abused and neglected its new generations.
2. If in the history of the family there are children who need protectors and advocates, there are also just as many parents who deserve purple hearts. From antiquity to the present, we find both children with parents they do not deserve and parents whose children are unworthy of them.
3. From surviving statistical records it can be inferred that the Middle Ages had less child abuse per capita than did the twentieth century, an inference that should humble modern historians and parents who believe effective childrearing is a very recent art.[2] That inference also suggests that parents and children in the past have something to teach the modern family today.

Sources

Since sources are everything in penetrating history, those for the study of the family must be carefully weighed. My early work in family history drew heavily on theological/catechetical and legal/admonitory texts. At first glance these sources seem to address childrearing nonempirically, in terms of the behavior recommended, or commanded, in ancient classical and sacred biblical texts, thus a discussion of an "ideal" child rather than a report

2. Shulamith Shahar, *Childhood in the Middle Ages* (London: Routledge, 1990), pp. 109-11; cf. Lloyd Demause, "The Evolution of Childrearing," *The Journal of Psychohistory* 28, no. 4 (2001): 362-452.

on "real" children. Upon closer inspection, however, the old codes of behavior do reflect a well-established parental consensus derived from hands-on childrearing. In training up a child in the way he or she should go, parents and educators in the past did not passively surrender their own observations and experience to abstract authorities.

Over the years I have sought out sources that provide the most direct and deepest access to the inner family circle. Among them are so-called "housefather books" and "how-to pamphlets," both devoted to the organization of the household and the definition of the roles individual family members properly should play. These sources also provide practical remedies for common problems and emergencies. They address animal husbandry from horses to bees, the science of housekeeping from slaughtering to soapmaking; maternal health from pregnancy to delivery and breastfeeding; the ailments of children from diaper rash and horsefly bites to epilepsy and intestinal worms; and rarer, exotic challenges such as the removal of a dead fetus from a mother's womb.

The raison d'être of the late medieval/early modern household was to bring children into the world and raise them up to be people useful to themselves and to others. Practically, that meant hands-on training for a self-sustaining vocation and the nurturing of moral and religious sensibilities requisite to a good citizen. All agreed that a worthy and successful human life heeded and honored parents, assisted neighbors, feared and trusted God, knew how to earn its own keep, and gave back to parents and society with the same generosity it was shown.

Discipline became the most important virtue of childhood because without it children neither retained the vital lessons of life, nor discovered their own selfish, possessive will, what previous generations called "the devil within them." Without such discovery a new generation grew to maturity without corresponding moral development and usefulness to society.[3]

Beginning in the fifteenth century, the growth of education and the availability of cheap paper and ink not only made the invention of the printing press possible, but it also gave family members the ability to correspond with one another and to record their innermost thoughts in private diaries. As sons and daughters departed the household in adolescence (7-14) and

3. Julius Hoffmann, *Die 'Hausväter-Literatur' und die 'Predigten über den christlichen Hausstand.' Lehre vom Hause und Bildung für das häusliche Leben im 16. 17. und 18. Jahrhundert* (Weinheim a.d.B., 1959), pp. 63-65, 87-90, 152-53; Johannes Colerus, *Oeconomia Ruralis et Domestica,* Part II (Frankfurt am Main: Schönwetter [Verlag], 1680), Bk. IV, xi, p. 350.

youth (14-20), these first-person documents began to accumulate in family archives. Today, they give historians a rare access to the inner family circle, particularly so during the passage through adolescence and youth, when the relationship between child and parent enters its most difficult years, with letters flying back and forth. In remembering those years of passage, parents and children documented the Jekyll-Hyde nature of adolescence and youth that is also familiar to modern parents.

One of many illustrative stories is that of Stephan Carl Behaim, the eldest son of a Nürnberg patrician family who failed his every vocational undertaking and moral choice. At 15, he flunked out of the nearby Altdorf Academy, thus becoming the first member of his family to fail at school. He then proved himself unfit for service at court and was relegated to waiting on tables during the remainder of his apprenticeship. Like many another failed burgher or patrician youth, Stephen Carl ended up in the military, later to die on a battlefield in Brazil at 26, while serving with the Dutch West India Company.

Evidence of a morally challenged child was there in adolescence. Learning of his debauchery, thievery, and resistance to discipline at school, his mother wrote him the following letter.

> Good evening. You have asked to know my thoughts about you . . . [Simply put they are] that God may have mercy upon you . . . I lie awake many a night because I cannot conclude otherwise than that your letters, with their pious citations of God's Word, are pure hypocrisy, used only to hide your shame. If you really took your behavior seriously, you would not be so bold and arrogant [as to boast to me] that you have eaten with the children at the "cat's table" [a separate table for unruly students] . . .
>
> Neither sin nor shame gives you pause. You have told me untruthfully that the water fountain [rather than the beer tap at the inn] is now your greatest joy. I have also learned that when you hear in church the word, "give . . ." you rather prefer [to take from the collection plate] a little money [for yourself]. By such thoughts you are steering a course of shame and vice which leads in the end to the gallows and hellfire . . . May God in his grace save you from such a fate . . . Alas, my admonitions so far have had little effect on you.[4]

4. Steven Ozment, *Three Behaim Boys: Growing Up in Early Modern Germany* (New Haven: Yale University Press, 1990), p. 168 (March 1629). Cf. Ozment, *Protestants: The Birth of a Revolution* (New York: Doubleday, 1991), pp. 206-7.

Such letters are snapshots of real days in the lives of families past. In such private sources one may glimpse the pendulum shifts in the generational divide as adolescent children and youth drop from the nest, either to fly or to fall to their deaths.

The Initiative of the Child

Having long and harshly scrutinized the childrearing practices of so-called "patriarchal" families and "monarchal" societies, it is fitting and refreshing to see new scholarship on the family discovering the kindred, positive side of historical parenting. It is also appropriate that equal attention is now being directed to the *child's* responsibility for his or her own maturation, vocational success, and advancement of the culture and civilization of his or her own generation. Once parents and society have equipped children to the best of their ability and resources, it then becomes the new generation's responsibility either to continue in the way it has been trained and warned, or freely to change that direction for what must and should be its own good reasons.

With the onset of adolescence and youth a child necessarily becomes the key player in his or her life and is no longer an innocent victim of parents or society. Having heretofore been artful and dutiful alter egos, parents at this point find themselves to be potential victims of their own offspring, something today's baby-boomer generation, like the late medieval "patriarchs" before them, are also discovering. In the past parents devised their own strategies and protections against unruly offspring and morally failed children. Yet, very few ever completely removed the safety net they had built under their children, and on those occasions when they did, it was not precipitously done, but came at the end of early and repeated warnings. As legal codes defining inheritance rights attest, historically youth have gained a lion's share of responsibility over both the lives and the legacies of their parents, and not always with and by good intentions.[5]

5. "Nürnberger Reformation," in *Quellen zur neueren Privatrechtsgeschichte Deutschlands,* ed. Wolfgang Kunkel (Weimar: H. Böhlaus Nachfolger, 1932-42), vol. 1, no. 15.2, 19-20; cf. Steven Ozment, "Inside the Pre-industrial Household," in *Family Transformed,* ed. Steven M. Tipton and John Witte Jr. (Georgetown: Georgetown University Press, 2005), pp. 225-43. On the readiness of society, guardians, and widowed mothers to bestow proper inheritances on offspring, cf. Ozment, *Three Behaim Boys.*

Conjunctions in History

Contemporary historical experience shapes the institution of the family just as it does those of the state and the church. Despite the stories Renaissance court historians tell, the institutions of family, state, and church do not spring up full-grown from antiquity. And despite the stories of modern historians, neither do they await enlightenments in the future to become all that they might be. At the intersection of past and future every age, in its age, creates its essential self, historically both a link and a divider, while holding a place of its own across centuries.

Historian Benjamin Kaplan has recently reminded us of the unifying power of civic experience in European civilization in the aftermath of the Reformation. His story is one of deeply sown, moral-communal values enabling ordinary laity in religiously divided cities and lands to maintain civility and political unity despite new confessional divisions.[6] Cities and lands that were then "divided by faith" spared their societies internecine warfare by applying the civic lessons instilled in adolescence and youth over generations. The resulting civic and political values shaped children and youth as effectively as catechetical instruction in the churches and the liberal arts curriculum in the schools. A resulting "our town first and last" belief held the body politic together.

Kaplan finds striking examples of Catholics, Lutherans, Calvinists, and even minority Anabaptists leading parallel religious lives despite their division by faith. Having lived together as burghers and neighbors in unity and peace for generations before the Reformation, these same Christian laity found ways to continue to live that same civic life, no matter the religious divide.

Kaplan calls this religious tolerance the "first tolerance" and traces its birth to the confessional rapprochement forced upon religiously divided Christian groups in the sixteenth century. Its foundation was laid when devout people of one religious confession agreed with devout fellow citizens of another to hold parallel services of worship under agreed-upon terms and conditions. Unlike modern toleration, which deems all religions to be equally true (or false), sixteenth-century tolerance did not neuter confessional differences. Recognizing alternative confessions as a new fact of life, dual and even plural confessions, none of which acknowledged the truth

6. Benjamin Kaplan, *Divided by Faith: Religious Conflict and the Practice of Toleration* (Cambridge, MA: Harvard University Press, 2007).

claims of the other(s), learned nonetheless to coexist together. Contrary religious beliefs were practiced by tacit, but firm, agreements within a contiguous community or land without reprisals and short of civil war, so long as the conditioning covenants were kept.

Neither assimilation to a religion one did not believe, nor agnosticism in the face of all religions, was then a true option. Yet, there was some "modern" watering down of religious faith on the fringes among rationalists (e.g., Erasmus and Servetus) and so-called spiritualists (e.g., Sebastian Frank). Rather than a modern pretense of a "hidden unity in all religions," a deeply engrained habit of civic allegiance and unity saved not a few late medieval and early modern communities from all-out religious warfare.

If a commonsense covenant was at work in the background helping prevent a Hobbesian war of all against all, a long, countervailing history of civic unity and pride held center stage. The civic goal was not suppression and conformity with one's fist, but accommodation and pluralism through one's fingers. In the sixteenth century, no confession had to give up its truth claims to survive the perceived heresy of another. Each had only to stand pat and practice "tolerance," which Kaplan describes as willingness to suffer, endure, and put up with what is objectionable to one's own religious faith for the sake of a greater civic and political good.

Like the modern political historians who deem the European world to have been blindly intolerant before the French and German Enlightenments, modern family historians have long invoked a belated modern "turn" to explain the emergence of loving, nonpatriarchal families. Philippe Ariès spoke for many of those historians when he dated the "discovery of the child" and the "triumph of the sentimental family" around the turn of the seventeenth century.[7]

For all the criticism one might heap on Ariès for so shortsighted a view of the history of the family, he did associate the rise of the modern family primarily with pragmatic changes in parent-child relationships — not the rise of grandiose secular philosophical ideas. That change was the vocational training of adolescents and youth in nearby schools rather than in apprenticeships in faraway homes and workshops. Because the new schools were more receptive to parental visits and children's journeys home, they made it possible for parents to be closer to their children for longer periods of time. This extended opportunity for parent-child intimacy in turn allowed par-

7. Steven Ozment, *Ancestors: The Loving Family in Old Europe* (Cambridge, MA: Harvard University Press, 2001), pp. 9-13.

ents to gain a better understanding of their children's developmental needs and abilities as they passed through adolescence and youth.[8]

So Kaplan's revision of the history of tolerance rings true with that of the history of the family. The rise of the sentimental family in the eighteenth century is just as much a myth as the rise of toleration in the eighteenth century. Tolerant societies and loving families preexisted the seventeenth century. While the citizens of late medieval Europe were finding ways to survive confessional division and religious warfare, parents in those same centuries found effective ways to guide their children through childhood, adolescence, and youth when historical circumstance and human nature threatened the unity and values of family life. Had Europeans in late medieval and early modern times been dependent on the French and German Enlightenments three centuries later in order to raise offspring in an effective, principled, and tolerant way, fewer of us would be alive today to appreciate it. There is an argument to be made that effective parenting began when the first newborn was placed in the arms of the first mother. The pressing historical question is not when such childrearing began, but what have been and remain its proven tactics.

Winning the Child's Heart and Mind

Getting an Early Start

Because it is no small effort of parental imagination to gain and hold a child's attention, proactive measures never come too soon or too frequently in the rearing of children. In the burgher households of Renaissance and Reformation Europe, the day of "divine quickening" (i.e., the moment the fetus moved perceptively in the womb, around the end of the first trimester) started the transformation of a not-yet-viable newborn into a future parent-pleasing, God-fearing citizen, something no one then believed the child to be by birth alone. Until delivery, there was much speculation on the infant's gender based on the astrological conditions existing on the day of the child's conception and any unusual food cravings and consumption that the pregnant mother had thereafter.[9]

8. Philippe Ariès, *Centuries of Childhood: A Social History of the Family,* trans. Robert Baldick (New York: Vintage, 1962), pp. 369-70.

9. Steven Ozment, *When Fathers Ruled: Family Life in Reformation Europe* (Cambridge,

As soon as "Little Hans" or "Little Gretchen" was known to be "in the oven" (i.e., the mother's womb), he, or she, was embraced by the entire household. Not only did its members talk *about* the infant in the womb, they also spoke directly to it. A full six months before delivery, while still unseen and unheard, the infant had already gained a place of honor in the household and was treated as a tablemate.[10] When pregnant women today sing and talk to the fetus in the womb, they are well in step with the wisdom of childbearing, childrearing women in the distant past.

According to the midwife's ordinance in ducal Saxony-Meiningen (1682), a practicing midwife approached the delivery of a child with the following prayer:

> May the fruit of this womb by your Gracious Will be well-shaped and formed so that it may be a good-natured child [i.e., a child of good breeding] and become in its lifetime a good soul.[11]

Once the newborn was delivered and secure *en scène,* every member of the household had their tried-and-true ways to comfort, cure, groom, and present the newborn properly to family and friends.[12] In the second month after the birth of his son Georg, Nürnberg counsel and diplomat Christoph Scheurl sat his two-month-old firstborn down on his lap, put a feather ink pen in his tiny hand, and guided it as the boy "wrote" a letter of gratitude to his cloistered great aunt and her convent for assisting his birth and survival through their prayers.[13] This was a father's first step toward teaching his son to be thoughtful and grateful, no matter the child's age and comprehension. Although seeming to expect too much too soon from the child, contemporaries believed that in the fullness of time, acts and deeds caught up with embedded ideas and concepts.

In the weeks after the birth of a child, neighbors and professionals from

---

MA: Harvard University Press, 1983), p. 114. Eucharius Roesslin, *Rosengarten* (1513), cited by Ozment, *When Fathers Ruled,* p. 113.

10. Hans Bösch, *Kinderleben in der deutschen Vergangenheit* (Leipzig: Diederichs, 1900), p. 7.

11. Bösch, *Kinderleben,* p. 7.

12. All knew, for example, that "when babies cry they should be comforted by offering the breast, or moving them about, now on the shoulders, now on the hands, now on the knees and lap. And one should also talk, whistle, and sing to them." Nicholas Orme, *Medieval Children* (New Haven: Yale University Press, 2001), pp. 62-63.

13. Steven Ozment, *Flesh and Spirit: Private Life in Early Modern Germany* (New York: Viking, 1999), p. 90.

the outside world extended their greetings and tendered their services. In burgher and patrician society, the first alien hand to touch the newborn's head was that of a city-certified midwife, whose job it was not only to guide the child safely through the birth canal, but also to swaddle and introduce it to the world outside the womb. In the birthing of the child the fifteenth-century midwife was arguably a kinder and gentler authority over the child than the commanding medieval patriarch and the more subtly controlling modern parent.

Swaddling literally straightened and shaped the newborn's limbs and seems a fitting start and symbol for the straight-and-narrow physical and moral development that lay ahead for the child. Against the modern critic's vision of swaddling as a constricting, crippling bondage, it is arguable that it twisted a child's body and mind far less than the regimens of modern disciplinary institutions and the permissive childrearing practices of more recent times, the former being too harsh, the latter too soft. Modern disciplinary institutions can push the child physically and psychologically to a desired perfection beyond his or her grasp, thus leaving behind a hardened or defeated child. And modern permissive childrearing is well known to praise the child for achievement unaccompanied by requisite sacrifice, thus leaving behind a "paper" adult.

By contrast, the fifteenth-century midwife "gently" swaddled the newborn infant with the intent to make its limbs strong and attractive. Viewed by contemporaries as a warm cocooning, swaddling was believed to alleviate the trauma of birth and to protect fragile, wobbly legs and arms from dirt, bumps, cuts, breaks, and animal predators. Contrary to much modern prejudice, swaddled children did not as a rule "steam" in their urine and feces for days on end. Both contemporary pediatric literature and parental instinct instructed mothers to allow their infants to kick freely at regular intervals during the day and to be frequently bathed.[14]

The second alien hand placed on the newborn's head was that of the church in the person of a priest, who administered the sacrament of baptism. As swaddling protected the newborn's body, baptism armored the soul, a spiritual rampart against sin, death, and the devil, giving the child a fighting chance against lifelong temptation. On the day of baptism, a rite of exorcism at the church door preceded the newborn's baptism inside the church. After commanding Satan to flee the child's soul, the priest thereafter invoked

14. Shahar, *Childhood in the Middle Ages*, pp. 86-88; Ozment, *When Fathers Ruled*, pp. 118-19.

the Holy Spirit to occupy that soul and protect it. Thereby, the eternal consequences of original sin were believed to be stricken, and a new foundation laid for the now Christian child's moral and spiritual growth.[15]

After birth, swaddling, and baptism, weaning occurred on or around the child's first birthday and was the last empowering, equipping, programming act administered to the newborn. Although a seemingly small event, weaning was an irrevocable step toward individuality and personal independence. Henceforth, the child would progressively receive solid food in place of mother's milk and learn to feed himself with his own hands.[16]

The Child at 7

Seven was the next big year in the life of a child. Medieval mirrors depict 7-year-old boys as loose cannons ("they lead their lives without cares, go about naked unashamedly, are quick to anger and to calm, and ruled only by their own appetites") and their female counterparts looser still ("swift wit, merciless, envious, bitter, deceitful, and quick to succumb to the pleasures of Venus"). Beyond infancy (0-7), the adolescent years (7-14) marked the beginning of the separation, stabilization, and earnest maturation of both sexes into adults.[17]

Newly self-reliant and now presumed able to choose between good and evil, 7-year-old boys put aside the unisex smock of childhood henceforth to wear the exclusive, sovereign male trousers. During adolescence and youth (7-20), boys were methodically integrated into the world of their fathers — a world of jousts and hunts, production and trade, politics and war, and courtship and marriage.

In step with their brothers, adolescent girls were absorbed into the world of their mothers and older female siblings, where they became proficient in the arts and crafts of home management and housekeeping, skills preparatory to marriage, service, and/or entrance into the cloister. For both sexes, these were years of very strict discipline and increased responsibility

15. Bösch, *Kinderleben*, pp. 25-26, 28; Ozment, *Flesh and Spirit*, pp. 78-79.

16. Orme, *Medieval Children*, p. 66; Ozment, *Flesh and Spirit*, p. 89.

17. Bartholomew the Englishman, "The Ages of Man," in Jacqueline Murray, *Love, Marriage, Family in the Middle Ages: A Reader* (Toronto: University of Toronto Press, 2001), pp. 447-48. "Late medieval theologians and lawyers thought a child of seven might be tonsured as a clerk, engaged to marry, charged with a crime, and (in the case of exceptional girls) become sexually active." Orme, *Medieval Children*, p. 68.

self and little about lying, deceit, drunkenness, gambling, cheating, fornication, and stealing.[21]

A contemporary of Menius was a Strasbourg physician, educator, and classical scholar named Otto Brunfels (1488-1534), author of a hugely popular classical-Christian tract on childrearing techniques. Therein, he distilled three tolerances without which he believed a child had scant hope of either personal or vocational success. Those tolerances were discipline *(Zucht),* mastery *(Kunst),* and honor *(Erbarkeit):* the well-prepared child was one who shows up, gains basic skills, and is reliable in word and deed. When parents and educators in the past wrote homiletically about "graftings and bendings of the twig," these were the traits, qualities, and temperament they wished to instill in the new generation.[22]

When contemplating the long transition into adulthood, parents in the past had no illusions about its difficulty. While not wishing to remain infants, adolescents and youth also did not easily surrender the idle pleasures of childhood.[23] In the eyes of their sterner elders, unproductive, childish play was at this point in life to be steadily challenged, and that challenge came in the form of daily manual labor and regular spiritual examination.

In these endeavors, parents did not as a rule coerce 7-year-olds into adult work beyond their abilities. Mindful of a child's stamina and level of skill, adolescent training, while steady and demanding, also remained incremental. Pre-adolescents helped around the house and performed doable out-of-doors chores. They herded sheep and geese, cleaned stalls, watered gardens, dug up beets, cleared paths, drove crows out of the cabbage patch, and the like.[24] Adolescent boys expanded such activities, while their sisters picked garden crops, prepared meals, wove cloth, and spun wool. By 12, most boys and girls had learned the rudiments of a craft, trade, or service. Their training occurred both at home and in the households of other families. There were both day jobs that returned them home at night and ap-

21. Menius, *An die hochgeborne Fuerstin/fraw Sibilla Herzogin zu Sachsen/Oeconomia Christiana/das ist von Christlicher Hausshaltung* (Nuremberg, 1530), pp. F1B; Bösch, *Kinderleben,* pp. 54-55; Ozment, *When Fathers Ruled.*

22. Brunfels, *Von der Zucht und Underweisung der Kinder/Ein Leer und Vermanung* (Strasbourg, 1525), A 4 b. See also the educational advice of Desiderius Erasmus in Ozment, *When Fathers Ruled,* pp. 136-37.

23. Orme, *Medieval Children,* p. 85. Adolescents were said to be "carefree . . . fearing no peril worse than a beating with a stick." Murray, ed., *Love, Marriage, and Family in the Middle Ages,* p. 447.

24. Bösch, *Kinderleben,* pp. 54-55.

prenticeships that took them far away from home for prolonged periods of time.[25]

Just as the physical ability of adolescents was accommodated in vocational training, there were also adjustments to intelligence and temperament in the spiritual development of the adolescent soul. Adolescent communicants also began confession at the age of 7. They were examined, however, on age-appropriate transgressions, which tested their caution, fidelity, and truthfulness, rather than scouring the adolescent soul for hardier adult sins. Children were asked if they had lied, cursed, dishonored, argued with, struck out at, or stolen from parents and teachers; whether carnal desires obsessed and tormented their minds; if they had endangered the lives of others while swimming or riding; or whether they had plundered the fields, vineyards, and/or gardens of others. The consensus of the confessors was that stealing, more than any other wrongdoing, was endemic among adolescents and youth![26]

Adolescents also received lighter penances than adults for the same transgressions. It is doubtful, however, that such adjustments calmed the fears of youngsters making their first confession. Still, the measure of gentility surely drew the novice penitent back to the Sacrament in the belief that the priest knew well what was in their hearts and minds, and had given them a fair shake at the confessional.

In the belief that it was better to harden a child than to spoil one, and to harden a presumed better child even more, the virtues of purity, discipline, and honor were methodically engrained in royal children more harshly. Young royals 6 years and older rose at 6:00 a.m., started their day with a prayer and a breakfast of meatless soup, buttered wheat meal, and an egg. From 9:00 to 11:45 a.m. they alternately prayed, read, sang, and busied themselves with puppets and other games.

The main meal of the day was served at 11:45. All present had to display clean clothes, hands, and faces. Complaining and joking about the food were not tolerated. Sharp and spicy foods were served in small amounts, while sweet foods (fruits, honey, and treats) only with parental permission. With each bite the child was reminded to thank God for what he received.

Elective walks were allowed in the afternoon. Supper was served at 6:00

25. Orme, *Medieval Children,* pp. 308-9; Ben-Amos, *Adolescence and Youth in Early Modern England,* ch. 2-6.

26. With an apparent eye on the Fifth Commandment ("Thou Shalt Not Kill"), one child's confessor tested agility and attentiveness by asking: "Did you recently kill the emperor with a double-bladed ax?" Ozment, *The Reformation in the Cities,* pp. 23-25.

p.m. followed by evening devotions at 8:00. Thereafter, the children washed up and went straight to bed, with a warning not to tell ghost stories into the night.[27]

For the vast majority of children in the premodern world the active life clearly trumped the contemplative life. Increasingly throughout adolescence and youth, one became what one could *do.* Abstract ideas and ideals of a philosophical or a spiritual nature held a hallowed but secondary place in preparing children for life in the workaday world. The Arts curriculum in the public schools and the religious catechism at church enlightened and consoled, disciplined and inspired the young with complementary forms of knowledge, but mundane work commanded the greater part of their time and sacrifice.

The Child as Father of the Man

In the sixteenth century, when grown children looked back on their childhoods, they had vivid memories of both good and bad times with parents, siblings, and peers, a memory bank that alternately sustained and haunted them into adulthood. An outstanding example is the memories of a Cologne civil lawyer, Hermann von Weinsberg (1518-1597), a well-known middle-class, anti-clerical Catholic burgher who deeply admired the Dutch humanist, Desiderius Erasmus. Consumed by a desire to immortalize and honor the Cologne Weinsbergs, Hermann wrote over his lifetime possibly the longest-surviving first-person biography of the sixteenth century. His goal was to make his middling burgher family as well known to posterity as any of Cologne's patrician and noble families.

He married twice and late in life, both times to women older than he, and his marriages were both unsatisfying and without children. However, before those marriages he sired an illegitimate daughter, Anna, out of wedlock with a family servant. Because of the circumstances of her birth, Anna spent her childhood in the home of a lower-class family and did not meet her father face to face until she was 10 years old. From that day on, Hermann progressively became a proud, doting, exemplary father, who saw to his daughter's material needs and arranged for her to receive a good education. When she turned 20, he endowed a place for her in a family cloister, where he visited her often with gifts, conversation, and love. The highlight of this be-

27. Bösch, *Kinderleben,* p. 52.

lated and stained parenthood came when Anna was elected the abbess of her cloister.[28]

Hermann's memories of his own childhood dated back to his third birthday, when he recalled receiving a blue coat and a red bonnet from his grandmother. He remembered most fondly the special times with his mother and father, whose childrearing was both thoughtful and aggressive, his mother erring on the side of consistency (including corporal punishment), his father rather more relaxed and inclined to cut the boy some slack. Once, when he was 6, his mother, "with [young Hermann's acknowledged] justification," slapped him hard "as [he claimed] she often did." On this occasion, it sent him screaming to his father, who asked him consolingly what he thought they should do about the incident: "Throw mother out of the house, or make her live in the basement, while we [men] live together in the large room upstairs?" When Hermann chose the latter course, his father praised his maturity for "not wanting to drive mother away because of a little spanking!"[29]

On the brighter parental side, his mother loved to recount the time when she was pregnant with Hermann. As he was her first pregnancy, she had wanted at the time to ensure a safe delivery by having the fruit of her womb blessed at the shrine in Aachen. Actually, the larger shrine in Trier had been her first choice, but she was too far along with her pregnancy to make that long journey, and thus had to go to the closer and lesser shrine in Aachen. Particularly on Hermann's birthday, she would endearingly tell the story of their pilgrimage to Aachen with closing words that sounded like a riddle: "In 1517, I was in Trier with you [Hermann], but I did not see the shrine there, and you were in Aachen with me, and you did not see the shrine there either."[30]

With such words, Frau Weinsberg amusingly recounted her disappointment for not having been able to see Hermann blessed at the shrine in Trier. Although physically in Aachen, her heart and mind were fixed on Trier — thus she was in Trier mentally but did not see the shrine. And Hermann, her first-

28. *Das Buch Weinsberg,* vol. 2, ed. Friedrich Lau (Leipzig: Publikation der Gesellschaft für Rheinische Geschichte, 1887), pp. 49, 83, 147-48, 164-67, 175, 191; vol. 3, ed. Friedrich Lau (Bonn, 1897), pp. 10-11; vol. 5, ed. Josef Stein (Bonn, 1926), p. iii.

29. *Das Buch Weinsberg. Kölner Denkwürdigkeiten aus dem 16. Jahrundert,* ed. Konstantin Höhlbaum, vol. 1 (Leipzig, 1886), p. 37; Bösch, *Kinderleben,* p. 39. Cf. Matthew Lundin, "The Mental World of a Middling Burgher: The Family Archive of Cologne Lawyer Hermann Weinsberg (1518-1597)" (dissertation: Harvard University, 2005).

30. *Das Buch Weinsberg,* vol. 1, p. 22.

born, who was physically in Aachen with her, did not see the shrine there because he was tucked away in the darkness of her womb. Later, as an adult, Hermann visited Aachen and while there confided to friends who had accompanied him that he had once before been in Aachen, "but had not seen it."[31]

Hermann also remembered equally endearing moments with his father. He recalled how, at 5, the two of them set out one day for Dormagen, three and half miles away, to visit his grandparents. Hermann quickly tired and could not keep up the pace. Noticing this, his father took a ball he had hidden in his shirtsleeve and threw it ahead of them on the road. The two of them would then race to fetch it. Father would then throw it down the road again. As this went on, Hermann forgot about his fatigue, regained his legs, and before he knew it, he was at his grandparents' house.[32]

Hermann's family had many mottos, most of them realism verging on pessimism. The one that appealed most to him had a small, saving grace, much like the silver lining scholars find in his often-cloudy life. It reads: "Always reach for a golden wagon. If you don't get the wagon, you may still grab a golden hitch."[33]

The Love of the Child, the Life of a Nation

A saying from the German Middle Ages suggests that a couple who cannot have children may be more burdened in life than a couple who do have children.

> Children bring grief and woe and often disturb parental peace: "no child, no worry." So do not complain so much just because your wife cannot bear a child.[34]

Historically couples without children have complained and grieved. Yet, for a half-century post–World War II Europeans have embraced either a "no child" or a "one child" family model. As a result of this negative birthrate, large and growing numbers of foreign workers have immigrated to Western

31. *Das Buch Weinsberg,* vol. 2, p. 104.

32. *Das Buch Weinsberg,* vol. 1, pp. 35-36.

33. *Das Buch Weinsberg,* vol. 5, pp. 197-98.

34. Bösch, *Kinderleben,* p. 21. On the anguish and joy childbirth brought early modern parents, see the trials of the Nürnberg husband and wife Scheurl, who had ten miscarriages or stillbirths over twelve years before a live birth of a son. Ozment, *Flesh and Spirit,* p. 72.

Europe to work jobs that native Europeans lack either the manpower or the desire to fill. The economic and social costs of that immigration have been high, and the civic and political consequences promise to become even more frightening if immigrant populations grow unchecked and a nonassimilating immigrant culture challenges that of its hosts.

In a gripping interview with *Die Zeit* (January 26, 2006, no. 5), Mathias Platzeck, then the SPD party chair, complained about the large numbers of Germans who no longer believe in the traditional family and traditional religion, to which one may add the traditional work ethic. That cannot be said of the immigrant communities confronting present-day Germany and Europe. Often eager to be fruitful and multiply, to confess and practice their historical faith, and to work longer hours for lesser pay in jobs their hosts avoid, the immigrant culture seems bound for power and success in the land of their hosts.

When questioned, Herr Platzeck doubted that religious faith, or the lack of it, had anything to do with Europe's low birthrates and regressive family formation, although a possible relationship intrigued him. At the end of his interview, speaking with refreshing candor, Herr Platzeck blamed negative German birthrates on the present-day desire of Germans to live unencumbered "for the fun-filled moment" *(Spass am Tag)*. For both good reasons and bad, a great many postwar-generation Germans want an untrammeled life, which childbearing and childrearing in every age and culture make difficult.

In his best interview moment, Herr Platzeck, echoing a more famous German (Wolfgang von Goethe), admonished his fellow countrymen and Europeans to let the tempting, ephemeral, self-indulgent moments go and reach out for something larger and more lasting, what he called "joy in life" *(Freude am Leben)*.

> Living for the moment does not help a society develop itself. It is children who give meaning to life. A society without children is a society without a future.[35]

The skills one needs to be a successful parent are also those required to raise up a mighty nation. The rearing of children in any age can only be as effective as the latter's "infrastructure," which is the overlapping network of family, religion, and state. Of these three, the family properly holds cen-

35. "Freude ist kein Spass," *Die Zeit On-Line*, 1/26/06, no. 5.

ter stage by virtue of its greater intimacy and commitment to its own. By comparison, the interventions of church and state have historically been a mixture of vital supporting roles, and intrusive crippling ones. In the rearing of children the wisdom of the ages has been to bundle them up early and often in the values of family and household before they become citizens and believers.

CHAPTER 5

The Duties of Love: The Vocation of the Child in the Household Manual Tradition

JOHN WITTE JR. AND HEATHER M. JOHNSON

Introduction

In his *Commentaries on the Laws of England* (1765), William Blackstone wrote: "The duties of children to their parents arise from a principle of natural justice and retribution. For to those who gave us existence, we naturally owe subjection and obedience during our minority, and honour and reverence ever after; they, who protected the weakness of our infancy, are entitled to our protection in the infirmity of their age; they who by sustenance and education have enabled their offspring to prosper, ought in return to be supported by that offspring, in case they stand in need of assistance. Upon this principle proceed all the duties of children to their parents, which are enjoined by positive laws."[1] The contemporaneous *Book of Common Prayer* (American Version, 1789) described the child's vocation thus: "To love, honour, and succour my father and mother: To honour and obey the civil authority: To submit myself to all my governors, teachers, spiritual pastors and masters: To order myself lowly and reverently to all my betters."[2] Hundreds of comparable sentiments can be found in standard textbooks of law and

1. William Blackstone, *Commentaries on the Law of England* (London, 1765), Book 1, ch. 16.
2. The Protestant Episcopal Church, *The Book of Common Prayer* (New York, 1789), p. x.

We wish to thank Mr. Timothy Rybacki for his excellent research assistance, and Mr. Will Haines and Ms. Kelly Parker for their fine library services. Another version of this chapter appeared in Patrick McKinley Brennan, ed., *The Vocation of the Child* (Grand Rapids: Eerdmans, 2008), pp. 266-91, and is used herein with permission.

theology in early modern times — both Catholic and Protestant, European and American.

The common source for many of these traditional legal and theological sentiments was the Bible, particularly the Commandment: "Honor your father and your mother, that your days may be long in the land which the Lord your God gives you" (Exod. 20:12; Lev. 19:5; Deut. 5:16) and its various New Testament echoes (Matt. 15:4; Mark 7:10; Eph. 6:1-2). Also important were the Bible's repeated admonitions to believers to "be subject to the governing authorities" (Rom. 13:1-7; Titus 3:1; 1 Pet. 2:13). But what precisely did it mean for a Christian child at various stages of development to "love, honor, and obey" or to "serve, succor, and sustain" parents, guardians, teachers, and other authorities? And what did "natural justice" (as Blackstone put it) add to these obligations of "biblical righteousness"? The answers to these questions came in sundry texts — in sermons, catechisms, and confessional manuals as well as in a growing early modern industry of legal texts on domestic relations.

In this chapter, we sample an interesting, but largely neglected, historical medium for teaching the duties and vocation of the child — the household manuals. These manuals were something of the spiritual "Dr. Spocks" of their day — pious "how to" manuals, usually written in the vernacular (unlike the Latin confessional manuals), sometimes highly illustrated (for the young child's benefit), and used regularly by priests and teachers, parents and guardians, tutors and catechists to instruct children at various stages of their development as budding communicants in the church and budding citizens of the state. These household manuals sometimes grew out of or merged into catechisms and religious teaching manuals, on the one hand, and books of etiquette, manners, and deportment, on the other. By the later sixteenth and seventeenth centuries, household manuals were increasingly recognized as their own distinct genre of literature, with the duties of love by and to children broken out in separate sections.

The earliest surviving household manuals in English that we have found are from the fourteenth century. The most famous was penned by the early English reformer, John Wyclif, *Of Weddid Men and Wifis and of Here Children Also* (1390). With the advent of the printing press in the fifteenth century, these manuals became more common, finding their way into myriad church, school, city, and home libraries, Catholic and Protestant alike. They also became more complex and comprehensive, reaching their apex in the massive 800-page tome of Anglo-Puritan divine William Gouge published in 1622. Scores of these household manuals have come down to us. They provide an illuminating window on what a late medieval or early modern child was taught to be his or her vocation in life, what rights and freedoms the child must enjoy in exercise of these duties, and what rights and duties the child's parents, guardians, teachers, and tutors had in helping the child achieve his or her vocation. These manuals helped to bridge law and theology, practice and theory, belief and action in Catholic and Protestant Europe and North America.

This chapter provides a brief tour of the highpoints of these household manuals. We sample nearly 100 manuals from the fourteenth to the nineteenth centuries that have survived in English.[3] We focus especially on the common and enduring Western formulations of the vocation of the child set out in these manuals — a rich latticework of virtues, values, and vocations that boys and girls respectively should consider at various stages in life.

The vocation of the child as revealed in these manuals consists of two main types of duties: (1) the duty of the child to love God, neighbor, and self and thereby to become beloved to others; and (2) the duty of the child to *be* loved by parents, guardians, and others. This latter duty was sometimes also cast as the child's right to be loved — though talk of a child's rights remained controversial in the manuals. While the child's basic duties to love did not change much over the five centuries of manuals that we have sampled, the child's duties and rights to be loved and to be beloved did change significantly in substance and form, as we note in the final section of this chapter.

The Child's Duty to Love

Love of God. The household manuals make clear that the first and most essential duty of the child is to love, revere, and worship God. The German Reformer Martin Luther put it thus in 1531: "[Y]ou must continually have God's Word in your heart, upon your lips and in your ears. Where the heart is unoccupied and the Word does not sound, Satan breaks in and has done the damage before we are aware."[4] For the First Commandment of the Decalogue is "that we are to trust, fear and love [God] with our whole hearts all the days of our lives."[5] An influential Catholic pamphlet *L'Instruction des*

3. See Appendix A for a list of the household manuals we studied.

4. Martin Luther, "Large Catechism" (1529), in *Luther on Education, Including a Historical Introduction and a Translation of the Reformer's Two Most Important Educational Treatises,* ed. and trans. F. V. N. Painter (St. Louis, 1928), p. 64.

5. *Luther on Education,* p. 65.

Enfans (1543) stated that the primary command for every child is to "love the Lord God with all your heart" and that the first responsibility of parents and siblings alike is to teach the child to obey that primal command.[6] Richard Baxter's *Rules & Directions for Family Duties* (1681) encouraged parents to "[w]isely break [children] of their own wills, and let them know that they must obey and like God's will" first and foremost.[7] Eleazer Moody's comprehensive manual *The School of Good Manners* (1775) listed as the first duty of a child the duty to "fear and reverence God."[8] The duty to face God daily with fearful and loving reverence, the vast majority of the manuals made clear, is the foundation of the Christian child's life.

The manuals often invoked the duty to love God to compel the child to fulfill his or her other duties, especially the duty to love parents, who are regularly described as God's "priests," "bishops," "kings," and "queens" to their children.[9] Of the duty to love parents, the Catholic *Christian Instructions for Youth* (1821) stated: "You cannot manifest your gratitude towards your parents by any other means but by loving them; this love must not be a natural affection only; it must be a rational love, and according to God; that is to say you must love them, because such is God's will, and you must give proofs of this love."[10] Thomas Becon, the sixteenth-century Anglican divine and confessor to Thomas Cranmer, wrote similarly that children must see their parents as gifts "by the singular providence and good-will of God," and they must love their parents "not feignedly, but from the very bottom of the heart and in wishing unto them all good things from God."[11] It is the child's duty "to honorably esteem them, godly to think of them, heartily to love them, humbly to obey them, [and] diligently to pray for them."[12]

While love of God and love of parents are conjoined, love of God is the primary commandment. Many of the household manuals make clear that when a parental command and a biblical command conflict, the child must

6. Anonymous, *L'Instruction des Enfans* (London, 1543), folios 1-2.

7. Richard Baxter, *Rules & Directions for Family Duties* (London, 1681), 1.

8. Eleazer Moody, *The School of Good Manners* (Boston, 1775); see also William Smith, *Universal Love* (1668), pp. 41-56.

9. See examples in John Witte Jr., *From Sacrament to Contract: Marriage, Religion, and Law in the Western Tradition* (Louisville: Westminster/John Knox Press, 1997).

10. Anonymous, *Christian Instructions for Youth,* 2nd rev. ed., trans. from French (London, 1821), p. 34; see also Richard Whitford, *The Werke for Householders* (1537), folios Ei-Fiii; Thomas Cobbett, *A Fruitful and Useful Discourse Touching the Honor Due from Children to Parents* (1656), pp. 9-68.

11. Thomas Becon, *The Catechism of Thomas Becon* [c. 1560] (Cambridge, 1844), p. 358.

12. Becon, *The Catechism of Thomas Becon,* p. 85.

follow the Bible. The manuals limited examples of such "wicked" commands of parents to obvious rejections of God or God's laws, such as a parental command that a child "forsake the true living God and his pure religion and to follow strange gods" or where parents, seeing a lucrative and evil opportunity, encourage their daughter "to play the whore."[13] God commands children to obey parents, and the corollary is that in obeying parents a child obeys God. However, "in a matter clearly contrary to the law of God, and to your conscience . . . you do not owe [parents] obedience; but be cautious on such occasions; and when in doubt of the justness of their commands, take the advice of prudent and discreet persons."[14] Later American Protestants like Samuel Phillips commented in his manual on *The Christian Home* (1860) that "the authority of God supersedes that of the parent. Obey God rather than man," but obey parents in "all things lawful and Christian."[15]

Honor and Obey Parents. Except in these cases of absolute conflict with divine law and conscience, the manuals stress the child's duty of showing "unhesitating obedience"[16] to her parents, often invoking the Commandment to "Honor your father and mother" and its elaborations in later biblical passages. The manuals required children to "obey your parents . . . do what they command, and do it cheerfully. For your own hearts will tell you that this is a most natural extension of honor and love."[17] One manual went so far as to say that children "should have no other will" than the will of their parents, and thus, even those things that are good and righteous should not be undertaken without the consent of the parents.[18] Luther explained the duty of love to parents thus: "God has exalted fatherhood and motherhood above all other relations under his scepter. This appears from the fact that he does not command merely to love the parents, but to honor them. As to our brothers, sisters, and neighbors, God generally commands nothing higher than that we love them. He thus distinguishes father and mother above all other persons upon earth and places them next to himself. It is a much greater thing to

13. Becon, *The Catechism of Thomas Becon,* p. 87.

14. *Christian Instructions for Youth,* p. 34.

15. Samuel Phillips, *The Christian Home as it is in the Sphere of Nature and the Church* (New York, 1860), p. 218.

16. Francis Wayland, "Early Training of Children," in *The Fireside Miscellany; and Young People's Encyclopedia* (February, 1864), pp. 60-61.

17. W. E. Channing, *The Duties of Children* (Boston, 1807), p. 5; see also Cobbett, *A Fruitful and Useful Discourse,* pp. 69-127; W.C., *A School of Nurture for Children: The Duty of Children in Honoring their Parents* (1656), pp. 1-62.

18. William Fleetwood, *The Relative Duties of Parents and Children* (London, 1716), pp. 2-3.

honor than to love."[19] Thomas Becon nicely summed up the parameters of the duty of obedience: "Not only to give them outward reverence, to rise up unto them, to give them place, to put off our caps, to kneel unto them, to ask them blessing . . . but also . . . charitably to conceal and hide their faults, in all honest things to gratify them, in their need to help and succor them, and . . . at all times to do all good things for them, whatsoever lieth in our power."[20]

For most manualists, the one-sentence commandment to "honor your father and mother" was the foundation for a whole range of forbidden activities from the obvious to the tenuously related: striking or kicking parents; desiring a parent's death; hating, mocking, or deriding parents; angering parents; failing to help parents who are in poverty; paying offerings to the church; keeping fasting days; nonconformity with the divine rights of rulers; fostering unrest or treason against their own rulers or against their city; and depriving someone of an honor or a favor and keeping him from something he is entitled to out of "brotherly love."[21] As this list of proscriptions makes clear, the manuals extended the duty to honor and obey parents to all other earthly authority figures. As the German Catholic Dietrich Kolde put it in *A Fruitful Mirror* (1470), this commandment "requires and teaches us to assist and serve our parents with a loving heart, a polite mouth, and a respectful body. This applies not only to our natural parents, but also to spiritual and earthly authorities."[22]

Obedience to parents requires submission to Christian correction. Children have a duty to submit to punishment when it is deserved and must not resent their parents for punishing them.[23] One manual warned: "Forget not, young people, that your parents and masters have a right to correct you. They are bound to correct you, when you deserve it; should a slight correction in this case be not sufficient, it is their duty to use more severity." Children are expected to love parents for correcting them because "they correct you solely for your good, and to make you discreet and virtuous."[24]

19. Luther, *Large Catechism,* p. 66.

20. Becon, *Catechism,* p. 85.

21. Kolde, *A Fruitful Mirror* (1470), in *Three Reformation Catechisms: Catholic, Anabaptist, Lutheran,* ed. and trans. Denis Janz (New York: Edwin Mellen, 1982), pp. 55-56.

22. Kolde, *A Fruitful Mirror,* pp. 55-56.

23. Henry Dixon, *The English Instructor* (Boston, 1746), p. 55; see also Richard Baxter, *Rules and Directions for Family Duties* (1681); Anonymous, *True and Faithful Discharge of Relative Duties* (1683); John Gother, *Instructions for Children* (1698); Benjamin Wadsworth, *The Well-Ordered Family* (1712), pp. 90-102; *Christian Instructions for Youth* (1821), pp. 51-55.

24. *Christian Instructions for Youth,* p. 36.

Some manuals took this duty further: "Should you not perchance have deserved that correction, suffer it patiently, remembering that it is less than your sins deserve; and that Jesus Christ, though innocent, suffered without complaint the torment of the cross, and death itself."[25] As we shall note further below, this duty of obedience even in the face of abuse was dangerous instruction in a world where children were abused, tortured, and sometimes fell to "death itself" at the hands of their parents. The danger of children thinking that their Christian duty required them to suffer at the hands of tyrannical parents is further complicated by instructions throughout the manuals to "charitably to conceal and hide" their parents' "faults."[26]

Obedience also requires that a child attend school and aim constantly for excellence in both spiritual and secular education. The manuals frequently admonished children, for their parents' sake, to work at school and aim at high standards of intellectual power and attainment. In the early manuals, this duty was simply one derived from obedience and the obligation to learn about God. Later manuals however, tied the need for good education to the child's duty to fulfill her social responsibility as well as her duty to find a calling that would help her recompense her parents should they fall into poverty or need aid in old age.

The duty to obey requires a child to seek the consent of his or her parents to court and marry another. Marriages without parental consent violate the law of God, both Catholic and Protestant manuals insisted repeatedly.[27] The ultimate authority for choosing at least a minor child's spouse rests with the parents. The child's wishes must be considered, Anglican preacher William Fleetwood advised in *The Relative Duties of Parents and Children* (1716), for children must have a say "with whom they are to live and die" and "with whom they are to venture being happy or unhappy all their days."[28] But, while parents are encouraged to respect their child's wishes, the parents' decision is absolute, and an obedient Christian child is ultimately bound by their decision.

Respect. The heart of the duty to honor and obey is to have respect for one's parents and other superiors — to develop what the popular American manualist William Ellery Channing called a "submissive deportment."[29] Channing explained in *The Duties of Children* (1807) that "[y]our tender, in-

25. *Christian Instructions for Youth,* p. 37.
26. Becon, *Catechism,* p. 85.
27. Fleetwood, *Relative Duties,* pp. 32-33.
28. Fleetwood, *Relative Duties,* p. 35.
29. Channing, *Duties of Children,* p. 3.

experienced age requires that you think of yourselves with humility . . . that you respect the superior age and wisdom and improvements of your parents" and "express your respect for [parents] in your manner and conversation. Do not neglect those outward signs of dependence and inferiority which suit your age." Such outward signs include a requirement to "ask instead of demand what you desire," and because children "have much to learn" they should "hear instead of seeking to be heard." Channing was not arguing for a "slavish fear" of parents: "Love them and love them ardently; but mingle a sense of their superiority with your love. Feel a confidence in their kindness; but let not this confidence make you rude and presumptuous, and lead to indecent familiarity. Talk to them with openness and freedom; but never contradict with violence; never answer with passion or contempt."[30]

Learning parental respect is a foundational duty of the child, because respecting parents eventually translates into learning the good manners, restraint, and decorum that are essential for later success in church, state, and society. To cultivate this respect, the manuals sometimes went to great lengths to dictate every aspect of the child's manners and accompanying emotions preparing the child for the norms and habits of adult life. In many of these manuals, the litany of duties is almost overwhelming: be pious, work in school with all your heart, beware of being beaten and corrected, do not offend the schoolmaster or schoolmates in word or deed, read continually, be eloquent in speech and writing, go hastily home from school each day without tarrying, learn the catechisms, pray often, honor the Sabbath, do household chores, set the table for dinner, keep yourself upright and proper at the table, walk modestly, avoid "unchaste women," dress neither too sumptuously nor too poorly, study diligently, avoid evil persons — and the list goes on.

Eleazer Moody's wildly popular *The School of Good Manners,* first published in the United States in 1715, outlines 163 rules for children's behavior — 14 rules for behavior at home, 43 for the table, 10 for at church, 41 for company or in public, 28 for speaking to superiors, and 13 for school. The directives range from the impossible ("approach near thy parents at no time without a bow"), to the practical dinner table instruction ("take no salt with a greasy knife"), to the amusing ("throw not anything under the table"), to the improbable ("be not hasty to run out" out of church "when worship is ended, as if weary of being there").[31] The *Christian Instructions for Youth*

30. Channing, *Duties of Children,* pp. 3-4.

31. Moody, *School of Good Manners,* pp. 7-8, 11-12.

(1821) devoted 258 pages to the duties of young persons ranging from how they should honor their parents, to how they should take correction, to the means of preserving their chastity, to choosing and maintaining friendships. Good manners also included a range of simple rules of etiquette: taking care to clean one's body, covering with clean and modest apparel, keeping elbows off the table at dinner, not drinking wine and ale excessively and preferably not at all, purity of speech in all encounters (not to swear, interrupt, or speak of vile things), not contending with another, keeping to one's own affairs, ignoring information one should not have overheard, and humility.[32]

According to many household manuals, humble and limited speech is a critical characteristic of a good and respectful Christian child. Evil speech and swearing are telltale signs of inner impurities and utter disrespect. But early manuals also warned children to limit their chatter (whether pure or not), speaking to their parents and other adults only when absolutely necessary. Out of the duty of obedience and good manners, children were also required to listen attentively to parents and never to speak to them with derision or mocking tones. Luther remarked that honoring parents requires "that they be esteemed and prized above everything else as the most precious treasure we have on earth. That, in conversation with them, we measure our words, lest our language be discourteous, domineering, quarrelsome, yielding to them in silence, even if they do go too far."[33]

Some of the early household manuals called for a child to have complete control over his or her emotions in order to demonstrate this requisite respect. In his *Little Book of Good Manners* (1554), the great Dutch humanist Desiderius Erasmus called children to be "merry and joyful" at the dinner table, and never "heavy-hearted." In his *The Civility of Childhood* (1560), Erasmus admonished children not to be "angry" when corrected or to "rejoice" when praised, for such habits were not becoming of a "courteous Christian child."[34] The child's duties to honor, love, obey, and respect parents, Erasmus insisted, require a child to exert and exercise full control over his emotional state, requiring tenderness in place of torment, happiness in place of heartache, and delight in place of despair.

Respect and Recompense. This calling of the child to respect parents contin-

32. See, e.g., Desiderius Erasmus, *A Little Book of Good Manners* (London, 1554); see also Desiderius Erasmus, *The Civility of Childhood* (1560); Robert Crowley, *The School of Virtue . . . Teaching Children and Youths Their Duties* (London, 1621); Robert Abbott, *A Christian Family Builded by God* (London, 1653).

33. Luther, *Large Catechism*, p. 66.

34. Erasmus, *The Civility of Childhood.*

ued into adulthood, even after the duty to obey parents in daily life had expired. American writer Timothy Shay Arthur made this point in his *Advice to Young Men on Their Duties and Conduct in Life* (1848), a highly popular manual, and often reprinted on both sides of the Atlantic: "Although the attainment of mature age takes away the obligation of obedience to parents, as well as the right of dependence upon them, it should lessen in no way a young man's deference, respect, or affection."[35] William Blackstone wrote similarly in his *Commentaries on the Laws of England* (1765) that as children we owe our parents "subjection and obedience during our minority, and honor and reverence ever after."[36]

One of the most important expressions of ongoing respect is the child's duty to "recompense his parents" for rearing him, especially if his parents fall ill or become poor. For younger children, the manuals insisted, the duty to recompense is bound up with the duty to obey. William Channing, for example, instructed children: "Do not expect that your parents are to give up every thing to your wishes; but study to give up every thing to theirs. Do not wait for them to threaten; but when a look tells you what they want, fly to perform it. This is the way in which you can best reward them for all their pains and labors."[37] The child's duty of recompense also requires "concealing, hiding, covering and interpreting all their parents' faults and vices." Further, it requires "never objecting nor upbraiding them by any thing done amiss; but quietly and patiently to bear all things at their hands, considering that in thus doing [children] greatly please God, and offer unto him an acceptable sacrifice." "It becometh a good and godly child not to display, but to conceal the faults of his father, even as he wishes that God should cover his own offenses."[38]

For mature and emancipated children, the duty to recompense also requires them to give their parents aid, comfort, and relief in accordance with their own means and their parents' needs. The Catholic manualist Barthelemy Batt put it thus in *The Christian Man's Closet* (1581): "To honor parents is to relieve and nourish their parents in case they fall into poverty and decay. And when they are old, to guide, lead, and bear them on their shoulders if need be." If the parents "shall fall into any grievous sickness, poverty or extreme old age, it shall be the children's duty willingly to relieve and comfort them by all possible means."[39] Luther taught similarly that

35. T. S. Arthur, *Advice to Young Men on Their Duties and Conduct in Life* (Boston, 1848), p. 100.

36. Blackstone, *Commentaries,* I.16.

37. Channing, *Duties of Children,* p. 7.

38. Becon, *Catechism,* p. 358.

39. Barthelemy Batt, *The Christian Man's Closet* (London, 1581), pp. 60-101, esp. 61, 71, 74.

honor is due to parents by our actions, "both in our bearing and the extension of aid, serving, helping, and caring for them when they are old or sick, frail or poor; and that we not only do it cheerfully, but with humility and reverence, as if unto God. For he who is rightly disposed to his parents will never let them suffer want and hunger, but will place them above and beside himself, and share with them all he has to the best of his ability."[40] Becon called for children "to requite their parents for . . . [the] great benefits as they have received of God by them and their labors." And "if their parents be aged and fallen by their own industry and labor, then ought the children, if they will truly honor their parents, to labor for them, to see unto their necessity, to provide necessaries for them, and by no means, so much as in them is, to suffer them . . . to lack for any good thing" because parents care and provide for children when they are unable to provide for themselves.[41]

A child must discharge this duty of recompense even if the parent does not deserve or appreciate it. Recompense is due to parents "in their old age" even when they were "hard and cruel" earlier in life, or if they now betray "unwieldy crookedness," wrote Heinrich Bullinger, the sixteenth-century Swiss Protestant.[42] Luther counseled similarly that "even though [parents] may be lowly, poor, frail, and peculiar, they are still father and mother, given by God. Their way of living and their failings cannot rob them of their honor."[43] Benjamin Wadsworth, American clergyman and later Harvard president, insisted in his *The Well-Ordered Family* (1712) that it was "a natural duty" for a child to take care of his parents, when they revert to the feeble and fragile state brought on by age and sickness, as a way of recompensing them for their earlier care of the child who was once just as feeble and fragile. You are "bound in duty and conscience" to "provide for them, nourish, support and comfort them."[44] "[T]he time is coming when your parents will need as much attention from you as you have received from them, and you should endeavor to form such industrious, obliging habits that you may render their last years as happy as they have rendered the first years of your existence."[45]

40. Luther, *Large Catechism,* p. 66.

41. Becon, *Catechism,* p. 358.

42. Heinrich Bullinger, *The Christen State of Matrimony Most Necessary and Profitable for All,* trans. Miles Coverdale (n.p., 1546).

43. Luther, *Large Catechism,* p. 66.

44. Benjamin Wadsworth, *The Well-Ordered Family, or Relative Duties* (Boston, 1712), pp. 98-99.

45. Channing, *Duties of Children,* p. 9.

The Duty (and the Right) to Be Loved

The child's duty to love, honor, obey, respect, and recompense his or her parents and other guardians and loved ones was only one-half of the domestic ethic envisioned by the household manuals. The manuals also spoke of a child's "duty to be loved" by his or her parents and others. The child was regarded as both an agent of love and an object of love — one who discharged the duties of love and one who induced parents and others to discharge their reciprocal duties of love to that child. These twin duties of love *by* and *of* a child were interdependent. The child had to discharge his duties of love in part in order to make himself beloved and thus to become the object of the love of his parents. But these twin duties of love were not mutually conditional. The child had to discharge her duty of love to parents even if the parents did not or could not reciprocate. The parents, in turn, had to discharge their duty of love to the child, even if the child was incapacitated, recalcitrant, or unruly.

The later manuals sometimes put these duties of parental love for their children in sweeping emotional terms. T. S. Arthur's *Advice to Young Men on Their Duties and Conduct in Life* (1848), for example, described a mother's love thus: "She watched over you, loved you, protected and defended you; and all was from love — deep, pure, fervent love — the first love, and the most unselfish love that has or ever will bless you in this life, for it asked for and expected no return. *A mother's love!* — it is the most perfect reflection of the love of God ever thrown back from the mirror of the human heart."[46] Such talk of emotional love was largely absent from the earlier Catholic and Protestant household manuals. More typically, the duty of the child to be loved was expressed as the set of duties that Christian parents, guardians, and other members of the community had to rear and raise the child properly so that he could prepare properly for his Christian vocation.

The later manuals also sometimes translated the child's duty to be loved into the child's right to receive love, support, education, and nurture. As Charles Reid shows in his chapter herein, some medieval canonists and moralists spoke of the rights of the child in these terms.[47] None of the early household manuals that we have sampled, either Catholic or Protestant,

46. Arthur, *Advice to Young Men*, p. 101 (emphasis in original).

47. See chapter by Charles J. Reid in this volume, and further exposition in Charles J. Reid Jr., *Power over the Body, Equality in the Family: Rights and Domestic Relations in Medieval Canon Law* (Grand Rapids: Eerdmans, 2004), pp. 213ff.

spoke of "children's rights." In fact, this language was sometimes explicitly rejected. Anglican Bishop Jeremy Taylor, author of *Bishop Taylor's Judgment Concerning the Power of Parents over Their Children* (1696), for example, put it thus: "So long as the son is within the civil power of his Father, so long as he lives in his house, is subject to his command, is nourished by his father's charge, [he] hath no distinct rights of his own, he is in his father's possession, and to be reckoned by his measures."[48] This was doubly true for daughters, whom the manualists and common lawyers alike readily treated as the property of their fathers and families.

Explicit talk of a child's rights to the love and support of his or her parents entered the manual tradition only at the turn of the eighteenth century, and it remained controversial. An early example was the 300-page English manual, *The Infant's Lawyer* (1697), which gave a detailed guide to the status of children at common law and contended that "the law protects children in their persons, preserves their rights and estates, executes their laches and assists them in their pleadings."[49] This manual, which was largely a set of instructions to litigators, showed how children may not be convicted of felonies until "the age of discretion," and how even minor children can be protected in their "estates and rights."[50] Such language became more popular with the rise of Enlightenment thought, particularly through the influence of John Locke and Jean-Jacques Rousseau, though, as we shall see, children's rights language was sometimes staunchly resisted, especially by Protestant writers.

The manuals' dominant genre was a discourse of parental duty to children. On the one hand, the manuals encouraged active parental involvement and attentiveness to children, and chastised parents for neglecting their children's temporal and spiritual needs. On the other hand, the manuals increasingly sought to prohibit abusive parenting.

Parental Duties of Love. The manuals rooted the parents' duty to love and care for their child in the Commandment that children must honor their fathers and mothers. The parents' duty to the child was the correlative and complement to the duty that the child owed parents — per this Commandment and many later biblical instructions for children.[51] Luther put it

48. Jeremy Taylor, *Judgment Concerning the Power of Parents over Their Children* (London, 1696).

49. Anonymous, *The Infant's Lawyer* (London, 1697), A2.

50. *The Infant's Lawyer,* pp. 15-16.

51. See the detailed biblical analysis in the chapter by Marcia Bunge in this volume, and in Marcia Bunge, ed., *The Child in Christian Thought* (Grand Rapids: Eerdmans, 2001).

thus: "Although the duty of superiors is not explicitly stated in the Ten Commandments, it is frequently dwelt upon in many other passages of Scripture, and *God intends it to be included even in this commandment, where he mentions father and mother.* . . . God does not purpose to bestow the parental office and government upon rogues and tyrants; therefore, he does not give them that honor, namely, the power and authority to govern, merely to receive homage. Parents should consider that they are under obligations to obey God and that, first of all, they are conscientiously and faithfully to discharge all the duties of their office; not only to feed and provide for the temporal wants of their children . . . but especially to train them to the honor and praise of God."[52] This was a typical sentiment of the household manuals, both Protestant and Catholic.

The manuals presented this parental duty to love their child as a duty owed first and foremost to God. A child is made in the image of God, and as one of God's own is to be embraced and loved as such. But the child is also made in the image of the parent, and thus to love and embrace that child is in a real sense to love oneself. The duty to love one's child, therefore, is one of the most sublime gifts by which a parent can live out the primal command to love God, neighbor, and self at once.[53]

Right rearing of children involves constant attentiveness, the manualists insisted. Parents must not be lulled into a sense that "the parental office is a matter of your pleasure and whim, but remember that God has strictly commanded it and entrusted it to you, and that for the right discharge of its duties you must give an account." Parents are not blessed with children as merely "objects of mirth and pleasure" or "servants to use, like the ox or the horse." Nor are parents to raise children "according to [their] own whims — to ignore them, in unconcern about what they learn or how they live."[54] Children must not be neglected, but should be "objects of conscientious solicitude." They must be cared for, but not coddled. "If we wish to have worthy, capable persons for both temporal and spiritual leadership, we must indeed spare no diligence, time or cost in teaching and educating our children to serve God and mankind." Parents must know that, under the threat of "loss of divine grace," their "chief duty is to rear . . . children in the fear and

52. Luther, *Large Catechism*, p. 77 (emphasis added).

53. Kolde, *Fruitful Mirror*, pp. 53ff.; see also Richard Baxter, *Rules and Directions for Family Duties* (1681).

54. Luther, *Large Catechism*, p. 77. See further such sentiments and other early Protestants in John Witte Jr., *Law and Protestantism: The Legal Teachings of the Lutheran Reformation* (Cambridge: Cambridge University Press, 2002), pp. 262-77.

knowledge of God; and, if they are gifted, to let them learn and study, that they may be of service wherever needed." "The children . . . we have are the children . . . we [must] rear." And, if we are negligent in this duty, not only will the child be harmed, but social discipline and peace will suffer.[55]

The manuals focused on four main duties of love and attentiveness that parents must discharge for their children. First, a parent must instruct the child about God and God's commands — by baptizing the children, taking them to church, and teaching them about sacramental and virtuous living, and guiding them through catechism to confirmation.[56] This duty, the manualists emphasized, begins as soon as the child is able to speak. In *Of Weddid Men and Wifis and of Here Children Also,* Wyclif opined that the greatest downfall of parents is in tending more to the temporal than the spiritual welfare of their children.[57] Kolde's *Fruitful Mirror* emphasized that parents must discharge this first duty both by good instruction and by setting a good example of doing virtuous works. Parents must not curse, nag, or scold a child or do anything else to set a bad example for their children. Nor should they "constantly torment or beat or kick their children," thereby "inducing them to have evil thoughts." Kolde emphasized that "carelessness and neglect by parents who do not instruct their children well when they are young . . . is the main reason why people are so evil in the world and why so many evil afflictions and plagues come over the world. When children grow up doing and being as they please, they are without fear and anxiety and shame. And so they remain hard-headed, horrible, obstinate and disobedient." When these children are grown, "they ruin their parents and themselves as well," becoming poor, criminal, and "often die in their sins and are damned. Thus they make themselves a whip and a rod to be beaten with."[58]

This points to the second main parental duty, viz., of subjecting children to proper Christian discipline and correction. A few of the early manuals, both Catholic and Protestant, countenanced severe discipline and violence against children. John Bradford's *A Letter Sent to Master A.B. from the Most Godly and Learned Preacher I.B.* (1548), for example, advocated violent beatings of children, and called parents to be "deaf" to their cries and moans of pain even while whipping and scourging "not only until the blood runs down, but even until we have left wounds in the flesh." Bradford believed

55. Luther, *Large Catechism,* p. 78.

56. John Wyclif, *Of Weddid Men and Wifis and of Here Children Also* (1390), reprinted in *Selected English Works of John Wyclif,* ed. Thomas Arnold (Oxford, 1871), pp. 195-97.

57. Anonymous, *A Glass for Householders* (London, 1542), n.p.

58. Kolde, *Fruitful Mirror,* pp. 114-15.

that severe discipline is the only way to save a rebellious child from eternal damnation. He adduced the Bible in support of his views. Deuteronomy 21:18-21,[59] he argued, gives parents the right to take their rebellious children of any age before the town's people, who may stone them to death.[60] While stoning may no longer be expedient, Bradford argued, this passage underscores that parents have absolute control over their children, including the power to "scourge" them severely as needed.

But even the Reverend Bradford insisted that such harsh treatment be reserved only for the most rebellious child who was "more than twenty years old" and should by now know better. He further qualified his remarks by chastising the parents to whom he addressed his letter for failing to punish this particular son at a younger age, which would have spared all of them this later and greater severity of treatment: "If you had brought up your son with care and diligence, to rejoice in obedience toward his parents; and on the other side to be afraid to do evil and shun disobedience, and to fear the smart of correction, you would then have felt those comforts which happy parents receive from their good and honest children."[61] Because these lax parents had allowed their child to "run the course of his own will" in his early years, and had "foolishly foregone to spend the sharp rods of correction on the naked flesh of his loins," they were now required to save him from hell by making "his blood run down in streams, scourged loins, and forty days of pain." Any further indulgence or forbearance would put their son "in hazards of bitter confusion" and most assuredly put them in judgment before the Lord for "carelessly and negligently bringing up their children."

Most manualists, particularly by the sixteenth century, called for more "reasonable" forms of discipline and correction. A good early example was Alberti's *Della Famiglia* (c. 1570). "Children must always be corrected in a reasonable manner, at times with severity, but always without anger or passion. We must never rage as some furious or impetuous [sic] fathers do, but

59. Deuteronomy 21:18-21 (NRSV) reads: "If someone has a stubborn and rebellious son who will not obey his father and mother, who does not heed them when they discipline him, then his father and his mother shall take hold of him and bring him out to the elders of his town at the gate of that place. They shall say to the elders of his town, 'This son of ours is stubborn and rebellious. He will not obey us. He is a glutton and a drunkard.' Then all the men of the town shall stone him to death. So you shall purge the evil from your midst; and all Israel will hear, and be afraid."

60. John Bradford, *A Letter Sent to Master A.B. from the Most Godly and Learned Preacher I.B.* (London, 1548), A-Cii (modernized spelling).

61. Bradford, *A Letter Sent to Master A.B.*, A-Cii.

must . . . not punish anyone without first putting anger aside." While "[i]t is a father's duty . . . to punish his children and make them wise and virtuous," punishment must be "reasonable and just." Similarly, William Gouge's *Of Domestical Duties* (1622) taught that parental authority should evoke fear in children, but parental love should evoke affection in children. "Love, like sugar, sweetens fear, and fear like salt seasons love."[62]

The call for moderate and reasonable correction was even more pronounced in later manuals. In his *The Christian Home* (1860), for example, Samuel Phillips called parents to find a moderate middle between "overindulgence" and "the iron rod of tyranny." Parents must take steps to rule their households and execute their commands, or children will "end up ruling them." But no household should feature "parental despotism," "making slaves of children, acting the unfeeling and heartless tyrant over them . . . and making them obey from motives of trembling fear and dread." That is not only "un-Christian" but ineffective, said Phillips. Parental despotism engenders in children "the spirit of a slave," rooting out "all confidence and love," and making their obedience "involuntary and mechanical." A proper Christian home must find a middle way between these extremes: "It is mild, yet decisive," and it is "not lawless, yet not despotic." It "combines in proper order and harmony, the true elements of parental authority and filial subordination." In the Christian home, "[l]ove and fear harmonize; the child fears because he loves; and is prompted to obedience by both."

Phillips condemned those who favored severe corporal punishment in reliance on the Proverbial adage that "he that spareth the rod, spoileth the child." The term "rod," in this passage, he argued, does not necessarily mean "the iron rod of the unfeeling and unloving despot" but instead could be interpreted as the "rod of a compassionate father" who "does not always inflict corporal punishment," and when he does, he does so out of love. Phillips argued that corporal punishment does more harm than good, resulting in "depravity" of character, resentment, and ultimately criminal acts against and by the children. "Christian correction is the interposition of love acting according to law in restraining the child." We should "correct but not punish" our children in a manner where "true severity and true sympathy . . . unite and temper each other."[63]

Third, beyond the parental duties of divine instruction and Christian

62. Leon Batista Alberti, *The Albertis of Florence: Leon Batista Alberti's Della Famiglia*, trans. Guido A. Guarino (Lewisburg, PA: Bucknell University Press, 1971), pp. 74-77.

63. Phillips, *The Christian Home*, pp. 218-31.

discipline, the manuals emphasized that parents must teach a child a "trade" or "occupation" — or what the Protestant manualists frequently called "a divine calling" or "Christian vocation."[64] Heinrich Bullinger's instruction was quite typical. He emphasized that teaching a child a proper Christian vocation was a matter of "mutual discovery" for the parent and the child. Parents must observe and assess the child's talents and inclinations, and prepare and place the child in the occupation for which the child is best suited. This vocation should be one that is not only most conducive to the child's abilities and interests but also the "most profitable and necessary" for the church and commonwealth. One of the chief parental responsibilities is to "place his children with expert and cunning workmen" who will "teach them some handicraft" and livelihood — or, as later manualists emphasized, to place them in a school to train them for their proper vocation. Placement in a job or a school should be determined by the "children's wit" and aptitude, and by mutual determination of where children would find the "most delight."[65]

Consideration of what vocation would bring the child the "most delight" became more explicit in later manuals — but principally for males. Most of the manuals restricted young women only to the vocation of being a wife and mother — or a nun or religious servant in a few of the late medieval Catholic manuals. Rather than seeking a vocation "most profitable and necessary for the commonwealth," the manuals encouraged parents to place daughters in a vocation "profitable for the family."

Fourth, the manuals emphasized the parents' duty to find a suitable mate for their children, the reciprocal of the child's duty to procuring parental consent before marriage. Bullinger insisted that while children "must" not marry without parental consent, "[s]o *should* not the parents without any pity compel their children to marry before their time, nor wickedly neglect them, nor leave them unprovided for in due season."[66] This was a common sentiment in early modern Protestant and post-Tridentine Catholic circles that insisted on parental consent for valid marital formation.[67] While the children "must"

64. Batt, *Christian Man's Closet,* p. 65; Bullinger, *Christen State,* pp. lxix-lxxii.

65. Bullinger, *Christen State,* pp. lxix-lxxii; Bullinger, "The Fifth Precept of the Ten Commandments" [c. 1542], in *Decades of Henry Bullinger, Second Decade* (Cambridge, 1849), pp. 267-98.

66. Bullinger, *Christen State,* pp. xv-xviii (emphasis added).

67. See examples in Witte, *From Sacrament to Contract;* John Witte Jr. and Robert M. Kingdon, *Sex, Marriage, and Family in John Calvin's Geneva I: Courtship, Engagement, and Marriage* (Grand Rapids: Eerdmans, 2005), pp. 165-201.

obey parents in this matter, at least when they are minors, the parents "should" act reasonably. Children objecting to their parents' choice of a mate should do so "comely and with good manner," and recognize that the parental word is final in the matter.[68] Similarly, Nathaniel Cotton's *Visions for the Entertainment and Instruction of Young Minds* warned young women "impatient of a parent's rule" not to rush into marriage without parental permission. Such foolish "rebels," Cotton warned, will only suffer a "joyless" life and, to add insult to injury, will become "barren."[69]

Evolving Ideals

Gender Roles. Not surprisingly, the manuals revealed the common double standards for men and women that prevailed in late medieval and early modern society. While much of the language in the household manuals was gender neutral and addressed to "children" or "youths," the manuals were directed principally at young men — as is clear from the prevalent warnings against "whoremongering" and the exhortations to court women properly. When the manuals did distinguish between gender roles, they generally called boys to learn to be bold and courageous and girls to be fearful and gentle. A 1542 manual made the father primarily responsible for rearing courageous and God-fearing young men and the mother responsible for raising gentle and virtuous females: "So in women . . . there is nothing more laudable than fearfulness and gentleness of manner. To the mother, your wife, give charge to do her duty in bringing up your women children virtuously and in the law and fear of God, as you do the men children."[70]

The Christian Man's Closet (1581) set out a typical list of duties that were "especially applicable to daughters." These included: (1) speaking and understanding (i.e., learning) only about the fear of God; (2) not using filthy words; (3) modesty in appearance (meaning limited makeup and natural hair color); (4) avoiding wine and overindulgence in food; (5) learning to make woolen and linen cloth; (6) donning appropriate apparel without focus on silks; and (7) avoiding unvirtuous ("light") maidens.[71] Typically, in the early manuals, the duties of young women also included "shamefast-

68. Bullinger, *Christen State,* pp. xv-xvii.

69. Nathaniel Cotton, *Visions for the Entertainment and Instruction of Young Minds* (Exeter, NH, 1794), p. 76.

70. Anonymous, *A Glass for Householders* (1542), n.p. (modernized spelling).

71. Batt, *Christian Man's Closet,* pp. 75-76.

ness," meekness, chastity, modesty, "sadness," and sobriety. The most important thing for a daughter to learn and to be taught, the manuals emphasized, is "how to please her husband through gentle behavior, discrete conversation, prudence, wisdom, and virtue." As to education, "[d]aughters should be instructed in prayer and Christian knowledge, but should not be too busy in teaching and reasoning openly."[72]

A few of the manualists had other vocations in mind for young women beyond demure marriage and dutiful motherhood. Juan Luis Vives' *Instruction of a Christian Woman* (1523), which appeared in some forty editions, was a good early example. Vives, a Spanish humanist and philosopher, recognized that many young women would pursue marriage, and their mothers had to teach them the proper ways and means of "keeping and ordering of a house." But other women "are born unto [learning], or at least not unfit for it." They were "not to be discouraged, and those that are apt should be heartened and encouraged." Vives acknowledged that "learned women are suspect to many." Thus "young women shall only study that which leads to good manners, informs her living and teaches the ways of a holy and good life." Eloquence and learnedness, while not necessary among women, is only shameful when it leads to indiscretion or deceit. Above all, women need goodness and wisdom. However, a woman is never to teach, because she is a "fragile thing," and, "like Eve," may be deceived by a weak argument.[73] These were only dim foreshadowings of the more ambitious vocations and aspirations for girls and young women projected by nineteenth- and twentieth-century feminist writers.

Enlightenment Influences. John Locke's *Some Thoughts Concerning Education* (1693) challenged many of the traditional notions of childhood, childrearing, and education. Locke advocated much more intimacy between parents and children. He rejected the idea that the child is marred by original sin, and instead saw the child as a free form ready to be shaped by experience and education. The parent's role was to guide and mediate those experiences for the benefit of the child. Education of children, Locke argued, is not simply for acquiring knowledge, but especially for building a virtuous and useful character. "Virtue is harder to be got than knowledge of the world; and, if lost in a young man, is seldom recovered." The aim of education is not simply knowledge, but to teach a child how to live life, and to live it well. Locke urged parents to teach their children self-discipline so

72. Bullinger, *Christen State*, p. xv (modernized spelling).

73. Juan Luis Vives, *Instruction of a Christian Woman* (London, 1585), pp. 8, 18, 25-30, 322.

that corporal punishment would be unnecessary. "I told you before that children love *liberty* and therefore they should be brought to do the things that are fit for them without feeling any restraint laid upon them. I now tell you they love something more: and that is *dominion*." He urged parents to restrain a child's cravings and desires by not giving in to the child's every whim.[74]

While Locke's treatise on education made a splash, Jean-Jacques Rousseau's *Emile* (1762) changed the tide of childhood education. Rousseau wrote: "Everything is good coming from the Creator, everything degenerates at the hands of men." Thus a child ought to be free to experience life in every respect irrespective of potential harm, for a child's "joy of freedom compensates for many injuries." Rousseau criticized the heavily duty-bound ethic of earlier household manuals, catechisms, and educational texts; parents and others, he insisted, should "[n]ever tell the child what he cannot understand."[75] He minimized the importance of book learning, and promoted instead the idea of educating a child's emotions and affections. Rousseau urged parents and teachers to focus on the passionate side of the child's human nature, something that earlier teachings had neglected, in his view. Like Locke, he specially recognized the virtue of a child's learning through experience — by trial and error, experiment and failure.

Rousseau's Enlightenment ideas of children and their education were highly controversial in their day, but they slowly found their way into the household manual tradition. Enos Weed's *The Educational Directory* (1803), for example, echoed Rousseau in arguing for a less rigid educational structure. Children should be exposed to a variety of experiences, and they must be allowed to question parents, teachers, and other authorities, especially as they grow older. Furthermore, while parents have a duty to correct children in all manner of wrongs, Weed warned against strict punishment. Good parenting requires taming an unruly will without breaking a child's spirit. A child's "trifling playish temper and disposition," which had been stifled by the strict traditional requirements, "should be encouraged, as being beneficial to them."

Weed, like Rousseau, criticized the heavily duty-bound ethic of the earlier manual tradition, calling for "very few" rules, lest the child's "natural development" be impaired and impeded. He had little sympathy for traditional instruction in decorum, etiquette, and manners, for this endless "heaping on

74. John Locke, *Some Thoughts Concerning Education* (London, 1693), sections 54-69.

75. Jean-Jacques Rousseau, *Emile* (Paris, 1769), pp. 292ff.

them a large number of rules about their putting off their hats or making legs or courtesies," which are mere "outward gestures to the neglect of their minds." Weed also railed against the earlier manualists' calls for emotional control of children, advising instead that children "should always . . . speak and act according to the true sentiments of their hearts." He despised compulsory use of courteous addresses made "for show and not from affection." Children should be free to express themselves to parents and other superiors according to the "true sentiments of their heart."[76]

Weed did not fully dispense with tradition. He thought that moderate corporal punishment to correct a child when necessary is best. He counseled that children should not be indulged in all their desires, and they should be taught to dress modestly, eat moderately, and avoid wicked speech and actions. Parents should likewise provide a good example for their children, a common theme of the earlier manuals.

Tennessee Celeste Cook went further in her chapter on children in *Constitutional Equality a Right of Woman* (1871). Cook was a feminist writer and reformer, most popular because her sister was the first woman to run for president of the United States. Cook wrote: "The teachings of Christianity are well; they have been taught persistently. But we have now arrived at that practical age of the world which demands adequate results as proofs of the validity of assumed positions." Among other things, practice has proved that while parental education and proper rearing of children are essential, "society is responsible for the character of the children which it rears." Heretofore, the household manuals had stressed the personal responsibility of the parent in rearing children, and the personal responsibility of the child to be well taught. Cook, following Rousseau and Locke, made this a paramount social duty as well, particularly through widespread schooling for young men and women.

Traditional schools, Cook argued, had failed to educate children in their duties as citizens of humanity: "We are arguing . . . [for] the rights of children . . . which shall make every child, male and female, honorable and useful members of society. . . . Scarcely any of the [traditional] practices of education . . . in regard to children are worthy of anything but the severest condemnation." Ignoring the child's "inherent rights," traditional schools cultivate virtues and "affections to the exclusion of all reason and common sense. They forget that the human is more than an affectional being; that he

76. Enos Weed, *The Educational Directory Designed for the Use of Schools and Private Families* (New York, 1803), pp. 21-22.

has other than family duties to fulfill, and that he belongs to humanity." Especially with respect to young women, Cook insisted, "[v]ery much of the fashionable external nonsense, which forms so great a part of young ladies' education might well be dispensed with, and they, instead, be instructed in their mission as the artists of humanity; artists not merely in form and feature, but in that diviner sense of intellectual soul." Cook viewed all children, male and female, as having both the ability and the responsibility to contribute to the common good. Indeed, she went so far as to urge the state to take children from parents not best suited to raise them in a vocation good for the commonwealth. "To make the best citizens of children, then, is the object of education, and in whatever way this can be best attained, that is the one which should be pursued, even if it be to the complete abrogation of the present supposed rights of parents to control them."[77]

While Weed and Cook were more radical than most, a number of more traditional manualists did absorb some of the Enlightenment concern for greater gender equality and greater respect for children's rights. A good example was the *Christian Home as it is in the Sphere of Nature and the Church* (1860), authored by American minister Samuel Phillips. Phillips called the Christian home "a little commonwealth jointly governed by the parents," rather than principally governed by the paterfamilias. It is "the right of the parents to command; and the duty of the child to obey," he insisted. But "parental authority" must be limited, and parents must not "enact arbitrary laws." While they should not be "despotic" to their children, they must also not be "indifferent" or "permit children to do as they please, and to bring them up under the influence of domestic libertinism." While children must obey their parents, "obedience of the child is not that of the servile, trembling subject." This "is not unnatural" and results in *"no infringement upon the rights and liberties of the child"* because "[h]is subordination to the parent is the law of his liberty." Indeed, "he is not free without it."[78] According to Phillips, a home "destitute of reciprocated affection" between parent and child is lacking Christian family values.

Some Christian manualists were more critical of these new Enlightenment views. For example, John Wesley, the father of Methodism, derided Rousseau's *Emile* as "the most empty, silly, injudicious thing that ever a self-conceited infidel wrote." Upon reading Rousseau on matters of education,

77. Tennessee Celeste Cook, *Constitutional Equality a Right of Woman* (New York, 1871), pp. 130-47.

78. Phillips, *The Christian Home*, pp. 213-17 (emphasis added).

Wesley harshly commented, surely "a more consummate coxcomb never saw the sun!"[79] Joseph Benson's *Hymns for Children,* collected from the works of John Wesley, included this hymn titled "Obedience to Parents," to be sung in services and Sunday schools: "Children your parents' will obey, the Lord commands it to be done; and Those that from the precept stray, To misery and ruin run. . . . The disobedient children meet the vengeance of the Lord Most High; His curse pursues their wand'ring feet, And ere they reach their prime, — they die!"[80]

New Protestant Emphases. While early manuals did speak of obedience to the political authorities as an extension of the duty of obedience owed to parents, eighteenth- and nineteenth-century American Protestant household manuals placed increasing stress on patriotism as a duty of children, especially young men.[81] Samuel Deane's *Four Sermons to Young Men* (1774), for example, instructed young men thus: "It is glorious to love your country. It is fashionable to profess this love. It is necessary that you abound in it, in the present distressed and alarming state of our public affairs. You can in no way so much befriend your country, I am sure, as by your being truly religious."[82] Similarly, Arminius Calvinus's *First Principles of our Religious and Social Duties* (1795) urged young men to esteem and emulate the virtues of love of country, exemplified by President George Washington, so that "future ages know his worth and venerate his memory."[83]

Likewise, while earlier manuals stressed good manners, affections, and recompense toward parents, eighteenth- and nineteenth-century manuals laid increasing stress on a child's charitable duties to others. John Barnard's *Discourses on the Great Concern of Parents and the Important Duty of Children* (1737) urged children to "cultivate and improve their natural disposition to pity and compassion." Charity was to be exercised in "inward affection" by showing love for God and all humanity, but especially to the "church family."[84] Charity also requires outward affection in the form of

79. John Wesley, "Entry of February 3, 1770," in John Wesley, *Journal and Diaries,* ed. W. Reginald Ward and Richard P. Heitzenrater, in *The Bicentennial Edition of the Works of John Wesley* (Nashville: Abingdon, 1975), vol. 5, p. 214.

80. Joseph Benson, *Hymns for Children* (London: Geo. Story, 1806), p. 32.

81. See e.g., Arminius Calvinus, *A Catechism Containing the First Principles of Religious and Social Duties* (Boston, 1795), p. 16.

82. Samuel Deane, *Four Sermons to Young Men* (Salem, 1774), p. 30.

83. Calvinus, *Catechism,* p. 18.

84. John Barnard, *Discourses on the Great Concern of Parents and the Natural Duty of Children* (Boston, 1737), pp. 57-58.

counseling and relieving the poor. Focusing more on the financial aspects of charity, Henry Dixon's *The English Instructor* (1746) required children to give to the poor as they are able.[85]

Summary and Conclusions

"We must not forget one very important admonition, which should be frequently inculcated to young students; that is, to pray often and fervently to God for his grace to know their vocation."[86] Amidst a litany of instructions, copious "how to's," and multitudes of good manner books, this simple counsel is the most timeless teaching of the household manuals.

The foundation of a child's Christian vocation is the love of God, most manuals insisted. The child truly loves God by living a life in profound, awe-filled reverence to God. This love for God involves a tenderness of feeling and a deep personal attachment to God that flows from God's power and majesty as the giver and sustainer of life. Love of God, in accordance with the first commandment of the First Table of the Decalogue, leads a child to honor of parents, in accordance with the first commandment of the Second Table. Children are called to obey and respect their parents as a gift of God, to accept their correction and direction in life and learning, to cultivate the habits and manners of Christian living, to offer them recompense and support in their time of need, to accept their counsel in choosing a mate and in preparing for their own vocation in church, state, family, and society.

The child's duty to honor and obey his or her parents also defines the parents' duty to nurture and educate their child. Parents are called to cherish their children as divine gifts who are images both of God and of themselves. They are to protect and support their children in their infancy, to teach them by word and example the norms and habits of the Christian life, to offer them correction and discipline, to prepare them for independence, and to direct them in their marriages and in their Christian vocations as adults.

Though sometimes quaint and idealistic, and occasionally offensive to modern ears, some of the lessons of these historical household manuals still ring true for young men and women struggling to find their direction and vocation in a world of conflicting loyalties and duties. On a practical level, the requirement that children be modestly dressed and primped says much

85. Henry Dixon, *The English Instructor* (Boston, 1746), p. 11.

86. *Christian Instructions for Youth*, p. 252.

to a culture numbed by the latest designer fashions for children. Cautions about moderation in food and drink provide an important message for a society with nearly half of its children suffering from obesity. The repeated instruction for children to work hard in school and to prepare for a vocation that serves the common good is good counsel for children who neglect or despise their education or parents who treat the school as a convenient child warehouse and daycare center. For the older child, the duty to recompense, care, and honor parents in old age is a valuable lesson as aged parents struggle on social security or live their twilight years lonely and isolated in nursing homes. On a social level, the requirement of parental attentiveness and attention to children alerts parents to the dangers of placing other vocational duties before their principal vocation as a parent.

There is also a hard, but enduring, lesson in the traditional teaching that the duties of love by and for a child are mutually dependent, but not mutually conditional. The manuals make clear that the failure of the parent does not alter the duties of the child to that parent. Indeed, a parent's failure increases, rather than diminishes, the child's duties to irresponsible parents. Children reared by wicked, abusive, or drunkard parents, the manuals emphasize, must cover up the faults of their parents and "meekly" admonish them to return to their duties. A Christian child must fulfill her duties to God, including the duty to honor and love her father and mother, even if the parents are undeserving. This traditional teaching goes entirely against modern views that children are less culpable for their personal failures when they suffer from poor parenting. The household manuals call children to rise above poor parenting, to set aside excuses, and to fulfill their duties of love, even when they are hated and despised. Their duty of love to God demands no less. Overcoming childhood adversity and taking responsibility can be a source of great empowerment. When the child understands that she belongs to God, she also realizes that her vocation belongs to her. Outside forces do not absolve the child of her duty, but they also cannot deprive the child of her vocation.

The rich history in the household manual tradition reminds us of something else that we might be apt to forget in a modern Western world voracious in its appetites for the latest technological innovations. Reading these manuals allows our minds to drift to a historical place where father, mother, son, and daughter taught and learned the Christian traditions together by the soft glow of candlelight at the common dinner table. There is a great benefit to be derived from the familial bonds created by dinner conversations rather than by TV dinners, as several recent social science studies again underscore.[87] The unspoken, unwritten, and invaluable lesson of the household manual tradition lies in how those lessons were transmitted — a direct and loving line of communication between parents and children that requires the sacrifice and commitment of all parties.

Appendix: List of Sampled Manuals in Order of Publication

John Wyclif, *Of Weddid Men and Wifis and of Here Children Also* (1390).
Dietrich Kolde, *A Fruitful Mirror* (1470).
Jacque LeGrand, *A Little Book of Good Manners* (1498).
Martin Luther, *The Law, Faith, and Prayer* (1517).
William Harrison, *Condemnations of Matrimony* (1528).
Martin Luther, *Small Catechism* (1529).
Martin Luther, *Large Catechism* (1529).
Richard Whitford, *The Werke for Householders* (1537).
Anonymous, *A Glass for Householders* (1542).
Anonymous, *L'Instruction des Enfans* (1543).
Heinrich Bullinger, *The Christen State of Matrimony* (1546).
John Bradford, *A Letter Sent to Master A.B.* (1548).
Erasmus of Rotterdam, *A Little Book of Good Manners* (1554).
Erasmus of Rotterdam, *The Civility of Childhood* (1560).
Leon Batista Alberti of Florence, *Della Famiglia* (?).
Barthelemy Batt, *The Christian Man's Closet* (1581).
Richard Greenham, *A Godly Exhortation & Fruitful Admonition to Virtuous Parents and Modest Matrons* (1584).
Juan Luis Vives, *Instruction of a Christian Woman* (1585).
Pierre Viret, *The School of Beasts* (The Good Householder) (1585).
Henry Smith, *A Preparative to Marriage* (1591).
Dudley Fenner, *The Order of Household Government* (1592).
Robert Cleaver, *A Godly Form of Household Government* (1598).
Stefano Guazzo, *The Court of Good Counsel* (1607).
William Perkins, *Christian Oeconomie* (1609).
William Phiston, *School of Good Manner* (1609).
Edward Topsell, *The Householder* (1610).
William Martyn, *Youth's Instruction* (1612).
Leonard Wright, *A Display of Duty* (1614).
Robert Crowley, *The School of Virtue . . . Teaching Children and Youths their Duties* (1621).
William Gouge, *Of Domestical Duties* (1622).

87. See the summary of recent research on the importance of family table talk by Robyn Fivush, "The Family Narratives Project: Building Strength Through Stories" (March 23, 2005), www.law.emory.edu/cslr/Fivushtext.pdf.

Thomas Carter, *Carter's Christian Commonwealth* (1627).
William Lily, *The Fairest Faring for a School-Bred Son* (1630).
Matthew Griffeth, *Bethel: A Form for Families* (1633).
Henry Peacham, *The Complete Gentleman* (1634).
Thomas Ridley, *A View of the Civil and Ecclesiastical Law* (1634).
Baron William Burghley, *Directions for the Well-Ordering and Carriage of a Man's Life* (1636).
Robert Abbott, *A Christian Family Builded by God* (1653).
Thomas Cobbett, *A Fruitful and Useful Discourse Touching the Honor Due from Children to Parents* (1656).
John Horn, *Brief Instructions for Children* (1656).
W.C., *A School of Nurture for Children: The Duty of Children in Honoring their Parents* (1656).
William Smith, *Universal Love* (1668).
Joseph Church, *The Christian's Daily Monitor* (1669).
Owen Stockton, *A Treatise of Family Instruction* (1672).
Peter Du Moulin, *Directions for the Education of a Young Prince till Seven Years of Age* (1673).
R. Mayhew, *The Young Man's Guide to Blessedness* (1677).
Samuel Crossman, *The Whole Duty of Youth* (1678).
Richard Baxter, *Rules & Directions for Family Duties* (1681).
Edward Lawrence, *Parents' Groans over their Wicked Children* (1681).
George Fox, *The State of the Birth, Temporal and Spiritual* (1683).
Anonymous, *True and Faithful Discharge of Relative Duties* (1683).
Henry Swinburne, *A Treatise of Spousals* (1686).
William Smythies, *Advice to Apprentices and Other Young Persons* (1687).
John Hart, *The School of Grace* (1688).
Bishop Jeremy Taylor, *Judgment Concerning the Power of Parents over Their Children* (1690).
John Locke, *Inculcating Self-Discipline* (1690).
Lancelot Addison, *The Christian's Manual in Three Parts* (1691).
John Hawkins, *The English School-master Completed* (1692).
Oliver Heywood, *Advice to an Only Child* (1693).
John Locke, *Some Thoughts Concerning Education* (1693).
James Kirkwood, *A New Family Book (Advice to Parents)* (1693).
James Kirkwood, *Advice to Children* (1693).
Anonymous, *The Infant's Lawyer* (1697).
John Gother, *Instructions for Children* (1698).
Church of England Catechism from Book of Common Prayer (1698).
Cotton Mather, *A Family Well-Ordered* (1699).
Benjamin Wadsworth, *The Well-Ordered Family* (1712).
William Fleetwood, *The Relative Duties of Parents & Children* (1716).
Benjamin Bass, *Parents and Children Advised and Exhorted to their Duty* (1729).
William Cooper, *Serious Exhortations Addressed to Young Men* (1732).
The New England Primer Enlarged (1735).

John Barnard, *Discourses on . . . the Important Duty of Children* (1737).
Henry Dixon, *The English Instructor* (1746).
Jean-Jacques Rousseau, *Emile* (1769).
Samuel Deane, *Four Sermons to Young Men* (1774).
Eleazar Moody, *The School of Good Manners* (1775).
Shippie Townsend, *Practical Essay: Part III — An Inquiry into the Case of Children* (1783).
Nathaniel Cotton, *Visions for the Entertainment and Instruction of Young Minds* (1794).
Arminius Calvinus, *A Catechism containing the First Principles of Religious and Social Duties* (1795).
John Willison, *The Mother's Catechism* (1795).
Enos Hitchcock, *The Parents Assistant* (1796).
Enos Weed, *The Educational Directory* (1803).
Joseph Benson, *Hymns for Children* (1806).
W. E. Channing, *Sermon Delivered on Lord's Day* (1812).
Christian Instructions for Youth (1821).
Francis West, *The Responsibilities and Duties of Children of Religious Parents* (1837).
Lydia H. Sigourney, *Do Your Duty to Your Brothers and Sisters* in *Youth's Magazine* (1837).
Thomas Becon, *The Catechism* (1844).
Mark Trafton, *The Duties and Responsibilities of Young Men* (1845).
Thomas Becon, *The Principles of Christian Religion.*
T. S. Arthur, *Advice to Young Men on their Duties and Conduct in Life* (1848).
Henry Bullinger, *The Fifth Precept of the Ten Commandments* in *Decades of Henry Bullinger, Second Decade* (1849).
Horace Bushnell, *A Milder and Warmer Family Government* in *Christian Nurture* (1849).
Sara Willis Payton, *Children's Rights* in *Fern Leaves from Fanny's Portfolio* (1853).
Francis Wayland, *Early Training of Children* in *The Fireside Miscellany* (1854).
Alfred Beach, *A Sermon Addressed to Parents* (1858).
Samuel Phillips, *The Christian Home* (1860).
Rev. Daniel Wis — , *The Young Man's Counselor* (1865).
Lady Tennessee Celeste Cook, *Constitutional Equality a Right of Woman* (1871).
Robert Speer, *A Young Man's Questions* (1903).

CHAPTER 6

The Right to Life and Its Application to the Welfare of Children in the Canon Law and the Magisterium of the Catholic Church: 1878 to the Present

Charles J. Reid Jr.

Introduction: Love and the Right to Life

Pope Benedict XVI, in his encyclical *Deus Caritas Est,* sees in the Incarnation the reconciliation of different ways of speaking about and understanding love. Adam, driven by *eros,* is compelled to seek a partner with whom he might become "one flesh."[1] The union he seeks, however, has not only physical qualities, but a transcendent, spiritual dimension — it is an act of self-giving, by which the parties unite for their own good and the good of the offspring to follow. This union, furthermore, has theological significance: "Marriage based on exclusive and definitive love becomes the icon of the relationship between God and his people and vice versa."[2]

The human person is thus summoned to imitate the divine union, which is perfectly creative and fruitful. And marriage becomes as well the metaphor by which to explain both the ultimate act of self-giving love which is Jesus' sacrifice of himself and the dedication and devotion that persons are called to demonstrate to one another in their everyday lives.

Any effort to understand the role the right to life plays in Catholic thought must begin with this call to self-giving and fruitful love. It is a love that is more than the passion one person might feel toward another. It is, rather, a commitment of self that can, at its highest level, give structure to entire human communities. Pope Paul VI thus spoke of a "civilization of

1. *Deus Caritas Est,* para. 11.
2. *Deus Caritas Est,* para. 11.

love" *(La civita dell'amore)* of which the Church, by virtue of its call to imitate Christ, is the guardian and the guarantor.[3] This is a love that is unequivocal, that does not condescend, and that binds all persons together — *dell'uomo per l'uomo,* as Paul put it. It is a love that is oriented toward the building of genuinely human — and humane — social structures.

Subsequent pontiffs have used similar language and images to discuss the love that should inform human relations and the respect for life that should follow upon the building up of communities of love. John Paul II, in *Dives in misericordia,* connected the divine act of self-giving love which is Christ's death on the cross to the "merciful love" that we must show "for the poor, the suffering and prisoners, for the blind, the oppressed, and sinners."[4] Joseph Ratzinger, in his tenure as prefect of the Congregation of the Doctrine of Faith, premised his instruction on the new reproductive technologies on the Church's "mission to serve the civilization of love."[5] The construction of a genuinely loving and fruitful community, on this account, requires respect for the sanctity of human life in all its stages. John Paul's encyclical *Evangelium Vitae* is probably the most comprehensive restatement of these ideas. Through our own experience of love, John Paul wrote, "every person — believer and non-believer alike — . . . come[s] to recognize . . . the sacred value of human life from its very beginning until its end, and can affirm the right of every human being to have this primary good respected to the highest degree."[6]

This paper is intended to examine the right to life as it pertains to children. Such an examination must begin with abortion, though it must also necessarily extend its reach to other threats to the life, health, and bodily integrity of children. The vocabulary of the right to life, as it is utilized in this paper, is of fairly recent vintage, although the ideas and principles it represents are quite old and venerable. But the adoption of this new vocabulary has allowed for the making of a number of affirmative claims on behalf of the child — to be free, for example, from the threats and dangers of war, or to have made available the medical care necessary to sustain life and well-being. The purpose of this paper is to trace the main lines of this development from nineteenth- and early twentieth-century canonistic condemna-

3. "Omelia Del Santo Padre Paolo VI," December 25, 1975.

4. *Dives in misericordia,* para. 8.

5. "Instruction on Respect for Human Life in Its Origin and on the Dignity of Procreation: Replies to Certain Questions of the Day," Congregation for the Doctrine of Faith (1987).

6. *Evangelium Vitae,* para. 2.

tions of abortion to the more recent expansions of this right to include a broad range of claims insisting upon the safety and well-being of children.

Abortion

"Thou Shalt Not Kill"

The Pio-Benedictine Code of Canon Law, envisioned by Pope Pius X and promulgated in 1917 by his immediate successor Benedict XV, condemned "procurers of abortion," including the mother, as subject to automatic excommunication.[7] The *Fontes* that accompanied the 1917 Code listed several sources for this penalty. The oldest sources included a text found in the twelfth-century *Decretum* of Gratian,[8] and the thirteenth-century *Liber Extra* of Pope Gregory IX.[9] The *Fontes* also cited the sixteenth-century decree *Effraenatum* ("Unrestrained") of Pope Sixtus V (1585-90), whose opening sentence connected abortion to a violation of the divine command "Do not kill." Even unborn children, the pope noted, were "made in the image of God" *(Dei imagine insignitam)* and so were worthy of the protection of the law.[10] And the law, he insisted, should draw no distinction between the ani-

7. 1917 Code, c. 2350. The penalty was reserved to the Ordinary, meaning in typical practice, only the bishop could lift the penalty of excommunication. A cleric who directly procured an abortion was, in addition to being excommunicated, deposed from office in the Church.

8. The *Fontes* cites C. 2, q. 5, c. 20, as its principal source in Gratian's *Decretum.* Written by Pope Stephen V between the years 886 and 889, the letter condemns as homicide "the destruction through abortion of what is conceived in the uterus" *(si conceptum in utero qui per aborsum deleverit, homicida est).*

9. The *Fontes* cite to X.5.12.5 and X.5.12.20. The first of these texts, c. 5, is an ancient text, known as *Si aliquis,* which condemned as homicides all those who, "filled with lust or premeditation, give to anyone, male or female, to prevent generation or conception, or to destroy the offspring so produced." John Noonan notes that this text has its origin in the early medieval penitentials and is first found in the works of the canonist and penitential writer Regino of Prüm (fl. 900-915). See Noonan, *Contraception: A History of Its Treatment by the Catholic Theologians and Canonists* 2nd enl. ed. (Cambridge, MA: Harvard University Press, 1986), pp. 168-69. The second of these texts was a letter of Pope Innocent III to a priory of Carthusian monks. Learning that a priest of that Order had gotten a girl pregnant and then secured an abortion, Innocent wrote that the priest should be adjudged a homicide if the fetus had shown "signs of life" *(vivificatus),* but he should not be adjudged a homicide if the fetus had not yet "become alive."

10. Pietro Cardinal Gasparri, ed., *Codicis Iuris Canonici Fontes* (Vatican City: Polyglottis Vaticanis, 1923), no. 165, vol. 1, p. 308.

mated fetus, which demonstrates fetal movement, and those fetuses who have yet to attain animation.[11]

Gasparri included in the *Fontes* two other pieces of papal legislation, a decree of Pope Gregory XIV and a text of Pius IX. Elected as the immediate successor to Sixtus V, Gregory's pontificate was a brief but active one of ten months' duration (1590-91). In that time, he ordered an end to slavery in the Philippines and insisted that reparations be made to the dispossessed of that land; he also became involved in the French Wars of Religion by extending the excommunication of Henry of Navarre when he proved dilatory in his promise to become Catholic. Gregory finally legislated on abortion by returning to the distinction, found in a decretal of Innocent III,[12] between animated and unanimated fetuses, and imposing the penalty for homicide only where the fetus was vivified.[13] Pius IX, in turn, relying upon a new scientific awareness of embryonic development, returned the law to the rigor imparted to it by Sixtus V when he decreed that those responsible for aborting a fetus at any stage of pregnancy were guilty of homicide and subject to excommunication.[14]

11. *Codicis Iuris Canonici Fontes* no. 165, vol. 1, p. 308. The medieval understanding of biological reproduction relied on Aristotelian science to distinguish between animate and inanimate fetal development. On the Aristotelian model, life was impossible before the detection of fetal movement (the old idea of "quickening"). This model for explaining fetal development was first seriously questioned by Thomas Fienus, professor of medicine at the University of Louvain and Paolo Zacchia, physician general of the Papal States, working independently in the early seventeenth century. See Donald DeMarco, *In My Mother's Womb: The Catholic Church's Defense of Natural Life* (Manassas, VA: Trinity Communications, 1987), pp. 12-15. Pope Sixtus's new synthesis could well have reflected the kind of questioning that was taking place in medical circles.

12. *Supra,* note 9.

13. *Codicis Iuris Canonici Fontes,* vol. 1, pp. 330-31.

14. Theologians as early as the closing decades of the seventeenth century were arguing that even "unanimated" fetuses could not be directly aborted, basing their claims not on biology but on theological intuition — Mary, for example, was free from original sin from the moment of conception, meaning that all other persons were laboring under this impediment to salvation from the very commencement of their physical existence. See John Connery, S.J., *Abortion: The Development of the Roman Catholic Perspective* (Chicago: Loyola University Press, 1977), pp. 189-210.

The modern science of embryology traces its beginnings to the early nineteenth century. A series of responses given by the Holy Office to a variety of problems generated by advances in medicine in the latter nineteenth century helped to cement the Church's position that even the indirect killing of the fetus in a medical procedure designed to save the mother's life was impermissible. Connery, *Abortion,* pp. 288-92.

Common to all of these sources was a recognition that where it could be established that human life was at stake, that life was deserving of a high level of legal protection. While the sources differed on determining when life actually came into being, the sources speak with one voice in imposing severe penalties upon those who abort any fetus found to be "vivified." The chief difference between Gregory XIV and Pius IX, it seems clear, has much more to do with developments in the biological sciences than with changes in Catholic doctrine.

The *Fontes,* however, are not the only source we have for canon 2350. To understand the *Fontes'* limitations, we need to appreciate the motives of Pietro Gasparri in collecting these texts. Employing an overly formalistic distinction between legislation and teaching, influenced in spite of his better instincts by the legal positivism of the day, which placed enormous stress on limiting the sources of law to identifiable acts of sovereign will, preoccupied with the high papalism of the First Vatican Council, Gasparri equated law with the acts of sovereigns and the bureaucracies under their command. The process by which texts were selected for inclusion in the *Fontes* reveals these jurisprudential commitments clearly. The Church's tradition on abortion, however, was larger and deeper than the texts mustered by Gasparri.

John Noonan has written clearly, cogently, and comprehensively on the Church's opposition to abortion from its earliest days. The *Didache,* a late first-century document that probably qualifies as the earliest Christian document not included in the New Testament, condemned abortion: "'You shall not slay the child by abortions *(phthora)*.'"[15] Tertullian (ca. 165-230) wrote in defense of Christian attitudes toward life: "'For us, indeed, as homicide is forbidden, it is not lawful to destroy what is conceived in the womb while the blood is still being formed into a man. To prevent being born is to accelerate homicide . . .'"[16] Stoic philosophy and Hippocratic medical principles provided support for these positions.[17]

Abortion, however, was probably not the principal means by which unwanted children were dispensed with in the ancient Greco-Roman world.[18]

15. John T. Noonan Jr., "An Almost Absolute Value in History," in John T. Noonan Jr., ed., *The Morality of Abortion: Legal and Historical Perspectives* (Cambridge, MA: Harvard University Press, 1970), pp. 1, 9 (translating the *Didache*).

16. Noonan, "An Almost Absolute Value in History," p. 12 (translating Tertullian).

17. Noonan, "An Almost Absolute Value in History," p. 17 (on the adaptation of Stoic thought); and pp. 4-5 (on the Hippocratic oath).

18. An important comparison of the relative degree to which adoption, abortion, exposure, and infanticide were made use of in the ancient world to address the problem of un-

That distinction belonged to exposure, the practice of which was pervasive. No less an authority than Seneca the Younger could recommend to friends that they should not feel grief or become emotionally distraught over destroying "weak and deformed" *(debiles monstrosique)* children.[19] Healthy but otherwise unwanted children were also routinely put out of the family, where they might die of exposure to the elements or be picked up by strangers for whatever purpose they might have in mind.[20]

Early Christianity condemned this practice with unequivocal vigor. The second-century Greek Christian Athenagoras attacked pagan criticism of Christians as ritual murderers and cannibals as unjustified, given that "Christians avoid gladiatorial games as akin to taking part in homicide, condemn abortion as the taking of human life, and treat as murderers fathers who expose their offspring."[21] Tertullian, for his part, condemned exposure for its inhumaneness — children were left to die "by cold, or by hunger, or by being torn apart by dogs, a crueler fate than simply taking the sword to them."[22] Other early Christian apologists were unanimous in expressing their moral outrage over exposure.[23]

---

wanted pregnancy is found in Konstantinos Kapparos, *Abortion in the Ancient World* (London: Duckworth, 2002), pp. 154-62.

19. Seneca, *De Ira,* I.15.2.

20. On the exposure of healthy children, see Charles J. Reid Jr., *Power Over the Body, Equality in the Family: Rights and Domestic Relations in Medieval Canon Law* (Grand Rapids: Eerdmans, 2004), pp. 70-71, and the sources cited therein. Additionally, one might consult William V. Harris, "The Theoretical Possibility of Extensive Infanticide in the Greco-Roman World," *The Classical Quarterly* 32 (n.s.) (1982): 114-16; and William V. Harris, "Child Exposure in the Roman Empire," *The Journal of Roman Studies* 84 (1994): 1-22.

The routineness of exposure is revealed by considering the casual and offhanded way Cicero used this practice as a metaphor for political life in the Roman Republic. Cicero, *De Legibus,* 3.19, in Clinton Walker Keyes, trans., *De Re Publica et De Legibus* (Cambridge, MA: Harvard University Press, 1977), pp. 480-81. The Roman law held an ambivalent posture on exposure. On the one hand, the second-century AD jurist Gaius wrote that parents held "the power of life and death" over their children. Francis de Zulueta, ed. and trans., *The Institutes of Gaius* (Oxford: Clarendon, 1946), Bk. 1, sec. 52, vol. 1, pp. 16-17. On the other hand, the third-century jurist Paulus condemned as "killing" *(necare)* not only the strangulation of infants but the practice of abandoning them in public spaces so as to arouse the sympathy of others. *Digest* 25.3.4. On the proper interpretation of this text, consult Max Radin, "The Exposure of Infants in Roman Law and Practice," *The Classical Journal* 20 (1925): 337, 339. Even Paulus, however, approved of the infanticide of deformed children in asserting that those who were "against human form" and "monstrous" should not be legally accounted as children. *Digest* 1.5.14.

21. Reid, *Power Over the Body,* p. 73.

22. Reid, *Power Over the Body,* p. 74.

23. Reid, *Power Over the Body,* pp. 73-74 (collecting and evaluating some of these sources).

This deep tradition, as well as the more formal legal sources arrayed by Gasparri, helped give content and shape to the 1917 Code's condemnation of abortion.

The twentieth-century canonists who commented on the 1917 Code were similarly supportive of the Church's condemnation. Some commentators did little more than repeat the canon with approval.[24] Other commentators provided helpful definitions. Abortion, it was repeatedly declared, was "the expulsion of the undeveloped human fetus from the uterus of the mother."[25] Still others raised provocative questions about what it meant to procure an abortion. A German commentator, Heribert Jone, thus asked whether a man, who in a fit of anger struck a woman and caused an abortion without intending to do so, was subject to the penalty; and he answered negatively.[26] Since intent was the foundation of culpability and the intent to abort was lacking in this instance, the excommunication was not incurred.[27] (Jone, however, perhaps to demonstrate his fidelity to the Church's teaching, immediately followed this hypothetical question by asserting that an abortion performed to achieve some other end, even the preservation of the mother's life, was to be considered criminal within the meaning of the canons.)[28]

One of the most detailed treatments found in the commentators was that of Charles Augustine.[29] Augustine distinguished between three types of

24. See, for example, T. Lincoln Bouscaren and Adam C. Ellis, *Canon Law: A Text and Commentary*, 2nd ed., rev. (Milwaukee: Bruce, 1951), p. 929.

25. "Abortus est foetus humani immaturi eiectio ex utero matris." Matteo Conte a Coronata, *Institutiones Iuris Canonici ad usum Utriusque Cleri et Scholarum* (Rome: Marietti, 1935), vol. 4, p. 458. Cf. R. P. Udalricus Beste, *Introductio in Codicem* (Collegeville, MN: St. John's Abbey Press, 1938), p. 953 (repeating Coronata's definition). An alternative definition was proposed by Saltelli and Di-Falco: "the violent interruption of the physical process of maturation of the fetus" *(L'aborto è ogni violenta interruzione del processo fisiologico di maturaz one del feto).* Carlo Saltelli and Enrico Romano Di-Falco, *Commento teorico-practico al nuovo Codice penale* (Turin: Unione Tipografico Editrice Torinese, 1931), n. 1124 (quoted in Coronata, vol. 4, p. 458, note 2).

26. P. Heribert Jone, *Commentarium in Codicem Iuris Canonici* (Paderborn: Schöningh, 1955), vol. 2, p. 530. Jone was not alone in raising this hypothetical question. See Felix Cappello, *Tractatus Canonico-Moralis De Censuris iuxta Codicem Iuris Canonici* (Rome: Marietti, 1933), p. 334. Cappello stressed that the man's actions should be condemned as "gravely evil" *(graviter malam),* but that the specific censure for abortion did not apply. In scholastic discourse, gravely evil acts amounted to mortally sinful behavior.

27. Jone, *Commentarium*, vol. 2, p. 530.

28. Jone, *Commentarium*, vol. 2, p. 530.

29. P. Charles Augustine, *A Commentary on the New Code of Canon Law* (St. Louis: Herder, 1931), vol. 8, pp. 397-402.

abortion — the accidental, which might be caused from "a fall, overexertion, or natural dislocation"; the criminal, which is "induced voluntarily for selfish reasons and by forbidden means"; and the artificial, which is "induced for medical-therapeutic reasons."[30] Abortion for criminal purposes obviously violated the canon, but so also did abortion for therapeutic reasons, since it might also "be criminal according to sound moral principles."[31]

Quite clearly, what is missing from these twentieth-century commentators is a deeper explanation of the principles at stake. For the most part, the commentators on the old 1917 Code tended to be legalistically minded individuals, who doubtlessly saw their task as the careful examination of rules. They took for granted the longstanding anti-abortion tradition of the Church and assumed without question that the protection of fetal life was of transcendent importance. But these assumptions remained untested; such questioning was avoided, it seems clear, because these formalistically trained men feared that they might as a consequence be led into the realms of philosophy and theology — disciplines that belonged to different parts of the university.

Indeed, to find a defense of the values at stake one must turn from the canonists to the magisterium of the Church. *Casti conubii,* Pius XI's encyclical in defense of marriage, published in 1930, might have been the most important papal pronouncement on abortion between the time of Sixtus V and the twentieth century. The purpose of the encyclical was to provide a comprehensive defense of marriage in the face of secularist and materialist challenges.[32] Marriage was divinely instituted for the achievement of certain transcendent ends.[33] And central to marriage was the place of children: "[A]mongst the blessings of marriage, the child holds first place."[34]

Abortion and contraception were incompatible with this vision of marriage. Allying himself with St. Augustine, Pius denounced "those wicked parents who seek to remain childless."[35] Abortion, however, was not the same as contraception. It was something even graver than the frustration of the natural fecundity of the marital relationship. It was, Pius made clear, the direct taking of innocent life and so immoral for that reason alone. Speaking of the extreme case of abortion to preserve the life and health of the mother, Pius declared:

30. P. Charles Augustine, *A Commentary,* p. 399.
31. P. Charles Augustine, *A Commentary,* pp. 399-400.
32. *Casti Connubii,* paras. 44-52.
33. *Casti Connubii,* paras. 5-10.
34. *Casti Connubii,* para. 11.
35. *Casti Connubii,* para. 65.

> [H]owever much we may pity the mother whose health and even life is gravely imperiled in the performance of the duty allotted to her by nature, nevertheless what could ever be a sufficient reason for excusing in any way the direct murder of the innocent? This is precisely what we are dealing with here. Whether inflicted upon the mother or upon the child, it is against the precept of God and the law of nature: "Thou shalt not kill." The life of each is equally sacred, and no one has the power, not even the public authority, to destroy it.[36]

Thus, Pius concluded, abortion, even abortion performed for therapeutic reasons or at the command of the state for eugenic reasons, was always immoral.[37] The invocation of the Ten Commandments' prohibition on killing and the description of abortion as murder made it clear that abortion was a crime not against marriage or fecundity but against life itself.

Thirty years later, the Second Vatican Council returned to these themes. The Council Fathers more optimistically, perhaps, than Pius, believed in the capacity of Christians to transform the world. This responsibility uniquely fell to the laity, who were "called by God . . . [to] contribute to the sanctification of the world."[38] One aspect of this sanctification that all were to work toward was the protection of innocent life, including the life of the unborn. Like Pius XI, the Second Vatican Council described abortion as a crime against life:

> God, the Lord of life, has entrusted to men the noble mission of safeguarding life, and men must carry it out in a manner worthy of themselves. Life must be protected with the utmost care from the moment of conception: abortion and infanticide are abominable crimes.[39]

The Right to Life

Around the time of the Second Vatican Council there took place a parallel development in philosophical circles — the development of a vocabulary that spoke of a "right to life" and that sought to apply this vocabulary specifically to the question of abortion. The linguistic expression "right to life" had long been a feature of both Christian and secular modes of discourse. Thus the thirteenth-century scholastic philosopher Henry of Ghent wrote

36. *Casti Connubii,* para. 64.
37. *Casti Connubii,* paras. 63-64.
38. *Lumen Gentium,* para. 31.
39. *Gaudium et Spes,* para. 51.

that all persons have a "right in accord with the law of nature" *(ius . . . secundum legem naturae)* to engage in acts of self-preservation.[40] This language was subsequently utilized by Thomas Hobbes and Samuel Pufendorf.[41] This language may have been in the back of Thomas Jefferson's mind when he wrote in the Declaration of Independence of "the right to life, liberty, and the pursuit of happiness." In ecclesiastical circles, one finds Pope John XXIII in his prophetic encyclical *Pacem in Terris* (Christmas 1962) writing of "Man['s] . . . right to live."[42] John, however, had in mind with this expression "the right to bodily integrity, and [the] means necessary for the proper development of life, particularly food, clothing, shelter, medical care, rest, and, finally, the necessary social services."[43]

At the beginning of the twentieth century one sees the first connection being drawn in the academic literature between the right to life and abortion. *The Right to Life of the Unborn Child,* which appeared in English in 1903 after having been published originally in Dutch under the title *Het Levensrecht der Ongeboren Vrucht,* consisted of an exchange of views among two Catholic physicians and a moral theologian on the subject of the licitness of therapeutic abortions to protect the health or life of the mother.[44] The substance of the debate is less important for our purposes than the use of the expression "right to life" in connection with abortion. Some sixty years later, this vocabulary was revived by the British statesman and philosopher, Norman St. John-Stevas (b. 1929). Now a member of the House of Lords, St. John-Stevas had studied for the Catholic priesthood as a young man and remains active in Catholic causes even today. In a slender book published in 1963 and titled *The Right to Life,* St. John-Stevas argued that abortion, euthanasia, suicide, and the killing that accompanies warfare should be analyzed in terms of a fundamental right to life, which he identified with the Christian civilization of the West.[45]

40. R. Macken, ed., *Henrici de Gandavo Quodlibet IX,* in vol. 13, *Opera Omnia* (Leuven: University Press, 1983), *quaestio* 26, col. 307. Cf. Brian Tierney, *The Idea of Natural Rights: Studies on Natural Rights, Natural Law, and Church Law, 1150-1625* (Atlanta: Scholars Press, 1997), pp. 78-89 (reviewing and evaluating Henry's arguments).

41. On Hobbes and Pufendorf, see Tierney, *Idea of Natural Rights, supra,* pp. 80-83.

42. John XXIII, *Pacem in Terris,* para. 11.

43. John XXIII, *Pacem in Terris,* para. 11.

44. Professor Hector Treub, M.D., Rev. R. van Oppenraay, D.D., S.J., and Professor Th. M. Vlaming, M.D., *The Right to Life of the Unborn Child* (New York: Joseph F. Wagner, 1903).

45. *The Right to Life* (London: Hodder & Stoughton, 1963). St. John-Stevas asserted, in a central paragraph in his work: "The respect for human life and personality that distinguishes Western society from the totalitarian societies of the East did not spring up out of nothing. It is

The magisterium came to adopt this vocabulary as its own over the next several decades. Pius XI and the Second Vatican Council were certainly concerned with the protection of the various forms of innocent life, but these sources did not make use of rights language in their utterances on abortion. This situation changed dramatically during the pontificate of Pope John Paul II, who spoke out many times about the right to life,[46] but whose most comprehensive explanation of this concept can be found in his 1995 encyclical, *Evangelium Vitae,* "The Gospel of Life."

The opening paragraphs of the encyclical adopt the phrase "right to life," and this vocabulary remains crucial to the entire text. The Gospel of Life, which John Paul defends, is foreshadowed by a birth — that of Jesus Christ in Bethlehem — which at the same time "reveals the full meaning of every human birth."[47] "[E]very person sincerely open to truth and goodness," John Paul II continued, "can, by the light of reason and the hidden action of grace, come to recognize in the natural law written in the heart (Romans 2:14-15) the sacred value of human life from its very beginning until its very end, and can affirm the right of every human being to have this primary good respected to the highest degree. Upon the recognition of this right, every human community and the political community itself are founded."[48] Abortion was a particular threat to the universal right to life: "Today there exists a great multitude of weak and defenseless human beings, unborn children in particular, whose fundamental right to life is being trampled upon."[49]

Indeed, Pope John Paul II warned against an encroaching "culture of death" that amounted "[in] a certain sense [to] a war of the powerful against

---

deeply rooted in experience and history. Above all it is rooted in religion. Ultimately the idea of the right to life, as is the case with other human rights, is traceable to the Christian doctrine of man" (pp. 15-16). St. John-Stevas first took up these themes in a law review article published three years before. See Norman St. John-Stevas, "A Roman Catholic View of Population Control," *Law and Contemporary Problems* 25 (1960): 445-69. His magisterial work, *Life, Death, and the Law: Law and Christian Morals in England and the United States* (Bloomington: Indiana University Press, 1961), dealt with contraception, euthanasia, artificial insemination, and suicide, but did not address abortion or warfare.

46. One might consult, for instance, the speeches John Paul II delivered on the occasion of his first visit to the United States, in October 1979. See "Pope John Paul II on Human Rights and Population," in *Population and Development Review* 5 (1979): 747-54 (providing excerpts from the pontiff's speeches).

47. *Evangelium Vitae,* para. 1.

48. *Evangelium Vitae,* para. 2.

49. *Evangelium Vitae,* para. 5.

the weak."[50] "[A] life which would require greater acceptance, love and care is considered useless, or held to be an intolerable burden, and is therefore rejected in one way or another."[51] John Paul feared a growing "conspiracy against life": "A person who, because of illness, handicap, or, more simply, just by existing, compromises the well-being or life-style of those who are more favored tends to be looked upon as an enemy to be resisted or eliminated."[52] An encompassing, robustly developed and defended right to life represented a bulwark against these threats.

Pope Benedict XVI has relied upon the premises of *Evangelium Vitae* in his statements on the moral requirement to respect the integrity of human life. Speaking to visiting Kenyan bishops in November 2007, he thus proposed that they should not succumb to secularizing trends evident in the West that depreciated and denigrated human life: "When you preach the Gospel of Life, remind your people that the right to life of every innocent human being, born or unborn, is absolute and applies equally to all people with no exception whatsoever."[53] In a 2007 address to the Pontifical Academy for Life, Benedict declared that the natural law and the gospel concurred in the need to "affirm the right of every human being to have this primary good [life] respected to the highest degree."[54] Speaking to the same group a year later, Benedict connected the right to life with the divine love that brought us all into being and called upon the entire Church, "with her already functioning institutions and new initiatives," to respect and conserve this right in its many dimensions.[55]

Expansion of the Right to Life

As the preceding discussion of popes John Paul II and Benedict has intimated, magisterial claims about the right to life have moved beyond the

50. *Evangelium Vitae,* para. 12.

51. *Evangelium Vitae,* para. 12.

52. *Evangelium Vitae,* para. 12.

53. "Address of His Holiness Benedict XVI to the Bishops of Kenya on their *Ad Limina* Visit," November 19, 2007.

54. "Address of His Holiness Benedict XVI to the Participants in the General Assembly of the Pontifical Academy for Life," February 24, 2007.

55. "Address of His Holiness Benedict XVI to the Participants of the Congress Organized by the Pontifical Academy for Life," February 25, 2008. The theme Benedict was addressing was "Close by the Incurable Sick Person and the Dying: Scientific and Medical Aspects." This theme gave Benedict the opportunity to apply the concept of the right to life to a range of concerns other than abortion.

abortion context and have begun to inform other aspects of Catholic social thought. In this way, the Church has acquired a deeper vocabulary with which to move from abortion to address a wide variety of morally problematic threats to human life and well-being. There was, after all, as Pope John Paul II noted, "[an] extraordinary increase . . . of threats to the life of individuals and peoples, especially where life is weak and defenseless."[56]

This was especially the case with children, who were the innocent victims of war, violent displacement, and an unjust distribution of resources leading to the deprivation of the necessities of life, such as adequate medical care.[57] Children are at risk in a multitude of contexts all over the globe. While many topics might be addressed, given requirements of length the remainder of this paper will be confined to only two of these many transcendent threats to the welfare of children: war and access to medical care.

The Right to Life and War

In his Angelus address for July 22, 2007, Pope Benedict XVI chose to reflect on the ninetieth anniversary of the issuance by his namesake Benedict XV of a Peace Note that called on the warring powers of Europe to cease the "useless slaughter" *(inutile strage)* of World War I.[58] War, Benedict XVI asserted, "is always justly considered a calamity in contrast with the project of God, Who created all things to thrive and, in particular, intended that the human race become one family."[59] Benedict consciously renewed the call of his predecessors, Paul VI and John Paul II, to look to the institutions of international law to resolve disputes.[60]

Increasingly, over the course of the Cold War and post–Cold War eras, the magisterium has adopted a skeptical view of the possibility that war might result in the affirmative doing of justice. In reflecting upon the inestimable damage war imposes upon the human race, the papal magisterium

56. *Evangelium Vitae*, para. 3.

57. *Evangelium Vitae*, para. 10: "And how can we fail to consider the violence against life done to millions of human beings, especially children, who are forced into poverty, malnutrition, and hunger because of an unjust distribution of resources between peoples and social classes? And what of the violence inherent not only in wars as such but in the scandalous arms trade . . . ?"

58. Benedict XVI, "Angelus," July 22, 2007.

59. Benedict XVI, "Angelus," July 22, 2007: "La guerra . . . è da sempre giustamente considerata una calamit? che constrasta con il progetto di Dio, il quale ha creato tutto per l'esistenza e, in particolare, vuole fare del genere umano una famiglia."

60. Benedict XVI, "Angelus," July 22, 2007.

has frequently recalled the slaughter of civilians, especially children, that modern war inevitably inflicts.[61]

In his New Year's World Day of Peace message for 2007, Pope Benedict XVI proposed the human person and human rights as the central organizing principles for understanding and eventually ameliorating conflict in the world.[62] The bodily and spiritual integrity of every person must be recognized and affirmed so that this end might be achieved.[63] "Peace," the pope pronounced, "is based on respect for the rights of all."[64] And the right that must be protected above all others, the pontiff insisted, was the *"right to life."*[65] This was especially true with respect to children, the innocent victims of war: "I invoke peace upon children, who by their innocence enrich humanity with goodness and hope, and by their sufferings compel us all to work for justice and peace."[66]

The Holy See's treatment of the rights of children in warfare has a number of dimensions. I have identified three particular organizing principles, although others certainly might have been used. These include: the destitution that warfare, especially on a massive scale, can cause; the use of child-soldiers, a particularly gruesome modern development; and the impact embargos and economic sanctions can have on the most vulnerable and innocent members of society, especially children.

The Destitute

Pope Benedict XVI's Angelus message provides a prism through which one might explain and understand the papal solicitude for the suffering of chil-

61. Many examples might be given, but one might cite in particular Pope John Paul II's Lenten message for 2004, which proposed to make the central theme for Lenten meditation in that year the scriptural verse, "Whoever receives one such child in my name receives me." John Paul II, "Message for Lent, 2004" December 8, 2003. War was among the human activities John Paul denounced as not only anti-human, but specifically anti-child.

62. Message of His Holiness Pope Benedict XVI for the Celebration of the World Day of Peace, January 1, 2007.

63. Message of His Holiness Pope Benedict XVI, para. 2: "Sacred Scripture affirms that 'God created man in his own image, in the image of God he created them; male and female he created them' (Genesis 1:27). *As one created in the image of God, each individual human being has the dignity of a person;* he or she is not just something, but someone, capable of self-knowledge, self-possession, free self-giving and entering into communion with others."

64. Message of His Holiness Pope Benedict XVI, para. 4.

65. Message of His Holiness Pope Benedict XVI, para. 5 (emphasis in original).

66. Message of His Holiness Pope Benedict XVI, para. 1.

dren in wartime that one can find in the sources from World War I to the present. Pope Benedict XV, who strove unceasingly to bring World War I to a just conclusion and to relieve the misery that that conflict spawned, issued an encyclical in November 1919, on the plight of the child-victims of that war.[67] The war in "Central Europe," by which the pope intended to include Belgium, France, Germany, the former Austro-Hungarian Empire, and other afflicted lands, had left children "deprived of food and clothing to a degree beyond all imagination."[68] Reminding his audience of the approaching Christmas season, Benedict XV continued:

> With the approach of the season of Christmas, commemorating the birth of Our Lord Jesus Christ, our thoughts spontaneously fly to the poor little children, especially in Central Europe, who are most cruelly feeling the wants of the necessities of life.[69]

Pius XII took up the same theme once again in his January 1946 encyclical *Quemadmodum,* which bore the subtitle "Pleading for the Care of the World's Destitute Children."[70] World War II, Pius asserted, had left "accumulated miseries that weigh on not a few nations."[71] Among these miseries was the plight of children. "[A] host of innocent children, millions of whom it is estimated in many countries without the necessities of life . . . are suffering from cold, hunger, and disease."[72] "Indeed, war has stolen from these children not only material well-being but the affections and tender emotions of parents and loved ones who are no longer present for them."[73]

The care for children in such circumstances, Pius continued, was a special responsibility for the Church:

67. Benedict XV, *Paterno Iam Diu.*

68. Benedict XV, *Paterno Iam Diu,* para. 1. The pope followed this letter with a second encyclical, published at Christmas 1920, in which he noted some amelioration of conditions in some European nations, but noted that the conflicts that were spawned in the wake of World War I left millions of other children worse off. See Benedict XV, *Annus Iam Plenus* (1920).

69. Benedict XV, *Paterno Iam Diu,* para. 2. The pope continued: "We embrace this tender age with all the more solicitude inasmuch as it exactly recalls the image of the Divine Infant supporting for the love of men in the cave at Bethlehem the rigour of winter and the want of all things." Benedict proposed that December 28, the Feast of the Holy Innocents, as an appropriate deadline for forwarding relief to the stricken lands (para. 3).

70. Pius XII, *Quemadmodum.*

71. Pius XII, *Quemadmodum,* para. 1.

72. Pius XII, *Quemadmodum,* para. 1.

73. Pius XII, *Quemadmodum,* para. 1.

> Let us recall that in every age the Church has exercised the most diligent care of the young and has rightly deemed this an official mission assigned in a very special way to her charity. And as she did this and continues to do it, she undoubtedly was following in the footsteps and obeying the injunctions of her Divine Founder, Who, gently gathering the children around Him, said to the Apostles who rebuked their mothers: "Let the little children come to me, and do not hinder them, for of such is the kingdom of God" (Mark 10:14).[74]

This commitment to the welfare of children uprooted and damaged by war has continued to our own day. One might consider, for example, Pope Paul VI's address to the Catholic school children of America, delivered in February 1972, reminding them of the millions of children left destitute because of fighting between India and Pakistan.[75] A 1999 intervention by then Archbishop (now Cardinal) Renato Martino, the Apostolic Nuncio to the United Nations, called attention to the fact that "[t]oday, there are over twenty million children who have been displaced by war within and outside their countries."[76] John Paul II undoubtedly had concerns of this sort in mind when he addressed the general effect of war on the material welfare of families and children in his 1994 Message for the World Day of Peace:

> [I]n many parts of the world, whole nations are caught in the spiral of bloody conflicts, of which families are often the first victims: either they are deprived of the main if not the only breadwinner, or they are forced to abandon home, land, and property and flee into the unknown; in any event they are subjected to painful misfortunes which threaten all security.[77]

Child-Soldiers

Child-soldiers have become an increasingly popular resource in the various armed struggles that have in recent years plagued the remoter corners of Africa, Asia, and the Middle East. Peter W. Singer, in grim detail, re-

74. Pius XII, *Quemadmodum,* para. 8.

75. "Appeal of Pope Paul VI to the Students of the Catholic Schools of the United States of America," February 16, 1972.

76. "Intervention by H.E. Archbishop Renato R. Martino, Promotion and Protection of the Rights of Children," October 28, 1999, before the Third Committee of the 54th Session of the General Assembly.

77. John Paul II, "Message for the XXVII World Day of Peace," January 1, 1994.

counts the ways in which these child warriors are exploited by their bloody-minded adult handlers. They are recruited, Singer notes, "[because] their lives are considered to be of less value than fully trained adult soldiers."[78] They are consequently "charged with tasks that entail greater hazard."[79] Children might be sent into minefields to locate explosive devices "through simple trial and error."[80] They might also be used "as direct shields at checkpoints or when ambushes or battles loom."[81] Children may also be used as "cannon fodder."[82] Children, even unarmed ones, are compelled to charge fortified positions in order to attract enemy fire and thus "distract the enemy from the real attack coming from another direction."[83] In all of these ways and in others children are among the most exploited victims of war.

The Holy See has been among the world's leaders in denouncing these practices and in proposing solutions. Pope John Paul II was especially responsible for this development. In a series of documents, spanning the final part of his pontificate, he returned repeatedly to the moral requirement that children not be used in combat. His 1996 and 1999 Messages for the World Day of Peace can thus be seen as foundational texts on this subject.[84]

Writing in 1996, John Paul II made children the centerpiece of his World Day of Peace Message. He expressed his hope that "all children of the world will be able to begin 1996 in happiness and to enjoy a peaceful childhood, with the help of responsible adults."[85] Regrettably, this was not yet the case. One of the most reprehensible developments of recent years, the pontiff noted, was the use of children as combatants:

> Children are not only victims of the violence of wars; many *are forced to take an active part in them.* In some countries of the world it has come to the point where even very young boys and girls are compelled to serve in the army of the warring parties. Enticed by the promise of food and schooling, they are confined to remote camps, where they suffer hunger

78. Peter Warren Singer, *Children at War* (New York: Pantheon, 2005), p. 106.

79. Singer, *Children at War,* p. 106.

80. Singer, *Children at War,* p. 107.

81. Singer, *Children at War,* p. 107.

82. Singer, *Children at War,* p. 107.

83. Singer, *Children at War,* p. 107.

84. "Message of His Holiness Pope John Paul II for the Celebration of the World Day of Peace," January 1, 1999.

85. "Message of His Holiness Pope John Paul II for the XXIX World Day of Peace," January 1, 1996.

and abuse and are encouraged to kill even people from their own villages. Often they are sent ahead to clear minefields. Clearly, the life of children has little value for those who use them in this way.[86]

John Paul II returned to this theme three years later. After grounding his call for peace on "the basic right to life,"[87] the Holy Father went on:

> I think with sorrow of those living and growing up against a background of war, of those who have known nothing but conflict and violence. Those who survive will carry the scars of this terrible experience for the rest of their lives. And what shall we say about children forced to fight? Can we ever accept that lives which are just beginning should be ruined in this way? Trained to kill and often compelled to do so, these children cannot fail to have serious problems in their future insertion into civil society. . . . Children need peace; they have a right to it.[88]

Returning to this theme near the end of his pontificate, Pope John Paul II expressed his outrage at the double horror that confronts children exposed to war, particularly in developing nations:

> In some corners of the earth, especially in the poorest countries, children and adolescents are the victims of a terrible form of violence: they are *enlisted to fight* in the so-called "forgotten wars."
>
> Indeed, they suffer a doubly scandalous aggression: they *are made victims of war,* and at the same time forced to *play the lead in it,* swept away in the hatred of adults. Stripped of everything, they see their future threatened by a nightmare difficult to dispel.[89]

John Paul II did not confine his criticism to these sorts of formal pronouncements but also encouraged his diplomatic corps to enlist the interna-

86. "Message of His Holiness Pope John Paul II for the XXIX World Day of Peace," January 1, 1996.

87. "Message of His Holiness Pope John Paul II for the XXIX World Day of Peace," January 1, 1996, para. 4. The pope continued: "Human life is sacred and inviolable from conception to its natural end. 'Thou shalt not kill' is the divine commandment which states the limit beyond which it is never licit to go. 'The deliberate decision to deprive an innocent human being of life is always morally evil'" (quoting *Evangelium Vitae,* para. 57).

88. "Message of His Holiness Pope John Paul II for the 14th World Day of Peace," January 1, 1996, para. 11.

89. John Paul II, "Angelus Message, Fifth Sunday of Lent," March 28, 2004.

tional community to act against outrages of this sort. One might take as an example of this effort a report prepared by Fr. Michael Blume on behalf of the Pontifical Council for the Pastoral Care of Migrants and Itinerant Peoples. This report called attention to the use of child-soldiers in places as diverse as Iraqi Kurdistan, the Democratic Republic of Congo, Liberia, and other world combat zones. The report makes chilling if also compelling reading in the ways in which it documents the ways that children — some enticed into combat by false promises, others kidnapped and forced to perform lethal functions — are used and discarded in modern war. It pleaded with the world community to address this crisis.[90]

Pope Benedict XVI, John Paul's successor, and the Roman Curia, have both taken up the cause of child-soldiers. Benedict thus took the occasion of the *ad limina* visit to Rome of the bishops of the Democratic Republic of the Congo to praise their efforts at reintegrating the child-soldiers of that land into society.[91] In June 2001, the Permanent Observer Mission of the Holy See at the United Nations organized a symposium that addressed the crisis of children in armed conflict.[92] And Stephen Fumio Cardinal Humao, on a fact-finding mission to Liberia and Sierra Leone, reported on the efforts of the local Church to deal with the problem of reintegration.[93] He singled out Catholic organizations such as Caritas Makeni and Children Associated with War for their success in this regard.[94] Both in arousing the larger international community to action and in mustering its own resources for the task, the Holy See has taken a leading role in the effort to eradicate the repugnant practice of using children to fight adult wars.[95]

90. Michael A. Blume, S.V.D., "Hidden Displacement: Child Soldiers," Pontifical Council for the Pastoral Care of Migrants and Itinerant People, December 1999.

91. "Address of His Holiness Benedict XVI to the Bishops from the Democratic Republic of the Congo, on their *Ad Limina* Visit," February 6, 2006.

92. The proceedings were subsequently published under the title of *Children in Armed Conflict: Everyone's Responsibility* (New York: Path to Peace Foundation, 2002).

93. "Pastoral Visit of Cardinal Humao to Liberia and Sierra Leone," Pontifical Council for the Pastoral Care of Migrants and Itinerant Peoples, August 2006.

94. "Pastoral Visit of Cardinal Humao."

95. Thus the Holy See has also called for the abolition of the international trade in "small-arms," noting their frequent use by child-soldiers. See, for instance, the "Statement of H.E. Monsignor Diarmuid Martin at the International Conference on War-Affected Children," September 16-17, 2000, Winnipeg, Manitoba. Cf. Statement of H.E. Monsignor Celestino Migliore, "Intervention by the Holy See at the United Nations Conference on Illicit Trade in Small Arms and Light Weapons," July 11, 2005.

Embargos and Economic Sanctions

Invoking the rights of the innocent, especially children, the Holy See has also taken a strong stand against the use of indiscriminate and disproportionate economic sanctions imposed by powerful countries to coerce smaller state actors either into changing their regimes or changing their conduct in the international arena. Explicitly invoking the endorsement of Pope John Paul II, Renato Martino announced the Holy See's position on the use of economic sanctions in international affairs:

> The Holy See considers it to be legitimate for the international community to resort to economic sanctions when confronted with a specific government that has acted in a manner that places world peace in danger. However, the Holy See holds that there are several conditions that must accompany the imposition of such sanctions, namely, sanctions may not be a means of warfare or punishment of a people; sanctions should be a temporary means of exerting pressure on governments whose choices threaten international peace; sanctions must be subjected to strict legal and ethical criteria. It is always imperative to foresee the humanitarian consequences of sanctions, without failing to respect the just proportion that such measures should have in relation to the very evil that they are meant to remedy.[96]

No clearer example of the use of these criteria to judge the morality of a coercive sanctions regime can be found than the consistent condemnations, expressed by the Holy See over a period of years, of the American-led economic embargo imposed on Iraq following the 1991 Persian Gulf War and sustained alike by Democratic and Republican administrations. The embargo had a devastating impact on the children of Iraq. A study conducted by the British medical journal *The Lancet,* published in 2000, found that childhood mortality significantly increased in most of Iraq following the imposition of sanctions, while other studies identified a range of pathologies associated with the embargo.[97]

96. "Intervention by Renato R. Martino at the 57th General Assembly of the United Nations On Unilateral Territorial Coercive Measures," October 16, 2002.

97. "Sanctions and Childhood Mortality in Iraq," *The Lancet* (May 27, 2000), p. 1851. The study found that in southern and central Iraq, which were subjected to the worst of the sanctions, "[i]nfant mortality rose from 47 per 1000 live births during 1984-89 to 108 per 1000 in 1994-99, and under-5 mortality rose from 56 to 131 per 1000 live births." The only exception to this increase in mortality was the autonomous Kurdish region in the north of the country,

John Paul II took the lead personally in condemning the impact the embargo had on the lives and welfare of the innocent people of Iraq. Greeting the diplomatic corps credentialed to the Holy See in January 1998, John Paul II declared:

> [A]n entire people is the victim of a constraint which puts it in hazardous conditions of survival. I refer to our brothers and sisters in Iraq, living under a pitiless embargo. In response to the appeals for help which unceasingly come to the Holy See, I must call upon the consciences of those who, in Iraq and elsewhere, put political, economic, or strategic considerations before the fundamental good of the people, and I ask them to show compassion. The weak and the innocent cannot pay for mistakes for which they are not responsible.[98]

Denunciations of this sort became a recurrent event of the latter years of John Paul II's pontificate. He clearly felt a powerful sense of solidarity with the innocent children of Iraq who were made to suffer extreme deprivations because of the economic embargo imposed on that nation.

In his greeting to the Chaldean bishops of Iraq, in December 2001, John Paul declared: "Dear Brothers, once again I want to express my compassion for your communities in Iraq, sorely tried like the entire population of the country, suffering for years from the severity of the embargo imposed on it. I implore the Lord to enlighten the minds and hearts of the leaders of nations so that they may work for the reestablishment of a just and lasting peace in this part of the world."[99] He spoke in similar terms in April 2001, when re-

---

which was not subjected to the severe sanctions imposed on the rest of the Iraqi nation. A review of previous studies conducted in 2004 found rampant malnutrition in Iraq. Thus we find that in 1999, "21% of children under 5 were underweight, 20% stunted, and 9% wasted." Shereen T. Ismael, "Dismantling the Iraqi Social Fabric: From Dictatorship Through Sanctions to Occupation," *Journal of Comparative Family Studies* 35 (2004): 333, 337. Cf. Shereen T. Ismael, "The Cost of War: The Children of Iraq," *Journal of Comparative Family Studies* 38 (2007): 337-59 (reviewing the range of consequences for children of sanctions, invasion, and occupation, from public health, to mental illness, to increased childhood cancers).

98. "Speech of His Holiness Pope John Paul II in Reply to the New Year Greetings of the Diplomatic Corps Accredited to the Holy See," January 10, 1998. In December 2001, John Paul II proclaimed a day of fasting by all Catholics in solidarity with the people of Iraq who had been "suffering for years from the severity of the embargo imposed upon it." "Address of John Paul II to the Bishops of the Chaldean Church on Their *Ad Limina* Visit," December 11, 2001.

99. John Paul II, "Address to the Bishops of the Chaldean Church on Their *Ad Limina* Visit," December 11, 2001. In March 2001, John Paul added, on the occasion of the *ad limina* visit of the Latin bishops of the Middle East: "In Iraq the embargo continues to claim victims; too

ceiving the credentials of the newly posted ambassador from Iraq to the Holy See: "I wish you to know of my esteem for the Iraqi people, whom I remember daily in my prayers, especially in light of the continuing difficulties which they face. As the embargo in your country continues to claim victims, I renew my appeal to the international community that innocent people should not be made to pay the consequences of a destructive war whose effects are still being felt by those who are weakest and most vulnerable."[100]

Speaking with a sense of fear and foreboding, anticipating the horrors that would accompany the American invasion of Iraq, John Paul II addressed the diplomatic corps posted to the Holy See in January 2003: "And what are we to say of the threat of a war which could strike the people of Iraq, the land of the Prophets, a people already sorely tried by more than twelve years of embargo?"[101]

Diplomats acting on behalf of the Holy See also spoke out forcefully against the use of indiscriminate sanctions to punish the people of Iraq. Renato Martino was especially vigorous in building upon John Paul II's solicitude for the innocent of Iraq:

> The fact that the leadership of a country has posed a threat to international peace and security and put obstacles to restoring peace "does not require that the entire population of that particular country, should be brought to suffer because of evil decisions of its leadership. . . . The tremendous humanitarian impact of economic sanctions on an entire popu-

many innocent people are paying for the consequences of a destructive policy whose effects continue to be felt by the weakest and most defenseless persons." John Paul II, "Address to the Latin Bishops in the Arab Regions, March 17, 2001.

100. "Address of the Holy Father to the New Ambassador of Iraq to the Holy See," April 28, 2001.

101. "Address of His Holiness Pope John Paul II to the Diplomatic Corps, January 13, 2003. In March 2003, Pope John Paul II engaged in a series of diplomatic moves in an effort to convince President George W. Bush not to go forward with the invasion. Pio Cardinal Laghi, who had once served as papal nuncio to the United States, was tasked with the responsibility of meeting with the President. See "Statement of Cardinal Pio Laghi, Special Envoy of John Paul II to President George Bush," March 5, 2003. In this statement, Laghi stressed that it was incumbent to "[take] into account the grave consequences of such an armed conflict: the suffering of the people of Iraq and those involved in the military operation, a further instability in the region, and a new gulf between Islam and Christianity." In a homily preached later that day, Cardinal Laghi urged Catholics to fast for the cause of peace because "through fasting we become one with those who are hungry, without homes and living without the basic necessities of life, conditions certainly caused by war." Ash Wednesday Homily of His Eminence Cardinal Pio Laghi, March 5, 2003.

> lation is not a matter to be easily overlooked by the international community. No doubt, impunity of atrocities and crimes cannot be tolerated. But justice demands that only the guilty be punished for their wrong-doing and not the innocent. The existing mechanism of economic sanctions causes only additional sufferings on the population in general and especially on members of vulnerable groups of the society, such as children, women, the sick, and the elderly."[102]

In an intervention in 2002, finally, Cardinal Martino explicitly connected the Holy See's opposition to sanctions with the right to life: "Mr. President, the position of the Holy See has not changed and it aligns itself with those other States who continue to call for the end of unjust and harmful measures directed at states . . . most especially on the basis of the recognition of the human dignity and the right to life, liberty, and security."[103]

In this body of material, one witnesses the magisterium coming to terms with the devastation that can be caused by the application of a coercive mechanism that fell short of the open and direct violence of war but still resulted in substantial infliction of harm, especially upon children and the vulnerable. Indeed, while combatants are the direct targets of open warfare, the magisterium made clear, economic sanctions posed even graver potential moral harm since the chief victims of sanctions, wrongly applied, are the weak and the innocent. The principle invoked to support this teaching was the right to life. Where that right was violated by the indiscriminate and disproportionate imposition of international sanctions, the Holy See was quick to respond as a voice of the voiceless.

102. "Intervention by H.E. Archbishop Renato R. Martino, Apostolic Nuncio, Permanent Observer Mission of the Holy See to the United Nations, Before the Second Committee of the 54th Session of the General Assembly of the United Nations on Item 99," October 19, 1999. Cardinal Martino's intervention the previous year was even blunter: "The Holy See recognized that there are legitimate reasons that the international community may resort to sanctions. But starvation may not be a means of warfare or the consequence of a legal decision. Sanctions must be proportionate to the goals they hope to achieve and they must always be accompanied by a dialogue between the parties involved." "Intervento dell Santa Sede, al Il Comitato Della 53 Sessione dell'Assemblea Generale dell'Onu," October 22, 1998.

103. "Intervention by H.E. Renato R. Martino at the 57th General Assembly of the United Nations on Unilateral Extraterritorial Coercive Measures," October 16, 2002. Another portion of this intervention is quoted and discussed above at note 76.

Healthcare

In October 1992, Pope John Paul II proclaimed that henceforth February 11 of every year, the feast on which the apparition of the Blessed Virgin occurred to St. Bernadette at Lourdes, would also serve as the World Day of the Sick. In subsequent messages in commemoration of this date, John Paul II developed a set of moral principles for the appropriate and just administration of healthcare. John Paul II was concerned, first, that the dignity of ill and suffering members of society be protected. In his inaugural World Day of the Sick message, Pope John Paul II emphasized that every human response to the sick among us must "draw on a transcendent vision of man which stresses the value and sacredness of life in the sick person as the image and child of God."[104] His initial message — and many subsequent messages — focused as well on the moral requirement to provide adequate healthcare to the neediest.[105]

The Right of Children to Medical Care

Even before the development of these principles in the context of the World Day of the Sick, however, the magisterium came to connect access to medical care to the right to life. In *Pacem in Terris,* Pope John XXIII declared adequate healthcare to be among the essential rights of all human persons. Since the person has a right to live, there follows in consequence of this fundamental right, subsidiary rights to "food, clothing, shelter, medical care, rest, and . . . the necessary social services."[106] Thus, Pope John continued, the person "has the right to be looked after in the event of ill health."[107]

104. "Message of the Holy Father Pope John Paul II for the First Annual World Day of the Sick," October 21, 1992.

105. "Message of the Holy Father Pope John Paul II for the First Annual World Day of the Sick," October 21, 1992: "[S]pecial attention [must] be reserved for the suffering and the sick by public authorities, national and international organizations, and every person of good will". Cf. "Message of the Holy Father Pope John Paul II for the World Day of the Sick," December 8, 1993: "About two-thirds of mankind still lack essential medical care, while the resources employed in this sector are too often insufficient." See also "Message of the Holy Father John Paul II for the World Day of the Sick for the Year 2001," August 22, 2000: "I . . . make a pressing appeal that everything be done to encourage the necessary development of health services in the still numerous countries which are unable to offer their inhabitants proper living conditions and appropriate health care."

106. John XXIII, *Pacem in Terris,* para. 11.

107. John XXIII, *Pacem in Terris,* para. 11.

Writing four years later, Pope Paul VI connected this right to the needs of children:

> "If a brother or a sister be naked and in want of daily food," says St. James, "and one of you say to them, 'Go in peace, be warmed and filled,' yet you do not give them what is necessary for the body, what does it profit?" [James 2:15-16]. Today no one can be unaware of the fact that on some continents countless men and women are ravished by hunger and countless children are undernourished. Many children die at an early age; many more of them find their physical and mental growth retarded. Thus whole populations are immersed in pitiable circumstances and lose heart.[108]

John Paul II developed this point further when he stressed in his 1982 apostolic exhortation that while the rights of all children must be respected, such respect is more urgently required "the smaller the child is and the more it is in need of everything, when it is sick, suffering, or handicapped."[109]

As with war, so with access to healthcare, one sees the Holy See taking numerous steps over the four decades since *Pacem in Terris* first connected medical care with the right to life to effectuate this vision of good health for all, even the neediest and most vulnerable children. In October 1983, John Paul II recommended to the world a "Charter of the Rights of the Family," drawn from principles of Catholic social thought and intended to give voice to the natural rights of all families. John Paul stressed at several points in this document principles that required society to provide all persons, but most especially children, social assistance that included by clear implication a right to appropriate medical care. "Children," he asserted, "both before and after birth, have the right to special protection and assis-

108. Paul VI, *Populorum Progressio,* para. 45. In the 1960s and early 1970s, Pope Paul VI wrote a series of letters to the Catholic school children of America. In his letter of March 3, 1965, Pope Paul wrote: "When one of your brothers or sisters is sick or in trouble, your parents want to give some special attention and care, and, we are sure, so do you. . . . How can you help us? This you can do again this year through Catholic Relief Services, the excellent organization which your good bishops have set up to help the poor throughout the world." "Address of Paul VI to the School Children of the United States of America." In his letter of February 24, 1971, Pope Paul called to his audience's attention "the millions of hungry, sick, and needy children around the world. . . . These boys and girls live in the poorest and neediest countries of the world. . . . Very often there are no schools where they can learn to read and write, no doctors to treat them when they are sick, and not enough food to build their little bodies." "Message of Paul VI to the Students of the Catholic Schools of the United States of America."

109. John Paul II, *Familiaris Consortio,* quoted in *Compendium of the Social Doctrine of the Church* (Vatican City: Pontifical Council for Justice and Peace, 2005), p. 110.

tance."[110] "All children," he added, "whether born in or out of wedlock, enjoy the same right to social protection, with a view to the integral personal development."[111] "Children who are handicapped have the right to find in the home and the school an environment suitable to their human development."[112] "Families have a right to a social and economic order in which the organization of work permits the members to live together, and does not hinder the unity, well-being, health, and stability of the family."[113]

One can also find frequent endorsements in diplomatic and curial pronouncements of the general principle of the right of children to healthcare. Speaking to the United Nations, Cardinal Alfonso López Trujillo has thus declared: "Everyone has the right to the highest attainable standard of health. Can the world say that its people have enjoyed that right? Too many people, far too many children die each day because they do not have access to the most basic of medicines or health care. Too many people suffer because they do not have clean water to drink or because they live in environments that are unsafe."[114]

The Holy See has also moved beyond general principles to express a series of more specific concerns about particular problems. From nearly the start of his pontificate, John Paul II expressed a kind of solidarity with the handicapped, particularly handicapped children. Speaking in Vancouver, British Columbia, in 1984, he declared: "The disabled and handicapped call forth energies from our hearts that we never suspected were there."[115] Fifteen years later, John Paul spoke on this subject once again: "The arrival of a suffering child is certainly a disconcerting event for the family, who are left deeply shocked by it. . . . Families clearly need adequate support from the

110. "Charter of the Rights of the Family," Article 4.

111. "Charter of the Rights of the Family," Article 4.

112. "Charter of the Rights of the Family," Article 4.

113. "Charter of the Rights of the Family," Article 10.

114. "Intervention by Cardinal Alfonso López Trujillo, "Meeting of Religious Leaders to the United Nations on the Occasion of the Special Session on Children," May 7, 2002.

115. "Address of Pope John Paul II to Young, Elderly, and Handicapped People," Vancouver, British Columbia, September 18, 1984. On the same trip to Canada, John Paul II addressed handicapped and sick children on a stop in Halifax, Nova Scotia. Speaking directly to the medical personnel who care for such children, John Paul declared: "Your loving devotion, your generous service, your medical and professional expertise — all these are acts of love for the child or the patient, and are acts of love for Christ who is mysteriously present in them. And your charity and devoted care bear witness to the dignity and worth of every human being, even the tiniest and most helpless baby." "Address of Pope John Paul II to the Handicapped and Sick Children, Izaak Walton Killam Hospital (Halifax)," September 14, 1984.

community. . . . Children deserve every care and this is especially true when they are in conditions of dificulty."[116] The following year, in an address recognizing the "Jubilee of the Disabled," John Paul II summoned the medical community to render necessary assistance: "Scientific research, for its part, is called to guarantee *every possible form of prevention*, while protecting life and health."[117]

The magisterium has sought to give voice to a basic right to medical care in at least two other contexts: with respect to children suffering from HIV/AIDS, and with respect to migrant families. The Holy See's call to respect the rights of migrant children is addressed in the next section. Regarding children afflicted with HIV/AIDS, Pope John Paul II wrote in a letter addressed to Kofi Annan on the occasion of a United Nations special session on HIV that "[t]he Catholic Church, through her Magisterium and her commitment to the victims of HIV/AIDS, continues to affirm the sacred value of life."[118] The Holy Father singled out two concerns in particular, both dealing with the right of children to life in the context of HIV/AIDS: "I am particularly concerned about two problems. . . . The transmission of HIV/AIDS from mother to child is an extremely distressing problem. While in developing countries there has been success in noticeably reducing the number of children born with the virus, thanks to suitable treatment, in developing countries, particularly in Africa, those who come into the world with the disease are very numerous and this is a cause of great suffering for families and the community. The second problem is that of access of AIDS patients to medical care, and as far as possible, to anti-retroviral treatment."[119] Subsequent curial pronouncements gave further substance to these concerns.[120]

116. "Address of the Holy Father to the Congress of Disabled Children," December 4, 1999.

117. "Address of John Paul II, Jubilee of the Disabled," December 3, 2000. Cf. "Address of Pope John Paul II to Meeting on Children with Brain Disorders," June 13, 1997 (calling upon the collaboration of states, families, and medical communities in order to work for "the rehabilitation of children born blind, deaf, and mute").

118. "Message of John Paul II to the Secretary-General of the United Nations," June 26, 2001.

119. "Message of John Paul II to the Secretary-General of the United Nations," June 26, 2001.

120. See, for example, "Address of Archbishop Javier Lozano Barragan, Head of the Holy See Delegation to the 26th Special Session of the General Assembly," June 27, 2001: "Unfortunately, in many countries it is impossible to care for HIV/AIDS patients due to the high cost of patented medicines. The Pope reminds us that the Church has consistently taught that there is a 'social mortgage' on all private property, and that this concept must also be applied to 'intellectual property.' The law of profit alone cannot be applied to essential elements in the fight

The Right to Life and Its Application to the Welfare of Children

The Right of Children of Migrants and Refugees to Healthcare

The Holy See has also used the rubric of rights, in particular the right to life, to stress the moral requirement to provide healthcare to the children of migrants, refugees, and those displaced from their homes by wars or by natural catastrophes. Pope Benedict XV, in his encyclicals on the moral requirement to provide for the children displaced by World War I, urged that they be provided not only with food and clothing but appropriate medical care.[121] Presciently recognizing the damage the Great War would cause in those theaters where it was fought, Benedict XV also proclaimed in 1915 a World Day of Migrants and Refugees — a commemoration honored every year since by the Holy See and by other nations and nongovernmental actors alike.[122]

Mention has also been made of Pius XII's encyclical *Quemadmodum,* which called upon the wealthy peoples of the world to relieve the medical as well as the nutritional and other needs of the child-victims of World War II.[123] In August 1952, Pius XII followed this encyclical with an apostolic constitution, *Exsul Familia Nazarethana* (literally, "The Exiled Family from Nazareth"), which proposed a theological framework within which to understand and implement the Church's mission to migrants and refugees. Mary, Joseph, and the infant Jesus, Pius proposed, must serve as "the models and protectors of every migrant, alien and refugee of whatever kind who, whether compelled by fear of persecution or by want, is forced to leave his native land, his beloved parents and relatives, his close friends, and to seek a

against hunger, disease, and poverty." Four and a half years later, Cardinal Barragan returned to this theme: "Faced with the difficult social, cultural, and economic situation in which many countries find themselves, there can be no doubt that a defense and promotion of health is required that is a sign of the unconditional love of everyone, in particular for the poorest and the weakest, and which meets the human needs of every individual and the community. As a result, those laws that do not take into sufficient consideration the equal distribution of conditions of health for everyone must be reformed." See Message of Cardinal Javier Lorenzo Barragan, "On the Occasion of World AIDS Day," December 1, 2005.

121. See Benedict XV, *Paterno Iam Diu* (1919) Benedict called for the urgent collection of "food, medicines, and clothing" to provide relief for the stricken children of World War I (para. 3). Cf. *Annus Iam Plenus,* calling for the collection of "necessaries" to relieve the hunger and sickness of the child-victims of the World War (para. 1).

122. See the remarks by Ellen Sauerbrey, Assistant Secretary for Population, Refugees, and Migration at Georgetown University, January 12, 2007 (http://state.gov/g/prm/rls/79036.htm).

123. Pius XII, *Quemadmodum* (1946): "Without home, without clothing, they shiver in the winter cold and die. And there are no fathers or mothers to warm and clothe them. Ailing, or even in the last stages of consumption, they are without the necessary medicines and medical care" (para. 11).

foreign soil."[124] Concerned principally with the Church's obligation to provide spiritual solace to those who have been displaced from their homes, the Constitution also stands as a moving statement of general principle. Incidentally, the Constitution also acknowledged the importance of Catholic charities for the relief of immigrants in the great migrations of the nineteenth century.[125]

Recent statements and calls to action by the Holy See have highlighted the needs and rights of children forced by circumstance to become refugees. Pope John Paul II helped to set the tone for these developments in a letter he addressed to the United Nations High Commissioner for Refugees in 1982.[126] John Paul II commended the High Commissioner for the United Nations' efforts to provide "food, lodging, . . . medical assistance, and the possibility of instruction" for at-risk children.[127] The Holy Father pledged that the Church would assist in these efforts, both by being a voice of conscience to the world, and by its own relief efforts.[128] John Paul II also used the occasion of one of his World Day of the Sick messages to call attention to dire needs of "whole populations tried by enormous hardships as a result of bloody conflicts whose highest price is often paid by the weak."[129]

An instruction issued by the Pontifical Council for the Pastoral Care of Migrants and Refugees built upon this letter and noted about refugees that "[t]he most striking fact is the presence of a vast majority of children and young people of both sexes, with serious problems of health, schooling, and education."[130] Noting also that Pope John Paul II had asserted that "helping refugees . . . is an essential task,"[131] the document called upon the world to effectuate the protections the United Nations sought to put into place on be-

124. Pius XII, *Quemadmodum* (1946), para. 1.

125. Pius XII, *Quemadmodum* (1946), para. 1: "It is well also to mention here, those numerous institutions for the education of boys and girls, the hospitals and other welfare agencies most beneficially established for the faithful of various language groups and national origins."

126. *Discours du Pape Jean-Paul II à Monsieur le Haut Commissaire des Nations Unies pour les réfugiés,* June 25, 1982.

127. *Discours du Pape Jean-Paul II à Monsieur le Haut Commissaire des Nations Unies,* para. 4: "alimentation, logement, . . . assistance médicale, et possibilités d'instruction."

128. *Discours du Pape Jean-Paul II à Monsieur le Haut Commissaire des Nations Unies,* paras. 6-7.

129. "Message of the Holy Father Pope John Paul II for the 3rd World Day of the Sick," November 21, 1994.

130. Pontifical Council for the Pastoral Care of Migrants and Refugees, "Towards a Pastoral Care of Refugees," para. 4.

131. "Towards a Pastoral Care of Refugees," para. 8.

half of refugees.[132] The document went on to stress its special concern "about the serious conditions in which so many Refugee minors live, and urges that their physical, psychological, and spiritual conditions be improved as much as possible."[133]

A more comprehensive document was issued by the same pontifical council nine years later.[134] The document called upon individuals and world leaders alike to "search for just and lasting solutions to what John Paul II has called 'perhaps the greatest tragedy of all the human tragedies of our time.'"[135] The human person, not international politics or other issues of expediency, should guide the handling of refugees.[136] Refugee camps, which should never be more than "emergency and . . . temporary solution[s]," must provide at least "a minimum of privacy, and medical, educational, and religious services."[137] States, particularly the affluent and developed states, had "concrete responsibilities" toward refugees, which includes a recognition of their human rights.[138] The Church should assume a special solicitude for children placed in such vulnerable settings: "A large percentage of refugees is made up of children, who are the most severely affected by the trauma experienced during their development; their physical, psychological, and spiritual balance is seriously jeopardized."[139]

In June 2000, the Pontifical Council issued a "Jubilee Charter of Rights of Displaced Persons," designed to call upon the world to give recognition to the fundamental rights of refugees and asylum-seekers.[140] These rights included:

132. "Towards a Pastoral Care of Refugees," para. 12.

133. "Towards a Pastoral Care of Refugees," para. 19.

134. Pontifical Council for the Pastoral Care of Migrants and Refugees, "Refugees: A Challenge to Solidarity." This document was produced with the collaboration of the Pontifical Council, Cor Unum.

135. "Refugees: A Challenge to Solidarity," quoting John Paul II, "Address to Refugees in Exile at Morong" (Philippines, February 21, 1981), *Acta Apostolicae Sedis* 73 (1981): 390.

136. "The first point of reference should not be the interests of the State, or national security, but the human person, so that the need to live in community, a basic requirement of the very nature of human beings, will be safeguarded" (para. 9).

137. "Refugees: A Challenge to Solidarity," para. 15.

138. "Refugees: A Challenge to Solidarity," paras. 20-21.

139. "Refugees: A Challenge to Solidarity," para. 28.

140. "Jubilee Charter of Rights of Displaced Persons." The website of the Holy See describes this document as one produced by a working group drawn from members of the Italian Episcopal Conference, the Jesuit Relief Service, the Italian Council for Refugees, and the United Nations High Commission for Refugees. Thus, the Pontifical Council notes, "It is not an official document of the Pontifical Council, but represents a consensus of various organizations on the most important rights of refugees."

> [T]he right of minors and the elderly to a special protection that takes account of their situation of greater physical, economic, and psychological vulnerability[.]
>
> [T]he right of children and of adolescents to education, medical care, and secure environment in which they can creatively develop their energies and potentials.[141]

There is every reason to believe that Pope Benedict XVI will continue to urge states and individuals to fulfill their responsibilities toward the displaced. Addressing the diplomatic corps posted to the Holy See, Pope Benedict proclaimed: "Among the key issues, how can we not think of the millions of people, especially women and children, who lack water, food, or shelter? The worsening scandal of hunger is unacceptable in a world which has the resources, the knowledge, and the means available to bring it to an end."[142] Pope Benedict stressed that war and the consequent displacements caused by conflict compounded the evils inherent in this unjust distribution of resources: "Another concern which looms ever larger is that of the movement of persons: millions of men and women are forced to leave their homes or their native lands because of violence or in order to seek more dignified living conditions."[143] In these statements, Pope Benedict is affiliating his own pontificate with what has become a powerful tradition on behalf of the right to life and well-being on the part of refugees.

Conclusion: Toward a Unified Theory of the Right to Life (and Love)

Recent pronouncements by Pope Benedict XVI point toward the development of a unified theory of the right to life. One might begin with his January 1, 2008 message for the World Day of Peace. Given a specific title, the speech was dedicated to the theme of "The Human Family: A Community of Peace."[144] A healthy, functioning family, Pope Benedict proposed, was a pre-

141. "Jubilee Charter of Rights of Displaced Persons."

142. "Address of His Holiness Pope Benedict XVI to the Diplomatic Corps Accredited to the Holy See," January 8, 2007.

143. "Address of His Holiness Pope Benedict XVI to the Diplomatic Corps Accredited to the Holy See," January 8, 2007.

144. Benedict XVI, "Message for the Celebration of the World Day of Peace, 2008" December 8, 2007.

requisite for any hope of achieving world peace. "The first form of communion between persons," Benedict wrote, "is that born of the love of a man and a woman who decide to enter a stable union in order to build together a *new family*."[145] The very language of the family, he continued, is the language of love. This is a love that is fecund, that replicates itself, and that promotes an awareness of peace through the loving interactions of its members.

But the family, Pope Benedict continued, is not only a community of love; it is a repository of rights and duties. To understand the rights proper to the family, the Holy Father declared, one should consult the "Charter of the Rights of the Family," issued by John Paul II in 1983.[146] Article IV of this document indicated that abortion was excluded from legitimate family life on account of the right to life of the unborn.[147] Article III added that "[t]he family has a right to assistance by society in the bearing and rearing of children."[148]

If the family and its rights and duties constitute the starting point for addressing issues of world peace and justice, Pope Benedict continued, it should also be understood as providing fruitful analogies by which one might develop the components of a proper and harmonious world order. Indeed, Benedict stressed, "Humanity is one great family."[149] Like any family that joyfully accepts new members and that tends to the old and infirm, the entire world should act on the basis of responsibility toward the most vulnerable. In this way, we live out "our lives in an attitude of responsibility before God."[150] "By going back to this supreme principle," Benedict wrote, "we are able to perceive the unconditional worth of each human being, and thus to lay the premises for building a humanity at peace." Absent acceptance of this principle, he stressed, we cease to be a community and become a "mere aggregation."[151]

Pope Benedict's address to the United Nations, delivered in April 2008, represents an expansion on these themes. Restating his understanding of the United Nations' Charter, Benedict declared that it was "capable of respond-

145. Benedict XVI, "Message for the Celebration of the World Day of Peace, 2008."

146. Benedict XVI, "Message for the Celebration of the World Day of Peace, 2008." Cf. "Charter of the Rights of the Family," 1983.

147. Article IV (a), "Charter of the Rights of the Family": "Abortion is a direct violation of the fundamental right to life of the human being."

148. "Charter of the Rights of the Family," Art. III (c).

149. Benedict XVI, "World Day of Peace Message, 2008."

150. Benedict XVI, "World Day of Peace Message, 2008."

151. Benedict XVI, "World Day of Peace Message, 2008."

ing to the demands of the human family."[152] In an allusion to both abortion and other forms of problematic reproductive questions, Pope Benedict declared that we must never allow science to overturn "the order of creation, to the point where not only is the sacred character of life contradicted, but the human person and the family are robbed of their natural identity."[153] Individuals, states, and societies alike have the "responsibility to protect" the dignity of every person and "the unity of the human family."[154]

These premises, Benedict insisted, are the mandatory starting point for further investigation of the operation of the international order. Only by embracing our common humanity, the dignity that flows from it, and our common responsibility to every human life, even the most vulnerable, can leaders of nations hope to understand the profound obligations they have toward the world. Invoking the contributions of the sixteenth-century Dominican Francisco de Vitoria, Benedict noted that the origins of modern international law lie in "the idea of the person as image of the Creator."[155] Protection of the human person in its rights thus becomes the foremost duty of the international order.

Benedict's logic becomes clear at this point and can be summarized in a series of propositions: we are all created beings; we gain our sense of what it means to be a created being in a family that authentically loves all of its members; we emerge from such a family with a heightened sense of responsibility toward all of God's creation; this responsibility requires respect for the rights of others, in particular, the right to life of all persons, beginning with the most vulnerable; this right thus begins with respect for the unborn but it does not end there; we remain duty-bound to protect the integrity of others in all stages of their existence; this duty to protect, and the concomitant right to be free of harm, embraces the many particular manifestations enumerated in this article; individual persons, families, communities, and states alike can put these insights to work in a way that might transform human relationships from the personal, to the local, to the global.

Benedict has now strongly associated himself and his pontificate with the role human rights have played in the international order since World War II. A particular focus of attention in his United Nations address was the *Universal Declaration of Human Rights*. Benedict made it clear that the rights

152. "Address of His Holiness Benedict XVI," at the General Assembly of the United Nations, April 18, 2008.

153. "Address of His Holiness Benedict XVI."

154. "Address of His Holiness Benedict XVI."

155. "Address of His Holiness Benedict XVI."

articulated in that document must be understood within the religious context of their origins:

> This document was the outcome of a convergence of different religious and cultural traditions, all of them motivated by the common desire to place the human person at the heart of institutions, laws and the workings of society, and to consider the human person essential for the world of culture, religion, and science. Human rights are increasingly being presented as the common language and the ethical substratum of international relations. At the same time, the universality, indivisibility, and interdependence of human rights all serve as guarantees safeguarding human dignity. It is evident, though, that the rights recognized and expounded in the *Declaration* apply to everyone by virtue of the common origin of the person, who remains the high-point of God's creative design for the world and for history.[156]

The *Declaration,* in short, must be interpreted in the light of its origins in the natural law. "Removing human rights from this context," the pope noted, "would mean restricting their range and yielding to a relativistic conception, according to which the meaning and interpretation of rights could vary and their universality would be denied in the name of different cultural, political, social, and even religious outlooks."[157]

"[R]ights are universal," Benedict concluded this line of analysis, just like "the human person, the subject of those rights."[158]

This analysis represents a significant step in the direction of unitary theory of the right to life; anything else, Benedict would claim, amounts to relativistic temporizing over matters that constitute permanent truths that should be given general acknowledgment and effect. In this way, Benedict asserts, not only individual rights but family harmony and the peace of the world might be achieved.

156. "Address of His Holiness Benedict XVI."
157. "Address of His Holiness Benedict XVI."
158. "Address of His Holiness Benedict XVI."

PART III

Philosophical and Theological Perspectives

CHAPTER 7

Collective Responsibility for Children in an Age of Orphans

CYNTHIA WILLETT

Introduction

What does it mean in an era of globalization to say that it takes a village to raise a child? Is there collective responsibility for children that extends beyond immediate families across communities and even continents? Do affluent middle-class Americans bear responsibility for Africa's orphans?[1] Given the practical circumstances, one could expect a negative response. The economic and social forces that render us a mobile workforce of individuals without strong roots and communities also attenuate feelings of obligation that social bonds sustain. Our weakened social bonds barely extend to supporting children in local communities, at least as measured in terms of adequate funding for public schools and the incarceration of adolescents. Hardly could we expect these weakened bonds to secure obligations across major geopolitical divides. There is more and more talk about rights, but not necessarily an accompanying sense of collective responsibility or social duty. In my contribution to this volume, I would like to define the best love of the child in terms of collective responsibility for children. The question for my

1. For a compelling account of Africa as a continent of orphans, see Melissa Fay Greene, *There Is No Me without You: One Woman's Odyssey to Rescue Africa's Children* (New York: Bloomsbury, 2006). As Greene emphasizes, many children who lose their parents have extended families who adopt and rear them. Hence, when I refer to children who are orphans, I mean to refer only to those who have no extended family who might care for them. Later in the text, when I use "orphan" as an image for the socially uprooted privileged adult, I mean to identify an icon for a social movement and not to literally identify adults as orphans.

essay is: What could generate a shared sense of social obligation when economic, social, and political forces make orphans, not only of children, but, in a certain sense, of us all?

Liberal Theories of Justice, Selfhood, and Rights

The weak sense of existential connection and social obligation in the United States goes hand-in-hand with a focus in Anglo-Saxon liberal theory on the justice claims of the rational individual. The individual who makes choices based on reason rather than external authority, and who is in this sense autonomous, lies at the center of our rights-oriented political discourse anchored in social contract theory. Such a political framework may secure freedom for individuals to make choices for their own lives; however, it obscures the ways in which individuals are dependent upon others in socioeconomic structures that demand social cooperation to function. These socioeconomic structures are held together by histories, cultures, and communities that typically slip into the background of political theory and yet provide sources for the motivations and meanings for individual choices.[2]

Political theory undervalues these shared sources of selfhood in favor of individual choices. Indeed, an individual whose basic motivations for decisions stem from external sources of meaning and unchosen sources of obligation appears, in our standard liberal discourse, to be lacking autonomy and selfhood. As a consequence, our political discourse centers its political demands on negative rights (or so-called "first generation rights") understood as various kinds of freedom from external interference, including rights to property, free speech, religion, and, more recently, privacy. The assumption that mature individuals are autonomous and not in some ways dependent on others can make it difficult to argue persuasively that positive liberties (so-called "second-generation rights") such as the right to healthcare, employment, and education are just as vital to freedom as negative liberties. Still, liberal theorists do with some success defend positive rights, arguing that these rights to secure basic needs for economic and social well-being are part of the meaning of freedom. Whatever success these

2. For two very different kinds of argument in favor of this view, see Judith Butler, *Precarious Life: The Power of Mourning and Violence* (New York: Verso, 2004), and Michael Walzer, *Politics and Passion* (New Haven: Yale University Press, 2004). I am especially grateful for a conversation with Martha Fineman that helped to clarify for me the value of equality in social justice theory.

theorists have in securing positive rights, they have less in accounting for the sources of connection and solidarity that might ground collective responsibility. In fact, many major political theorists neglect to develop these sources and their accompanying rights ("third-generation rights") altogether.[3]

The reason for the inadequate attention to positive rights and rights to solidarity can be explained in part through the underlying equation of political subjectivity with the capacity for choice rather than with having a range of options and social relationships that, arguably, make choices meaningful and materially possible in the first place. This equation leads many liberal theorists to consign positive liberties to background conditions for the flourishing of mature individuals who are envisioned predominantly as separate individuals rather than as relational individuals with commitments, affiliations, histories, or even sexual desires that connect them with others in ways that they do not always choose. There are significant social and historical strands of our relational identities that cannot be denied except in bad faith. In the United States, current social identities, for example, reflect the history of slavery and its aftermath in Jim Crow and institutional racism. However, the standard liberal framework renders it difficult to conceptualize any clear alternative to resting political principles on the economic and moral independence of the individual other than in terms of relinquishing freedom through some form of authoritarianism or dependence upon the state.[4] As feminists have argued, one consequence is that those persons who are visibly dependent upon others for either their livelihood or for decisions regarding their lives, including children but also the disabled, are not rendered "subjects of justice" but "objects of care."[5] While a rights-based theory

3. On the distinction between the three generations of rights, see Stephen P. Marks, "Emerging Human Rights: A New Generation for the 1980s?" *Rutgers Law Review* 33, no. 2 (Winter 1981): 435-42; Karl Vasak, "A 30 Year Struggle," *The UNESCO Courier* (November 1977); and also Karl Vasak, "Pour une troisième génération des droits de l'homme," in *Études et essais sur le droit international humanitaire et sur les principes de la Croix-Rouge en l'honneur de Jean Pictet/Studies and Essays in International Humanitarian Law and Red Cross Principles in Honor of Jean Pictet*, ed. Christophe Swinarski, 1984. For a defense of the priority of positive rights over negative rights, see Joy Gordon, "The Concept of Human Rights: The History and Meaning of Its Politicization," *Brooklyn Journal of International Law* 23, no. 689 (1998).

4. Isaiah Berlin, "Two Concepts of Liberty," in *Four Essays on Liberty* (Oxford: Oxford University Press, 1969), pp. 118-72.

5. See Martha Nussbaum, *Frontiers of Justice: Disability, Nationality, Species Membership* (Cambridge, MA: Belknap Press, 2006); henceforth cited in the text as *FJ;* Eva Feder Kittay, "Human Dependency and Rawlsian Equality," in *Feminists Rethink the Self*, ed. Diana T. Meyers (Boulder, CO: Westview, 1997), pp. 219-66; and her *Love's Labor: Essays on Women, Equality, and*

may support rights for dependents, the focus of rights theory is on independent adults who make rational choices. Given this focus, liberal theory has not been able to generate a strong sense of social obligation for dependents. As it stands, liberal theory renders the care of dependents a private virtue and not a public obligation. Liberal political systems cannot generate a sufficiently strong sense of a collective, political obligation to dependents without altering the grounds for selfhood. Hence, I am proposing that justice theory begin by reenvisioning mature adults as in some sense like children, needy and dependent, or alternatively, to render visible the invisible networks of support for apparently self-standing individuals, and then, on this radically altered basis, address questions of social responsibility to children.

My aim, of course, is not to lay the groundwork for an authoritarian society, one that fails to support basic liberties and renders us all dependents of the state, but on the contrary to deepen our understanding of liberty and its paradoxes. Most important, I am arguing that the very ties that bind us can also in a sense make us free. This appears less paradoxical once we build a theory of justice that roots the core identity of individuals in social as well as economic relationships and locates freedom in strengthening diverse social bonds rather than weakening them, as Anglo-Saxon theories of freedom would typically do. My aim is to shift our focus to a political and ethical framework that intertwines freedom with responsibility more fundamentally than has Anglo-Saxon liberalism. In this altered framework, individual choices would be viewed as interwoven with the negotiation of relationships and the ethical obligations that these relationships impose. Among these obligations would be collective responsibility for children, inflected through multiple social relationships and networks of care. Responsibility for children, including not just our own but also orphans, would then not be exclusively or even primarily privatized but would function through the empowerment of local communities, particular cultures, and a network of primary and secondary nurturers, childcare providers, and teachers.

John Rawls's classic *Theory of Justice* exemplifies the tendency of liberal theory to prioritize negative liberties of independent individuals free from external interference at some expense to those forms of liberty that entail positive rights while neglecting solidarity rights altogether.[6] Under his vision, liberal theory does insist upon public assistance for covering basic eco-

---

Dependency (New York: Routledge, 1999); Nancy Folbre, *The Invisible Heart* (New York: New Press, 2001); Susan Moller Okin, *Justice, Gender, and the Family* (New York: Basic Books, 1989).

6. John Rawls, *A Theory of Justice* (Cambridge, MA: Harvard University Press, 1971).

nomic and social needs in order to secure the material conditions of freedom. The satisfaction of these needs through the allocation of primary social goods allows individuals to exercise their negative liberties and make moral choices. However, it is clear that for Rawls liberty itself is primarily understood in negative terms. That is, freedom is freedom from external interference and is measured in terms of the ability to make choices, and not measured primarily in either the range and quality of options (positive freedom) or in networks of cooperation (solidarity). The commitment to autonomy may be consistent with promoting sufficient material conditions for individual well-being for those whose social network of support functions well and disappears into the background of their personal lives. However, my claim is that this emphasis on autonomy provides very little basis for understanding any deeper social obligation to care for dependents or, in the terms that I prefer, for understanding wide-scale social solidarity.

Nussbaum's Critique of Rawlsian Liberalism and the "Capability Theory" Alternative

This failure of standard liberal theory to include dependents as subjects of justice goes right to the heart of the concerns of Martha Nussbaum's critique of Rawlsian liberalism. Nussbaum argues quite forcefully that the Rawlsian emphasis on negative liberties of mature, rational individuals renders care for children as well animals and the mentally and physically disabled anomalies for a liberal theory of justice (*FJ*, p. 19). As long as standard liberal theories of justice locate the primary bearer of rights and liberties in rational individuals, and not in dependents of any kind, care for dependents will be a secondary concern. Indeed, as Nussbaum painstakingly establishes, Rawls's theory of justice fails to take up the political claims or basic needs of dependents in his account of the basic principles of justice. This liberalism consigns dependents to objects of private concern or charity, not concerns of justice.

In order to account for how dependents could be the subjects of justice claims, and not merely objects of private concern, Nussbaum turns to a specific type of rights theory that she, along with Amartya Sen, term "capability theory."[7] The theory is anchored in Aristotle's account of the virtues (or

7. Amartya Sen, "Capability and Well-Being," in *The Quality of Life,* ed. Martha Nussbaum and Amartya Sen (Oxford: Clarendon, 1993), pp. 30-53.

excellences) that allow for human flourishing. Nussbaum revises Aristotle's list, proposing ten capabilities for the human species including life, emotions, thought, affiliation, play, and control over the environment, and she argues that a liberal theory of rights should serve to justify at least a minimum degree of functioning in all ten categories.

The classical origin of capability theory in Aristotle's conception of the person as fundamentally social and affective reemerges in the early Marx, where this conception poses a romantic alternative to Enlightenment conceptions of the person as rational and nonrelational. At the same time, like Marxist theories of justice, capability theory grows out of egalitarian Enlightenment sentiments regarding our equal moral worth as persons. Beyond both Aristotle and Marx, capability theory allows us to understand how dependents of our own species as well as animals might be considered to have rights and entitlements based on their capabilities rather than simply be subordinate objects of care.

I think that we can strengthen our conception and commitment to rights and responsibilities regarding children with a stronger view of how normal adults are in some crucial ways, no less than children, dependent on others.[8] In order to emphasize this otherwise rather minor difference with Nussbaum and feminists who aim to augment liberalism with a political ethics of care for dependents, I approach the concerns of dependency through a political ethics based on solidarity. My claim is that a sense of our own fundamental dependence should not rest on conditions such as childhood or disability inasmuch as these conditions are viewed as "not normal" and hence not relevant for the basic way in which we think about ourselves and frame our political ethics. On the contrary, our sense of our own dependence should grow out of an awareness of how each and every one of us is sustained by, and hence also vulnerable to, larger forces that we do not control. These forces include but are not by any means limited to the impact of the environment on our private lives, past and contemporary social traumas (including American slavery and the prison system) that harm the social milieu that we live in, and the dehumanizing effects of globalization. The aim is to offer some thoughts on transforming the individualism of our normative framework, where individuals are viewed as autonomous moral agents, to a framework in which vital moral decisions regarding any matter that has an impact on others is

8. And at the same, we need to understand how children are also agents. See, for example, Bonnie J. Miller-McLemore, *Let the Children Come: Reimaging Childhood from a Christian Perspective* (Hoboken, NJ: John Wiley & Sons, 2003).

viewed as achieved through dialogue and negotiation with those others, including those who may not share the same basic intuitions; and that this need for dialogue and negotiation, rather than private decision making, is viewed as the norm because of our interdependence. I intend these thoughts to counter the neoliberal tilt of current Anglo-Saxon frameworks of justice. True, normal adults possess critical powers of reasoning, experiences, and skills that render them self-sufficient in ways that differ from those who are mentally and/or economically dependent upon others. However, we are all significantly bound to others as well. This altered perspective on who we are should, I am arguing, enable us to strengthen the project of rendering children subjects of justice rather than merely objects of care, but not by treating children as radically different from ourselves. We are all in one sense or another dependent on networks of cooperation and care, and recognition of this vulnerability should alter our sense of what justice is. Solidarity is a universal condition for well-being, not just a secondary concern for a system of justice that focuses on autonomy. In this respect, I think that Nussbaum's critique of Rawlsian liberalism does not go far enough.

This is because Nussbaum maintains the standard liberal commitment to treating "normal adults" as separate individuals. Given this commitment to some strong degree of ontological separatism, Nussbaum finds the need to anchor political principles of justice, including responsibility for dependents, in moral sympathy. The notion of moral sympathy is not based on an underlying connectedness but on the assumption that mature individuals are morally and economically independent, and in this sense ontologically disconnected and separate. Moral sympathy, and not economic or social and cultural forms of affective dependence, functions as the glue to unify us. My question is whether this thesis regarding our nature along with the subsequent reliance on moral sympathy for principles of justice adequately captures our social, economic, and affective nature and therefore provides a sufficiently strong basis for collective responsibility, the kind of basis that I am seeking under the term "solidarity."

Interestingly, Nussbaum does on occasion mention a view of the person as at its core interdependent, but whatever this interdependence might mean, capability theory, as Nussbaum develops it, focuses on individuals and their choices, and not on relationships, structures, or histories that condition social justice. My contention is that a theory of justice that takes interdependence seriously should attend more centrally to ways in which we find ourselves through ongoing entanglements, burdens, and debts that are not fully chosen and yet entail through our very identities social obligations.

Nussbaum, however, aims instead to preserve individual choice as the existential center of the person. Socially or historically inflected theories of human nature, such as those found in Aristotle and Marx, which focus not on separate individuals who make choices but on individuals in relationships whose judgments are informed by social conditions, offer an alternative framework for political ethics, one that should be able to significantly augment what capability theory can do. This alternative framework provides a firmer ground for the possibilities as well as the limits of social cooperation, including the care of dependents.

We can clearly see that the basis for social cooperation remains underdeveloped in Nussbaum's theory, in her claim that it is an advantage of capability theory that it focuses not on responsibility but on entitlements. She explains that establishing basic entitlements to social goods is a much more straightforward task than discerning wherein lies the responsibility to secure them. She urges us to consider the example of worker exploitation under global capitalism. It is easier to determine the degree to which capitalism has stunted the worker's capabilities, she argues, than to agree on who has the duty or responsibility to prevent this harm from happening. Moreover, Nussbaum seems fairly confident that a list of basic entitlements might generate international consensus in the near future, at least if the list is kept relatively vague and open-ended. A theory of capabilities allows us to avoid controversies and attain the degree of international agreement on basic normative claims that would move justice forward.

This is not to say that there should not be social obligations, according to Nussbaum. On the contrary, she argues that there are social obligations to care for dependents, and in fact to assure actual functioning of normal human capabilities in children. The larger social obligations are best exercised not by individuals or specific parties, she argues, but by institutions based partly in nations and finally in the world community. In particular, women should not be coerced or manipulated to continue shouldering the primary burden of caregiving.

Consensus on matters of justice at any level is hard to come by. Any claim that strong agreement — indeed overlapping international consensus — can be generated on basic normative claims should raise some suspicions. In the United States alone, conflicting views on basic moral issues from gay rights and abortion to children's rights hardly rest easily with the assumption that there might be some objective basis for transcending religious and other metaphysical differences for a shared stance on political principles. Any concrete or substantial proposal regarding basic rights let alone responsibilities cannot avoid controversy, and will require some kind of political process of dialogue and negotiation to work out a compromise as well as a significant degree of local control. Nussbaum, however, preempts the process by appealing to objective natural standards that presumably would allow us to transcend some of our religious and other deeper differences. However, this assumption, that there are natural standards that transcend religious and other differences, does not reflect the fact that many if not most people hold religious or other metaphysical beliefs near the core of their concepts or intuitions of justice. These people disagree not only on what values are most real but also on what values are natural and even to what degree to respect values that in some sense are natural and immanent rather than transcendent. Moreover, as soon as Nussbaum gives her theory of capabilities any degree of concrete interpretation or application, she is in trouble. Liberal theorists cannot avoid controversies, and to the extent that they do, they avoid core issues of justice as well as the dialogues and other political processes required to generate social cooperation.

Even apart from the assertion of particular rights for adults, the claim that children, animals, and the mentally disabled have individual rights is controversial. Nussbaum's appeal to our universal capacity for moral sympathy along with judgment to secure these claims is too simple. Not only is this appeal to universal sympathy likely to fail to generate agreement through dialogue and negotiation with others — we typically have sympathy only for those we believe to be deserving of sympathy — but the appeal to compassion to secure rights claims for dependents does not adequately support the aim of establishing dependents as subjects of justice rather than as objects of charity. Let me explain why I think this is so, and how I think we might return to Aristotelian and Marxist traditions to move capability theory beyond an appeal to moral sentiments to more substantial demands for justice through solidarity.

A Critique of Nussbaum and the Limits of Altruism

Nussbaum aims to account for how we discern the basic needs and entitlements of children, the disabled, and nonhuman species as claims of justice rather than as private moral or religious concerns. However, as she points out, it is difficult to rest any theory of justice on the assumption that human behavior is motivated by moral sympathy between otherwise detached individuals. Social contract theories tracing back from Rawls to

Hobbes do not rely on altruism, compassion, or benevolent sentiments of any kind to secure agreement to principles of justice or produce action in accordance with just political principles. These theorists maintain that people are far more likely to be motivated by egotistic considerations, and that for this reason they rest their political principles on appeals to mutual advantage. Nonetheless, Nussbaum argues that mutual advantage is not likely to secure a place for children and other dependents as subjects, and as a consequence the major liberal theories consign dependents to objects of unpaid and disempowered care work. This is a consequence that has unfair implications for both children and caregivers. For example, under this view, primary caregivers become one more class of dependents. And children cannot make claims on their own behalf.

My question is how we might argue persuasively to adults who perceive themselves as morally and economically independent that the claims of dependents are of equal significance to their own? Nussbaum writes that it is highly unlikely to expect with John Stuart Mill that "people can be taught to think that the happiness of all the world's people is part of their own happiness" (*FJ*, p. 412). For, as she points out, people act out of motives of envy or aggression toward others at least as often as they act through feelings of benevolence. The right institutions help to sustain better behavior, she argues. However, Nussbaum observes that Kant is right on one important point: it will be difficult see how we can expect consistently moral behavior to happen unless people join "churches of the right sort, which turn out to mean a type of church that has never yet existed" (*FJ*, p. 408). Still, Nussbaum does insist and rightly so that our species is capable from time to time and in specific contexts of acting upon a sense of fellowship not based on mutual advantage alone. Individuals often make tremendous sacrifices for others. The question is how to secure fellowship for all (including orphans) beyond mutual advantage in a way that is realistic?

Nussbaum herself brings her observations on liberalism and autonomy to a quick end with appeals to altruism (*FJ*, p. 412). She does not presume that people automatically develop moral sentiments of sympathy for others, but she does believe that a "society aspiring to justice . . . must devote sustained attention to the moral sentiments and their cultivation — in child development, in public education, in public rhetoric, in the arts," and of course she is partly right (*FJ*, p. 414). And while she does not claim that she has yet established either the political or psychological grounds for this education of the moral sentiments, she closes her argument with a plea for its necessity and a promise to attend to its possibility in her future work.

While there is no doubt that a society that cultivates a moral climate of sympathy and compassion rather than, say, greed and arrogance or even the narrow if fair-minded pursuit of self-interest, is a significant part of any stable progressive social change, a theory of justice that turns too quickly to sympathy to link otherwise separate individuals does not draw fully on either classical or dialectical insights into human sociality and our economic, psychological, and social interdependence. Rather than assume that individuals are ontologically separate, we might consider the implications of reframing political ethics in the concern for the well-being of individuals who are, in the first instance, related economically, culturally, and socially to others, and who are fundamentally needy and dependent, and not just needy because of temporary conditions such as immaturity or because of abnormal circumstances of development.

We could contrast two views with regard to the origins of the sense of our obligation to others. The first picture borrows from Nussbaum, and poses normal people (those who have met minimal standards of functioning as indexed to our species norm) as capable of making moral choices on their own apart from the guidance of external authorities or built-in obligations due to, say, historical debts or social positions that they might occupy. As Nussbaum explains, according to this view individuals are not defined in their core identity as belonging to a people or larger group, not at least in any way that a theory of justice would have to acknowledge. Still, Nussbaum insists, these otherwise detached individuals do not make decisions on the basis of reason alone but are affective and social creatures. Accordingly, these individuals forge their connections to others through sympathy. There is no original experience or language of connectedness, only an original ontology of separate identity. Any larger social, historical, or economic bonds, at least those that have import for theories of justice, emerge at best through cultivating our quasi-biological species potential for altruism and making individual moral choices accordingly. My concern is that species altruism and choices based on altruism as well as self-interest (in fact, on the basis of this dichotomy) are fairly thin for developing a notion of shared responsibility (solidarity) in the face of ongoing racial, religious, and geopolitical conflicts and the finitude of our fellow-feeling.

While Nussbaum aims for capability theory to reflect what she argues to be the underlying links between negative and positive rights, or first- and second-generation rights, in stronger terms than standard liberalism, her theory does not approach solidarity rights at all. This failure points to its major weakness. Nussbaum makes occasional references to social fellowship based on friendship rather than self-interest (*FJ*, pp. 284, 270, 350); she even at one point mentions in passing that we might develop our human functioning for the sake — not of the self per se — but of friendships and social relationships (*FJ*, p. 364). But any strong assumptions regarding interdependence would not cohere with her overall ontological separatism. I assume that her relatively strong allegiance to a separatist ontology stems from her firm stance against utilitarianism, and in particular its willingness to subordinate the interests of individuals to the larger interests of society. But regardless, her ontology obscures a full treatment of the range of socially informed motivations and interests that shape individuals. In lieu of a thorough consideration of how capabilities are thickly mediated by culture, history, and other social processes, and at the same time, the obligations that our social identities entail, Nussbaum gives pride of place to individual moral choice and relies upon a single moral sentiment to enlarge individual responsibility beyond the self.

Moreover, in a gesture that seems to avoid the larger social processes required to deal with conflicting moral perspectives on basic questions of justice, Nussbaum claims that the basic claims of justice can rest on quasi-biological species norms. The appeal to a quasi-biological notion of our human capabilities, including the possibility of altruism, is meant to secure the claim that these capabilities are universal and that normative judgments based on them should generate agreement. The problem is that this quasi-biological appeal to species norms is way too vague to do any really normative work apart from an understanding of larger social processes, processes that seem at least at this time to generate conflict rather than mutual sympathy. Conflict and competition seem to be just as quasi-biological as sympathy. I would think that only after diverse groups of people examine capabilities and limitations across particular historical, cultural, and socioeconomic conditions, can the more difficult work of finding a basis for establishing norms across major geopolitical sources of conflict begin. And even then, agreement will require negotiation, reparations, and compromises to generate social cooperation. Any simple appeal to objective norms as quasi-biological and universal preempts the hard-won process necessary for social cooperation, and, consequently, such an appeal undertaken apart from this process appears to be naïve or hubristic.

The gestalt switch in our political framework from individual autonomy (ontological separatism) to connected individuals (or, a relational ontology) requires shifting our focus from individual capabilities or activities (*FJ*, p. 346) to functioning relationships, or at least, to individuals with the capability to function in cooperative relationships, relationships that are currently consigned to the backdrop of our thinking. This shift in focus of background and foreground prepares us to argue more forcefully for the interconnection of freedom and responsibility.

Care for Children and Justice in Social Relations

Let's return to the particular problem of care for children. As we have said, Nussbaum insists that the care of children is a responsibility of the world community (*FJ*, p. 321), and in a basic way this seems right. However, the attempt to anchor this rather vague duty through an equally vague appeal to moral sympathy could benefit from a gestalt shift to socioeconomic and even, as I shall claim, cultural structures of dependency. Consider the reliance of the developed nations (and therefore of individuals who thrive in developed nations) on overseas markets and immigrant labor to sustain high levels of consumption and productivity, and the effect of U.S. tariffs on cotton or the availability of affordable medication on the well-being of families in Africa. Appeals to species altruism might strengthen commitments to justice in these diverse spheres, but apart from an economic grasp of intertwined social identities, and moral obligations that grow out of these economic dependencies, we may lack the means to check the greed, arrogance, or ignorance that readily undo any simple appeals to justice through sympathy. Even worse, apart from an understanding of the way that seemingly self-sufficient individuals and nations depend upon poorer nations for cheap resources and labor, well-intentioned acts of the world citizens to assist others may appear to the rest of the world as gestures of power and privilege, not humility. Justice for dependents on the part of the world community would need to avoid the social hubris of rich northern nations rescuing brown children from failing brown families.

A justice theory that focuses on social relationships rather than individual moral choice should allow us to take into account these kinds of considerations, at least more so than a view that focuses on individuals and consigns their relationships and dependencies to the background of normative thought. The alternative picture might begin with the Aristotelian assumption that individuals, like children, fail to thrive apart from friendships or families as well as communities, and that even mature adults depend for their sense of self on a sense of belonging that is cultural as much as social. A biology-based theory of evolution might support the need for individuals to define themselves as part of groups in order to survive. Certainly an Aristotelian approach would emphasize the significance of cultivating friendly networks of cooperation and the attitudes and habits that sustain them; and for Marxism, this is the goal of social change. Moreover, it is important today to expand the human need to belong to an emerging world community. However, I am arguing, the appeal to moral sympathy to sustain this world community remains too abstract and vague to account for the concrete and substantial ways in which our sense of belonging (and survival) requires a multilayered social infrastructure and a developed sense of our social and cultural identities.[9] The cultivation of moral sympathy for humanity should be part of any theory of justice, but this appeal cannot afford to skip over the multilayered social infrastructure required to hold together specific cultures, communities, or peoples, and thus the need for a fully developed relational ontology.

Moreover, this social infrastructure is not the result of altruistic gestures of moral sympathy from one individual to another individual. This structure expands from concrete sources of social identity, beginning with family-based caregiving to the work that holds together neighborhoods and tribal associations, maintains cultural and educative efforts in schools, and finally the work of citizenship that sustains nations as well as international organizations and social movements. As a part of this larger network of care, the work of caring for and educating children along with other care work is misrepresented if it is viewed too simply as charity, instinctual (maternal) love, or unskilled labor.

That is, care for dependents should not be viewed as merely an act of justice at all. Care work is work and should be viewed as such. Indeed, it is part of the work that sustains not only families but also communities and cultures. Care work, whether performed by kin or immigrant nannies and daycare workers, should be understood as contributing to the economy just as teaching, artistic creation, medical intervention, or any other labor that may or may not be a labor of love. The fact that work traditionally associated with women is not typically viewed as real work, work that requires a degree of skill and training, and that creates social value, is a major source of injustice. One problem with the view of caregivers as dependent creatures in contrast

9. On the importance of local networks of care to sustain both children and a larger cosmopolitanism, see Sylvia Ann Hewlett and Cornel West, *The War Against Parents* (Boston: Houghton Mifflin, 1998); and Cynthia Willett, "Parenting and Other Human Casualties in the Pursuit of Academic Excellence," in *Theorizing Backlash*, ed. Anita M. Superson and Ann E. Cudd (Lanham, MD: Rowman & Littlefield, 2002), pp. 119-32.

with the rest of us who work for a living is that it sustains this injustice rather than directly challenging it. The appeal to solidarity rights on the basis of a norm of mutual dependency aims to counter this source of inequity.[10]

Apart from a conception of our interdependence, and the various forms of work that generate social cooperation, capability theory falls short of providing a moral basis for world community. Instead, we are left with a cosmopolitanism that is stripped of any concrete cultural, social, or economic infrastructure as well as recognition for some of the kinds of care work and some of the responsibilities that maintaining this infrastructure requires. The simple and direct moral appeal for the world community to secure entitlements for children along with other dependents does not suffice to deal with the ethical questions and political disagreements that a thick social infrastructure poses.

The world community should support the flourishing of children, but not by just acknowledging that children, like adults, have entitlements. Instead, the world community should view these children, like adults, as connected to the families, communities, and institutions that sustain them. The first priority of justice for children should be to support in economic and social terms the work of care, and the relationships that care work builds, including local communities, neighborhoods, and cultures. Examples of this kind of support include those practices found in Mexico and Africa of awarding cash payments to parents who bring in their children for routine medical care or assist their children with their homework. Adopting AIDS orphans rebuilds families, but sustaining the original families and communities — in part by procuring AIDS medicines and AIDS prevention measures — is even more important. Immigration and economic policies should reflect the need to sustain and strengthen communities and families in other ways as well. Care work should be viewed as real work and remunerated as such.

From these networks of care emerges the sense of social obligation that should define the context of our individual choices. A direct and unmediated appeal to sympathy along with negative and positive rights cannot gen-

10. For an extended argument on awarding appropriate cash payments for care work, including parenting, see Cynthia Willett, *The Soul of Justice* (Ithaca, NY: Cornell University Press, 2001), pp. 80-98; for an argument that care work should be a universal citizen duty, but one that unfortunately incorrectly attributes to me the view that childcare should not be paid work if performed by a biological parent, see Allison Weir, "The Global Universal Caregiver," in *Constellations* 12, no. 3 (2005): 308-30. See also Nancy Fraser, "After the Family Wage," in *Justice Interruptus* (New York: Routledge, 1997), pp. 41-66.

erate sufficient motivation and orientation to social responsibility unless our identities have already been developed in terms that are relational.

The rendering visible of the labor of care not only in families but in communities reveals the way in which not just children but all of us are dependent upon networks that sustain meaningful connection. Without these core connections for sustaining individual identities, feelings of emptiness and alienation render flourishing difficult, whether we explain this flourishing in classical or romantic terms. Principles of justice require not only moral sympathy but also a sense of the self as embedded in cooperative relationships and the rights and responsibilities that are based on sustaining these relationships.

Moral sympathy for dependents readily slides into a downward-looking pity for those perceived as weak, and for this reason among others has not proved to be useful, for example, in concerns for justice articulated in some aspects of feminism or in critical race theory. Moral outrage, in contrast, may more likely express respect for the moral equality of the victim of harm and suggest a shared perspective and even underlying connection. As I have argued extensively in *The Soul of Justice,* such a stance of connection can also lead to developing a sense of collective responsibility that does not rest, as do predominant models, on either guilt or economic considerations alone, but on richer relational identities.

Models of Collective Responsibility and Our Care for Children

I am claiming that rich ethical conceptions of collective responsibility require a political ethics that is not based on the autonomous individual but on the relational one. There are two existing and apparently opposed models of collective responsibility that take us close to where I would like us to be. I would like to incorporate insights from both of these models but move yet one step further.

The first model, known as the liability model,[11] is used in the United States in debates over reparations for slavery. This model turns on a sense of debt, unacknowledged benefits, or unearned privileges based on social identity (e.g., being white in the U.S.), and the accompanying sense of guilt for political crimes or social harms committed not by individuals but by groups

11. Joel Feinberg, "Collective Responsibility," in *Doing and Deserving: Essays in the Theory of Responsibility* (Princeton: Princeton University Press, 1970), pp. 221-51.

to which one belongs. These arguments turn on our inability to avoid connection and identity with larger groups, and they demand acknowledgment and/or reparations for crimes or damages to victim groups. This model offers one part of a larger notion of collective responsibility, one that emerges from a fully relational conception of the self.

A second, and apparently alternative, notion of shared responsibility has been developed most recently by Iris Young, who terms it the social connection model.[12] Young argues that first-world consumers share political responsibility for third-world workers based on socioeconomic interdependence. Consumers in wealthy nations are not to blame for the working conditions in sweatshops or factories in underdeveloped nations, but they are part of a larger socioeconomic system from which they benefit, and they share responsibility for the effects of this system on working conditions. Any individual who participates in the socioeconomic system has the obligation to assure that the system works fairly. This strikes me not as simply an alternative but as a second part of a larger notion of collective responsibility.

Neither of these two models of responsibility fully accounts for collective responsibility for children, the disabled, or animals. The first model focuses on reparations for past crimes, whereas the collective responsibility for children aims to ensure that children in the present flourish. The second model focuses on mutual dependence in systems that produce material wealth or satisfy material needs. Except as child laborers, children do not count as agents under the socioeconomic model of social connection. Our connection with children is often based more on affective and cultural sources of identity and not primarily on economic calculations of material needs.

A model of collective responsibility, one that extends to children, might instead address the affective and cultural center of our identities as both adults and children. Instead of viewing adults as rational autonomous agents, and children as immature adults, this model would require that we view both children and adults as socially connected, affective persons who are driven in part by a need to belong to something larger than themselves. Adults and children share meaningful forms of interdependencies. Not only are children and adults part of a global socioeconomic system; they are also social and emotional creatures who participate in a network of affective, cultural, and socio-psychological relationships. Children are more like adults

12. Iris Marion Young, "Responsibility and Global Labor Justice," *Journal of Political Philosophy* 12, no. 4 (2004): 365-88.

and adults more like children than standard models of justice assume. This means giving more attention to the affective, cultural, and economic networks of solidarity necessary for adults no less than children to flourish. This model of collective responsibility should prioritize "no family left behind" policies (living wages, community-based and culturally rich public education, investment in cities, alternatives to incarceration, and a strengthened family) over a narrow focus either on mature and rational citizens or on individual children and their needs. In this way, we might counter the extreme tendencies of a neoliberal politics of self-interested individualism and yet do so without relying precipitously on the universal compassion or moral sympathy of world citizens without a culture or a history of meaningful connections. Instead of the individual or the universal, we might turn direct resources to multilayered networks of care work — networks that would serve to enhance our solidarity with uprooted, disconnected orphans. And ironically, this sense of solidarity should bear not only on faraway children but also on those orphans that we are, in a sense, ourselves. We never outgrow the need to belong.

CHAPTER 8

Original Sin and Christian Parenting: A Constructive Proposal

RICHARD R. OSMER

Introduction

During my daughter's first year of high school, she took a required course on American history. In this course, she was asked to read only one text by a theologian of the colonial period: Jonathan Edwards's sermon, "Sinners in the Hands of an Angry God." Her response was telling: "That's a pretty scary sermon. It was kind of hard to be a Christian when we talked about it in class. You and Mom never taught me that God is so angry and threatening. What do you think of Edwards?" I remember quite vividly my ambivalence as a parent about how to respond.

On the one hand, I longed for my daughter to learn the vocabulary of the Christian faith, a vocabulary that includes the concept of sin. I wanted her to go beyond a lingering cliché of the Enlightenment still found in textbooks, media, and art, that Christianity is totally preoccupied with sin, fear, guilt, and divine wrath. The selection of this sermon by Edwards as a window on American Puritanism is a case in point. The textbook did not contain even a hint of Edwards's extensive writings on divine grace and beauty or on human discernment, affections, and virtue. Yet Edwards's use of the language of sin in this sermon only makes sense within the broader context of his theology and practice. I remember wondering how I might help my daughter learn the richness of concepts like sin in the face of one-sided portraits like this one, common in our society today.

On the other hand, I remember being equally concerned about a very different set of issues. The concept of sin, especially original sin, has lent itself to a wide range of abuses in Christian parenting and education. In the name of saving their children from human nature's tendency toward sin, parents and teachers have sometimes used extremely harsh methods of punishment, attempting to literally beat the hell out of their children. They have also sometimes labeled "natural" emotions and desires like anger, self-assertion, positive self-esteem, and sexual attraction as manifestations of sin. They have advocated breaking the will of the child or enforcing strict moral codes that suppress such emotions and desires — all in the name of saving the child from sin. Such attitudes and practices do not, I believe, reflect God's love of children, and I did not want my daughter to accept the understanding of sin on which they are based.

My ambivalence as a parent is not unique. If curriculums on Christian parenting and sex education are any indication, this ambivalence is widespread in mainline Protestant denominations. Such programs have downplayed or eliminated the language of sin altogether. This is especially the case with regard to the concept of original sin, so central to classical Christianity. In this chapter, I explore this concept and its potential contribution to Christian parenting in a manner appropriate to practical theology.[1] I begin with present practice, proceed to the articulation of an action-guiding, normative perspective, and conclude by indicating the implications for present practice.

Original Sin: The Discordant Language of a Missional Church

A number of years ago, I heard the historian of religious education, Robert Lynn, develop an image comparing the ecology of Christian education in nineteenth-century America with that of the present.[2] Imagine a circle, he said, composed of four institutions that contribute to education: the family, church, common school, and media. For much of the nineteenth century, all of these institutions included a significant component of Christian educa-

1. Broadly speaking, this approach is found in Don Browning, *A Fundamental Practical Theology: Descriptive and Strategic* Proposals (Minneapolis: Fortress Press, 1991); Johannes van der Ven, *Practical Theology: An Empirical Approach* (Kampen: Kok Pharos, 1993); and Richard Osmer, *Practical Theology: An Introduction* (Grand Rapids: Eerdmans, forthcoming).

2. Robert W. Lynn, Sprunt Lectures, Union Theological Seminary. Lynn was drawing on the ecological approach to American education articulated by Lawrence Cremin in such books as *American Education: The Colonial Experience, 1607-1783* (New York: Harper & Row, 1970).

tion. For example, *The New England Primer* was used in many common schools and taught children theology along with their ABCs:[3]

A In Adam's Fall
  We sinned all.
B Thy Life to Mend
  This Book Attend.

It intermingled lessons and moral stories with the Apostles' Creed, the Lord's Prayer, the Westminster Shorter Catechism, and the Ten Commandments put to rhyme for easy memorization:

1. Thou shalt have no more gods but me.
2. Before no idol bend thy knee.
3. Take not the name of God in vain.
4. Dare not the Sabbath day profane,
5. Give both thy parents honor due.
6. Take heed that thou no murder do.
7. Abstain from words and deeds unclean.
8. Steal not, though thou be poor and mean.
9. Make not a willful lie, nor love it.
10. What is thy neighbor's dare not covet.

Lynn portrayed this ecology of educational institutions as emerging out of the Reformation of the sixteenth century, an ecology in which families, common schools, media, and congregations worked together to provide young people *both* general and Christian education. He then invited the audience to walk around this circle today. Virtually none of these institutions contribute much in the way of Christian education. Secularization and the successive disestablishments of religion in the United States have eliminated public education and the mainstream media as sources of Christian education.[4] Congregations vary greatly in the extent to which they offer young people quality Christian education. Moreover, research repeatedly has found that many Christian parents do relatively little in the way of teaching and

3. *The New England Primer* was first printed in Boston in 1690 by Benjamin Harris. Over five million copies of the book were sold.

4. Robert Handy has described the various disestablishments of religion in the United States in a variety of writings, including *Undermined Establishment: Church-state Relations in America, 1880-1920* (Princeton: Princeton University Press, 1991).

practicing the faith with their children.[5] Typically, the last thing to go is prayer at bedtime and meals, but even this has become relatively rare in Christian families, which frequently do not even eat together, much less pray together.

Lest this sound like a trip down nostalgia lane, let me state directly that I am not advocating here a return to the older ecology. Nor was Lynn. This is not possible in a social context characterized by a high degree of cultural and religious pluralism — though research on Roman Catholic schools by James Coleman helps us imagine new ecologies of education.[6] Rather, my point is to underscore the tremendous challenge facing contemporary Christian education. Not only does more of the burden fall on congregations and families today, but it does so in the face of daunting institutional pressures. Over the past hundred years, children in the West have begun to spend more time per day and more years of their lives in educational institutions than at any other time in history. Over the past sixty years, the revolution in microprocessors and electronic communication has extended the reach of the media into virtually every part of life, increasing their influence on young people enormously.[7] Just as families and congregations are asked to do more in the way of Christian education, they have less social capital with which to work in terms of time, resources, social status, and personnel. They also must carry out Christian education in the face of values and beliefs often experienced as quite different than those of the Christian community, communicated through institutions of education and media that are more powerful than ever. We have moved a long way from an educational ecology in which common schools included teaching like "In Adam's fall, we sinned all" to one in which such teaching is characterized as indicative of the "stern and somewhat morbid Protestantism of that time and place."[8]

5. Peter Benson et al., *What Kids Need to Succeed* (Minneapolis: Free Spirit Publishing, 1998). For an excellent discussion of the implications of this study, see Karen Marie Yust, *Real Kids, Real Faith: Practices for Nurturing Children's Spiritual Lives* (San Francisco: Jossey-Bass, 2004), ch. 1.

6. James S. Coleman, *Equality and Achievement in Education* (Boulder, CO: Westview, 1990).

7. See *Youth, Religion, and Globalization: New Research in Practical Theology*, ed. Richard Osmer and Kenda Creasy Dean (Berlin: LIT Verlag, 2007), which traces the enormous impact of the global media on adolescents around the world.

8. *The New England Primer* is characterized by J. B. Hare in this fashion at http://www.sacred-texts.com/chr/nep/.

From a Christendom Church to a Missional Church

Responding to this shift in the ecology of education requires a great deal more than a new program or curriculum of Christian education. It will take nothing less than a paradigm shift in our understanding of the church and its teaching ministry. It requires congregations to move *from a Christendom ecclesiology to a missional ecclesiology.* This entails a new approach to the teaching ministry that is integrally related to the spiritual formation taking place in congregations and families. Or to use Paul's terms, it means that we must view the teaching ministry as a form of edification, of building up families and congregations to serve as witnesses to the gospel.

The shift from a Christendom ecclesiology to a missional ecclesiology signals the clear recognition that American congregations no longer operate in the societal or even the civilizational context of Christendom, which Douglas John Hall defines quite simply as "the domination or sovereignty of the Christian religion."[9] Hall continues:

> Today Christendom, so understood, is in its death throes, and the question we all have to ask ourselves is whether we can get over regarding this as a catastrophe and begin to experience it as a doorway — albeit a narrow one — into a future that is more in keeping with what our Lord first had in mind when he called disciples to accompany him on his mission to redeem the world through love, not power.[10]

The shift to a missional ecclesiology entails a change in expectations on the part of congregations. Sociologically, they can no longer expect the dominant institutions of the surrounding culture to privilege their values and beliefs. They must learn to think and act like minority communities, which foster a strong subcultural religious identity among their members.[11] They must take responsibility for creating "plausibility structures" that embody the be-

9. Douglas John Hall, *The End of Christendom and the Future of Christianity* (Eugene, OR: Wipf & Stock, 1997), p. ix. The term "Christendom" is used by those involved in the missional church discussion as a kind of shorthand expression for the period stretching from Constantine to modernity. They recognize that this encompasses a wide variety of cultural contexts in which the church, culture, and state were related in diverse ways. The shorthand expression captures the dominance of Christianity across these contexts, as Hall's definition indicates.

10. Hall, *The End of Christendom,* p. ix.

11. For an excellent discussion of the importance of fostering subcultural religious identities in modern social contexts, see Christian Smith, *American Evangelicalism: Embattled and Thriving* (Chicago: University of Chicago Press, 1998).

liefs and practices of the Christian way of life.[12] Theologically, congregations face the task of breaking with Christendom understandings of their identity and mission.[13] They must undertake the demanding theological task of clarifying their understanding of God's mission of redemptive love toward the world. They must discover their own mission within God's mission, seeking to embody an alternate set of possibilities of fellowship, love, and hope that give witness to God's redemption in Christ in a particular time and place.

The concept of sin is an important part of the interpretive framework by which Christians have understood God's mission of redemptive love. It allows them to understand the Father's sending of the Son to a humanity that has turned away from its Creator and stands in need of reconciliation and forgiveness. It also helps them grasp the sending of the Holy Spirit for the renewal and healing of creation in anticipation of the consummation. The distinctive vocabulary of scripture and Christian tradition, which includes the concept of sin, is not something Christians or congregations can do without. It is essential to their self-understanding and discernment of their own mission within the mission of God.

Moving from a Christendom ecclesiology to a missional ecclesiology requires recognizing that the distinctive vocabulary and conceptual framework of the Christian faith will not necessarily find cultural support or sanction. It is the discordant language of a missional church and may even be ridiculed and caricatured at times. When my daughter is asked to read a textbook that reduces the thinking of Jonathan Edwards and American Puritanism to a single sermon on human sin and divine wrath, I need to learn to respond as part of a missional community. I need to help her develop a good "crap detector," to put it colloquially, and to understand what is at stake in the Christian concept of sin. Thinking as a minority, I might even risk call-

12. The concept of plausibility structures comes from Peter Berger and Thomas Luckmann, *The Social Construction of Reality: A Treatise on the Sociology of Knowledge* (Garden City, NY: Anchor Press, 1967). Berger initially portrayed secularization and cultural pluralism as eroding the plausibility structures of Christianity and as resulting in various forms of individualization; that is, every individual faces the task of *choosing* his or her own beliefs. See Peter Berger, *The Heretical Imperative: Contemporary Possibilities of Religious Affirmation* (Garden City, NY: Anchor Books, 1979). Berger later moved away from this position.

13. For an introduction to the missional church discussion, see the following: *Missional Church: A Vision for the Sending of the Church in North America*, ed. Darrell Guder (Grand Rapids: Eerdmans, 1998); Darrell Guder, *The Continuing Conversion of the Church* (Grand Rapids: Eerdmans, 2000); *Treasure in Clay Jars: Patterns in Missional Faithfulness*, ed. Lois Barrett (Grand Rapids: Eerdmans, 2004); David Bosch, *Transforming Mission: Paradigm Shifts in Theology of Mission* (Maryknoll, NY: Orbis Books, 1991).

ing her teacher's attention to the one-sided treatment of Christianity in a required textbook. I might gently ask for the same level of accuracy and fairness afforded other religions in her high school.

The Teaching Ministry of a Missional Church

Teaching my daughter the distinctive vocabulary and interpretive framework of the Christian faith is not something that I or any parent can do on our own. It requires the support of a Christian community. What does this look like in a missional church? What sorts of changes might need to take place in the inherited patterns of Christian education?[14] Among Protestant churches influenced by the Reformation, the teaching ministry clustered around educational activities such as catechetical instruction in church and home *and* Christian education in common schools and universities. With the rise of the Sunday school movement, the church school was added to this mix and, eventually, eclipsed older practices in many congregations. During the first decades of the twentieth century, the Religious Education movement drew on the emerging fields of modern psychology and education to professionalize the teaching of Sunday schools. The unspoken assumption of *all* of these developments was the support of a Christian social context and the broader ecology of Christian education. The breakdown of this ecology during the twentieth century is one indication of the end of Christendom, as described by Hall. Three changes are required in the teaching ministry of a missional church.

First, it involves the clear recognition that the congregation is the primary source of spiritual formation. As Lesslie Newbigin aptly put it: "The only hermeneutic of the gospel is a congregation of men and women who believe it and live by it."[15] No amount of education in the catechism or church school can take the place of a community that is attempting to live out the gospel, struggling to embody a missional identity and way of life. Conceptually, then, the primary language of the teaching ministry is spiritual formation, not education. This points to the Holy Spirit's role in uniting the members of a Christian community to Christ and one another and in forming and transforming them toward Christ's image. It affirms that indi-

14. An overview of this history is found in Richard Osmer, *Confirmation: Presbyterian Practices in Ecumenical Perspective* (Louisville: Geneva Press, 1996), chs. 4-6.

15. Lesslie Newbigin, *The Gospel in a Pluralist Society* (Grand Rapids: Eerdmans, 1989), p. 227.

viduals are built up in Christ through the Spirit through the relationships and practices of communities. Spiritual formation is a matter of learning to participate in Christ's mission in a particular community of faith. Education is no substitute for this sort of spiritual formation. The congregation is a hermeneutic of the gospel. Its way of life teaches its members how to interpret the gospel, for better or worse.

This entails a second shift in the teaching ministry. Its primary purpose is to "equip the saints for the work of ministry, for building up the body of Christ" (Eph. 4:12). Obviously, building up a congregation to carry out its mission is not the task of the teaching ministry alone. It is the purpose of many forms of ministry — of preaching, worship, and fellowship, for example. What is the special contribution of the teaching ministry in equipping the saints for ministry?

Elsewhere, I have drawn on Paul's letters to identify three core tasks of the teaching ministry in the missional communities of early Christianity: (1) catechesis — handing on of scripture and tradition; (2) exhortation — moral formation and education; and (3) discernment — teaching practices by which to discern the guidance of the Spirit in situations of uncertainty and decision.[16] Today, it is imperative that we recover the missional orientation of these tasks, viewing them as equipping Christians to make their contribution to the church's mission within the mission of God. Let us see what this might involve in the study of scripture, central to catechesis.

Eugene Peterson captures the essence of this quite nicely: "In our reading of this book [the Bible] we come to realize that what we need is not primarily informational, telling us things about God and ourselves, but formational, shaping us into our true being."[17] He unpacks what this means:

> My emphasis is on the cultivation of understandings and practices that make us receptive listeners to the living Trinitarian voice that brought these words onto the pages of our text in the first place, but also brings them off the pages into our lives. The emphasis is on the cultivation of understandings and practices that make us better *followers* of Jesus into the story he speaks into being so that we find ourselves at home in it, both now and in eternity. Participation is required.[18]

16. Richard Osmer, *The Teaching Ministry of Congregations* (Louisville: Westminster/John Knox, 2005), ch. 2.

17. Eugene Peterson, *Eat This Book: A Conversation in the Art of Spiritual Reading* (Grand Rapids: Eerdmans, 2006), pp. 23-24.

18. Peterson, *Eat This Book*, p. 62.

This is a shift from "learning about" scripture to "participating in" the story it tells. It is a matter of finding our story within God's story, of discovering our gifts and vocations as we participate in the mission of the triune God. As Peterson notes, this sort of Christian education is formational, not informational. It equips the members of the Christian community for ministry within the mission of the church.

A third break with inherited patterns of Christian education is required as congregations struggle to make the transition from a Christendom ecclesiology to a missional ecclesiology. It is no longer adequate to view the teaching ministry as taking place exclusively in class-like settings — in the church school, confirmation classes, or Bible studies. While such settings remain important, they are no substitute for the sort of "on-the-job" training that is essential to becoming a missional community. Let me illustrate what I have in mind.

In *Welcoming the Stranger,* Patrick Keifert invites congregations to come to terms with the new challenges of worship in a post-Christendom context.[19] On a given Sunday, he notes, many congregations have unannounced visitors who are "checking out" their Sunday morning worship. Today, such visitors may include people with no Christian background or people from a new apartment complex near the church who are quite different than the average member. Such visitors may find the "in-house" language of worship bewildering or the formality of the music off-putting. Whether members like it or not, congregational worship has become a moment of evangelism every bit as much as the nurture of the congregational family. As congregational leaders develop new forms of worship that extend hospitality to the strangers in their midst, they face an educational task. They must teach the members of their congregation to understand the changes taking place and why these are an effort to help the congregation become more faithful in its mission. Moreover, in my own research on the leaders of missional congregations, I discovered that they are deeply aware that such changes are risky and often fail.[20] They struggle with the educational task of helping their congregations "learn how to learn" from their failures, as well as their successes. This is much closer to the trial-and-error learning of on-the-job training than formal classroom instruction. Yet it is essential to a congregation's dis-

19. Patrick R. Keifert, *Welcoming the Stranger: A Public Theology of Worship and Evangelism* (Minneapolis: Augsburg Fortress, 1992).

20. This ongoing research is part of the Missional Pastors Project, funded by an internal grant from Princeton Theological Seminary. Special thanks to Darrell Guder for assistance in this project and to Drew Dyson, who served as my research assistant.

cernment of its mission. It is especially important in churches making the transition from a Christendom ecclesiology to a missional ecclesiology.

We have traveled quite far from the personal incident with which I began. Yet I have come to believe that my daughter's experience in high school and my ambivalence in how to respond are illuminated by the foregoing discussion of the present context of Protestant Christian education. This is a context in which congregations face the challenge of moving beyond Christendom and forging new understandings of their identities and practices as missional communities. They can no longer count on a broader ecology of education to teach young people the Christian faith. They must take greater responsibility for such teaching themselves, often in the face highly persuasive alternatives that distort or caricature Christian beliefs and values. Perhaps more than ever, Christian parents and teachers need the assistance of theologians who retrieve the teachings of scripture and tradition with integrity and render them intelligible in dialogue with the intellectual resources of contemporary culture. To illustrate what this involves, I want to explore the continuing relevance of the concept of original sin. What sort of understanding of this concept might have equipped me to better respond to my daughter's questions?

Original Sin: Interpreting Human Vulnerability and Evil

Ernst Cassirer once noted that "the concept of original sin is the most common opponent against which the different orientations of the Enlightenment unite."[21] To many Enlightenment thinkers, the very idea of original sin was paradigmatic of the features of classical Christianity they found most questionable. It was based on the authority of scripture and church tradition, not human reason; it relied on a mythological story of a primeval paradise, not modern science; and it offered a pessimistic assessment of the human condition, not an optimistic, progressive portrait of human potential. In the face of this sort of criticism, is the concept of original sin worth retrieving? Does it necessarily encourage practices by parents and teachers at odds with God's love of children? These are the questions I will explore in the remainder of this chapter.

To orient us to this topic, let us begin with a basic definition of original sin found in a standard dictionary of religion:

21. Ernst Cassirer, *The Philosophy of the Enlightenment* (Boston: Beacon Press, 1955), p. 141.

> The doctrine that throughout the history of the human race, human nature has been flawed and disordered in every human group and every human individual. The flaw has several dimensions, and we most often think of it as a moral flaw. But in calling it sin, we are recognizing that fundamentally it is a separation from God, the Creator and Sustainer of life. The gravity of original sin lies in the fact that it means that human life is cut off at the very roots, and that all particular sins and wrongdoings of the race arise from this deep disablement.[22]

It is important at the outset of this discussion of original sin to indicate its relationship to reconciliation and forgiveness. Reconciliation is the restoration of right-relatedness to God and neighbor accomplished in the life, death, and resurrection of Jesus Christ. It is an act of divine grace taking the form of a free gift. Those who accept this gift become participants in God's ministry of reconciliation in their personal relationships, communities, and larger social systems. The forgiveness of sins is a critical part of reconciliation, as we shall see. It involves the acknowledgment of wrongdoing, intentional and otherwise, and the possibility of starting anew, freed from destructive patterns of hatred and enmity.

Reconciliation and forgiveness have theological priority over sin in the Christian tradition for several reasons. First, the love of God in Jesus Christ is more powerful than sin. Human beings may turn away from and separate themselves from their Creator, but God's love does not give up on them. This is the heart of the gospel. Second, human sin only becomes apparent in the light of God's love. It is analogous to a family that is trapped in destructive patterns of communication. It takes the outside intervention of a therapist to open up new possibilities of communication. Only later, in retrospect, is it apparent to family members how dysfunctional their past relationships have been. So too, it is the "outside intervention" of God in Christ, revealing the depths of God's love and the form of true humanity, that allows human beings to realize how trapped they are in the destructive cycles of sin and death. While the concept of sin — especially original sin — receives most attention in the remainder of this chapter, it is important to keep its secondary, derivative status in mind. The first and last word is the reconciling, forgiving love of God; sin has its place within this more comprehensive framework.

22. *The Dictionary of Bible and Religion,* ed. William Gentz (Nashville: Abingdon, 1986), p. 761.

The Emergence and Development of Original Sin in the Christian Tradition

The language of original sin is not explicitly found in Christian scripture. Like the Trinity and other important doctrines, it emerged gradually as Christian theologians reflected on scripture and on the beliefs and practices of the church. Scriptural warrant for the development of this concept drew heavily on the story of Adam and Eve (Gen. 3) and Paul's reflections in the first five chapters of Romans. It also was based on Paul's portrait of Christ's redemption as freeing humanity from the enslaving bondage of sin and death (e.g., Rom. 8:21-23; 6:17, 20). Since many parts of scripture deal with sin, theologians also appealed to numerous passages that seem to imply its universal scope, like Psalm 51:5; John 1:10, 29; and 1 John 1:8. It was the universal scope of sin as a human condition that was to become the focus of later theological reflection on original sin. Such reflection had already begun to emerge in the early church as it struggled with three practical questions.

The first question was: Why do we proclaim the gospel to all people? The Gospel of Matthew portrays the risen Jesus as telling his followers to go "and make disciples of all nations" (28:19). Quite quickly, the church viewed its mission as extending beyond the boundaries of Israel. The gospel of Jesus Christ was interpreted as having a universal thrust, addressing all people in all cultures who share a common human plight: the reality of human sin and evil. As Paul put it: "All have sinned and fall short of the glory of God" (Rom. 3:23). Likewise, according to John's Gospel: "He was in the world, and the world came into being through him; yet the world did not know him." Jesus is described as the Lamb of God who "takes away the sin of the world" (1:10, 29). As the early church thus reflected on its mission, it began to describe its mandate to proclaim the gospel to all nations as a response to the universal scope of sin. Since all of humanity is trapped in sin, all stand in need of God's redemption in Christ Jesus.

A second question evoking reflection on the universal scope of sin in the early church was: How do we appropriately signify our continuity with Israel, God's chosen people? Clearly a decisive break had taken place. The early Christian movement quickly spread beyond Palestine and formed communities of Gentiles and Jews. Yet its leaders portrayed these communities as standing in continuity with Israel. What were appropriate ways of signifying this continuity? Some believed that Gentile converts should accept traditional markers of Jewish identity, like circumcision and dietary regulations. This position was strongly opposed by Paul in Galatians. Romans 1–5, however, offers the most elegant statement of his position.[23] He argues that Jews and Gentiles alike are caught in sin and are both therefore justified by faith in Christ, not obedience to the Law. Traditional markers of Jewish identity like circumcision are no longer relevant in congregations called into being by the gospel. Rather, the true offspring of Abraham are those who, like Abraham, accept God's promise in faith (Rom. 4). Paul underscores the "caughtness" of Jews and Gentiles in sin and their common need for faith by developing an Adam Christology in Romans 5:12-21 (cf. 1 Cor. 15:22). He portrays the trespass of one man, Adam, as leading to "condemnation for all" and the "act of righteousness" of the one man, Jesus Christ, as leading "to justification and life for all" (v. 18). Paul's allusion to the story of Adam and Eve's disobedience of God and expulsion from Eden would prove decisive for later theological reflection. This story had received little attention or elaboration in Israel's scripture. Christian theologians would make it central to their interpretation of original sin as a universal condition.

A third question evoking reflection on the scope of sin was: Why do we baptize infants? This was not merely an academic question in an era of high infant mortality. It rose in response to practices that were already taking place. It is not clear when the church began to baptize infants. Some theologians have argued that this practice was part of the church's life from the beginning, pointing to passages in the New Testament that speak of the baptism of "households" (e.g., Acts 16:15, 33; 18:8; 1 Cor. 1:16). It is clear that infant baptism emerged quite early, even while the baptism of adult converts remained the norm. Hippolytus's *Apostolic Tradition*, a very early liturgical instruction book, tells church leaders: "They shall baptize the little children first. And if they can answer for themselves, let them answer. But if they cannot, let their parents answer or someone from their family."[24] Moreover, it is evident that, quite early, infant baptism evoked reflection on infants' participation in sin. In *First Apology*, for example, Justin Martyr (d. 165 CE) argued for the necessity of infant baptism because of the wayward inclinations of

23. See Brendan Byrne, *Romans*, Sacra Pagina (Collegeville, MN: Liturgical Press, 1996). In part, I am following here the so-called "new perspective" on Paul, articulated initially by E. P. Sanders, *Paul and Palestinian Judaism: A Comparison of Patterns of Religion* (Philadelphia: Fortress, 1977), and subsequently developed by James Dunn and many others. For a nice summary, see Frank Matera, "Galatians in Perspective: Cutting a New Path Through Old Territory," *Interpretation* 54, no. 3 (July 2000): 233-45.

24. Geoffrey Cumming, *Hippolytus: A Text for Students* (Nottingham, UK: Grove Books, 1976). See my discussion of the difficulties in identifying the author, church context, and exact date of this text in *Confirmation*, pp. 41-42.

infants.[25] Indeed, Tatha Wiley argues that this perspective gradually represented a consensus among early Christian theologians.[26] The church baptizes infants because they are born in sin, participating in the "primeval fall" of Adam and Eve.

While Augustine is rightly acknowledged as formulating the most influential statement of original sin during the patristic period, he was not the first theologian to make use of this concept. Justin Martyr, Tertullian, Origen, Cyprian, Gregory of Nazianzus, Gregory of Nyssa, Theodore of Mopsuestia, and others contributed to its development. Augustine's formulation of the doctrine of original sin, however, was to exert enormous influence on Western Christianity. In the councils of Carthage (418) and Orange (529), which dealt with Pelagianism, much of Augustine's thinking on original sin became normative for the official teaching of the Western church. During the Middle Ages, prominent theologians like Anselm and Aquinas continued to reflect on this doctrine, seeking to clarify the effects of the fall on human nature with the tools of philosophy. The Reformers of the sixteenth century continued this line of theological reflection, making concepts like bondage of the will prominent. Even in the face of the sustained critique of the Enlightenment, at least some prominent liberal theologians like Friedrich Schleiermacher and Walter Rauschenbusch attempted to reinterpret this doctrine for modern Christians. In the twentieth century, the dialectical theologians of Europe and Christian realists in the United States retrieved certain elements of the Reformers' position. It is not too much to say, then, that the concept of original sin has figured prominently in the central theological currents of Christianity. In many eras and contexts, theologians have found it to be a compelling way of interpreting why humans are as they are and what they need.

Retrieving and Reinterpreting the Concept of Original Sin

It is beyond the scope of this chapter to trace in detail the various ways this concept has been portrayed theologically across the Christian tradition, a task ably carried out by others.[27] Rather, I want to enter into a dialogue with

25. *The First Apology of Justin Martyr,* trans. John Kaye (London: Griffith, Farran, Okeden & Welsh, 1889).

26. Tatha Wiley, *Original Sin: Origins, Developments, Contemporary Meanings* (Mahwah, NJ: Paulist Press, 2002), p. 49.

27. See Wiley, cited immediately above; Henri Rondet, *Original Sin: The Patristic and Theological Background* (Shannon, Ireland: Ecclesia Press, 1972); W. E. Wibby, *Original Sin and*

central tenets of the Augustinian-Calvinist line of interpretation. Moreover, I am especially interested in exploring ways this concept might be retrieved and reinterpreted to make sense to contemporary Christians. I will carry out this dialogue in the form of seven theses.

1. The concept of original sin calls attention to the universal scope of human sin and evil.

Reinhold Niebuhr once remarked that "the doctrine of original sin is the only empirically verifiable doctrine of the Christian faith."[28] This sentiment aptly captures the perspective of Augustine and Calvin, both of whom offer poignant observations on the breadth and depth of human sin and evil. This should not be taken as implying that human beings and institutions are incapable of goodness, which is empirically verifiable as well. Rather it means that such goodness is deeply ambiguous. It is caught in conditions of sin and evil that precede and compromise it. To describe this condition, Augustine and Calvin describe original sin along two lines: as *originating* sin, the primeval fall of Adam and Eve, and as *originated* sin, the fallen state in which human beings find themselves.

We live in a world that has largely discarded confidence in modern myths of progress and human perfectibility. It is difficult to contemplate the prospects of humanity at the beginning of the twenty-first century without a deep sense of foreboding. The threats posed by weapons of mass destruction, population growth, ecological disaster, and religious conflicts are too obvious to be avoided. People are aware that they live in a "risk society," to borrow a term from the sociologist Ulrich Beck.[29] They also are aware that there is really no place to run and hide. These problems are truly universal in scope and they implicate us all. The concept of original sin as both originating and originated has plausibility in our present context. It not only draws our attention to the reality and universal scope of human evil, but also to the ambiguous and compromised nature of grand solutions to such evil.

Redemption: A Brief Review of the Doctrine in the Light of Modern Thought (London: Faith Press, 1926).

28. Reinhold Niebuhr, *Man's Nature and His Communities* (New York: Scribner's, 1965), p. 24.

29. Ulrich Beck, *Risk Society: Towards a New Modernity* (London: Sage Publications, 1992).

2. To speak of originating sin is to describe the condition of the human species in the face of vulnerability and the misuse of human freedom. It portrays sin as essentially a spiritual, not a moral, problem.

The concept of original sin does not stand in isolation. It is developed in concert with the depiction of creation as essentially good. Drawing on the story of Adam and Eve, Augustine and Calvin distinguish the original goodness of human beings as part of the created order and their "fall," the origin of sin.[30] This is a very important part of Augustine's argument against Manicheanism, which portrayed evil as part of a cosmic conflict between Light and Darkness and identified the material world with the latter. In contrast, Augustine argues that sin is a departure from original goodness and refuses to identify the material world as inherently evil. Human beings are created for relationship with God, as a part of an essentially good world. The heart of sin is turning away from this relationship. This "vertical," or spiritual, dimension is primary. Only in consequence of turning away from God do human relationships become distorted, the "horizontal" dimension. Augustine and Calvin tend to portray this broken relationship in terms of pride: Adam and Eve's willful refusal to obey God's command ("but of the tree of the knowledge of good and evil you shall not eat") and their desire to usurp God's place ("you will be like God").

Many contemporary interpreters follow the important distinction made here between the essential goodness of human beings as part of creation and human sin and evil. They also affirm the depiction of sin as fundamentally a spiritual matter, as a turning away from God. However, many do not believe that the Genesis story should be taken as a literal account of the origin of sin, narrating a time in the past when the "primal parents" of the human race disobeyed God and caused its downfall. Rather, they believe Genesis 3 makes use of mythological material that must be interpreted symbolically.[31] The origin of sin lies in the universal human experience of the contingencies of

30. Augustine, *The City of God,* trans. Marcus Dods (New York: The Modern Library, 1950), pp. 407-11; John Calvin, *The Institute of the Christian Religion,* trans. Ford Lewis Battles (Albany, OR: Books for the Ages Software, 1998), vol. 2, p. 10.

31. Gerhard von Rad, *Genesis* (Philadelphia: Westminster Press, 1972); Bernard Anderson, *Understanding the Old Testament* (Englewood Cliffs, NJ: Prentice-Hall, 1966) and *Creation and Chaos: The Reinterpretation of Mythical Symbolism in the Bible* (New York: Association Press, 1967); Brevard Childs, *Biblical Theology of the Old and New Testaments: Theological Reflection on the Christian Bible* (Minneapolis: Fortress Press, 1992), ch. 2. For an excellent discussion of the interpretation of the mythological material of Genesis 3 symbolically, see Paul Ricoeur, *The Conflict of Interpretations* (Evanston, IL: Northwestern University Press, 1974), part 4.

finite existence by a species with the capacities of self-transcendence and consciousness. Human beings are aware of the contingent nature of life, especially death, and grow anxious in the face of the experience of human vulnerability.[32] Rather than trusting the Creator to meet their needs in life and death, they use their freedom to alleviate this anxiety in an attempt to secure their existence. Turning away from God, they trust in some part of the created world. While pride is one form this takes, many contemporary theologians believe it should not be viewed as the exclusive paradigm of original sin. Indeed, some make this point by appealing to the thinking of Augustine and Calvin, noting the primacy the former gives to false love and the latter to idolatry.

3. Human beings are "caught" in the condition of originated sin.

Augustine and Calvin describe the results of the primal fall in a wide variety of ways. These include idolatry (worshiping as God that which is not God), concupiscence (inordinate love of the sensual, resulting in disordered desires), sloth (spiritual indifference, the failure to do and be what one can in relation to God), and rebellion (actively working against God's will; joining the "league of the Devil"). Moreover, both describe originated sin as an active force, as something that binds and holds human beings in its grip both internally and externally. Calvin, for example, describes human nature as a "perpetual factory of idols."[33]

To describe human beings as "caught" in originated sin is to depict their participation in a condition that is not their own making but which, through their choices and actions, is something in which they participate and to which they contribute. In his interpretation of the Adam myth, Paul Ricoeur captures what is at stake in the metaphor of "caughtness":

> [I]f any one of us initiates evil, inaugurates it . . . each of us also *discovers evil,* finds it already there, in himself, outside himself, and before himself. . . . In tracing back the origin of evil to a distant ancestor, the myth discovers the situation of every man: evil has already taken place. I do not begin evil; I continue it; I am implicated in evil. . . . Hence, the myth unites . . . the reality of sin anterior to every awakening of conscience, the

32. This line of interpretation is found in Niebuhr, *Nature and Destiny,* vol. 1, pp. 179-86, and Edward Farley, *Good and Evil: Interpreting a Human Condition* (Minneapolis: Fortress Press, 1990). Farley does a particularly nice job of portraying human vulnerability in its personal, interhuman, and social dimensions.

33. Calvin, *Institutes,* vol. 1, p. 152.

communal dimension of sin, which is irreducible to individual responsibility, and the impotence of will that surrounds every actual fault.[34]

4. Sin as a condition in which human beings are "caught" is to be distinguished from particular sins. The former is categorical; the latter is actual and admits of degrees.

Augustine and Calvin are very careful to distinguish between sin as a condition and the particular sins that flow from this condition. One way of clarifying what they have in mind is to distinguish between sin as categorical and as actual. As categorical, sin is unconditional. It is like death or pregnancy. You cannot be a little dead or a little bit pregnant. Likewise, you are either a sinner or not. Original sin is categorical in affirming that all persons are "caught" in the condition of sin. Reinhold Niebuhr refers to this as "equality in sin."[35] Yet, sin is also actualized in particular ways and is a matter of degree. Not all sins are equal. Anger and murder are not the same, though both may be sin in the sight of God (Matt. 5:22). Telling a lie to get out of doing something is not the same as telling lies in leading a country to war. Niebuhr describes this as "inequality in guilt."[36]

The distinction between categorical and actual sin, or sin as a condition and the particular sins of individuals and communities, is important. It allows us to distinguish "classical" understandings of sin from the moralistic views of much American Protestantism, which reduce sin to the violation of conventional norms of good behavior. Sin as a condition is more basic. It is a matter of turning away from God in the face of human vulnerability and the "caughtness" of human beings in a web of sin and evil that influences their choices and actions. As Reinhold Niebuhr pointed out, moralistic understandings of sin commonly are an expression of pride in the form of religious self-righteousness.[37] In effect, those who hold this view say: We good people, who are free of sin, are in a position to point out your sinfulness.

The distinction between categorical and actual sin also throws light on the theological status of victimization, with which some contemporary theologians virtually equate sin. Sin is a theological term; victimization is a social, political, and moral term, which describes the experience of injustice or abuse on the part of the innocent. Theologically, social or personal vic-

34. Ricoeur, *Conflict of Interpretations,* p. 284.
35. Niebuhr, *Nature and Destiny,* vol. 1, p. 219.
36. Niebuhr, *Nature and Destiny,* vol. 1, p. 219.
37. Niebuhr, *Nature and Destiny,* vol. 1, pp. 199-203.

timization should be construed as an expression of the actualization of sin in particular forms and circumstances. Those complicit in perpetrating injustice face the sin of *avaritia* (avarice, greed, rapacity, covetousness). Those enduring the innocent suffering of victimization face the sin of *acedia* (apathy, sloth, spiritual torpor). Yet perpetrators and victims alike participate in the universal condition of sin. God may be said to stand in solidarity with victims but in eternal judgment over sinners.[38]

5. The scope and effects of originated sin are universal, affecting both individuals and human associations.

One of the most important features of Augustine's and Calvin's treatment of original sin is the way they portray it as encompassing all forms of human life. Human associations, as well as individuals, are "caught" in the web of originated sin. While they view duly constituted authority as playing an important role in human associations, they are wary of the ways such authority can be abused, especially when power is unchecked. Their sentiment is echoed in the well-known comment by Lord Acton that power tends to corrupt and absolute power tends to corrupt absolutely. In *The City of God,* for example, Augustine portrays the government as a providential measure established to restrain the disruptive forces unleashed by the fall. Yet, he also offers many passages in which the Roman Empire and all political institutions are depicted as "power-hungry organizations for wicked domination and oppression by the powerful."[39] All forms of association need duly constituted authorities, but even more, they need rulers and laws that embody justice. As Augustine puts it in *The City of God:* "Justice being taken away, then, what are kingdoms but great robberies?"[40]

Calvin sometimes is viewed as advocating theocratic absolutism, with the execution of Servetus as the prime datum. Fredrick Carney argues that Calvin's perspective is consistent with later Calvinist political thought, which is neither individualist nor absolutist:

> It begins neither with the self-evident rights of individuals nor with the *a priori* authority of rulers. Rather it asks what is the vocation (or purpose) of any association, and how can this association be so organized as to accomplish its essential business. Authority (or rule) becomes a function of vocation; and great care must be taken to provide constitutional structures, both

38. Hunsinger, *Theses on Sin* (unpublished manuscript), p. 4.

39. Chadwick, *Augustine* (Oxford: Oxford University Press, 1986), p. 99.

40. Augustine, *City of God,* p. 112.

> ideological and institutional, that authority not become unduly weak or corrupt. One can therefore properly say that Calvinist associational thought involves at its very roots both the acknowledgement of a high calling and *the recognition of ever-present finitude and sin.* (emphasis added)[41]

Like Augustine, Calvin affirms the role of duly constituted authorities in various forms of human association but is aware that such authorities have a tendency toward corruption under the power of sin. This was a point articulated more forcefully in later Calvinist political thinking. It is one of the intellectual sources of modern constitutionalism and the recognition of the importance of balancing power and authority in various branches of government. What is true of government is true of other forms of association as well. This has important implications for our understanding of exercise of authority in families.

6. Originated sin is transmitted.

One of the best-known and most ridiculed features of Augustine's understanding of original sin is his depiction of its biological transmission through sexual intercourse. No doubt, this reflects the influence of neo-Platonism on his thinking and his personal struggle with sexual temptation. Because sin is biologically transmitted, he argues, infants are born in sin. This is the primary reason he believes they should be baptized as quickly as possible. In *The Confessions,* Augustine reports observing sin at work in a baby who grows jealous of his foster-brother nursing at his mother's breast.[42] If babies are innocent, he writes, "it is not for lack of will to do harm, but for lack of strength."[43] Calvin follows Augustine in this line of thinking. As he puts it, "Even infants themselves, while they carry their condemnation along with them from the mother's womb, are guilty not of another's fault but of their own. For, even though the fruits of their iniquity have not yet come forth, they have the seed enclosed within them."[44]

41. Fredrick Carney, "Associational Thought in Early Calvinism," in *Voluntary Associations: A Study of Groups in Free Societies, Essays in Honor of James Luther Adams* (Richmond: John Knox Press, 1966), pp. 39-53. See Carney's comments about the continuity between Calvin and later Calvinist political theology on p. 40. For an overview of different perspectives on this issue, see Daniel Elazar, *Covenant and Commonwealth* (New Brunswick, NJ: Transaction Publishers, 1996), chs. 8-9, especially pp. 177-79.

42. Augustine, *Confessions,* trans. R. S. Pine-Coffin (London: Penguin Books, 1961), p. 28.

43. Augustine, *Confessions,* p. 28.

44. Calvin, *Institutes,* vol. 2, p. 12.

This dimension of original sin has received severe criticism for a variety of reasons. It implies a negative view of human sexuality and propagation. It ascribes guilt to children before they reach the age of discretion. It leads adults to label the "natural" impulses and needs of children as sinful and may encourage adults to take harsh actions to curb them. Accordingly, many modern theologians abandoned altogether the idea that sin is transmitted. However, this makes it difficult for them to describe the "caughtness" and universality of sin as a condition into which human beings are born and which has them in its grip from the beginning. For this reason, some contemporary theologians have attempted to reinterpret the transmissive dimension of originated sin in dialogue with the natural and social sciences. This is a helpful way of making this concept intelligible as long as it is clear that these are *analogies* of a condition that can only be described theologically, not *explanations* of sin on other grounds. While I cannot develop these analogies in depth in this chapter, I will describe several found in contemporary theology.

The first analogy is the human species as the planetary killer in the web of life, an image taken from the life sciences.[45] It portrays the natural and human worlds as an interconnected web of systems that support and interact with one another. Individual organisms, including human beings, participate in these systems from the very beginning of life. It is therefore impossible to describe human beings apart from the web of life, which precedes their existence, is transmitted to them, and shapes every facet of their existence. Their organic systems are formed by the very air they breathe and the nutrition they receive; their sense of self and life course is shaped by the cultural and social systems in which they participate. In the Social Gospel movement and, more recently, liberation and feminist theologies, theologians have drawn attention to the transmission of human evil through social systems that condition the life chances of individuals and groups. Others have called attention to the devastating effect of human beings on natural systems. The human species alone is a "planetary killer," to borrow Edward Wilson's term, which wipes out biodiversity and entire species to promote its own short-term survival.[46] The very web of life into which human beings are born is conditioned by their species' propensity to appropriate the earth's resources for its own purposes with little respect for the sanctity of life. This is a powerful analogy of originated sin.

The second analogy is the fall "upward" in evolution. In recent decades

45. Fritjof Capra, *The Web of Life: A New Scientific Understanding of Living Systems* (New York: Doubleday, 1996).

46. Edward Wilson, *The Future of Life* (New York: Alfred Knopf, 2002).

biological evolution has been extended backward to the evolution of the universe (cosmology) and forward to the evolution of society (cultural evolution).[47] Within this broad perspective, the movement from one phase of evolution to another is described as the emergence of new forms of complexity.[48] The appearance of *Homo sapiens* is marked by two new forms of complexity: (1) cognitive complexity, which rests on the unique human brain and central nervous system making consciousness possible; and (2) the complexity of human culture, which encodes and transmits units of cultural information. While the genetic and cultural inheritance of human beings has co-evolved, it is a persistent source of tension and dissonance.[49] The central nervous system, for example, includes a much older evolutionary heritage — sometimes referred to as the reptilian and paleo-mammalian components of the brain — in addition to the neocortex, which is primary in the formation of culture.[50] It is not difficult to discern the many possible ways the "higher" inheritance and capacities of culture stand in tension with the "lower" inheritance bequeathed by our genes. The latter includes response strategies like aggression, and desires like unfettered sexual expression characterizing young males. Broadly speaking, this account is similar to that offered by psychoanalysis, which portrays the ego as situated between the desires of the libido and the repression necessitated by civilization, which results in the ego's defensive structuring.[51]

47. Contributors to this synthesis of perspectives are many. For excellent overviews of this literature, see Nancey Murphy and George F. R. Ellis, *On the Moral Nature of the Universe: Theology, Cosmology, and Ethics* (Minneapolis: Fortress Press, 1996), and J. Wentzel van Huyssteen, *Alone in the World? Human Uniqueness in Science and Technology* (Grand Rapids: Eerdmans, 2006).

48. Philip Clayton, *Mind and Emergence: From Quantum to Consciousness* (Oxford: Oxford University Press, 2004).

49. Philip Hefner, *The Human Factor: Evolution, Culture, and Religion* (Minneapolis: Fortress Press, 1993); Denis Edwards, *The God of Evolution: A Trinitarian Theology* (New York: Paulist Press, 1999).

50. This reference is to Paul MacLean's famous account of the triune brain found in "The Brain's Generation Gap: Some Human Implications," *Zygon: Journal of Religion and Science* 8 (March 1973): 113-27. His work has been surpassed by others, including Antonio Damasio, *The Feeling of What Happens: Body and Emotion in the Making of Consciousness* (New York: Harcourt Brace & Co., 1999).

51. This is one of the reasons theologians influenced by neo-Reformation understandings of sin in the mid-twentieth century drew so heavily on psychoanalytic thought. See, for example, David Roberts, *Psychotherapy and a Christian View of Man* (New York: Scribner's, 1950), and Albert Outler, *Psychotherapy and the Christian Message* (New York: Harper & Brothers, 1954). This connection was sparked by the work of Paul Tillich.

In these accounts, the human species is portrayed as "falling upward" over the course of evolution. The very advances making human consciousness and culture possible stand in tension with other parts of its genetic and cultural inheritance. Paul Tillich, among others, has portrayed this sort of movement as a kind of *felix culpa* (blessed fault or happy fall).[52] The "fall" of the human race from childhood innocence (repeated in every individual) is a necessary step in the emergence of consciousness and human maturity. This comes perilously close to identifying human finitude, which necessarily includes growth, with sin. In contrast, the emergence of greater complexity over the course of the evolution of the universe, including human consciousness, might be interpreted as inherent to the dynamism of continuing creation. The admixture of past and present, or "higher" and "lower" — e.g., genetic inheritance and the development of consciousness, inherited cultural norms and the challenges of developing new cultural patterns — is not best viewed as inherently sinful or fallen but as a condition that "tempts" human beings to sin. From this perspective, the emergence of human consciousness is not so much a "fall upward" as a further unfolding of continuing creation, with its own potentials for good and evil.

The third analogy is addiction and bondage of the will. The analogy between alcohol addiction and original sin is not as comprehensive as the first two. Nonetheless, it provides a powerful image of human vulnerability to a condition that is transmitted and can result in the bondage of the will.[53] Research on alcoholism has revealed the likelihood that it rests on a genetically transmitted vulnerability. Genes do not "cause" alcoholism, any more than they cause any other specific form of behavior. Rather they *predispose* people to alcohol addiction if they begin to consume alcohol on a regular basis. People with this genetic vulnerability drink more and more without intending to do so. Indeed, the predictable course of this disease is to gradually disable the ability to control the use of this drug. Active alcoholics often are deeply aware of the pain their addiction is causing others, as well as themselves. But no matter how hard they try or how good their intentions, they cannot stop their drinking. This is why their first step toward recovery is admitting that they do not have control of this drug. The analogies with original sin are not difficult to discern. Like the condition of sin, alcoholics must

52. Paul Tillich, *Systematic Theology*, vol. 2 (Chicago: University of Chicago Press, 1957), pp. 31-35.

53. I am following here James Nelson, *Thirst: God and the Alcoholic Experience* (Louisville: Westminster/John Knox, 2004), and Linda Mercadante, *Victims and Sinners: Spiritual Roots of Addiction and Recovery* (Louisville: Westminster/John Knox, 1996).

cope with a condition that is not of their own making, one rooted in an inherited vulnerability. Like actual sin, active alcoholism is set in motion by human choices and cultural attitudes toward drinking. Like the "caughtness" of sin, once people are addicted their wills are quite literally disabled and in bondage to alcohol. While it is a mistake to equate sin with addiction, as some have done, it does provide a poignant analogy to certain features of original sin.[54]

7. "Caught" in originated sin, human beings cannot save themselves. Their redemption is a gift of grace through the one who overcomes sin on their behalf and in their stead. Receiving this gift in faith through the power of the Holy Spirit, they are gradually set free from sin's bondage, though they will struggle with its internal and external power for the duration of their lives.

Augustine and Calvin are pessimists with regard to human nature but optimists with regard to God's grace. "Caught" in the web of sin, they argue, human beings cannot save themselves. The harder they struggle, the more they become entangled. Yet they affirm that God's grace is more powerful than human sin. In his incarnation, death, and resurrection, Christ entered fully into the condition of human sin — though he remained sinless — and overcame it. Augustine and Calvin frequently explain this with imagery derived from Israel's priesthood, which is used throughout the New Testament. Christ's self-offering is portrayed as a sacrifice for the sins of the world, bearing the burden of humanity's guilt and reconciling human beings to the Creator from whom it has turned away. The accent is on the substitutionary, representative, and vicarious nature of Christ's reconciling work. What humanity cannot do for itself, God in Christ has done on its behalf and in its stead. This can only be received in faith as a free gift of grace. Augustine and Calvin, however, go on to portray the effects of God's grace as real and tangible, using the imagery of healing, renewal, and sanctification to portray processes that unfold throughout life because of the continuing power of internal and external sin. Both describe the primary effect of grace as the restoration of relationship with God. God created human beings for this relationship and, as Augustine puts it, "Our hearts are restless until they find themselves in thee." The Holy Spirit unites us to Christ and through him to the Father.

54. Gerald May, for example, equates sin and addiction in *Addiction and Grace: Love and Spirituality in the Healing of Addictions* (San Francisco: HarperSanFrancisco, 1988). He is criticized by Mercadante and Nelson, cited immediately above, for doing so.

Original sin, then, is neither the first nor last word in Augustine's and Calvin's theologies. They portray this concept as pointing to a departure from God's desire for communion with human beings in creation and as the restoration of this communion through Christ's salvation and the Spirit's renewal. Appropriately understood, it need not issue in fatalism, other-worldliness, or the abuse of power. It can be interpreted as issuing in a realism about the scope and depth of human evil and the only source of humanity's redemption.

Original Sin and Christian Parenting

I conclude this chapter by exploring the implications of this understanding of original sin for Christian parents in the present American context. As we have seen, original sin frequently is portrayed as the source of some of the worst abuses by Christian parents and educators, a charge that is not completely without foundation. But is this necessarily the case? Might a better understanding of this concept actually enhance the way parents embody God's love toward their children? Drawing on the previous section, I will argue that this, in fact, is the case. Reclaiming the discordant language of original sin, missional congregations face the task of equipping families today along five lines.

First, congregations will do well to take the ministry of families more seriously, equipping parents to serve as partners in teaching the Christian faith. This guideline harks back to the earlier discussion of the broken ecology of Christian education and the all-important role of congregations and parents in the present American context. Parents cannot carry out Christian education by themselves. Congregations provide their children with their first and most important "hermeneutic of the gospel," to recall Newbigin's way of putting it. The congregation, not the family, is the primary form of Christian community.[55] Yet congregations cannot accomplish Christian education by themselves either. Several hours on Sunday morning in the church school and worship are no substitute for parents who talk about their faith and live it out in the home. This mutual need is best pictured as a partnership of reciprocal support. At a minimum, it entails that congregations

55. For two somewhat different discussions of the congregation as embodying the gospel, see Miroslav Volf, *After Our Likeness: The Church as the Image of the Trinity* (Grand Rapids: Eerdmans, 1998), and Hans Küng, *The Church* (New York: Sheed & Ward, 1967).

will equip parents to interpret the faith to their children, helping them to grow in their understanding of Christian beliefs and practices and how best to communicate the faith in age-appropriate ways. Such equipping cannot avoid helping parents understand the meaning of sin, even original sin. In a cultural context that often caricatures Christianity as obsessed with sin, guilt, and divine wrath, parents must be ready to provide an account of sin that reflects the richness of scripture and tradition.

Second, it is important that congregations help Christian parents recognize that their families are places where spiritual formation takes place. Teaching is important but secondary in relation to the formative power of family life. What parents *say* will take root only if it is embodied in what they *do* and how they *live*. By spiritual formation, I recall my earlier comments about the way the Holy Spirit works through the relationships and practices of communities to form and transform people toward the image of Christ. Christ must take visible and concrete shape in the ways parents relate to their children and one another, their regulation of the patterns and practices of family life, and the values they live out. Together, such actions and practices are avenues of formation, which teaching subsequently interprets.

Third, congregations will do well to encourage Christian parents to develop an authoritative style of parenting, which embodies the spirit of Christ's redemptive love in the face of human evil and sin. I ended the previous section by affirming that the power of God's love is greater than the power of sin and evil. This is the good news of the gospel. The primary task of parents in relation to their children is to give witness to this love, fully cognizant of the condition of human sin and evil addressed by God's redemptive love. In the context of contemporary America, I believe that this entails equipping and encouraging Christian parents to develop an authoritative style of parenting. What I have in mind can best be explained with recent research discussed by Johannes van der Ven in *Formation of the Moral Self*.[56]

This research studied the ways parents relate to their children along two axes: support and control. Support has to do with forms of parental investment in children that demonstrate active interest in their activities, abilities, and needs. It also involves attitudes of warmth and care. Control has to do with the ways parents discipline their children: the sorts of rules and expectations they form, how they communicate them, and the way they respond

56. Johannes A. van der Ven, *Formation of the Moral Self* (Grand Rapids: Eerdmans, 1998), pp. 49-52.

to misbehavior. Using these two axes, four styles of parenting were identified. One style is characterized by neglect, in which parents offer neither support nor control. Indulgent parenting offers high support and low control, and authoritarian parenting, high control and low support. Authoritative parenting is characterized by *both* high support and high control. As van der Ven notes, this body of research reveals that, generally speaking, authoritative parenting is associated "with positive aspects of child development such as activeness, independence, taking initiative and responsibility, spontaneity, social competence in interaction with peers, and lesser levels of impulsiveness, aggression, or inclination to withdraw."[57]

On theological grounds, why does it make sense for American congregations to encourage parents to develop an authoritative style of parenting? Indulgent parenting, in effect, ignores the power of sin, both within the child and in the surrounding culture. It fails to acknowledge that children need discipline for a variety of reasons: to learn self-control, to resist temptation, and to take account of the needs of others, to name but a few. Christian love takes account of the realism of sin and the need for restraint. Authoritarian parenting, on the other hand, fails to acknowledge that love demands investment in the child as the recipient of God's gracious care. Discipline unaccompanied by warmth and interest may motivate obedience out of fear but not as an expression of affection and gratitude toward the parent. Nor does it help children learn how to regulate their own behaviors when authority figures are not around. Moreover, authoritarian parenting fails to take account of the parent's potential corruption by sin. Who will discipline the disciplinarian? Without idealizing authoritative parenting, it has the potential of representing a middle way that acknowledges the need for control and discipline and the equal need for support and interest. Both are an expression of love; both are necessary in the face of sin.

Fourth, congregations will do well to encourage families to practice mutual forgiveness in the home as a sign of God's reconciling love. More than once in my teaching career, I have driven to school after an angry exchange with my wife or children and put on my public persona as a caring professional. I doubt that I am alone in this experience. The darkness of the human heart often shows itself most clearly in our families. It is crucial, then, for Christian families to learn how to practice mutual forgiveness. Parents must model this. A willingness to make apologies and amends must begin here. But it also must become an expectation of children as well. This should in-

57. Van der Ven, *Formation of the Moral Self,* p. 50.

clude not only learning to say they are sorry, but also, learning to accept in good faith the apologies of others, to offer forgiveness, and to start anew.

This sort of mutual forgiveness in the home, potentially, is the seedbed of practices of reconciliation in the neighborhood, nation, and global community. It is a critical dimension of Christian witness in a world "caught" in various forms of enmity across racial, cultural, and religious lines. Families will need to rely on their congregations to help their children extend outward the practices of forgiveness and reconciliation. But unless these are first learned in the home, it is unlikely to be seen as relevant or even possible in other, riskier relationships.

Fifth, congregations will do well to equip parents to interpret evil to their children. Scholars of developmental psychology and folklore have long noted that children pass through a stage in which they divide the world into simple patterns of good and evil. The archetypal patterns of fairy tales appeal to this cognitive style, offering evil stepmothers, giants, and kings, on one side, and good children, fairy godmothers, and princes, on the other. The cognitive psychologist Howard Gardner argues that adults often revert to these simple "Star Wars" scripts in crisis situations.[58] Indeed, leaders often appeal to this tendency by encouraging their followers to see the crisis as caused by forces of evil "out there" and to view themselves as among the forces of good who must combat this evil.

The concept of original sin does not lend itself to this way of interpreting evil. It complexifies the motives of all parties in crisis situations and portrays the actors as complicit in events and conditions that are not entirely of their own making. Goodness and evil are found on both sides. Even those actors who may be judged as doing what is right can rarely pursue goodness without unintended, negative consequences for themselves and others. One of the best examples of this way of interpreting evil is found in a series of articles written by H. Richard Niebuhr during World War II.[59] Niebuhr implored the American Christian community to resist demonizing their Axis enemies and to acknowledge their own complicity in the conditions leading up to war. God's judgment, he says, falls on both sides in this conflict. Though the United States was right to enter the war, the Christian community must resist the widespread tendency to identify the Allies' cause com-

58. Howard Gardner, *The Unschooled Mind: How Children Think and How Schools Should Teach* (New York: Basic Books, 1991).

59. H. Richard Niebuhr, "War as the Judgment of God," *The Christian Century* 59 (1942): 953-55; "War as Crucifixion," *The Christian Century* 60 (1943): 513-15. Cf. "The Grace of Doing Nothing," *The Christian Century* 49 (1932): 378-80.

pletely with God's. They too will cause the innocent to suffer and thereby make their own contribution to the evils of the war. In these articles, Niebuhr offered a clear alternative to simple "Star Wars" scripts at a time when Americans were quite vulnerable to this way of interpreting evil. He was informed by a long tradition of reflection on the universal scope and power of human sin. Certainly, Americans today are no less vulnerable and in need of equally rich interpretations of the evil. Not only is this a task for the preacher and teacher, but also for Christian parents. Congregations will do well to prepare them to help their children recognize the complicity of their own nation in sin and the ambiguity of all responses to evil.

I began this chapter by sharing my daughter's encounter with a sermon by Jonathan Edwards in a required course in high school and my ambivalence in how to respond. Many Christian parents today are in a similar position. I have argued that they need the support of congregations that have moved beyond the assumptions of Christendom and become more intentional about discovering their mission as Christian communities within the mission of God. Missional churches must equip parents to better understand the richness of concepts like sin as part of a broader effort to support the spiritual formation of families.

CHAPTER 9

"Best Practices" for Nurturing the Best Love of and by Children: A Protestant Theological Perspective on the Vocations of Children and Parents

Marcia J. Bunge

Introduction

One of the central questions of this volume on "the best love of the child" and of many parents and caregivers today is: How do we raise children to be loving and compassionate members of the community? How do we help cultivate in them altruism and a deep sense of our common humanity?

In many Christian communities today and in the past, questions about "the best love of the child" include attention not only to an adult's love of children and a child's love of and compassion for others but also God's love for humanity and humanity's love of God. Within the Christian tradition, love of self and others is always intertwined with love of God, who is seen as the source and font of all love. Furthermore, although perspectives about Jesus Christ vary among and within denominations, Christians generally believe that Jesus clearly revealed God's love in his teachings and in his own life and death.

Thus, Christian parents and others working with or on behalf of children might rephrase questions about the "best love of the child" in these kinds of ways: How do we love children and raise them in such a way that they grow up loving God and loving and serving the neighbor? How do we cultivate in children a love of God, self, and neighbor? How do we help children become disciples of Christ who are empowered to love and serve others, even their enemies? Such questions build upon the sayings of Jesus and other biblical passages about love of others and about the responsibilities of parents and other caring adults for children. For example, Jesus commanded his followers to "love the Lord your God with all your heart, and with all your soul, and with all your mind, and with all your strength" and to "love your neighbor as yourself" (Mark 12:28-24; Matt. 22:34-40; Luke 10:25-28). The Bible also states that parents and other adults are to "train children in the right way" (Prov. 22:6) and bring them up "in the discipline and instruction of the Lord" (Eph. 6:4). They are to tell children about God's faithfulness (Isa. 38:19) and "the glorious deeds of the Lord" (Ps. 78:4b). They are to teach children the words of the law (Deut. 11:18-19; 31:12-13); the love of God with the whole heart (Deut. 6:5); and just and fair behavior (Gen. 18:19; Prov. 2:9). Although Christians have carried out these commands in different ways, and although they have had diverse approaches to childrearing, nurture, teaching, and discipline, they do share a common conviction that any discussion about the love of children or a child's love of others must include attention to God's love for us and our love of God.

One of the particular ways that many Protestant Christians have understood the tasks of childrearing and of cultivating a child's love of God and others is through the concept of calling or vocation. Today "vocation" is commonly used to refer either to one's profession (such as the calling to be a teacher, professor, or medical doctor) or to full-time service in the church (such as the calling to ordained ministry, the priesthood, or the monastic life). However, within many Protestant traditions, vocation is understood as a rich theological term that embraces far more than the adult world of paid work or ordained ministry. Most Protestant theologians claim that the concept of vocation, rightly understood, addresses our deepest human longings for purpose and meaning in life and encompasses the totality of our lives. It is also a term that applies to everyone — regardless of gender, race, class, or age.

The notion that vocation or calling applies to everyone, including parents and children, was articulated during the Reformation. Since that time, Protestants have often stated in various ways that all people have a "vocation" or "calling" in two senses.[1] On the one hand, they are all called to follow Christ and to love God and to love and serve the neighbor, especially those in need. This is their common vocation or calling: it is, as some Protestants have said, a "general" or "spiritual" vocation that all Christians share. It is the call to discipleship and to unity with Christ. On the other hand, people

1. William C. Placher, ed., *Callings: Twenty Centuries of Christian Wisdom on Vocation* (Grand Rapids: Eerdmans, 2005), p. 206. Placher's book is an excellent introduction to various understandings of vocation in the history of Christianity.

are also called by God to particular "vocations": to specific "offices," "stations," or "places of responsibility" in which they use their gifts and talents to serve the well-being of others, whether at home, at work, at church, or in civic life. They serve others in particular ways — for example, as spouses and parents, doctors and lawyers, pastors and deacons, or politicians and teachers. This is sometimes called their "particular" or "external" vocation. Within this understanding of vocation, all work that benefits the community holds equal religious value. As Martin Luther stated: "There is no true, basic difference between laymen and priests, princes and bishops, between religious and secular, except for the sake of office and work, but not for the sake of status."[2] Furthermore, all people, regardless of age, have a vocation. Everyone has a calling and takes on specific "roles" or "offices" — whether given or chosen, for as one contemporary Protestant ethicist notes, "all significant social relationships are places into which God calls us to serve God and the neighbor."[3]

Building on this theological understanding of vocation, Protestants have viewed parenting itself as a sacred and divine calling, and they have articulated the task of loving and raising children in terms of vocation. They hold parenting as equally sacred and important as any other particular calling in life. A priest or pastor does not have a "higher calling" than a mother or father, because all roles and positions that serve the neighbor and benefit the community are equally sacred and worthy callings.

Furthermore, from a Protestant perspective, children also have particular vocations and callings as children, and adults do not have a "higher calling" than them. Children, like adults, have specific roles and responsibilities within their families and communities. They carry out tasks in their particular "station" in life that serve others and contribute to the common good.

Given this perspective on vocation, the most pressing questions within many Protestant traditions regarding childrearing and "the best love of the child" would be: How do we raise children who have a strong sense of voca-

2. In this passage Luther continues, "They are all of the spiritual estate, all are truly priests, bishops, and popes. But they do not all have the same work to do. . . . Further, everyone must benefit and serve every other by means of his own work or office so that in this way many kinds of work may be done for the bodily and spiritual welfare of the community, just as all the members of the body serve one another." See Martin Luther, "To the Christian Nobility," in *Luther's Works* (LW), ed. Jaroslav Pelikan and Helmut Lehmann (St. Louis: Concordia Publishing House, 1955-1986), 44:129-30.

3. Douglas Schuurman, *Vocation: Discerning Our Callings in Life* (Grand Rapids: Eerdmans, 2004), p. xi.

tion or calling? How do we raise children who know they are loved and forgiven by God and who also use their particular God-given gifts and talents to love and serve the neighbor in specific ways? How do we help cultivate the gifts and talents of children so that they contribute to the common good in the future? How do we help parents understand that raising children is just as important and sacred as one's professional work or as the calling to be a pastor? How can we support parents in their sacred calling as parents?

Although Protestants have long honored parenting as a divine and sacred calling, contemporary Protestant systematic theologians and ethicists have written little about parenting or child-parent relationships. They have left issues of parenting, children, and spiritual and moral formation primarily to religious educators or pastoral theologians, and they have focused much more attention on other, albeit related issues, such as abortion, contraception, reproductive technology, or sexuality. Those who have turned their attention directly to children and childrearing tend to focus on the tasks of "teaching" children or "disciplining" them. As a result, their views of children, parents, and adult-child relationships are often too narrow. For example, when the main task of parents is understood as teaching, children are seen principally as ignorant or immature beings. Or when the task of parents is viewed primarily as disciplining, children are viewed largely as sinful or defiant. Such perspectives fail to take into account the rich and complex views of parents, children, and adult-child relationships that are found both within the Bible and within Protestant theological understandings of vocation. They also weaken other areas of the church's work with or on behalf of children, whether in children's ministry, religious education, or child advocacy.

Thus, there is an urgent need for contemporary Protestant theologians to articulate stronger theological understandings of the best love of the child, and they can do so by building upon and critically mining resources from the Bible, their own theological traditions about vocation, and insights from the burgeoning areas of "theologies of childhood" and "child theologies." This distinction is just emerging among Christian theologians and ethicists who are concerned about children.[4] "Theologies of childhood," on the one hand, aim to provide sophisticated understandings of children and childhood and our obligations to children themselves. On the other hand, "child theologies" reexamine not only conceptions of children and obliga-

4. For a fuller discussion of current trends, see Marcia J. Bunge, "The Child, Religion, and the Academy: Developing Robust Theological and Religious Understandings of Children and Childhood," *Journal of Religion* 86, no. 4 (October 2006): 549-79.

tions to them but also fundamental doctrines and practices of the church.[5] Drawing on analogies to feminist, black, and liberation theologies, child theologies have as their task not only to strengthen the commitment to and understanding of a group that has often been voiceless, marginalized, or oppressed — children — but also to reinterpret Christian theology and practice as a whole.[6] In this way, child theologies aim to offer new insights into central themes of the Christian faith, such as God, creation, Christology, theological anthropology, sin, salvation, faith, the Word, worship, sacraments, missiology, and eschatology.

Recent developments in these areas and in the area of Childhood Studies in general provide resources for Protestant theologians concerned about children and also raise some challenging questions that should be addressed, especially regarding the "agency" of children. These questions include but are not limited to the following: In what ways do children teach

5. Studies in the areas of ethics, systematic theology, historical theology, and practical theology that are helping to shape and strengthen both "theologies of childhood" and "child theologies" include, for example, Herbert Anderson and Susan B. W. Johnson, *Regarding Children* (Louisville: Westminster/John Knox Press, 1994); Jerome Berryman, *Godly Play: An Imaginative Approach to Religious Education* (San Francisco: HarperSanFrancisco, 1991); Marcia J. Bunge, ed., *The Child in Christian Thought* (Grand Rapids: Eerdmans, 2001); Pamela Couture, *Seeing Children, Seeing God: A Practical Theology of Children and Poverty* (Nashville: Abingdon, 2000); Marva Dawn, *Is It a Lost Cause? Having the Heart of God for the Church's Children* (Grand Rapids: Eerdmans, 1997); Dawn DeVries, "Toward a Theology of Childhood," *Interpretation* 55, no. 2 (April 2001); Kristin Herzog, *Children and Our Global Future: Theological and Social Challenges* (Cleveland: Pilgrim Press, 2005); Timothy P. Jackson, ed., *The Morality of Adoption: Social-Psychological, Theological, and Legal Perspectives* (Grand Rapids: Eerdmans, 2005); David H. Jensen, *Graced Vulnerability: A Theology of Childhood* (Cleveland: Pilgrim, 2005); Kathleen Marshall and Paul Parvis, *Honouring Children: The Human Rights of the Child in Christian Perspective* (Edinburgh: Saint Andrews Press, 2004); Scottie May, Beth Posterski, Catherine Stonehouse, and Linda Cannell, *Children Matter: Celebrating Their Place in the Church, Family, and Community* (Grand Rapids: Eerdmans, 2005); Joyce Ann Mercer, *Welcoming Children: A Practical Theology of Childhood* (St. Louis: Chalice Press, 2005); Bonnie Miller-McLemore, *Let the Children Come: Reimagining Childhood from a Christian Perspective* (San Francisco: Jossey-Bass, 2003); Jürgen Moltmann, "Child and Childhood as Metaphors of Hope," *Theology Today* 56, no. 4 (2000): 592-603; Deusdedit R. K. Nkurunziza, "African Theology of Childhood in Relation to Child Labour," *African Ecclesial Review* 46, no. 2 (2004): 121-38; Merton P. Strommen and Richard Hardel, *Passing on the Faith: A Radical New Model for Youth and Family Ministry* (Winona, MN: St. Mary's Press, 2000); Karen-Marie Yust, *Real Kids, Real Faith: Practices for Nurturing Children's Spiritual Lives* (San Francisco: Jossey-Bass, 2004); and John Wall, "Childhood Studies, Hermeneutics, and Theological Ethics," *Journal of Religion* 86, no. 4 (October 2006).

6. Bunge, "The Child, Religion, and the Academy," p. 554.

adults to be more loving and compassionate toward others? In what ways are adults shaped morally and spiritually by children? In what ways are children active social agents in the community and already contributing to the common good?

Given these questions, a strong Protestant theological understanding of childrearing and the best love of the child should address the following:

1. What is the best love of the child by adults? How do parents help children to live out their vocations — to use their particular gifts and talents to love God, to love and serve the neighbor, and to "care for creation"? How can other caring adults and the community support parents in this task?
2. What is the best love of others by the child? How does a child best carry out his or her vocation here and now? What do adults learn from children about how best to use their gifts and talents to love God, to love and serve the neighbor, and to care for creation? How are children examples or models for adults? What are other primary duties and responsibilities of children? What is their role in the family, congregational life, and the community?

The aim of this chapter is to address these questions and to offer the beginnings of a robust theological understanding of child-parent relationships by mining resources from the Bible and from selected Protestant understandings of vocation. The chapter is divided into three parts. The first part provides an introduction to the concept of vocation and the specific callings of children and parents. It explores the questions: What are parents and children called to do? What does it means to say that both parents and children have a sacred calling or vocation?[7] The second part focuses on how parents can help children to live out their vocations, and it outlines ten central responsibilities and "best practices" emphasized in the Bible and the Christian tradition for raising children to love and serve God and the neighbor and to care for creation. The third part examines some of the central ways children

7. Parts one and three of this chapter build heavily on my essay "The Vocation of the Child: Theological Perspectives on the Particular and Paradoxical Roles and Responsibilities of Children," in *The Vocation of the Child*, ed. Patrick Brennan (Grand Rapids: Eerdmans, 2008), pp. 31-52. Another helpful resource on Lutheran perspectives on children, education, and vocation is "Our Calling in Education," a recently adopted social statement of the Evangelical Lutheran Church in America (ELCA).

can carry out their particular vocations here and now, thereby showing love to God and the neighbor and contributing to the common good.

Although this paper builds mainly on a Lutheran theological understanding of vocation, it illustrates the possibility of critically retrieving other theological concepts from various strands of the Christian tradition, thereby strengthening our theological language of child-parent relationships in ways that not only honor the sacred task of parenting and the important role of parents in the spiritual formation of children but also honor the dignity and complexity of children and their roles and responsibilities in the community. Above all, this exploration of vocation shows that any strong theological understanding of parenting must be integrally connected to a vibrant and complex theological understanding of children and childhood. Exploring the vocation of parents and children is also a rich and fruitful way to challenge common and often narrow conceptions of children and parents; to deepen our understanding of who children are and the significant roles they play in families and community life; to highlight the important role of parents in the moral and spiritual development of children; and to strengthen our commitment to both children and parents.

Parents, Children, and Their Sacred Callings

Given his expansive view of vocation that includes both professional and familial roles and relationships and people of all ages, Martin Luther speaks meaningfully about the sacred task and calling of both parents and children. Although Luther knows that parenting can be a difficult task and is often considered an insignificant and even distasteful job, he believes parenting is a serious and divine calling that is "adorned with divine approval as with the costliest gold and jewels."[8] In one often-quoted passage, he says the following:

> Now you tell me, when a father goes ahead and washes diapers or performs some other mean task for his child, and someone ridicules him as an effeminate fool . . . God, with all his angels and creatures, is smiling — not because that father is washing diapers, but because he is doing so in Christian faith.[9]

Luther further underscored the importance of parenting by claiming:

8. LW 45:39.
9. LW 45:40-41.

> Most certainly father and mother are apostles, bishops, and priests to their children, for it is they who make them acquainted with the gospel. In short, there is no greater or nobler authority on earth than that of parents over their children, for this authority is both spiritual and temporal.[10]

According to Luther, as priests and bishops to their children, parents have a twofold task: to nurture the faith of their children and to help them develop their gifts to serve others.[11] He also helped parents in this task by preaching about parenting and by writing the "Small Catechism," which was intended for use in the home.

Children and young people, in turn, have a sacred calling here and now. They are to honor their parents, learn about the faith, live out their faith here and now by serving others in their midst, and discern and develop their gifts and talents so that they can effectively serve both church and society later in life.

Followers of Luther also spoke meaningfully about the sacred task of parenting and the vocations of both parents and children. August Herman Francke, the eighteenth-century German pietist from Halle, for example, claimed that the primary goal of parents is to lead their children to godliness. They are to help children grow in faith, empowering them to use their gifts and talents to love and serve God and the neighbor and to contribute to the common good.[12] Children, in turn, are to honor their parents and to cultivate their gifts and talents through diligent study.

There are many other examples in the Protestant tradition of theologians who took seriously the role of parents in the spiritual formation of children and who emphasized that the primary goal of parenting is to help children strengthen their faith and their calling to love God and to love and serve others. For example, in his popular book, *Christian Nurture,* Horace

10. LW 45:46.

11. For a full discussion of Luther's views on parenting, see, for example: Jane E. Strohl, "The Child in Luther's Theology: 'For What Purpose Do We Older Folks Exist, Other Than to Care for . . . the Young?'" in Bunge, ed., *The Child in Christian Thought,* pp. 134-59; William Lazareth, *Luther on the Christian Home: An Application of the Social Ethics of the Reformation* (Philadelphia: Muhlenberg Press, 1969); Steven Ozment, *When Fathers Ruled: Family Life in Reformation Europe* (Cambridge, MA: Harvard University Press, 1983); F. V. N. Painter, *Luther on Education* (Lutheran Publication Society, 1889); and Gerald Strauss, *Luther's House of Learning.*

12. See Marcia Bunge, "Education and the Child in Eighteenth-Century German Pietism: Perspectives from the Work of A. H. Francke," in Bunge, ed., *The Child in Christian Thought,* pp. 247-78.

Bushnell, a nineteenth-century congregational pastor and scholar, emphasized that parents are the primary agents of a child's spiritual formation. "Religion," he claimed, "never penetrates life until it becomes domestic."[13]

"Best Practices" for Nurturing the Moral and Spiritual Lives of Children and Cultivating Their Sense of Vocation

If parents, indeed, have a specific calling, then what does it look like? What is their "work" or "office"? In what specific ways do parents and other caring adults help children to live out their vocations? What are the best ways for raising children to live out their vocations — to use their particular gifts and talents to love God, to love and serve the neighbor, and "care for creation"? What are the specific duties, roles, and responsibilities of parents that help children and contribute to the life of the community?

The Bible and various Christian traditions emphasize what we might call ten "best practices" and responsibilities of parents for nurturing the moral and spiritual lives of children and helping them live out their callings in life. Attending to these ten practices and responsibilities is not a guarantee that children will "turn out okay" and be faithful, service-oriented, and compassionate adults. Christians generally agree that despite any child's upbringing (whether good or bad), children continually surprise us, and God can work in their lives. However, Christians from various traditions have used these ten particular duties and practices to foster the moral and spiritual formation in children. Recent sociological and psychological studies on moral or spiritual development also confirm the value of these kinds of activities for children and young people today. These are ten valuable ways of creating a space for the Holy Spirit to work in the lives of children and adults. Although perhaps the first four are most familiar and most emphasized in the Christian tradition,[14] all ten have been important in the tradition for cultivating faith and service to others.

13. Horace Bushnell, *Christian Nurture* (New York: Charles Scribner, 1861; reprint, Cleveland: Pilgrim Press, 1994), p. 63. For a full discussion of Bushnell, see Margaret Bendroth, "Horace Bushnell's *Christian Nurture*," in Bunge, ed., *The Child in Christian Thought*, pp. 350-64.

14. The first four practices are most familiar and have been emphasized by several institutes that focus on faith formation in children, such as the Search Institute and the Youth and Family Institute.

1. *Reading and Discussing the Bible and Interpretations of It with Children*

Luther, John Calvin, Friedrich Schleiermacher, Horace Bushnell, and many other Protestant theologians have emphasized the importance of reading and discussing the Bible with children. Regardless of their view of biblical authority or biblical interpretation, so-called conservative and liberal Protestant Christians today would all agree that the Bible is the central text for the Christian church and contains truths and stories that parents or caring adults need to tell and to teach children. Adults will read different Bible stories to children in different ways, but no matter what their approach, they should cultivate in children the practice of "religious reading" — reading and rereading the texts, "digesting" them, and viewing the Bible as a vast and abundant goldmine of wisdom that can never be fully excavated.[15]

2. *Worshiping with a Community and Carrying Out Family Rituals and Traditions of Worship and Prayer*

Protestants have also emphasized that parents should worship regularly with their children. They should "remember the Sabbath and keep it holy" and participate in corporate worship. Rituals of worship and prayer at home are also important. Many Protestant theologians have emphasized praying daily with children, and they have written special prayers that can be said before and after meals and at bedtime. They have also carried out particular rituals and family traditions during seasons of the liturgical year, such as Lent and Advent.

3. *Introducing Children to Good Examples, Mentors, and Stories of Service and Compassion*

Like other Christians, Protestants have recognized the importance of good examples in the lives of children. Within Protestant traditions, being a good

15. Here we can learn from the contemporary thinker, Paul Griffiths, who makes a distinction between "religious reading" (which is done slowly, repeatedly, and with the aim of gaining wisdom for life from the text) and "consumerist reading" (which is done quickly and with the aim of getting information). See Paul Griffiths, *Religious Reading: The Place of Reading in the Practice of Religion* (Oxford: Oxford University Press, 1999).

example means that parents or caregivers are believers themselves and strive to live out their faith in their everyday lives. Other important examples for children are often teachers, coaches, or other adults who have cared for children and taken an interest in them.

4. Participating in Service Projects with Parents or Other Caring Adults; and (Connected to Service) Teaching Financial Responsibility

Christian theologians have also encouraged parents to serve others in the community with their children and to reach out to those in need. The family is not understood as an isolated, self-satisfied, or enclosed entity; it is not a fortress but rather a community that reaches out to those in need. Many theologians have emphasized the notion that the family should serve others in need by speaking about it as a "little church." For example, John Chrysostom, an important figure in the fourth-century church and for Eastern Orthodox communities of faith today, spoke about the family as a little church or a "sacred community." For him, this means that parents should read the Bible to their children, pray with them, and be good examples. However, being a little church also means that the family reaches out to the poor and needy in the community. Chrysostom ranks the neglect of children among the greatest evils and injustices.[16] For him, neglect of children includes inordinate concern for your own needs and affairs above those of your children. He also believes that we neglect children when we focus on secular standards of success, which at that time, as today, means mainly financial success, or when we are preoccupied with accumulating possessions.

Parents and other caring adults teach children much about their faith and values when they find ways to help the poor or to carry out service projects together with children. This can be done in formal or informal ways, such as helping a neighbor, visiting the sick, or helping poor communities. In the United States, for example, many young people and their families serve in a soup kitchen or participate in a Habitat for Humanity project. The value of this kind of mutual service was underscored in a survey that found that "involvement in service proved to be a better predictor of faith maturity than participation in Sunday School, Bible study, or worship services."[17]

16. Vigen Guroian, "The Ecclesial Family: John Chrysostom on Parenthood and Children," in Bunge, ed., *The Child in Christian Thought*, pp. 64, 73.

17. Strommen and Hardel, *Passing on the Faith*, p. 95.

Because service is related to financial responsibility, and because we do live in a consumer culture, it is important for parents to speak to their children about money and financial responsibility. In the United States today, a country in which children are daily bombarded with commercials, we now have more shopping malls than schools, the favorite activity of 95 percent of high school girls is shopping, and the number one reason that students must drop out of college is credit card debt. Parents must realize that financial responsibility goes along with service to and love of others: knowing how to spend money wisely and using it to help others.

5. *Singing Together and Exposing Children to the Spiritual Gifts of Music and the Arts*

The arts, especially music, have always been an important vehicle of moral and spiritual formation in the Protestant tradition. Martin Luther, for example, believed that music was not simply an ornament for worship service but rather a vital element of human existence, an instrument of the Holy Spirit, and a powerful vehicle for spreading the gospel. He emphasized the value of music in these bold words: "Next to the Word of God, music deserves the highest praise."[18] Because of the vital role of music and the arts in spiritual life, he specifically encourages Christians to sing with children and to train them in music and the arts. In one passage Luther claims, for example, "I would like to see all the arts, especially music, used in the service of Him who gave and made them. I therefore pray that every pious Christian would be pleased with this [the use of music in the service of the gospel] and lend his help if God has given him like or greater gifts. As it is, the world is too lax and indifferent about teaching and training the young for us to abet this trend."[19]

6. *Appreciating the Natural World and Cultivating a Reverence for Creation*

There are many examples within the Christian tradition, other religious traditions, and our own experience of how close contact with the natural world has been a source of spiritual growth and inspiration. Many biblical passages

18. Foreword to Georg Rhau's *Symphoniae iuconudae,* in LW 53:323.
19. "Preface to the Wittenberg Hymnal" (1524), in LW 53:316.

emphasize the beauty and goodness of creation and the importance of going to the wilderness for spiritual renewal, cleansing, or insight. Early in the Christian tradition, monks retreated to the wilderness to meditate and wrote eloquently about the insights they gained about God's creation and their place in it. The important relationship between the spiritual life and the natural world is also found in the works of Celtic Christians, medieval mystics, St. Francis, and many contemporary Christian writers today, such as Leonardo Boff or Wendell Berry. Many young Christians today attend Bible camps or wilderness retreats, and such experiences not only help cultivate a love of others but also a love and respect for the natural world.

7. Educating Children and Helping Them Discern Their Vocations

Many Protestant theologians, such as Luther and Francke, would add that we nurture faith in children by helping them discern their gifts and talents and by providing them with a good liberal arts education so that they can better use their gifts to love and to serve others. Both believe a strong liberal arts program will help children develop their God-given gifts and talents, enabling them to serve both church and society.[20] Parents and caring adults are to help children find their vocation: not just help them see what is fulfilling or makes the most money, but how they can best use their talents to make a difference in the world and to contribute to the common good. In a letter to the councilmen, Luther underscores the importance of education by saying:

> Now the welfare of a city does not consist solely in accumulating vast treasure, building mighty walls and magnificent buildings and producing a goodly supply of guns and armor. Indeed, where such things are plentiful, and reckless fools get control of them, it is so much the worse and the city suffers even greater loss. A city's best and greatest welfare, safety, and strength consist rather in its having many able, learned, wise, honorable, and well-educated citizens.[21]

20. For Luther's ideas on education, see, for example, his "Sermon on Keeping Children in School" (1530) and his "To the Councilmen of All Cities in Germany That They Establish and Maintain Christian Schools" (1524). For Francke's view of education, see Bunge, "Education and the Child in Eighteenth-Century German Pietism."

21. Martin Luther, "To the Councilmen of All Cities in Germany That They Establish and Maintain Christian Schools," in *Martin Luther's Basic Theological Writings,* ed. Timothy F. Lull (Minneapolis: Fortress, 1989), pp. 712-13.

Given their views of education and vocation, both Luther in the sixteenth century and Francke in the eighteenth, in contrast to many in their time, were advocates of excellent schools and education for all children (including girls and the poor). They prompted real educational reforms that continue to influence German schools today. As Luther stated, "We must spare no diligence, time, or cost in teaching and educating our children" to serve God and the world.[22] In the Jewish tradition, too, one of the major responsibilities of parents is to provide their children with an education that prepares them for a trade or a profession. Thus, many theologians and religious leaders in both the Jewish and Christian traditions have started or supported schools and colleges, fought for educational reform, and demanded that all children be given an excellent education.

8. Fostering Lifegiving Attitudes toward the Body, Sexuality, and Marriage

Although the Christian tradition has a somewhat ambivalent legacy regarding the body, the Jewish and Christian traditions both affirm the goodness of our bodies and our sexuality and the goodness of the natural world in general. Because of this conviction, and because young people and even very young children today are bombarded with messages about sex in the news, TV, and other forms of technology, parents and other caring adults should therefore help children understand from an early age that taking care of their bodies is part of honoring God and God's gifts to us. They should also help children understand the proper context for the expression of sexuality and speak to them about Christian understandings and expectations of marriage and sexual activity.

Protestant theologians in the past have also typically encouraged parents to do more to help young people think about and find a mate. Luther considered this to be one of the central duties of parents. Jews today also consider this to be one of the primary duties of parents.[23] Today, Protestants do not tend to speak about this as a parental duty, since they want children to choose their own mates. But helping children find a mate is not the same as promoting forced marriages. It is simply saying that just as we "make

22. "The Large Catechism," 388.

23. Elliot N. Dorff, *Love Your Neighbor and Yourself: A Jewish Approach to Modern Personal Ethics* (Philadelphia: Jewish Publication Society, 2003), pp. 143, 150-54.

sure" our children have good friends or a good education or music lessons, we need to "make sure" we talk to them about sex and marriage, help them learn from both our mistakes and positive experiences in relationships, introduce them to potential mates, and ensure that when and if they become engaged, they take advantage of strong premarital programs offered in the church today.

9. *Listening to and Learning from Children*

Adults also cultivate faith in children by listening to their questions, insights, and concerns. In this way, faith can be taken to heart and appropriated.

Furthermore, as several biblical texts illustrate, parents should recognize that children can also nurture, deepen, and challenge the faith of adults. For example, several Gospels depict children in striking and even radical ways as moral witnesses, models of faith for adults, sources or vehicles of revelation, and representatives of Jesus. These passages turn upside down common assumptions held in Jesus' time and our own: that children are to be seen but not heard and that the primary role of children is to learn from and obey adults. In contrast, these and other biblical passages remind us that children can teach and challenge adults, prophesy, and praise God. They can be models of faith and even paradigms for entering the reign of God. "Unless you change and become like children, you will never enter the kingdom of heaven," Jesus warns. "Whoever becomes humble like this child is the greatest in the kingdom of heaven. Whoever welcomes one such child in my name welcomes me" (Matt. 18:2-5). Viewing children as models for adults or vehicles of revelation does not mean that they are creatures who are "near angels," "closer to God," or "more spiritual" than adults. However, these passages and others do challenge adults to be receptive to the lessons and wisdom that children offer them, to honor children's questions and insights, and to recognize that children can positively influence the community and the moral and spiritual lives of adults.

The idea that children can be teachers, bearers of revelation, or models of faith has often been neglected in Christian thought and practice. However, throughout the tradition and today, we do find theologians who have grappled seriously with these New Testament passages, forcing them to rethink their assumptions about children and exploring what adults learn from them. For example, Friedrich Schleiermacher, the nineteenth-century German Protestant theologian, emphasized that adults who want to enter the kingdom of God need to recover a childlike spirit. For him, this childlike spirit has many components that we can learn from children, such as "living fully in the present moment," being able to forgive others, or being flexible.[24]

10. Taking Up a Christ-Centered Approach to Discipline and Authority; and Recognizing That, in the Tradition, Parental Authority Is Always Limited

Another part of a parent's vocation within the Protestant tradition is taking up a Christ-centered approach to discipline and parental authority. Although some Protestants today equate "disciplining children" with physically punishing them, true discipline has much more to do with becoming followers and disciples of Christ.

Furthermore, although most Protestants claim that parents have authority over children, they also recognize that this authority is never absolute. It is always limited. Theologians generally qualify absolute parental authority because they recognize that parents are sometimes sinful, unjust, or just plain inept. They also recognize that as children grow and develop, their moral capacities and responsibilities also grow and develop, and children must be prepared to challenge the authority of their parents and even political and ecclesiastical authorities if they lead to injustices. Thus, parents are given authority over their children, but this authority is limited, and it is never an excuse for treating children unjustly or unkindly.

Although Luther, for example, compared the authority of parents to God's own authority, he gave examples of the abuse of parental authority. Building on scripture, he believed that even though children should generally tolerate the injustices of their parents and obey them, they could under certain circumstances and in good conscience act contrary to the will of tyrannical or unjust parents.[25] He believed, for example, that parents should neither force nor hinder the marriage of their children and asserted:

24. For an excellent discussion of Schleiermacher, see Dawn DeVries, "'Be Converted and Become as Little Children': Friedrich Schleiermacher on the Religious Significance of Childhood," in Bunge, ed., *The Child in Christian Thought*, pp. 300-328; and Dawn DeVries, "Toward a Theology of Childhood," pp. 165-66.

25. Martin Luther, "That Parents Should Neither Compel nor Hinder the Marriage of Their Children, and That Children Should Not Become Engaged Without Their Parents' Consent," in LW 45:385-93.

> Parental authority is strictly limited; it does not extend to the point where it can wreak damage and destruction to the child, especially to its soul. If then a father forces his children into a marriage without love, he oversteps and exceeds his authority. He ceases to be a father and becomes a tyrant who uses his authority not for building up — which is why God gave it to him — but for destroying. He is taking authority into his own hands without God, indeed, against God. The same principle holds good when a father hinders his child's marriage, or lets the child go ahead on his own, without any intention of helping him in the matter.[26]

The Specific Vocation of Children: Primary Duties and Responsibilities

If children, too, have a specific calling, then what does it look like? What are their specific duties, roles, and responsibilities that contribute to the life of the community and show compassion for others? What is their specific "work" or "office"? How do they use their gifts and talents here and now to love and serve others and to care for creation?

The Bible and the tradition emphasize that the specific vocation of the child contains at least six almost paradoxical elements. Each of these elements is built on a complex theological understanding of the nature of children, and each one corresponds to duties and responsibilities of parents and other caring adults as outlined above.

1. *Honor and Respect Your Parents*

Throughout the Christian tradition, one of the most commonly cited duties of children is to honor and respect their parents. The fourth commandment is "Honor your father and mother so that your days may be long in the land that the Lord your God is giving you" (Exod. 20:12; Deut. 5:16), and several other biblical passages command children to honor and respect their parents (Lev. 19:3; Eph. 6:2-3; Heb. 12:9). The term for honor in Hebrew literally means "to make heavy," and the fourth commandment calls children to regard their parents as worthy of this weighty respect and dignity.

Corresponding to this first duty of children are also particular assump-

26. LW 45:386.

tions about the nature of children and the duties of parents. It assumes that children are dependent and vulnerable beings, and parents, in turn, are to love, serve, and protect them by providing them with food, clothing, and other basic needs. It also indicates that children are capable of gratitude and giving thanks for others.

Children should honor their parents, in part, because parents must do so much for them to nourish them, protect them, and keep them alive. Luther states, for example, that God commands children to honor their parents because parents have "nourished and nurtured them," and they owe their parents "body and life" and "every good." Without parents a child would have, as Luther says so delicately, "perished a hundred times in his own filth."[27] He believes that even young children can honor their parents by being grateful for the love and protection of their parents or guardians. For him, children have a duty "to show gratitude for the kindness and for all the good things we have received from our parents."[28] He believes that children should not grumble, and they should remember the many blessings they have already received.

However, the commandment to honor and respect parents does not stop with childhood, and the particular vocation of the "child" includes some duties that are lifelong. This particular duty of the "child" continues into adulthood, since as long as one's parents are alive, one still has an obligation to honor and respect them. Indeed, Jewish scholar Elliot Dorff has stated that the rabbis understood the commandment to honor and respect parents as "primarily governing the interactions of adult children of elderly parents."[29] Thus, adult children of elderly parents have an obligation to provide food and clothing for them, and they honor their parents by caring for them as they grow older.[30]

2. *Obey Your Parents*

Another duty of children often cited in the Christian tradition is that children are to obey their parents. They are commanded: "Children, obey your parents in everything, for this is your acceptable duty in the Lord" (Col. 3:20). They are to obey their parents "in the Lord, for this is right" (Eph. 6:1). Obedience also includes recognizing the authority of parents over their chil-

27. Luther, "The Large Catechism," 383.
28. Luther, "The Large Catechism," 382.
29. Dorff, *Love Your Neighbor and Yourself,* p. 128.
30. Dorff, *Love Your Neighbor and Yourself,* pp. 127-43.

dren. The "younger must accept the authority of the elders" and "clothe" themselves with humility (1 Pet. 5:5-6). The New Testament also lists disobedience to parents as a particular vice (Rom. 1:30; 2 Tim. 3:2).

The duty to obey assumes that children are not yet able to discern fully right from wrong, and they need to learn from and follow the example of their parents and other adults in authority. They need to be told what is right and wrong and what God requires of them (Mic. 6:6). Parents, in turn, have an obligation to be good examples to their children and to be their moral and spiritual teachers. Given their authority and significance in a child's life, they should also understand that their example and actions can influence not only a child's relationship to other human beings but also his or her understanding of God.

Many Protestant theologians have emphasized that children should honor and obey their parents to such a degree that they regard them as God's representatives. Luther, for example, states that children should honor and revere their parents "as God's representatives" and hold them in distinction and esteem above all things "as the most precious treasure on earth."[31] In the twentieth century, the Protestant theologian Karl Barth also spoke of parents as "God's representatives." "From the standpoint of children parents have a Godward aspect, and are for them God's primary and natural representatives."[32] For Barth, parents are really the "elders" in relation to their children, and they represent not only their own knowledge and experience to children "but that conveyed to them by their own predecessors." Thus, children are to heed and obey them. This does not mean, Barth clarifies, that children are the parents' "property, subjects, servants or even pupils." Rather, children are their parents' "apprentices, who are entrusted and subordinated to them in order that they might lead them into the way of life. The children must be content to accept this leading from their parents. In general outline, this is what the command of God requires of them."[33]

3. *Disobey Your Parents and Other Adult Authorities*

Although almost all Protestant theologians today and in the past would emphasize that children should honor and obey their parents, they often ne-

31. Luther, "The Large Catechism," 379-80.

32. Karl Barth, *Church Dogmatics*, II/4, ed. G. W. Bromiley and T. F. Torrance (Edinburgh: T. & T. Clark, 1961), p. 243.

33. Barth, *Church Dogmatics*, II/4, p. 243.

glect a third and corresponding responsibility of children that is also part of the tradition: children have a responsibility and duty *not* to obey their parents, if their parents or other adult authorities cause them to sin or to carry out acts of injustice. Although children should honor and obey their parents, their ultimate loyalty is to God, and their primary task is to love and serve others and to care for creation.

Several examples in the Bible illustrate that parents are sometimes unjust and unfaithful or that children must follow God's law above the commands of parents when the two conflict. Ezekiel, for example, commands children, "Do not follow the statutes of your parents, nor observe their ordinances, nor defile yourselves with their idols. I the Lord am your God; follow my statutes, and be careful to observe my ordinances, and hallow my Sabbaths" (Ezek. 20:18-19). In the New Testament, Jesus also points out potential conflicts between parents and children, when one is called to follow him.[34] Speaking to his disciples, he says "You will be betrayed even by parents and brothers, by relatives and friends; and they will put some of you to death. You will be hated by all because of my name" (Luke 21:16-17).

Building on such passages, Protestant theologians generally qualify absolute obedience to parents, just as they qualify parental authority. Barth, for example, states that "no human father, but God alone, is properly, truly and primarily Father. No human father is the creator of his child, the controller of its destiny, or its savior from sin, guilt and death."[35] Parents and other caring adults therefore have a duty to recognize that they are certainly not gods on earth, and they should not demand blind obedience from their children.

Related to the notion that children should at times disobey their parents is an understanding that children (whether young children or adults) are not ultimately subject to their parents. Rather, children are made in the image of God (not primarily in the image of their parents); they are thus worthy of respect from the start. Even as young children, they are active moral agents with growing moral capacities and responsibilities of their own. Their ultimate loyalty is to God and not to any adult authority, and showing love and compassion to others is more important than loyalty to family. As fully human moral agents who are made in God's image, their primary task is to love

34. For a fuller discussion of the tension between obedience to parents and following Jesus, see John T. Carroll, "'What, then, will this child become?': Perspectives on Children in the Gospel of John," in *The Child in the Bible,* ed. Marcia J. Bunge, Terence Fretheim, and Beverly Gaventa (Grand Rapids: Eerdmans, 2008), pp. 177-94.

35. Barth, *Church Dogmatics,* II/4, p. 245.

and serve the neighbor and to care for creation, even if their actions conflict with the expectations or demands of their parents.

4. *Fear and Love God*

Consonant with children's responsibility to evaluate adult demands and to disobey unjust authority is the call to fear the Lord. Although parents are to be honored and obeyed, God alone is to be feared and held in reverence. Again and again, the biblical texts emphasize that everyone, including children, is called to "fear the Lord" (Deut. 4:10; 6:1-2; 14:23; 17:19; 31:12-13). "The fear of the Lord is the beginning of knowledge; fools scorn wisdom and instruction" (Prov. 1:7; cf. 9:10). As the biblical scholar William Brown notes in Proverbs, the "fear of God is eminently edifying and life-enhancing" (Prov. 10:27; 14:27; 19:23).[36]

The duty of children to fear God is connected to the notion that both parents and children are to fear God. Here is where true security for both children and parents has its root: "In the fear of the Lord there is strong confidence, and one's children will have a refuge" (Prov. 14:26). Here is where love of others has its foundation.

5. *Go to School and Study Diligently for the Future*

The Protestant tradition often emphasizes a fifth duty or responsibility of children: to go to school, to study diligently, and to cultivate their unique skills, gifts, and talents so that they can love and serve others and contribute to the common good in the future.

This duty is directly tied to the idea of vocation and built on the notion that children are uniquely created with diverse gifts and talents that enable them to serve others, thereby offering families and communities hope for the future. Indeed, many people today and in the past speak about children as our future or as our hope. As Jürgen Moltmann and others have recognized, the child and childhood are powerful metaphors for hope, and chil-

36. William Brown, "To Discipline without Destruction: The Multifaceted Profile of the Child in Proverbs," in Bunge, Fretheim, and Gaventa, eds., *The Child in the Bible*, p. 73. For further discussions of the "fear of the Lord," see also Patrick Miller, "That the Children May Know: Children in Deuteronomy," in *The Child in the Bible*, pp. 45-62, in the same volume.

dren themselves give us hope and open up new possibilities for the future.[37] This responsibility of children corresponds to the parental duty (discussed above) to help children discern and name their gifts and to provide them with good schools and a solid education. By doing so, they prepare children to use their gifts in service to others, thereby strengthening the community and building for the future.

6. Play and Be in the Present

Finally, although children are to cultivate their gifts and talents to serve others in the future, at the same time they have a role of strengthening and enlivening families and communities here and now simply through their openness, playfulness, and ability to laugh and be in the present. This aspect of their vocation or calling is another positive social role they serve as children right here and now.

This dimension of their specific calling is informed by the biblical conviction that children are gifts of God and sources of joy and that adults should cherish, enjoy, and be grateful for children as they are now — not for what they will become in the future. The Bible and the Christian tradition often depict children as gifts of God and sources of joy who ultimately come from God and belong to God. Many passages in the Bible speak of children as gifts of God or signs of God's blessing who are gifts not only to parents but also to the community.[38] They will grow up to be not only sons and daughters but also husbands, wives, friends, neighbors, and citizens. Viewing children as gifts of God to the whole community radically challenges common assumptions of them as "property" of parents or as "economic burdens" to the community. Related to this notion that children are gifts and signs of God's blessing, the tradition speaks of them as sources of joy and pleasure. Here, too, there are many examples.[39] Sarah rejoiced at the

37. Jürgen Moltmann, "Child and Childhood as Metaphors of Hope," *Theology Today* 56, no. 4 (2000): 592-603.

38. For example, Leah, Jacob's first wife, speaks of her sixth son as a dowry, or wedding gift, presented by God (Gen. 30:20). Several biblical passages indicate that parents who receive these precious gifts are being "remembered" by God (Gen. 30:22; 1 Sam. 1:11, 19) and given "good fortune" (Gen. 30:11). To be "fruitful" — have many children — is to receive God's blessing. The Psalmist says children are a "heritage" from the Lord and a "reward" (Ps. 127:3).

39. Other passages include Jeremiah's recollection that the news of his own birth once made his father Hilkiah "very glad" (Jer. 20:15) and the promise to Zechariah and Elizabeth that their child will bring them "joy and gladness" (Luke 1:14).

birth of her son Isaac (Gen. 21:6-7). In the Gospel of John, Jesus says, "When a woman is in labor, she has pain, because her hour has come. But when her child is born, she no longer remembers the anguish because of the joy of having brought a human being into the world" (John 16:20-21).

Furthermore, the notion of children at play is tied to visions of restoration and peace and to the notion of divine wisdom itself. For example, the prophet Zechariah included the image of children at play in his vision of a restored Zion. At a future time, when Jerusalem is restored as a faithful city, "the streets of the city shall be full of boys and girls playing in its streets" (Zech. 8:5). In Proverbs, divine wisdom, often portrayed solely as a woman, is also depicted as a child who is playing, delighting, and growing:[40]

> When [God] established the heavens, I [Wisdom] was there,
> When he circumscribed the surface of the deep,
> When he secured the skies above,
> When he stabilized the spring of the deep,
> When he assigned the sea its limit,
> Lest the waters transgress his command,
> When he carved out the foundations of the earth,
> I was beside him growing up.
> And I was his delight day by day,
> Playing before him always,
> Playing in his inhabited world,
> And delighting in the human race. (Prov. 8:27-31)

As Brown notes, such imagery highlights the "primacy of play when it comes to the sapiential way of life. The authority that wisdom embodies is not 'grave' but creative, and playfully so."[41]

We all recognize that children often have a sense of awe and wonder that delights and refreshes us. They are also often far more forgiving than adults and can often bring humor to difficult situations and help adults move forward. As some contemporary philosophers have recognized, children are also gifts in the sense that they offer us fresh and open perspectives. They often ask fundamental questions about life that open our eyes to new possibilities in our thinking. They are like the new employees in a company who can ask, "Why do you do things like this?" Their questions force us to reevaluate

40. Brown, "To Discipline without Destruction," pp. 78-79.

41. Brown, "To Discipline without Destruction," p. 79.

our priorities and to reexamine "business as usual." The biblical texts go further to suggest that play, too, is an aspect of true wisdom.

Implications and Conclusion

By examining the vocations of both parents and children, we have explored ways that both parents and children express forms of "best love" to their families and their communities. The specific duties, practices, and responsibilities outlined above are all ways that parents and children are able to love God and to show love and compassion to others both within and outside their own households. Furthermore, we have discovered that a robust understanding of the child-parent relationship must be built on a vibrant theological understanding of children themselves.

A sound theological understanding of vocation that incorporates these elements and others and thereby offers a complex view of the child and adult-child relationships has several positive implications for our understanding and treatment of children in both church and society.

For example, a strong theological understanding of the vocation of children and parents can encourage the church to be a stronger national and international advocate for child well-being in areas such as healthcare and education. It stresses the need for parents and the community to provide for the needs of children — not just the needs of their own children but of all children in need. It also emphasizes that the common good of society requires educated citizens, that all children should receive a good education, and that the education of young people is a shared responsibility.

At the same time, reflecting on the concept of the vocation of children also deepens our understanding of children as social agents and citizens themselves. Based on a Protestant understanding of vocation, children clearly have a responsibility to serve others now — not just in the future when they are "grown up." Furthermore, they are also called to name and to reject injustices in their own families and communities. Although they are to honor and respect their parents, they also have a responsibility to disobey them and any other adults who ask them to cause or to perpetuate injustices.

Even as a Christian understanding of vocation heightens the child's role as social agent and citizen, it also leaves room for some of the other important qualities of children that heal and help families and communities. Part of their vocation and their genuine gifts to communities is their sense of play, their ability to be in the present, and their awe and wonder at what adults sometimes regard as mundane and ordinary.

A strong concept of the child's vocation also prompts both parents and children to recognize that they are on a mutual journey of faith, striving together to fear God, to love the neighbor, and to care for creation. With this as their common focus, both children and parents might speak more intentionally and frequently about their beliefs and values, carry out central religious practices that nurture faith in their homes, and listen to and learn from one another. In general, when we also consider that in our current consumer culture adults and now even very young children are the targets of intense and highly sophisticated marketing campaigns, vying for their money and brand loyalty and shaping their values and assumptions, adults and children all have an important role to play in helping one another continually examine and assess values and priorities in their families and communities.

This chapter has provided only a brief sketch of one theological view of the vocations of children and parents, yet even this short sketch reminds all of us — regardless of our philosophical or religious backgrounds or convictions — that children, too, have vocations. Like people of all ages, races, gender, and social classes, children are meant to and already do participate in and contribute to the life of their families and communities. Furthermore, any strong view of the vocation of parents can be built only by cultivating, at the same time, a vibrant and complex understanding of children themselves that includes attention not only to their vulnerabilities and weaknesses but also their gifts and strengths. Finally, reflection on the vocations of children and parents challenges us to think more seriously about our own duties and responsibilities to all children in our midst — whether or not we have children of our own.

PART V

Legal Perspectives

CHAPTER 10

What's Love Got to Do with It? (Part I): Loving Children in Cases of Divorce or Death in the Jewish Tradition*

Michael J. Broyde

Introduction

Although Jewish law is replete with mandates to "love," from loving the convert[1] to loving one's wife,[2] understanding why helps frame the basic perspective of this chapter. Love as a legal response must be limited to those cases where law gives you the right to choose whom you will love. One can be forced to love one's spouse precisely because one can choose him or her, and if one does not love that person, one should not marry him or her.[3] The same is true for loving the convert — which is essentially a voluntary relationship between an individual and the Jewish people.[4] As I have noted else-

*See Wikipedia, "Tina Turner," which notes that Ms. Turner is commonly known as the Queen of Rock 'n Roll. To my dismay, this is the first citation to Tina Turner in my work or, as far as I can tell, other works of Jewish law.

1. Deuteronomy 10:18.

2. This obligation is derived rather than biblical. Yet even the obligation not to hit one's wife stems not from an obligation to love her, but from the obligation to honor and respect her; see Rabbi Joseph Karo, *Beit Yosef, Even HaEzer* 154:[3]. This only reinforces the point that the term "love" is not taken by Jewish law sources to generate obligations in action — in contrast to terms like "honor," "respect," "heed," and "obey."

3. See Babylonian Talmud, *Gittin* 89a-b, which records a three-way dispute about the exact standards for divorce. The normative view is that even the slightest fault can be grounds for divorce, as love is gone in those cases.

4. For more on this, see Michael Broyde, "Proselytism and Jewish Law: Inreach, Outreach, and the Jewish Tradition," in *Sharing the Book: Religious Perspectives on the Rights and Wrongs of*

where, the same can be claimed to be true for one's relationship with one's adopted children.[5] Since choice is a central criterion in each of these relationships, love — an emotion that one frequently cannot regulate and rarely can compel — can be required to be part of the obligation. Even the ultimate mandate — to love God — is based in the Jewish tradition on the covenantal choice made by the Jewish people to choose to be Jewish and accept the commandments at Sinai. Only because we have chosen to accept, can we be asked to love.

Such is not the case in the parent-child relationship. Children are sometimes unwanted, the unintended byproduct of love of one's spouse or inattention to the details of birth control or one (actually, two people[6]) having too much to drink. Whatever the cause, the Jewish legal tradition mandates that parents care for their children and act in their best interest, whether or not they love them. Indeed, love is essentially unmentioned in the Jewish law discussion of children and their rights, duties, and obligations. The legal duty of guardianship, and hence the way true love is manifest in the many different situations where children are born, is found in the obligation to care for one's children. Love without a duty would be perceived as a somewhat empty obligation. Law — even Jewish law[7] — cannot compel love. But it can compel manifestations of love in terms of the parents' obligation to care for and support a child.

More than twenty years ago, the late professor Robert Cover of Yale Law School noted a crucial difference between the rights-based approach of common law countries and the duties-based approach of Jewish law. He remarked:

> Social movements in the United States organize around rights. When there is some urgently felt need to change the law or keep it in one way or another a "Rights" movement is started. Civil Rights, the right to life, wel-

---

Proselytism, ed. John Witte Jr. and Richard C. Martin (Maryknoll, NY: Orbis Books, 1999), pp. 45-60.

5. See Michael Broyde, "Adoption, Personal Status, and Jewish Law," in *The Morality of Adoption: Social-Psychological, Theological, and Legal Perspectives,* ed. Timothy Jackson (Grand Rapids: Eerdmans, 2005), pp. 128-47. The present chapter is intended as a companion and complement to that one.

6. There is an ongoing dispute in Jewish law as to whether a married couple may have sexual relations if one or both of them is drunk; see *Arba'ah Turim, Even HaEzer* 25 and commentaries ad loc.

7. For more on Jewish law as a system that requires ethical duties see, e.g., J. David Bleich, "Introduction: The *A Priori* Component of Bioethics," in *Jewish Bioethics,* ed. Fred Rosner and J. David Bleich (Brooklyn, NY: Hebrew Publishing Company, 1985), pp. xi-xix.

> fare rights, etc. The premium that is to be put upon an entitlement is so coded. When we "take rights seriously" we understand them to be trumps in the legal game. In Jewish law, an entitlement without an obligation is a sad, almost pathetic thing.[8]

This same point can be made in reflecting on a contrast between the Jewish legal tradition and many common understandings of Christian jurisprudence. Professor Saiman of Villanova University School of Law has written insightfully about the sources of these fundamental differences and how they still resonate today in a number of ways.[9] He notes:

> The Christian (particularly the contemporary Protestant) mode inhabits a very different discursive realm. Law is not the correct platform through which to analyze and decide important religious and social issues. It is thought to be overly restrictive, and unjustifiably replaces faith and love with rules and precedents. Rather, the reasoning process is directed inward, and exhibits more overtly religious, spiritual and subjective modes of reasoning and analysis.[10]

His observation echoes that of Professor Cover. Many religious movements in the United States identify love as an overarching guiding principle. When there is some urgently felt need to change a doctrine or keep it in one way or another, "love" is frequently pointed to as a way to modify law.[11] The premium that is to be put upon a religious entitlement is so coded. When Christianity takes love seriously, we often understand that to mean that love trumps other values and creates some sort of entitlement. But Jewish law[12]

8. Robert M. Cover, "Obligation: A Jewish Jurisprudence of the Social Order," *Journal of Law and Religion* 5 (1987): 65-74, at p. 67 (footnotes omitted).

9. Chaim N. Saiman, "Jesus' Legal Theory — A Rabbinic Interpretation," *Journal of Law and Religion* 23 (2007): 97-130. (This article argues that the polarized positions in many contemporary debates within American law — law vs. equity, procedural vs. substantive justice, rules vs. standards, formalism vs. instrumentalism, and textualism vs. contextualism — can be seen as manifestations of a fundamental disagreement between the rabbinic Jewish understanding of law and Christian jurisprudence as represented in the Gospels.)

10. Saiman, "Jesus' Legal Theory," p. 106.

11. Consider the frequent references in contemporary Christian literature to the homosexual and love, or this conference's insistence that love is a key value for dealing with children.

12. "Jewish law," or *halakha*, is used herein to denote the entire subject matter of the Jewish legal system, including public, private, and ritual law. A brief historical review will familiarize the new reader of Jewish law with its history and development. The Pentateuch (the five books of Moses, the Torah) is the touchstone document of Jewish law and, according to Jewish

embodies an approach where "an entitlement without an obligation is a sad, almost pathetic thing."[13]

With regard to our particular issue, the Jewish tradition would rather speak about the duties of parents and children — and love cannot be a duty or an obligation; indeed, it cannot even be the predicate for other duties and obligations, lest one exempt oneself from the many technical obligations of parenthood by claiming that one does not love one's children. Who needs a heart if a heart can be broken, indeed?

This is just one manifestation of the stark contrast between the Jewish law view and the Christian approach. In the Jewish tradition, love-based

---

legal theory, was revealed to Moses at Mount Sinai. The Prophets and Writings, the other two parts of the Hebrew Bible, were written over the next seven hundred years, and the Jewish canon was closed around the year 200 before the Common Era (BCE). The time from the close of the canon until 250 of the Common Era (CE) is referred to as the era of the *Tannaim*, the redactors of Jewish law, whose period closed with the editing of the *Mishnah* by Rabbi Judah the Patriarch. The next five centuries were the epoch in which the two Talmuds (Babylonian and Jerusalem) were written and edited by scholars called *Amoraim* ("those who recount" Jewish law) and *Savoraim* ("those who ponder" Jewish law). The Babylonian Talmud is of greater legal significance than the Jerusalem Talmud and is a more complete work.

The post-talmudic era is conventionally divided into three periods: (1) the era of the *Geonim*, scholars who lived in Babylonia until the mid-eleventh century; (2) the era of the *Rishonim* (the early authorities), who lived in North Africa, Spain, Franco-Germany, and Egypt until the end of the fourteenth century; and (3) the period of the *Aharonim* (the latter authorities), which encompasses all scholars of Jewish law from the fifteenth century up to this era. From the period of the mid-fourteenth century until the early seventeenth century, Jewish law underwent a period of codification, which led to the acceptance of the law code format of Rabbi Joseph Karo, called the *Shulhan Arukh*, as the basis for modern Jewish law. The *Shulhan Arukh* (and the *Arba'ah Turim* of Rabbi Jacob ben Asher, which preceded it) divided Jewish law into four separate areas: *Orah Hayyim* is devoted to daily, Sabbath, and holiday laws; *Even HaEzer* addresses family law, including financial aspects; *Hoshen Mishpat* codifies financial law; and *Yoreh Deah* contains dietary laws as well as other miscellaneous legal matter. Many significant scholars — themselves as important as Rabbi Karo in status and authority — wrote annotations to his code, which made the work and its surrounding comments the modern touchstone of Jewish law. The most recent complete edition of the *Shulhan Arukh* (Vilna: Ha-Almanah veha-Ahim Rom, 1896) contains no less than 113 separate commentaries on the text of Rabbi Karo. In addition, hundreds of other volumes of commentary have been published as self-standing works, a process that continues to this very day. Besides the law codes and commentaries, for the last twelve hundred years Jewish law authorities have addressed specific questions of Jewish law in written *responsa* (in epistolary, question-and-answer form). Collections of such *responsa* have been published, providing guidance not only to later authorities but to the community at large. Finally, since the establishment of the State of Israel in 1948, the Rabbinical Courts of Israel have published their written opinions (Piske Din) deciding cases on a variety of matters.

13. Cover, "Obligation: A Jewish Jurisprudence of the Social Order," p. 67.

commandments are weak and obligation-less. Thus, the requirement to love the convert or even to love God seems to be magnificent in the Jewish tradition, but really is somewhat powerless — until it is actualized in terms of a duty and an obligation. Maimonides' *Book of Commandments* lists four love-based commandments: to love God,[14] to sanctify God's name (in demonstration of that love),[15] to love one's neighbor,[16] and to love a convert.[17] None of them ever directs one to a concrete action,[18] with the exception of the sanctification of God's name, which is understood by Maimonides as allowing one to be killed rather than violate specific aspects of Jewish law.[19] This stands in contrast to other code words such as "respect" or "fear" or "remember," each of which is understood to direct concrete actions in the Jewish tradition. Parents are entitled to be respected and obeyed by operation of the Jewish law duty imposed on children to respect them. Children are entitled to be fed, clothed, taught Judaism, given a profession, and generally taught to be competent adults, grounded in the obligations imposed on parents. Nowhere is love mentioned.

Why this is so in the Jewish tradition reflects an underlying sense of what Jewish law aims to accomplish. Unlike other religious systems and like other legal systems, Jewish law is focused on the practical. Love is at its core a commandment that can never be mandated. Even the biblical verses directing one to love God generate an enormous literature in the Jewish tradition about what that means and how to fulfill it.[20] Instead, the Jewish tradition,

14. Moses Maimonides, *Book of Commandments,* Positive Commandment no. 3.

15. Maimonides, *Book of Commandments,* Positive Commandment no. 9.

16. Maimonides, *Book of Commandments,* Positive Commandment no. 206.

17. Maimonides, *Book of Commandments,* Positive Commandment no. 207.

18. Consider, for example, the obligation to love one's neighbor as oneself. This certainly does not mean that when I have two dollars in my wallet and I am going into a store to buy myself a banana (which I love), and I am with my neighbor and he loves bananas too, I should buy him one as well.

19. Which is, at its core, a passive activity and not an active one.

20. Contrast, e.g., *Notes of Nahmanides to the Book of Commandments,* Positive Commandments nos. 1, 5, and 9, together with the explanatory notes of R. Hayyim Heller to Maimonides' *Sefer HaMitzvot* (Jerusalem: Mosad Harav Kuk, 1980), with the view of R. Sa'adia ben Joseph Gaon in his *Sefer HaMitzvot* and the illuminating comments of R. Jeroham Fishel Perla to that work (Jerusalem: Keset, 1973). This literature focuses on whether this and other abstract, action-less *mitzvot* are even to be enumerated as commandments. Nahmanides, for example, reinterprets a whole host of *mitzvot* to make them tangible, though in essence he distances many of these commandments from their simple understanding. To him, love of God is manifest in the particulars of regular worship, though it is far from clear whether that truly can be considered a duty of "love" in any classical sense.

when it focuses on the parent-child relationship, sets forward obligations and responsibilities so that parents should be compelled to act in a manner that is in the best interests of the child.

Continuing this rabbinic sense that love is manifest only through concrete rules that govern the conduct between individuals, this essay will explore the basics of this issue through the lens of a complex problem — namely when parents cannot jointly raise their children together, which parent (or third party) shall be given the rights, duties, and obligations of the caregiver. Conceptually, this essay is the sequel to an article I wrote explaining why the Jewish tradition has no legal category called adoption.[21] The contrast between how Jewish law views natural children and adopted children is profound, as adopted children are exactly *chosen* and natural children are not. These two essays thus constitute twin takes on the same issue, albeit studies in contrast.[22]

This article will survey Jewish law's approach(es) to several complex matters of Jewish law, each of which focuses on who bears the duty and obligation to care for children — the concrete manifestation of love.[23] Specifically, this

21. Broyde, "Adoption, Personal Status and Jewish Law."

22. This concretizing of "love" into real obligations, when coupled with the revival of the Rabbinical Court system in the United States, has returned the topic of child custody from the theoretical to the practical in Jewish America; Jewish law courts now are hearing child custody matters and issuing rulings in this area. In fact, these determinations are among the most difficult to make as they pose many of the classical difficulties related to mixed fact and law determinations.

23. A number of excellent articles address the unique mixture of law and fact found in this area and survey the applications of the various practical rules developed. The most complete of these is Professor Shochatman's excellent article; see Eliav Shochatman, "The Essence of the Principles Used in Child Custody in Jewish Law," *Shenaton LeMishpat HaIvri* 5 (5738 [=1978]): 285-301 (Hebrew).

In addition, a number of articles address various issues in the field; see Rabbi Chaim David Gulevsky, "Question on the Custody of Children," in *Sefer Kavod Harav: Essays in Honor of Rabbi Joseph B. Soloveitchik*, ed. Moshe D. Sherman (New York: Student Organization of Yeshiva, 5744 [=1984]), p. 104 (Hebrew); Ronald Warburg, "Child Custody: A Comparative Analysis," *Israel Law Review* 14 (1978): 480-503; Maidi Katz, "A Reply to Ronald Warburg" (manuscript on file with the author) (1992); Basil Herring, "Child Custody," in *Jewish Ethics and Halakhah for Our Time* (New York: KTAV and Yeshiva University Press, 1989), p. 177; Israel Tzvi Gilat, "Is the 'Best Interest of the Child' a Major Factor in a Parental Conflict over Custody of a Child?" *Bar Ilan Law Studies* 8 (1990): 297-349 (Hebrew).

In particular, Professor Shochatman's article is a complete analysis of this area with in-depth collection and discussion of the many Jewish law authorities and a near complete review of the *responsa* literature. Each of the articles listed above (except perhaps Gulevsky's), as well as this article, in one way or another is responding to or complementing the analysis found in Professor Shochatman's article.

article is divided into four substantive sections: the first addresses the theoretical basis for child custody determinations, the second discusses disputes between parents as to who should have custody, the third assesses the status of relatives and strangers[24] in child custody disputes, and the fourth draws certain theoretical conclusions based on the previous three sections.

Of course, all reasonable[25] legal systems must acknowledge that certain people are unfit to be custodial parents of their children, and Jewish law accepts this fact. That does not, however, minimize the importance of certain purely legal questions that are raised in all child[26] custody determinations.

Determinations of Custody between Parents

The Babylonian Talmud[27] seems to embrace three rules that govern child custody disputes between parents:

1. Custody of all children under the age of six is to be given to the mother;
2. Custody of boys over the age of six is to be given to the father;[28]

24. The word "stranger" need not mean a person unknown to the children, but rather denotes a person having no prior legal claim to custody of the children; see the fourth section of this article.

25. Certainly Jewish law rejected Roman law's rule that parents have a "property" right or interest in their children no different than an ownership interest in any other object. For a discussion of Roman law, see Jay Einhorn, "Child Custody in Historical Perspective: A Study of Changing Social Perceptions of Divorce and Child Custody in Anglo-American Law," *Behavioral Sciences and the Law* 4 (Spring 1986): 119-35. According to Roman law, ownership of the child apparently included the right to terminate the child's life; see, e.g., *The King v. Greenhill*, 111 Eng. Rep. 926 (1836).

26. According to Jewish law, minors are emancipated at the age of 12 for girls and 13 for boys if these ages are also accompanied by signs of physical maturity. "Child" custody issues thus only discuss arrangements prior to legal emancipation. The question of the theoretical basis for custody of adolescence in Jewish law is a complex one and will be addressed in a forthcoming piece.

27. See Babylonian Talmud, *Eruvin* 82a, *Ketubot* 65b and 122b-123a.

28. *Shulhan Arukh, Even HaEzer* 82:7 seems to indicate that the mother may keep custody of the children in all circumstances if she is willing to forgo the father's financial support. Thus, according to *Shulhan Arukh*'s way of understanding the rule, children are placed according to these presumptive rules and parents are obligated to support them in these circumstances. Should one parent wish to keep custody beyond the time in which it is in the children's own best interest to stay with the parents, the other parent would cease being obligated to pay for their support; Rabbi Moses Alsheikh, *Responsa* 38. As has been noted (see R. Yom Tov ben Mo-

3. Custody of girls over the age of six is to be given to the mother.[29]

Thus, the mother presumptively is given custody 72 percent of the time when the rules are strictly applied.[30]

The Babylonian Talmud (*Ketubot* 59b) also indicates that these ideal rules of child custody presuppose that both the mother and the father desire custody of the children and that both are financially capable of custody.[31] Jewish law, however, rules as a matter of law that mothers (at least upon termination of the marriage) are under no legal obligation to financially support and maintain their children, whereas fathers are under such an obligation.[32] These rules are codified in Maimonides' code[33] and in *Shulhan*

ses Tzahalon, *Responsa Maharitatz* 1:16, 2:232 and others), most authorities reject this rule and state that the mother may not keep custody of the children beyond the time in which it would be in the children's own best interest, even if she were willing to do so without child support payments from the father. This appears to be the majority opinion; for a long discussion of this topic see Shochatman, "The Essence of the Principles Used in Child Custody in Jewish Law," pp. 297-303, and Sylvan Schaeffer, "Child Custody: Halacha and the Secular Approach," *Journal of Halacha and Contemporary Society* 6 (1983): 33, 36-39, at page 39.

29. For a detailed discussion of the background of these rules, see Herring, "Child Custody," pp. 180-87, where the basic texts are translated into English, and Shochatman, "The Essence of the Principles Used in Child Custody in Jewish Law," pp. 289-92. While there is much discussion in the literature (see articles cited in note 23 above) of how precisely these rules have been interpreted, this article focuses instead on what the theoretical underpinnings of these rules are.

30. For a boy, the mother is the presumptive custodial parent for six of his thirteen years of childhood. For a girl, the mother is the presumptive parent all twelve years of her childhood. Thus, the mother is the presumptive parent eighteen years out of twenty-five, or 72 percent of the time (assuming boys and girls are born in equal numbers and that the sequence of children born or their sex has no correlation with the likelihood of divorce).

31. In classical Jewish law a father provided child support payments, but not alimony. Instead, the wife was paid a lump sum upon divorce or the death of her husband.

32. Maimonides, *Mishneh Torah, Sefer Nashim, Hilkhot Ishut* (Laws of Marriage), 21:17-18; *Shulhan Arukh, Even HaEzer* 82:6, 8. This presupposes that others can and will raise and support the children if the mother does not. However, in a situation in which a child is so attached to a particular parent that if this parent does not care for the child, the child will die, Jewish law compels one to take care of the child, not because of a special legal obligation between a parent and a child, but because of the general obligation to rescue Jews in life-threatening situations. This situation arises when a woman has been nursing her child and does not wish to continue nursing the child; if the child will not nurse from another and thus will die absent the mother's nursing, Jewish law compels the mother to care for the child and nurse it as part of the general obligation of not standing by while one's neighbor's blood is shed; see, e.g., R. Jacob ben Asher, *Tur, Even HaEzer* 82.

33. Maimonides, *Mishneh Torah, Sefer Nashim, Hilkhot Ishut* 21:17.

Arukh,[34] and are the basis of much of the discussion found among the later authorities.[35]

The above talmudic rules, read in a vacuum, appear to provide no measure of flexibility at all and mandate the mechanical placement of children into the appropriate category. However, as has been demonstrated by others,[36] Jewish law never understood these rules as cast in stone; all decisors accepted that there are circumstances where the interest of the child overwhelmed the obligation to follow the rules in all circumstances.

It is apparent that this interpretation of the talmudic precepts, which turns these rules into mere presumptions — and allows custody to be given contrary to the talmudic rules — is understood by the various authorities in different ways. Two different issues need to be addressed. First, in what circumstances may one reject the talmudic presumption? Need the presumptive custodial parent be "unfit," or is it enough that others are "more fit"? Second, in cases where the talmudic presumption has been rejected, who should then be assigned custody? Is that determination based purely on the "best interests of the child," or must custody be granted to the other parent as a matter of law, assuming that the parent is "fit"?[37]

The circumstances in which the talmudic presumptions can be rejected are often not explicitly stated; thus it may be unclear in any particular case whether the parent designated to presumptively receive custody but denied

34. *Shulhan Arukh, Even HaEzer* 82:7. It is worth noting that the view of Rabbi Abraham ben David of Posquières (Ravad), who explicitly takes issue with the first rule above (see *Commentary of Ravad, Hilkhot Ishut* 21:17) is not quoted as normative by any authority; but see Rabbi Eleizer Waldenburg, *Tzitz Eleizer* 15:50.

35. Indeed, of the major review articles published in the area, all of them use these principles as the organizational framework for their discussion; see Shochatman, "The Essence of the Principles Used in Child Custody in Jewish Law"; Gilat, "Is the 'Best Interest of the Child' a Major Factor in a Parental Conflict over Custody of a Child?"; Herring, "Child Custody."

36. See Warburg, "Child Custody: A Comparative Analysis," pp. 495-99; Shochatman, "The Essence of the Principles Used in Child Custody in Jewish Law," pp. 308-9; and Herring, "Child Custody," pp. 207-19.

37. This article will not address the extremely important question of *how* Jewish law determines parental fitness; for an excellent discussion of that topic, see Rabbi Gedalia Felder, *Nahalat Tzvi* 2:282-87 (2nd ed.), where he discusses the process that should be used by a rabbinical court (beth din) to make child custody determinations. Rabbi Felder discusses the practical matters involved in child custody determinations, and he adopts a format and procedure surprisingly similar to that used by secular tribunals in making these determinations. He indicates that a beth din should interview the parents, consult with a child psychologist, and conduct a complete investigation.

that right is "unfit," or merely that the other parent is "more fit." However, an examination of the *responsa* literature and decisions of the Rabbinical Courts in Israel does indicate that two schools of thought exist on this issue. Many decisors maintain that these presumptive rules are relatively strong ones and may be reversed only when it is obvious that the parent who would be granted custody (or already has custody) is unfit. Other decisors adopt a lower standard and permit granting custody contrary to the talmudic rules when these presumptions are not in the best interest of the specific child whose case is being adjudicated.

For example, Rabbi David ben Solomon ibn Avi Zimra (Radvaz) discusses a case where a couple was divorced and the mother assumed custody of the seven-year-old daughter (in accordance with the rules discussed above). After a short time the mother became pregnant out of wedlock and the father sought to regain custody of his child based on the moral delinquency of the mother. Radvaz rules in his favor; however, an examination of his language indicates that it is based on the *unfitness of the mother* to have custody of the children and not merely on the fact that the father could do a better job raising the children.[38] Many, including Maharival[39] and Rabbi Ovadia Hadaya,[40] agree with this method of analysis.[41]

The contrary approach, based on the best interests of the child, can be found in the *responsa* of Rabbi Moses ben Joseph di Trani (Mabit) and Rabbi

38. Rabbi David ben Solomon ibn Avi Zimra, *Radvaz* 1:263, cited by R. Abraham Zvi Hirsch Eisenstadt, *Pithei Teshuva* 82:(6). He concludes that if the mother is sufficiently unfit, even had the father not sought custody he would remove the child from the mother's home. See also Gulevsky, "Question on the Custody of Children," pp. 122-23, who indicates that the standard is "unfitness" rather than "best interest." Katz, "A Reply to Ronald Warburg," pp. 9-16, claims that this school of thought is represented in the Israeli Rabbinical Courts.

In a different *responsum,* Radvaz reaches a different result and uses language closer to the best interest of the child; see *Radvaz* 1:126. See note 83 for a discussion of this.

39. Rabbi Joseph ben David ibn Lev, *Responsa Maharival* 1:58.

40. Rabbi Ovadia Hadaya, *Yaskil Avdi, Even HaEzer* 2:2(4) (additional section).

41. See Gilat, "Is the 'Best Interest of the Child' a Major Factor in a Parental Conflict over Custody of a Child?" pp. 328-35. It can occasionally be found in judgments of the Rabbinical Courts of Israel, see e.g., P.D.R. *(Piskei Din Rabbani'im)* 4:332, although as noted in Warburg, "Child Custody: A Comparative Analysis," it is not the predominant approach; but see Katz, "A Reply to Ronald Warburg," pp. 1-6.

Excluded from this analysis are those cases where the father denies paternity. The standard of review for those cases involves completely different issues in that Jewish law hesitates to assign custody (and even visitation rights) to a person who denies paternity, even if as a matter of law that person is the presumptive father. For precisely such a case, see P.D.R. 1:145 and Katz, "A Reply to Ronald Warburg," n. 57.

Samuel ben Moses de Medina (Maharashdam).[42] Mabit describes a mutually agreed-upon child custody arrangement between divorced parents that one parent now seeks to breach. Mabit states that it appears to him that the agreement is not in the best interest of the children and thus no longer ought to be enforced, and that custody is to be granted contrary to the agreement. He understands the "standard of review" to be the best interest of the child and not unfitness of the parent.[43] So too, Maharashdam evaluates the correctness of a (widowed) mother's decision to move a child to another city away from the family of the father based on the best interest of the child. He concludes by prohibiting such a move, as it is not in the child's best interest.[44] This approach can also be found in the works of many additional authorities.[45] Both Shochatman and Warburg maintain that this is the predominant school of thought among judges in the Israeli Rabbinical Courts[46] who often issue statements supporting this approach. For example, one Rabbinical Court noted:

> The principle in *all* child custody decisions is the best interest of the child as determined by the beth din [Rabbinic Court].[47]

42. Rabbi Moses ben Joseph di Trani, *Responsa of Mabit* 2:62, and Rabbi Samuel ben Moses de Medina, *Responsa of Maharashdam, Even HaEzer* 123; For a list of similar rulings, see Shochatman, "The Essence of the Principles Used in Child Custody in Jewish Law," nn. 115-16.

43. This issue becomes a little perplexing, since it is not the practice of Jewish courts to second-guess decisions of parents as they relate to their children; as noted by the Supreme Rabbinical Court of Israel, "As a general rule the court will not decide against the judgment of the parents merely based on a disagreement of judgment," P.D.R. 2:300 quoted in Shochatman, "The Essence of the Principles Used in Child Custody in Jewish Law," n. 115; but see Rabbi Gedalia Felder, *Nahalat Tzvi* 2:282-87, who justifies this practice. He notes that there is no *res judicata* or law of the case in child custody matters. In addition, a conceptual difference is present between a mutually agreed upon arrangement between parents which they both seek to honor, but with which the Beit Din disagrees, and an agreement between the parents which one parent now seeks to void.

44. Rabbi Samuel ben Moses de Medina, *Responsa of Maharashdam*.

45. See e.g., Rabbi Meir Melamed, *Responsa Mishpat Tzedek* 1:23, Rabbi Moses Albaz, *Responsa Halakhah LeMoshe, Even HaEzer* 6, and Shochatman, "The Essence of the Principles Used in Child Custody in Jewish Law," nn. 100-102, for a list of decisors and Rabbinical Court rulings accepting this line of reasoning.

46. Shochatman, "The Essence of the Principles Used in Child Custody in Jewish Law," pp. 311-12; Warburg, "Child Custody: A Comparative Analysis," throughout the article. For an example of a bifurcated *responsa* on this topic reflecting both standards of review, each in the alterative, see R. Eliezer Waldenburg, *Tzitz Eleizer* 15:50.

47. P.D.R. 1:55-56 (emphasis added).

plained below, two very different theories, one called "parental rights" and one called "best interest of the child," exist in Jewish law. These two theories are somewhat in tension, but they lead to similar results in many cases, as the best interests of the child often will coincide with granting parents rights.

There is a basic dispute within Jewish law as to why and through what legal claim parents have custody of their children. Indeed this dispute is crucial to understanding why Jewish law accepts that a "fit" parent is entitled to child custody — even if it can be shown that others can raise the child in a better manner.[57]

Rabbi Asher ben Yehiel (R. Asher),[58] in the course of discussing the obligation to support one's children, adopts what appears to be a naturalist theory of parental rights. R. Asher asserts two basic rules. First, there is an obligation (for a man)[59] to support one's children and this obligation is, at least as a matter of theory, unrelated to one's custodial relationship (or lack thereof) with the child or with one's wife or with any other party.[60] A man who has children is biblically obligated to support them. Flowing logically from this rule, R. Asher also states[61] that, *as a matter of law,* in any circumstance in which the marriage has ended and the mother is incapable of raising the children, *the father is entitled to custody of his children.* Of course, R. Asher would agree that in circumstances in which the father is factually incapable of raising the children — is a legally unfit father — he would not be the custodial parent.[62] However, R. Asher appears to adopt the theory that

57. This article will not address the crucial question of how a legal system determines who is "fit" and who is not and which environment would be in the best interest of a particular child. These determinations are essentially "fact" determinations, and beyond the scope of this article; see also note 37.

58. Known by the Hebrew acronym "Rosh," R. Asher (1250-1327) was a late Tosaphist who emigrated from Franco-Germany to Barcelona, then Toledo, Spain.

59. See text accompanying note 90 for an explanation of why this is limited to a man, at least as a matter of Torah law. R. Asher might claim that the talmudic rule, which transferred custody of children (of certain ages) from the husband to the wife, did so based on a rabbinic decree and that this rabbinic decree gave the custodial mother the same rights (but not duties) as a custodial father; for a clear explication of this, see Rabbi Samuel Alkalai, *Mishpetei Shmuel* 90, and Gilat, "Is the 'Best Interest of the Child' a Major Factor in a Parental Conflict over Custody of a Child?" pp. 316-18.

60. Rabbi Asher ben Yehiel, *Responsa of Asher* (Rosh) 17:7; see also Rabbi Judah ben Samuel Rosannes, *Mishneh LeMelekh, Hilkhot Ishut* 21:17.

61. *Responsa of R. Asher* 82:2.

62. This could reasonably be derived from the Babylonian Talmud, *Ketubot* 102b, which mandates terminating custodial rights in the face of life-threatening misconduct by a guardian.

the father is the presumptive custodial parent of his children based on his obligations and rights as a natural parent, subject to the limitation that even a natural parent cannot have custody of his children if he is factually unfit to raise them. For the same reason, in situations where the Sages assigned custody to the mother rather than the father, that custody is based on a rabbinically ordered transfer of rights.[63] While this understanding of the parents' rights is not quite the same as a property right, it is far more a right (and duty) related to possession than a rule about the "best interest" of the child. The position of R. Asher seems to have a substantial basis in the works of a number of authorities.[64]

There is a second theory of parental custody in Jewish law, the approach of Rabbi Solomon ben Abraham Aderet (Aderet).[65] Aderet indicates[66] that Jewish law always accepts — as a matter of law — that child custody matters (upon termination of the marriage) be determined according to the "best interests of the child." Thus, he rules that in a case where the father is deceased, the mother does not have an indisputable legal claim to

63. For a longer discussion of this issue, see *responsa* of Rabbi Ezekiel Landau, *Noda BeYehudah, Even HaEzer* 2:89, and Rabbi Yitzhak Weiss, *Minhat Yitzhak* 7:113, where these decisors explicitly state that, even in cases where the mother was assigned custodial rights, the father has a basic right to see and educate his male children, and if this right is incompatible with the mother's presumptive custody claim, his rights and obligations supersede hers and custody by the mother will be terminated. This issue is addressed in more detail in the third and fourth sections of this article.

64. See, e.g., Rabbenu Yeruham ben Meshullam, *Toldot Adam veHavah* 197a, in the name of the *Geonim;* Rabbi Isaac de Molena, *Kiryat Sefer* 44:557, in the name of the *Geonim;* and Rabbi Joseph Gaon, *Ginzei Kedem* 3:62, where the theory of custodial parenthood seems to be based on an agency theory derived from the father's rights; see also Gulevsky, "Question on the Custody of Children," pp. 110-12. R. Asher, in his theory of parenthood, seems to state that typically the mother of the children is precisely that agent. When the marriage ends, the mother may — by rabbinic decree — continue if she wishes to be the agent of the father, because Jewish law perceives being raised by the mother (for all children except boys over six) as typically more appropriate than being raised by the father.

Interestingly, a claim could be made that this position was not accepted by Rabbi Judah ben R. Asher, one of Rabbi Asher's children; see *Zichron Yehudah* 35, quoted in *Beit Yosef, Hoshen Mishpat* 290.

65. Known by the Hebrew acronym "Rashba," Aderet (1235-1310) of Barcelona, Spain, was an eminent and prolific decisor.

66. *Responsa of Rashba Traditionally Assigned to Nahmanides,* 38. Throughout this work, the theory developed in this *responsa* is referred to as Rashba's, as most later Jewish law authorities indicate that Aderet wrote these *responsa* and not Nahmanides; see Rabbi David Halevy, *Turei Zahav, Yoreh Deah* 228:50, and Rabbi Hayyim Hezekiah Medina, *Sedei Hemed, Klalei HaPoskim* 10:9 (typically found in volume 9 of that work).

custody of the children. Equitable factors, such as the best interest of the child, are the *sole* determinant of the custody. In fact, this *responsum* could well be read as a general theory for all child custody determinations.[67] Aderet accepts that all child custody determinations involve a single legal standard: *the best interest of the child*, regardless of the specific facts involved.[68] According to this approach, the "rules" that one encounters in the field of child custody are not really "rules of law" at all, but rather the presumptive assessment by the talmudic Sages as to what generally is in the best interest of children.[69]

An enormous theoretical difference exists between R. Asher and Aderet. According to Aderet, the law allows transfer of custodial rights (even from their parents) in any situation where it can be shown that the children are not being raised in their best interests and another would raise them in a manner more in their best interest.[70] According to R. Asher, parents (or at least fathers)[71] have an intrinsic right to raise their progeny. In order to remove children from parental custody, it must be shown that these parents are unfit to be parents and that some alternative arrangement to raise these

67. For example, see *Otzar HaGeonim, Ketubot* 434, where this rule is applied even when the father is alive.

68. One might suggest that the deeply searing psychological trauma involved in being removed from one's parental home makes it never in the best interest of the child to be taken from one's parent, so long as that parent is fit. Consequently, even according to Aderet, this seemingly broad rule — that custody is granted in the best interest of the child — is properly interpreted to mean that Jewish law would not allow the removal of children from the home of their parents to be raised in the house of another who apparently is better capable of raising them. For a brief examination of this rule, see Schaeffer, "Child Custody: Halacha and the Secular Approach."

69. See Warburg, "Child Custody: A Comparative Analysis," pp. 496-98, and Shochatman, "The Essence of the Principles Used in Child Custody in Jewish Law," pp. 308-9.

70. As a matter of practice, this would not happen frequently. Indeed, this author has found no *responsa* that actually permit the removal of children from the custody of parents who are married to each other.

71. See Katz, "A Reply to Ronald Warburg," pp. 16-19, for a discussion of whether this analysis is genuinely limited to fathers or includes all parents. It is this author's opinion that later authorities disagree as to the legal basis of the mother's claim. Most authorities indicate that the mother's claim to custody of the daughter is based on a transfer of rights from the father to the mother based on a specific rabbinic decree found in the Talmud; see note 59 above. On the other hand, many later authorities understand the mother's claim to custody of boys under six to be much less clear as a matter of law and are inclined to view that claim based on an agency theory of some type, with the father's rights supreme should they conflict with the mother's; see also sources cited in note 64.

children consistent with the parents' wishes and lifestyle (either through the use of relatives as agents or in some other manner[72]) cannot be arranged.[73]

This legal dispute is not merely theoretical: the particular *responsa* of Rabbis Asher and Aderet, elaborating on these principles, contain a distinct contrast in result. Aderet rules that when the father is deceased, typically *it is in the best interest of the child to be placed with male relatives of the father rather than with the mother;* R. Asher rules, that as a matter of law, when the mother is deceased, *custody is always to be granted to the father (unless the father is unfit).* To one authority, the legal rule provides the answer, and to another equitable principles relating to best interest do.

These two competing theories, and how they are interpreted by the later authorities, provide the relevant framework to analyze many of the theoretical disputes present in prototypical cases of child custody disputes. Indeed, it is precisely the balance between these two theories that determines how Jewish law awards child custody in many cases.[74]

Strangers and Relatives Seeking Custody

The Jewish law rules for situations where those competing for custody are not the mother and father but legal strangers to the children raise a very interesting issue as a matter of law: Are relatives considered strangers? Do family members other than parents (siblings, siblings-in-law, or grandparents) have a presumptive claim of custody to the children (based on their relationship with the parents), which is terminable only on the same grounds as the parents' claims?[75]

72. For example, sending a child to a boarding school of the parent's choosing; see e.g., P.D.R. 4:66 (1959), where the Rabbinical Court appears to sanction granting custody to the father, who wishes to send his child to a particular educational institution (a boarding school) that will directly supervise the child's day-to-day life.

73. It is possible that there is a third theory also. Rabbenu Nissim (Hebrew acronym "RaN," commenting on Babylonian Talmud, *Ketubot* 65b) seems to accept a contractual framework for custodial arrangements. R. Nissim appears to understand that it is intrinsic in the marital contract *(ketubah)* that just as one is obligated to support one's wife, so too one is obligated to support one's children. This position does not explain why one supports children out of wedlock (as Jewish law certainly requires, see *Shulhan Arukh, Even HaEzer* 82:1-7) or what principles control child custody determinations once the marriage terminates. *Mishneh LeMelech, Hilkhot Ishut* 12:14 notes that R. Nissim's theory was not designed to be followed in practice.

74. See also the fourth section of this article.

75. Alternatively, relatives merely compete with all others under the rubric of "best interest of the child."

The answer to this question is disputed by the various authorities, with numerous decisors supporting each position. The remarks of Rabbi Moses Isserles (Rama) in *Shulhan Arukh* provide the framework for this discussion. After Rabbi Karo states that a daughter resides with her mother even after the mother remarries and the father dies, Rabbi Isserles adds:

> Only if it appears to the court that it is good for the daughter to remain with her mother; however, if it appears to them that it is better for her to reside in the house of her father, the mother cannot compel the daughter to remain with her.[76] If the mother dies, the maternal grandmother cannot compel that her grandchildren be placed with her.[77]

Rabbi Moses ben Isaac Lima in his commentary *Helkat Mehokek* explains Rama's first rulings by stating that Rama does not rule that the daughter *cannot* reside with her mother, but merely that *it is not obvious* that she must. He adds that if the daughter wishes to be with her paternal grandparent, she is entitled to do so; if she has no opinion, the court should contemplate whether it is appropriate to uproot the talmudic rule that daughters reside with their mother.[78] He explains the second rule as limited to a case where the father is alive; however, if both parents are dead, the maternal grandmother has a stronger claim to custody of the girls throughout childhood and of the boys until they are six.[79]

Thus, these rules do appear to grant relatives some greater claim than strangers. It would seem reasonable that these rules implicitly are based on the notion that grandparents have the same rights (except vis-à-vis the parents) as their now-deceased children.[80]

The legal basis for these preferences is addressed in the *responsa* literature in some detail. Four basic legal theories have been set forth. The first as-

76. Rabbi Elijah of Vilna (Gra) rules that the proper resolution of this case depends solely and completely on the wishes of the daughter; *Biur HaGra Even HaEzer* 82:11. This is the only case encountered in which the desires of the minor child are deemed to be the sole relevant factor by any decisor.

77. Rabbi Moses Isserles, Comments of *Rama, Even HaEzer* 82:7.

78. Rabbi Moses ben Isaac Lima, *Helkat Mehokek, Even HaEzer* 82:10.

79. Lima, *Helkat Mehokek, Even HaEzer* 82:11.

80. Thus, the maternal grandmother does not usurp the father's claim, as he is a parent. However, the maternal grandmother has a stronger claim than a paternal grandmother to children that would normally go to the mother, since the maternal grandmother "inherits" (in some form) her daughter's claim. For the same reason, it would seem likely that the paternal grandfather has a greater claim than the maternal grandfather to boys over the age of six.

serts that the basic rights and duties of parents are obligations and privileges that are similar to rights and duties that transfer to heirs of the estate (other than one's spouse[81]). Thus, in a case where a man dies who would have custody of his children if he were alive, his father inherits the right-obligation-*mitzvah*-duty[82] to educate the grandchildren; along with that obligation-right-duty-*mitzvah* he is given custody. Similarly too, if a woman who would have custody were she alive dies, her mother would be entitled to custody assuming she is fit, even if others are more fit.[83]

A second theory can be found in the *responsa* of Rabbi Mordecai ben Judah Halevi addressing a situation common in our society.[84] The *responsum* concerns a man who had just ended his second marriage; his first marriage ended in divorce, and his second marriage ended in the death of his second wife, with whom he had had a number of children. Being unable to take care of these children himself, he arranged for them to be raised by his first wife, *whose marriage with him had ended in divorce.* The children's maternal grandparents, from whom the husband was estranged, sought custody. The author of *Darkhei Noam* ruled that since the father was alive, his rights to the children still existed and so long as his custodial arrangements were satisfactory, others (perhaps even others capable of providing a better home) could not seek to subrogate his rights.[85]

81. In Jewish law, spousal inheritance laws differ from those of blood relatives in significant ways, in that they are fundamentally grounded in contract rather than classical biblical notions of inheritance. This complex matter is well beyond our topic but deserving of treatment in a future article.

82. This author is uncertain which term to use, as none of these privileges are classically heritable. Rather, it is assumed that those authorities who treat the matter in this way understand this to be part of the decree of the Sages. Indeed, different terms might best be used to denote roles of different people seeking custody; see also note 90.

83. See *Helkat Mehokek* 82:11, who states this principle as a matter of law rather than as a matter of best interest of the child; but see Herring, "Child Custody," p. 205, who indicates that this is a rule based on best interest rather than law.

The explanation of Rama advanced by *Helkat Mehokek* is the one most consistent with Rama's elaboration on this topic found in his commentary on *Tur, Darkhei Moshe, Even HaEzer* 82. It is also consistent with the comments of Rabbi Meir ben Isaac Katzenellenbogen, *Responsa Maharam Padua* 53, who is the source for Rama's ruling. It is possible that this same result is reached by others based on a best-interest analysis; see *Radvaz* 1:123, and Rabbi Simeon ben Tzemah Duran, *Tashbetz* 1:40.

84. Rabbi Mordecai ben Judah Halevi, *Responsa Darkhei Noam, Even HaEzer* 26.

85. It is apparent that *Darkhei Noam* invokes the additional concept of "the best interest of the child"; however, the repeated focus of the *responsum* is on the rights of the father who is the surviving parent. While there is language used in this *responsum* that could be interpreted

According to this approach, relatives have greater rights solely because they are most likely to be appointed agents of the parents. Thus, when a particular parent is alive and entitled to presumptive custody of a child,[86] but is in fact incapable of being the custodial parent, the primary legal factor used to determine which stranger shall receive custody is who is designated as an agent of the parent.[87] Thus, this *responsa* adopts a theory of agency rather than guardianship as it relates to parental rights. While the author of the *responsa* does not phrase the discussion precisely this way, it is manifest that his analysis is predicated on the ability of the father to appoint someone to watch his children (in the absence of the mother).[88] This approach accepts the ruling of R. Asher discussed above, as it addresses these issues from the perspective of parental rights. Such a position is explicitly adopted by Rabbi Moses ben Joseph di Trani (Mabit) who primarily analyzes custody of children as a matter of inheritance of rights and agency law according to Jewish law.[89]

The third theory indicates that all levels of relatives are equal to each other, but in legal advantage to the complete stranger. The earliest source for this appears to be *Otzar HaGeonim* (Ketubot 59b), which states that when both parents are unavailable (either unfit for custody, unwilling to take custody, or dead) the court should decide between the maternal and paternal grandparents who desire custody based on the "best-interests-of-the-child"

---

as favoring a pure best-interest analysis, a reading of the whole *responsum* indicates that *Darkhei Noam* is not using a pure best-interest analysis. In this writer's opinion, *Darkhei Noam*'s oft-repeated insight that all custody arrangements are subject to review by Beit Din for the best interest of the child must be limited to cases of unfitness or other disqualification, rather than pure value judgments as to where a child would be best off.

Indeed, more generally, this author finds it difficult as a matter of halakhic jurisprudence to accept that, notwithstanding the precepts found in the codes, one can ignore the rules simply based on a showing that "more likely than not" the rule is not beneficial to this particular child. Rather, based on Babylonian Talmud *Ketubot* 102b, it seems reasonable that some higher standard must be used; see note 95 for a possible way to resolve this difficulty.

86. According to the rules explained in text accompanying notes 27 to 30 above.

87. See also *Ginzei Kedem* 3:62, where the right of the father to appoint a relative is explicitly mentioned as an option in a case where the father is not capable of raising the child.

88. Indeed, the notion of agency is implicit in R. Asher, and can be found also in works of others; see note 64.

89. Rabbi Moses ben Joseph di Trani, *Mabit* 1:165. There are reasons why one would not adopt a pure inheritance approach. One might accept that, for example, a paternal grandfather is entitled presumptively to custody of a male child above six even as against the mother. Such a result is found in *Mabit* 1:165 and *Maharitatz* 1:16, 2:232. As explained above, all agree that in a case of unfitness to be a parent, custody is denied or abrogated. Thus, unlike ownership of a cow or house, there are situations that can abrogate one's "rights."

rationale. There is no acknowledgment of the legal possibility that the children can be placed with complete strangers. This approach seems to be the one most easily consonant with the wording of Rama on *Shulhan Arukh* 82:7 and the explanation of *Helkat Mehokek*, and it also draws support from *Beit Yosef*.[90]

The final possibility, explicitly found in Aderet,[91] is that in the case of orphans, based on the principle "the court is the guardian of orphans," a pure best-interest-of-the-child analysis is made. Indeed, it is precisely in this category of case that Aderet explicitly states the best-interest-of-the-child rule. He writes:

> As a general rule, the beth din (court) must closely inspect each case [of child custody] very closely; since the court is the guardian of orphans, it is to find out what is in their best interest.

Similar observations can be found in the words of many authorities who discuss the status of relatives or strangers in child custody matters.[92] In the case

90. Commenting on *Tur, Even HaEzer* 82; see also Rabbi Simeon ben Tzemah Duran, quoted in *Beit Yosef, Even HaEzer* 82. This theory is a little difficult to harmonize with the lack of legal obligation imposed upon the mother according to Jewish law. One could read this position as simply being the best interest of the child, with a presumption that when parents are incapable of retaining custody, grandparents are those adults most likely (as a matter of fact) to function in the best interest of the child. If one understood this to be the view of the *Geonim*, one could easily assert that in modern times, when other couples might more readily take custody of the children, the *Geonim* would fall into the camp of Aderet and rule that child custody determinations are made purely in the best interests of the child.

Alternatively one could posit that grandparents are merely presumed agents or heirs and thus this position is identical as a matter of theory with *Darkhei Moshe*'s rule, with the psychological insight that grandparents are very likely to be appointed.

It is possible to distinguish between the obligation of the mother and the obligation of the father. The mother, if she desires custody, is entitled by rabbinic decree to custody in those cases explained in the third section of this article. However, she is under no obligation to accept such custody. To her, Jewish law treats custody as a privilege or right without a concomitant duty; see note 32 above. The father, however, has certain duties and obligations based upon Jewish law's requirements that he support his children. Custody to him is a right and a duty; see also note 82.

91. *Responsa of Aderet (Rashba) Traditionally Assigned to Nahmanides* 38.

92. Rabbi Meir Abulafia, *Responsa of Ramah* 290; Rabbi Isaac ben Moses of Vienna, *Or Zarua* 1:746; Rabbi Simeon ben Tzemah Duran, *Tashbetz* 2:216. For a long list of authorities who accept this rule, see Shochatman, "The Essence of the Principles Used in Child Custody in Jewish Law," n. 51. As explained in note 85, one could read such an approach into *Darkhei Noam* as well. In this author's opinion, *Darkhei Noam* uses a pure best-interest analysis only once parents are deceased, but in the presence of both parents, the rule "*beit din* is the guardian of orphans" is simply completely inapplicable and not used by him. Indeed, one could go further and claim that even Aderet would not disagree with that claim; however, Aderet is commonly

of orphans, where potential custodians are strangers, it would appear that most authorities accept the opinion of Aderet.[93]

Conclusion

This article has analyzed various basic disagreements among the Jewish law authorities regarding the application of halakhic rules in child custody determinations. Essentially three disputes were discussed: by what standard may one remove a child from the custodial parent; who then is entitled to custody; and what is the status of relatives in custody determinations. All of these disagreements can be regarded as manifestations of the theoretical dispute between R. Asher and Aderet discussed in the third section of this article (although the *responsa* rarely acknowledge the dichotomy explicitly).

According to R. Asher and those who accept his rule, parents are always entitled to custody if they are fit, even if others would be more fit.[94] So too, when one parent is incapacitated, dead, or otherwise unfit, the other parent may assert rights against strangers. Some would go even further with R. Asher's theory by incorporating some sort of concept of transferable rights to children; upon the death or incapacity of the parents, the children can be transferred to an agent or heir according to the wishes of the parent.[95] R.

---

interpreted as advancing a general rule, one that is not limited to orphans; see Shochatman, "The Essence of the Principles Used in Child Custody in Jewish Law," pp. 307-11, and Herring, "Child Custody," pp. 207-19; see also *Otzar HaGeonim, Ketubot* 434.

93. See, e.g., *Shulhan Arukh,* Hoshen Mishpat 290, and Herring, "Child Custody," pp. 194-95. Thus, the more distant one is from the parents, the more likely one is to have to prove that one's custody actually is in the child's best interest.

94. Indeed R. Asher states this clearly in *Responsa of Asher* 82:2. In this writer's opinion, R. Asher makes no distinction between mother and father for the purposes of this rule when they are both alive. While it is true that a strong claim can be made that as a matter of Torah law this is only true for the father (see Gulevsky, "Question on the Custody of Children," p. 106, and notes accompanying that section), one could easily claim that the nature of the rabbinic decree giving the mother custody transfers to her those rights.

95. The crucial issue might be why the Baraita quoted in Babylonian Talmud *Ketubot* 102b, which indicates that children whose father is deceased do not get placed with paternal relatives lest these children be killed to produce an inheritance, is not normative in Jewish law. As noted by Shochatman, "The Essence of the Principles Used in Child Custody in Jewish Law," p. 296, this rule is not followed by nearly all codifiers. The rejection of this rule must indicate that some sort of additional analysis is taking place. It could be that, absent this talmudic source, children would have had to be transferred according to inheritance laws. Once the Talmud indicated that this need not be done, the crucial question is in what circumstances chil-

Asher's analysis accepts that the talmudic rules are generally to be followed unless they lead to custody being given to one who is not fit or capable.

According to Aderet, the presumed rule is not one of rights but of best interest of the child. In this approach, the beth din accepts the talmudic rules as presumptively correct and then seeks to ascertain what actually is the best interest of the child by determining whether the general talmudic presumptions are applicable to the particular child. It is not a system of rights, but a system that seeks to do the best for children — and not for their parents. It thus actually rejects "rule-based" determinations and insists that custody will be given to the most fit caretaker, rather than the one designated by the father (or mother). Thus, fewer default rules and no absolutely concrete ones are found in this system, at least once the parents are divorced, separated, or incapacitated.

Absent from the entire discussion of the relationship between caregivers and children as portrayed in Jewish law is the notion of love — perfect, complete, or otherwise. As we have seen throughout this chapter, no authority discusses who can love the children more or better. Jewish law never addresses the question of who is obligated to love a child and what the nature of that love is. Indeed, it even imposes no requirement upon parents to love their children or for children to love their parents. Rather, Jewish law places an obligation upon parents to take care of their children and upon children to honor and respect their parents. Love is too fleeting an emotion for the Jewish tradition to put its faith in when discussing children, the most important asset any society and any family might have.[96]

---

dren may be transferred contrary to the technical requirements of unchanged Torah law. R. Asher would claim that we reject the talmudic law of placing children with their parents only in cases of unfitness, whereas Aderet must state that this talmudic precedent allows for the transfer of children according to their own best interest.

96. Marriage, too, in the Jewish tradition is not based on an unbreakable, unyielding bond of love but on mutual agreement between the husband and wife. Marital roles and duties are thus established contractually at the outset of a marriage with the *ketubah* document and are subject to negotiation between the parties. Most significantly, marriages in the Jewish tradition are ultimately dissolvable by divorce; see Michael Broyde, "The Covenant-Contract Dialectic in Jewish Marriage and Divorce Law," in *Covenant Marriage in Comparative Perspective,* ed. John Witte Jr. and Eliza Ellison (Grand Rapids: Eerdmans, 2005), pp. 53-69.

Even the covenantal relationship between God and the Jewish people has been presented as requiring reaffirmation following the destruction of Solomon's Temple. According to the Babylonian Talmud, *Shabbat* 88a, even though the Jews accepted the Torah at Sinai, the Sages understood exegetically from the Book of Esther that the Jews reaffirmed and reaccepted it again in the time of the Persian king Ahasuerus (Artaxerxes), several generations into the exile.

Though there certainly is a deep connection between love and care, the Jewish tradition generally and Jewish law specifically — given its deep, nitty-gritty concern that abstract principles be made concrete — choose to concentrate their energies in the parent-child arena, not on the inchoate and intangible manifestations of the word "love" or even to contemplate who will love a child more. These are impossible to measure, the Jewish tradition avers. What we can measure is who will best care for the child, and that is the approach of Jewish law. This is consistent with the general worldview of the Jewish tradition, a religion that focuses on deed as the central manifestation of the godly in this world.[97]

Indeed, the inclination toward care as the measure of parental fitness underlies the classic biblical story in which King Solomon wisely suggests to "split the baby." This incident, recounted in 1 Kings 3:16-28, involves the custody determination of an infant contested by two women, each of whom claims to be the biological mother. The Jewish tradition, I think, does not deny that both of these women "love" this baby, but it sees that one of them is prepared to love the baby to life and the other to love the baby to death. The one who loves the baby to life is entitled to custody, whereas the one prepared to love the baby to death should not have custody in fact. In other words, King Solomon was not seeking to determine who is the true mother, but who is the true and proper caregiver.

I opened the chapter by making reference in the title to the refrain of a Tina Turner hit — what's love got to do with it — that summarizes one half of the Jewish law view on parents and children, namely what the relationship is *not* based upon. I will now end with the signature song/lyric of the Queen of Soul, Aretha Franklin, one that I think better encapsulates the Jewish tradition's understanding of what the basis of the relationship *is*. Ultimately, it is not love that matters, but R-E-S-P-E-C-T.[98]

97. Secular law has chosen to adopt the Jewish law view here and also focus on the best interest of the child exactly because love — particularly as it is used in the Christian tradition — remains difficult to quantify, easy to fake, hard to mandate, and prone to manipulation in front of a judge. Thus, one never sees courts adjudicating matters of child custody asking who will love the child more or better; instead, courts focus on the best interest of the child as manifest through indicia of care. No other structure can actually provide for the best interests of the child.

98. See Wikipedia, "Aretha Franklin." To my dismay, this is also the first citation to Aretha Franklin in my work or, as far as I can tell, other works of Jewish law. It should be noted that although "Respect" was first written and recorded by Otis Redding in 1965, Ms. Franklin's cover recording of the song, recasting it as a feminist ballad, lent it enduring popularity; see Wikipedia, "Respect (song)."

CHAPTER 11

What's Love Got to Do with It? (Part II): The Best Interests of the Child in International and Comparative Law

RANA LEHR-LEHNARDT AND T. JEREMY GUNN

[A]lthough a pragmatic approach was needed for children's problems, an important point was being missed in the general human rights debate: the substantive provisions of the Convention [on the Rights of the Child] made no reference to the emotion of love. . . . Disabled children needed love more than anything else, yet the Convention dealt only with rights and was addressed to Governments.[1]

Introduction

With the ratification of the United Nations Convention on the Rights of the Child, the best-interests-of-the-child standard has been elevated from being a widely accepted legal norm in the domestic law of a significant number of countries around the world to becoming the prevailing international legal norm as well.[2] Although the best-interests standard has been increasingly ac-

1. Committee on the Rights of the Child, General Discussion on the Rights of Children with Disabilities, Oct. 7, 1997. CRC/C/SR.419, ¶19.

2. The best-interests-of-the-child doctrine is used in courts and administrative agencies to determine various issues relating to child welfare, especially upon the dissolution of marriage or the termination of parental rights. In deciding the best interests of the child, often, multiple factors are weighed against each other to determine which combination works to the greatest advantage of the child and her development. Countries using the best-interests-of-the-child doctrine (to varying degrees and with varying terminology) in their laws include countries from every continent, including countries of the European Union, countries with a foun-

cepted worldwide, criticism of it has been raised and some scholars and child advocates search for ways to improve or modify it. Inasmuch as the best-interests standard serves as the dominant standard for addressing a certain range of legal issues affecting children, and inasmuch as substantial psychological and sociological research has demonstrated a child's need for love[3] to survive and thrive,[4] it is worth considering what role the emotive elements of love and affection do play and should play on the standard as understood and applied at the national and the international levels. We focus on the visible aspects of love (i.e., affection, attachment, and care), because the research and legal history have addressed these components of love — perhaps because actions associated with emotion or affection can be observed and quantified whereas love as an abstract notion cannot be measured.

In this chapter we will consider whether the visible aspects of love and affection could sensibly be incorporated in a limited way within the best-

dation in English common law (including the United States, Canada, Australia, New Zealand), countries in the Middle East (including Israel, Egypt, Morocco, Tunisia), countries of Asia (including China, Taiwan, Japan, South Korea), countries of South Asia (including India, Sri Lanka, Bangladesh), countries of Africa (including Nigeria, Uganda, South Africa, Ghana, Kenya), and countries of South America (including Brazil, Argentina, Chile).

3. Love is generally divided into four types: *eros* (romantic love), *philia* (brotherly love or friendship), *agape* (Christ-like or unconditional love), and *storge* (familial love). Much research regarding children and love focuses on affection, physical contact, and separation, which are all visible and measurable occurrences. See note 4 below. Likewise, the law focuses on aspects of love that are visible and measurable: affection, attachment, and care. As such, when we use the term "love" in this chapter, we are referring to the unconditional love a parent feels for a child, often visible to others via acts of affection, physical contact, and care. It also includes the unconditional love a child feels for a parent.

4. See chapters in this book by Peter Benson, Annette Mahoney and Ken Pargament, and Robyn Fivush that focus on the psychological and sociological need for love and affection. See generally, Harry F. Harlow, "The Nature of Love," *American Psychologist* 13 (1958): 673-85 (describing experiments on macaque monkeys and their responses to and needs for affection); John Bowlby, papers read to the British Psychoanalytic Society: "The Nature of the Child's Tie to His Mother" (1957), "Separation Anxiety" (1959), "Grief and Mourning in Infancy and Early Childhood" (1959) (revealing a need for intimate physical contact, which is initially associated with the mother); Joseph Goldstein et al., *The Best Interests of the Child: The Least Detrimental Alternative* (New York: Free Press, 1996) (proposing that children in child custody and adoption disputes remain with the psychological parent, the parent with whom the child has the deepest attachment); Sandra Kaler and B. Freeman, "Analysis of Environmental Deprivation: Cognitive and Social Development in Romanian Orphans," *Journal of Child Psychology and Psychiatry* 35, no. 4 (1994): 769-81; S. Wang, J. V. Bartolome, and S. M. Schanberg, "Neonatal Deprivation of Maternal Touch May Suppress Ornithine Decarboxylase via Down Regulation of Proto-Oncogenes C-Myc and Max," *Journal of Neuroscience* 16 (1996): 836-42.

interests standard and thereby produce benefits for children and society. Next, we will probe the Anglo-American roots of the tender-years and best-interests doctrines and consider the perhaps surprising role that love and affection played therein. We will consider the historical development of children's rights in international norms that have incorporated the best-interests standard, and find that love and affection rarely have been raised either in the process of drafting international norms or in decisions interpreting international instruments. Following, we will acknowledge that there are some important criticisms that have been made against the best-interests standard. Finally, we will conclude by suggesting that not only was love and affection an integral feature during the development of the best-interests standard in the domestic arena, but love and affection should be an important consideration when deciding family-law disputes that involve children and also should be included as part of the best-interests standard when deciding family law issues in international bodies.

Intersections of Children and the Law

Issues involving children and the law arise principally in six interrelated areas: first, in the family law context (or "personal law" in the Civil Law), which focuses on disputes involving issues such as child custody or inheritance; second, where the state might guarantee by law certain social services or benefits to children (e.g., education, medical care, housing, etc.); third, where the law requires children to engage in certain activities (e.g., compulsory education, vaccinations, etc.); fourth, where the law restricts the ability of children to engage in activities that would be permitted for adults (e.g., voting, entering into contracts, joining the military, etc.); fifth, in the context of the criminal law, where children are subject to different (typically less harsh) standards of behavior and where punishments might be lighter; sixth, in the "rights" context, where the state (or an international instrument such as the Convention on the Rights of the Child) articulates certain rights that a child might have in relationship to the state (e.g., the right not to be subjected to physical abuse). In most modern societies these six areas of law generally presume that children should be subjected to a different standard of treatment than adults inasmuch as their judgment, personality, or levels of education are not fully developed. In some cases they are given additional benefits (or solicitude), while in others they are denied rights that are available to others.

While the best-interests language may have some applicability to each of the six areas, albeit with different connotations in each, the love and affection factor would seem to be of relevance only in the context of family law (or personal law), and even there only in certain specific applications. While we presumably would not want judges in child custody disputes, for example, to make decisions based on how much they personally loved the child whose future was in question, we would want them to take into account the extent of the emotional bonds between parents and children and whether parents are able to provide an environment of love and affection. This emotive factor is thus important, and may in some cases be decisive, in determining the best interests of the child in family law. Such concerns, as will be shown below, already are present in many national laws and are referenced with terms including "love," "affection," "emotional attachment," "emotional ties," "emotional well-being," "emotional welfare," and "emotional needs." The love and affection component is always considered as a factor between a child and parents or other guardians, never between a child and state actors associated with the child.

Love and affection would certainly seem to be less applicable to the other five intersections between children and the law for the obvious reason that the state (as opposed to parents and family) plays the primary role in each of them. It would be odd, for example, for a legislator to opine that the voting age should be reduced to sixteen on the grounds that she loves children. We would expect legislators, when enacting laws, to focus on concern for children and the best interests of children as measured by objective social science standards rather than using love as the basis of their votes. In the other five areas the state is the actor responsible for providing the social and physical benefit, protection, or restriction on actions, and is not the actor responsible for loving the child. Love of an individual child, or even children generally, is not an advisable obligation to impose on states because states are quite obviously incapable of loving and states need to act in the interest of society generally. Love and affection belong within family law — in judicial or administrative decisions that affect families. And this love needs to be directed toward the relationship between parents/guardians and children.

The remainder of the chapter will consider love and the best-interests standard in the critically important but clearly circumscribed family law context, both historically and currently, and in both national courts and international tribunals.

Historical Development of Children's Rights and Parental Authority

Children as Chattel

Roman law influenced Western legal systems well after its demise. It was especially influential on the European continent and in the Byzantine Empire, but less so in England and subsequently the United States.[5] A main component of the Roman Law of Persons is *patria potestas,* or the absolute power given to the patriarch over family members and over all property. Only a male Roman citizen could be a *paterfamilias,* the oldest living male ancestor of a family who exercised *patria potestas.*[6] He alone decided the fate of all descendants, including sons, daughters, in-laws, grandchildren, and all other descendants. The *paterfamilias* had virtual control over the members of his family and could legally punish them with banishment, slavery, and death.[7] This legal control over descendants did not end upon descendants' attainment of the age of majority. The Twelve Tables of ancient Roman law declare: "The father has power to imprison or to scourge his son, to keep him at work in fetters, and even to put him to death. This is his power although the son should hold the highest office in the state."[8] Children and grandchildren could not own property, retain their wages, or exercise legal control over their own children.[9] Ultimately, "there was no legal limit to the *patria potestas.*"[10] The *paterfamilias*'s control ended only upon his death or loss of citizenship.[11] Upon the death of the *paterfamilias,* each son became the *paterfamilias* of his own household until his own death.[12]

The *patria potestas* weakened during the first centuries of the common era.[13] Alexander Severus, emperor from 222 to 235, limited the *paterfamilias*'s

5. William L. Burdick, *The Principles of Roman Law and Their Relation to Modern Law* (1838; reprint, Clark, NJ: Lawbook Exchange, 2004), pp. 35-86.

6. Burdick, *The Principles of Roman Law,* p. 241.

7. Burdick, *The Principles of Roman Law,* p. 255 (listing several recorded instances of a *paterfamilias* executing sons and daughters for various reasons).

8. Burdick, *The Principles of Roman Law,* p. 254 (quoting Table IV of the Twelve Tables).

9. Andrew Stephenson, *A History of Roman Law* (1912; reprint, Littleton, CO: Fred B. Rothman & Co., 1992), pp. 26-28.

10. Stephenson, *A History of Roman Law,* p. 28.

11. Stephenson, *A History of Roman Law,* p. 27.

12. Stephenson, *A History of Roman Law,* p. 259.

13. Other sources date the first legislative restriction of punishing children to 364-375 CE as contained in the constitution of Valentinian and Valens. Sheldon Amos, *The History and Prin-*

legal ability to punish family members to only physical chastisement.[14] Constantine agreed with this limitation and declared that a father who willfully killed his son should receive harsh punishment — drowning in a sack with a viper, cock, and ape.[15] Children and grandchildren acquired some autonomy from the *paterfamilias* as common practice developed that allowed them to retain their earnings and private possessions, though the legal title of all property was still in the *paterfamilias*.[16] Despite mild improvements in ancient Roman law, children, especially those below the age of majority, continued to be treated as chattel.

Introducing Restraints on Parental Action

Based in part on the Roman tradition, Western legal systems typically classified children as chattel until the mid-1800s.[17] However, restraints on parental authority, mild though they were, could be found in the law. While children could be indentured, gifted, beaten, or exploited, fathers were not authorized to kill their children. In fact, in eighteenth- and nineteenth-century common law England, one of the only sure ways a father would lose custody of his children was if he endangered his child's life or limb.[18] In the *Skinner* case of 1824, the King's Bench opined that a father, even an unfit father, who was in possession of the child, could not be denied custody unless the father posed a threat to the life and limb of the child.[19] An English court, in 1827, stated that once the father has physical custody of a child, even if obtained by stratagem and force, only extreme ill treatment of the child would justify removal of the child from the father's custody.[20] Another limit on a father's authority was introducing a child into an immoral situation, specifically dealing with a pre-

---

ciples of the Civil Law of Rome: An Aid to the Study of Scientific and Comparative Jurisprudence (1883; reprint, Littleton, CO: Fred B. Rothman, 1987), p. 268.

14. Burdick, *The Principles of Roman Law*, p. 258.

15. Burdick, *The Principles of Roman Law*, pp. 258-59.

16. Burdick, *The Principles of Roman Law*, pp. 256-57.

17. See generally Philippe Aries, *Centuries of Childhood: A Social History of Family Life* (New York: Knopf, 1962); Lloyd deMause, ed., *The History of Childhood* (New York: Psychohistory Press, 1974).

18. Danaya C. Wright, "The Crisis of Child Custody: A History of the Birth of Family Law in England," *Columbia Journal of Gender & Law* 11 (2002): 225.

19. Wright, "The Crisis of Child Custody," pp. 195-96; *Ex parte* Skinner, 27 Eng. Rep. 710, 718 (1824).

20. Ball v. Ball, 2 Sim. 35, 36-37, 57 Eng. Rep. 703, 704 (ch. 1827).

marital sexual relationship. This limit is demonstrated by a case from the King's Bench in which the court refused to return a teenaged daughter to her father's custody because the court believed the father was knowledgeable or complicit in the placement of his daughter in the home of a wealthy elderly gentleman for the purpose of becoming his mistress.[21]

In nineteenth-century America, several states struggled with how to deal with excessive parental discipline. Beginning in about 1825, several cities and states penned laws permitting public authorities to intervene on behalf of a child who was severely mistreated or grossly neglected by parents.[22] In 1874, the case of Mary Ellen brought notoriety to child abuse. Mary Ellen was placed in foster care where she was severely and regularly beaten by her "mamma," which resulted in scars, burns, bruises, and stunted growth from malnutrition. New York had laws against assault, but they had never been used on behalf of a child in the home. With police unable or unwilling to intervene, the president of the New York Society for the Prevention of Cruelty to Animals brought suit on behalf of Mary Ellen, who testified of the daily beatings and starvation. She was promptly removed from the family by a special warrant under the Habeas Corpus Act, as no child abuse law was available.[23] The abusive mother was found guilty of felonious assault in a separate criminal trial and was sentenced to one year of hard labor.[24]

A year after the Mary Ellen case, a court in another state declared that physical punishment of children by parents was legal as long as it was moderate.

> The right of parents to chastise their refractory and disobedient children is so necessary to the government of families, to the good of society, that no moralist or lawgiver has ever thought of interfering with its existence. . . . But, at the same time that the law has created and preserved this right, in its regard for the safety of the child it has prescribed bounds beyond which it shall not be carried. In chastising a child, the parent must be careful that he does not exceed the bounds of moderation and inflict cruel and merciless punishment; if he do, he is a trespasser, and liable to

21. In Rex v. Sir DeLavel, 97 Eng. Rep. 913 (K.B. 1763) (acknowledging a day after its initial comments that sufficient information had been provided to the court to establish that the father was neither knowledgeable nor complicit in the placement of his daughter as a mistress).

22. John E. B. Myers, *Child Protection in America: Past, Present, and Future* (New York: Oxford University Press, 2006), p. 13.

23. Myers, *Child Protection in America,* p. 30 and note 5.

24. Lela B. Costin, "Unraveling the Mary Ellen Legend: Origins of the 'Cruelty' Movement," *Social Service Review* 65, no. 2 (1991): 203-23; Myers, *Child Protection in America,* pp. 27-33, and accompanying notes.

> be punished by indictment. It is not, then, the infliction of punishment, but the excess, which constitutes the offence.[25]

Other courts that attempted to balance the parental "right" of chastisement with child protection created a definition of criminal child abuse that resulted in permanent injury of the child.[26] These views — that parents may chastise their children within prescribed (if vague) limits and that the state may punish parents not for the act of chastising, but for excessive force and duration — are still valid in many parts of the United States and in many other countries around the world, though the understanding of excessive force has evolved through the years.

Most states have codified child abuse laws, though each state defines abuse differently and provides for some parental exemptions when it is the parent's own child. The relevant Texas statute, for example, provides that the parent's use of force against a minor child is permitted if the force used is not deadly.[27] Until recently, English law permitted the caning of children through its reasonable chastisement exception to child abuse laws.[28] Section 58 of Britain's Children Act, 2004, removed the defense of reasonable chastisement from various offenses causing bodily harm, but retained the defense for minor forms of assault on children that leave only fleeting marks on the body.

Another restraint on parental authority was the legal obligation to maintain one's children.[29] Parents could not legally abandon children or withhold from them necessary nourishment, clothing, and shelter whenever they possessed the financial means to provide for the children. In a case from eighteenth-century England, the King's Bench denied custody to a father who was not in possession of the child and who did not provide financially for the child. "The natural right is with the father; but if the father is a bankrupt, if he contributed nothing for the child or family, and if he be improper . . . the Court will not think it right that the child should be with him."[30]

A final restraint on parental authority appeared in the form of child la-

25. Johnson v. State, 21 Tenn. 283, 283 (1840).

26. State v. Jones, 95 NC. 588, 592 (1886).

27. Tex. Penal Code Ann. § 9.61 (West 1974) (justification section of penal code).

28. A. v. United Kingdom, 1998-VI Eur. Ct. H.R. 2692 (1998).

29. Sir William Blackstone, "Of Parent and Child," ch. 16 in *Commentaries on the Laws of England* (1765-69), book 1, p. 435; Chancellor James Kent, "Of Parent and Child," lecture 29 in *Commentaries on American Law,* vol. 2 (1827).

30. Blisset's Case, 98 Eng. Rep. 899, 900 (K.B. 1774).

bor laws.[31] During the early 1900s every state in the United States had some limitation on child labor. The federal government passed the Federal Fair Labor Standards Act in 1938, which prohibited most child labor for juveniles under the age of sixteen. Parents could no longer send their young children to work for long hours or in dangerous conditions.

In the U.S. Supreme Court case *Sturges & Burn Mfg. Co. v. Beauchamp,*[32] an employer was found to have violated an Illinois law of 1903, which prohibited the employment of children under the age of sixteen in various hazardous jobs. In another lawsuit, a father of two sons below the age of sixteen alleged that a specific federal law intended to prevent interstate commerce of the products of child labor violated the Constitution.[33] A reasonable assumption for the father's opposition to the federal statute, which was supposedly crafted to protect his sons from exploitation, was the father's desire for his children to work and earn wages to pay for necessities for the family, even if the working conditions were not ideal for teenage boys. In a later and now famous Supreme Court case, *Prince v. Massachusetts,*[34] a mother who had allowed her foster daughter to sell religious tracts on the street with her was found guilty of violating child labor laws. The Supreme Court stated that a parent's "sacred private interests" in exercising authority in the household and rearing one's children were tempered by society's interests to protect the welfare of children.[35] "Rights of parenthood are [not] beyond limitation."[36]

These few limitations on parental authority over one's children constituted important steps toward creating a broader legal standard that would consider the best interests of the child. Below, we will see that parental love and affection soon played a role in the development of that standard.

Parental Love and Affection

Although a few restraints were crafted into the chattel theory in the eighteenth, nineteenth, and early twentieth centuries, parents still retained almost

31. Concern for child welfare was not the only reason, and perhaps not the primary reason for child labor laws. Difficult financial times in the United States and a desire to make more jobs available to adults were players in this legal reform.

32. 231 U.S. 320 (1913).

33. Hammer v. Dagenhart, 247 U.S. 251 (1918). The statute was Act of September 1, 1916, ch. 432, 39 Stat. 675 (1916).

34. 321 U.S. 158 (1944).

35. 321 U.S. 165 (1944).

36. 321 U.S. 166 (1944).

total control over their children. But eighteenth-century England began to voice a separate and different rationale; this new rationale was based on love. Although the origin of the second rationale is to some extent the *opposite* of the chattel theory, its practical consequences would in many circumstances prove to be identical — parents were given almost total control over children. This new theory was based on the belief that parental love and affection toward one's children naturally inspire the best decisions on behalf of children. Thus, parents make decisions on behalf of their children not because of a proprietary reason, but because they love their children and want the best for them. A leading eighteenth-century English legal scholar, Sir William Blackstone, voiced the importance of parental love as an uncodified element of family law. Specifically, Blackstone recognized the "natural affection" parents have for their children and how this natural affection directs parents in fulfilling their duties of maintenance, guidance, and education. He stated,

> The municipal laws of all well-regulated states have taken care to enforce [the parental duty to maintain one's children]: though providence has done it more effectually than any laws, by implanting in the breast of every parent that natural *sopyn,* or insuperable degree of affection, which not even the deformity of person or mind, not even the wickedness, ingratitude, and rebellion of children, can totally suppress or extinguish.[37]

Blackstone did not think it necessary to provide evidence of this natural affection; it is stated as if it were self-evident.

More than half a century later, an American legal scholar, Chancellor James Kent, also recognized the importance of parental love in family law matters. He opined, "The duties that reciprocally result from this connection [of parent and child], are prescribed . . . by those feelings of parental love and filial reverence which Providence has implanted in the human breast. . . ." He continued, "The obligation of parental duty is so well secured by the strength of natural affection, that it seldom requires to be enforced by human laws."[38]

These comments on parental love and affection by two leading legal scholars of the eighteenth and nineteenth centuries illustrate a philosophical change in legal reasoning and provide a backdrop for the legal atmosphere in which the best-interests standard began its development. This philosophical change from viewing parents (particularly fathers) as property owners of

37. Blackstone, "Of Parent and Child," p. 435.

38. Kent, "Of Parent and Child."

children to seeing parents (particularly mothers) as concerned and affectionate protectors of children is perhaps one reason why the best-interests and accompanying tender-years doctrines contained significant discussion of parental love and affection.

Challenging Parental Authority

In the years following Blackstone's and Kent's comments on parental love, lawmakers began to chip away at Roman law vestiges and at common law practice that had largely deferred to parental authority, particularly in two major areas: compulsory public education and life-saving medical decisions. The state laws would come to supersede parental decisions in these two areas not because of any perceived lack of parental love or any supposed neglect, but because the state found that it had significant interests in both the child individually and society generally.

Compulsory Education

As early as 1846, the framers of the Wisconsin constitution supported a uniform public education system to inculcate values in children in order to preserve American liberties.[39] But attendance at the uniform Wisconsin schools was not made mandatory in the state constitution. A few years later, in 1852, Massachusetts passed the first modern compulsory attendance of public education law in the United States.[40] As counties and states improved their public school systems, all of the states ultimately adopted compulsory attendance laws by the early 1900s, and the colonial practice of parents educating their children in the home essentially ended.[41]

However, as governments attempted to increasingly interfere with parental involvement in their children's education, parents challenged this infringement on their once-unquestioned parental authority. The courts responded by carving exemptions for parents, many of which have been codified.

39. Michael S. Ariens and Robert A. Destro, *Religious Liberty in a Pluralistic Society* (Durham, NC: Carolina Academic Press, 1996), p. 404.

40. William M. Gordon et al., *The Law of Home Schooling,* NOLPE Monograph Series, no. 52 (Topeka, KS: National Organization on Legal Problems of Education, 1994), p. 7.

41. See Christopher J. Klicka, *The Right to Home School: A Guide to the Law on Parents' Rights in Education,* 3rd ed. (Durham, NC: Carolina Academic Press, 2002), p. 2.

Nebraska mandated compulsory education, and in 1919 it adopted a new law making it illegal to teach any subject in a language other than English.[42] The purpose of the law was to ensure children learned what the state believed to be most important for children: the English language and ideals that promote democracy.[43] In response, the U.S. Supreme Court declared that it is within parental rights, as part of their duty to educate their children, to choose to have their children taught in a language other than English.[44]

A few years later, the U.S. Supreme Court held that an Oregon law requiring compulsory education at a *public* school "unreasonably interferes with the liberty of parents and guardians to direct the upbringing and education of children under their control."[45] Parental authority included the right to send one's child to a private religious school.

Nearly fifty years later, Amish fathers raised religious objections to the compulsory education of their children after the eighth grade. In *Wisconsin v. Yoder*,[46] the U.S. Supreme Court stated, "the values of parental direction of the religious upbringing and education of their children in their early and formative years have a high place in our society."[47] As such, the Court found that compulsory education of Amish youth after the eighth grade violated the parents' and children's religious liberties.

Medical Interventions

State interests have also trumped parental authority regarding medical decisions.

Vaccinations became increasingly mandatory in Europe during the nineteenth century.[48] Similarly, individual states or local jurisdictions within the United States began requiring all persons to be vaccinated against communicable diseases. In 1902, Cambridge, Massachusetts, passed one such law

42. Meyer v. Nebraska, 262 U.S. 390 (1923); see also Farrington v. Tokushige, 273 U.S. 284 (1927) (invalidating a law of the Territory of Hawaii barring private schools that taught languages other than English for violating the Fifth Amendment).

43. *Meyer*, 262 U.S. 397-98, 401 (1923).

44. *Meyer*, 262 U.S. 400 (1923).

45. Pierce v. Society of the Sisters of the Holy Names of Jesus and Mary, 268 U.S. 510, 534-35 (1925).

46. 406 U.S. 205 (1972).

47. 406 U.S. 213-14 (1972).

48. Bavaria was the first to mandate vaccinations in 1807, followed by Denmark in 1810, Sweden in 1814, various German states in 1818, Prussia in 1835, England in 1853, Romania in 1874, Hungary in 1876, and Serbia in 1881. See Jacobson v. Massachusetts, 197 U.S. 11, 31 n.† (1905).

and imposed criminal liability for failure to comply. Three years later, the U.S. Supreme Court upheld this law in a case brought by a conscientious objector who was concerned about the possible negative effects of vaccinations.[49] In 1944, the U.S. Supreme Court stated in dicta that religious beliefs would not circumvent a compulsory vaccination law.[50]

Current child abuse statutes require parents to seek life-saving medical intervention for their minor children.[51] Courts ordinarily defer to parental decisions for non-life-threatening medical issues. However, some courts have overridden parental decisions even in cases where the medical intervention was not immediately necessary to preserve the child's life. Judges have used neglect statutes to make the child a ward of the state for the one issue of approving necessary medical care. In one such case, the court declared a mother negligent for refusing medical intervention that could have reduced the disfiguring effects of a tumor on the face and neck of her son.[52] The tumor was caused by an incurable but non-life-threatening disease. Over the mother's religious objections to blood transfusions, the court ruled the surgery necessary to afford the boy a chance at a normal and productive life. Many Western nations, including all fifty states of the United States, now mandate childhood vaccinations. But most nations, including Australia, Canada, the United Kingdom, and the United States, provide exemptions for religious, medical, or personal reasons.[53]

Case law and statutes partially exempt parents from seeking medical intervention when the failure to do so is based on sincere religious beliefs. New provisions of the Child Abuse Prevention and Treatment Act Amendments of 1996 specify that nothing in the Act is to be construed as establishing a federal requirement that a parent or legal guardian provide medical service or treatment that is against the religious beliefs of the parent or legal guardian.[54] But religious exemptions are only partial; they do not apply to life-saving medical interventions.[55] For example, the Colorado statute provides that children

49. *Jacobson,* 197 U.S. 11.

50. Prince v. Massachusetts, 321 U.S. 158, 166 (1944).

51. For an example of one such statute, see, Colo. Rev. Stats. § 19-3-102(1)(d) (2005).

52. See *In Re Sampson,* 323 N.Y.S.2d 253 (N.Y. App. Div. 1971), aff'd, 278 N.E.2d 918 (N.Y. 1972).

53. For a list of vaccination exemption requirements and forms, see http://www.unhinderedliving.com/statevaccexemp.html.

54. 42 U.S.C. § 5106i.

55. Additionally, approximately thirty-one states, the District of Columbia, Puerto Rico, and Guam provide an exemption from the definition of neglect for parents who choose not to seek medical care for their children because of religious beliefs. Sixteen of these states, and

shall not be deemed neglected, and therefore will not fall under the custody of the state, because they are receiving "treatment solely by spiritual means through prayer in accordance with a recognized method of religious healing. . . . However, the religious rights of a parent, guardian, or legal custodian shall not limit the access of a child to medical care in a life-threatening situation or when the condition will result in serious disability."[56]

In recent history, several parents have been criminally prosecuted for the death of their children that resulted from their reliance on spiritual healing rather than seeking medical intervention.[57] The Supreme Court addressed this by stating that parents may choose to become martyrs, but they have no right to make their children martyrs.[58] Thus the parents' right to religious practice does not include the right to expose their children to ill health or death,[59] which echoes the eighteenth-century nascent concern for a child that was expressed in the legal restriction that a father could not endanger his child's life or limb.

Rights of the Child in International Thought

With restraints on parental authority and a new philosophical foundation for that parental authority, societies began to recognize that children deserved to be treated humanely. Internationally, the first document to mention children's rights was the Declaration of the Rights of the Child, commonly known as the Declaration of Geneva, adopted by the League of

---

Puerto Rico, authorize the court to order medical treatment for the child when the child's condition warrants intervention, and five states require mandated reporters to report instances when a child is not receiving medical care so that an investigation can be made. Child Welfare Information Gateway, *Definitions of Child Abuse and Neglect: Summary of State Laws* (2009), pp. 5-6, available online at http://www.childwelfare.gov/systemwide/laws_policies/statutes/defineall.pdf.

56. Colo. Rev. Stat. § 19-3-103 (1) (2005).

57. See, e.g., Walker v. Superior Court, 763 P.2d 852 (Cal. 1988) (affirming the criminal conviction of a mother who treated a child's illness with prayer rather than medical care where the child died of acute purulent meningitis after a seventeen-day battle); Hermanson v. State, 604 So.2d 775 (Fla. 1992) (vacating guilty verdict and sentence for child abuse resulting in third-degree murder for failing to provide daughter with conventional medical treatment, which resulted in her death from juvenile diabetes; the court reasoned that the confusion in the statutes regarding religious exemption to medical care violated the parents' due process rights).

58. *Prince*, 321 U.S. at 170 (1944).

59. *Prince*, 321 U.S. at 166-67 (1944).

Nations in 1924.[60] "Rights" included in this document are: (1) "The child must be given the means needed for its normal development"; (2) children should be fed, sheltered, helped, and reclaimed if errant; (3) "the child must be first to receive relief in times of distress"; (4) the child must be protected from exploitation and afforded opportunity to earn a livelihood; and (5) the child should be taught to serve others. League members were encouraged to apply the Declaration's five principles as guiding points in their decisions.[61] The Declaration lacks legal force even though the Declaration's title is "*Rights* of the Child" (emphasis added), and even though the document declares that "mankind owes to the child the best that it has to give" and in support lists five "rights." This foundational piece for children's rights does not mention "love" or "best interests of the child," but it did formalize ideals that children deserve protection, opportunities, and necessities. Although love and best interests were not part of this Declaration, the listed rights point in that direction. Indeed, the five rights are in every child's best interests. Even the concept of love arguably could be included in the first right as part of "the means needed for its normal development."

The idea of children's rights was greatly developed and debated during the drafting of the Convention on the Rights of the Child (CRC), which will be discussed below, along with the 1959 United Nations Declaration of the Rights of the Child, which influenced the language of the CRC. But prior to evaluating these two international documents, we will first delve into the historical development of the best-interests-of-the-child standard, which appears in the 1959 Declaration and is used extensively throughout the CRC. The 1924 Declaration of Geneva acted as one of the foundation stones, along with developing national laws, in the development of the best-interests-of-the-child standard nationally and then internationally.

Historical Development of the Best-Interests Standard: An Anglo-American Innovation

The best-interests-of-the-child doctrine originated as a principle of Anglo-American family law that is applied by state courts and quasi-judicial tribu-

60. The Declaration was drafted by Eglantyne Jebb and promulgated by Save the Children International Union.

61. Nigel Cantwell, "The Origins, Development and Significance of the United Nations Conventions in the Rights of the Child," in Henry J. Steiner and Philip Alston, *International Human Rights in Context: Law, Politics, Morals,* 2nd ed. (New York: Oxford University Press, 2000), p. 512.

nals in proceedings concerning matrimony, adoption, fostering, and the guardianship of minors — issues of child custody.[62] Emotive factors, such as love and affection, were integral considerations in judicial decisions during the historical development of the best-interests standard.

Parens Patriae

The best-interests doctrine evolved over several centuries in English courts. The first step toward the creation of the best-interests-of-the-child principle was the unwritten doctrine in English courts called *parens patriae,* which refers to the public policy power of the state to usurp the rights of natural parents or legal guardians and act as the state parent of any child in need of protection.[63] The King's Bench and later the chancellors applied this doctrine to children throughout the seventeenth and eighteenth centuries. It is this principle that enables governments to limit parental authority and mandate compulsory education, vaccinations, and restrictions in child labor laws.[64] It is also through *parens patriae* that most jurisdictions make the best interests of the child the first and sometimes single most important concern of the courts in deciding the outcome of disputes involving children.

Pre–Tender-Years and Best-Interests Doctrines

During the formative years of the best-interests doctrine, which includes the tender-years doctrine, leading legal scholars on both sides of the Atlantic drew attention to the intersection of the law with parental love and affection. Because of the presumption of underlying parental love, parents were deemed likely to maintain and protect their children and seek their chil-

62. Claire Breen, *The Standard of the Best Interests of the Child: A Western Tradition in International and Comparative Law* (The Hague: Martinus Nijhoff, 2002), p. 16. French scholars also point to laws that developed the concept of best interests of the child. See Jacqueline Rubellin-Devichi, "The Best Interests Principle in French Law and Practice," in *The Best Interests of the Child: Reconciling Culture and Human Rights,* ed. Philip Alston (Oxford: Oxford University Press, 1994), p. 260. As the concept of best interests evolved, the best interests of childhood or children collectively developed, which was perceived to thus serve the general interests of society. The focus slowly changed to the individual child in the nineteenth century.

63. Lynn D. Wardle and Laurence C. Nolan, *Fundamental Principles of Family Law,* 2nd ed. (Buffalo, NY: William S. Hein, 2006), pp. 863-64.

64. *Prince,* 321 U.S. at 166.

dren's interests even without being legally compelled to do so.[65] These comments on parental love and affection by Blackstone and Kent, cited previously, provide a backdrop for the legal and social atmosphere in which the best-interests and tender-years doctrines developed.

Although financial concerns were the principal reason for interfering with fathers' rights,[66] by the end of the eighteenth century, "judges spent less time trying to justify their power to interfere and more time analyzing the healthiness of the childrearing environment and the culpability of the father in not providing adequate support, abusing his children, or precipitating the mother's separation."[67] The judges' inquiry into the home and potential financial opportunities for the children amounted to a skeletal best-interests standard directed toward the welfare of the child. But the following century witnessed a backward slide in children's rights and in the development of the best-interests standard as courts stated that fathers (not mothers) knew what was in the best interests of the child. This belief became so entrenched during the nineteenth century that, as late as 1883, a chancery court stated the well-established rule that "[i]t is not the benefit to the infant as conceived by the court, but it must be the benefit to the infant having regard to the natural law which points out that the father knows far better as a rule what is good for his children than a Court of Justice can."[68]

During the nineteenth century, English courts (King's Bench and Chancery) reverted more to the common law rule that fathers presumptively had a right to the custody of their children, which they could forfeit by endangering the life or limb of the child, as seen in the *De Manneville* case[69] from the first years of the nineteenth century. In 1804, Mrs. De Manneville petitioned the King's Bench and Chancery for custody of her infant child, who literally was snatched from her while breastfeeding by her estranged husband.[70] Perhaps basing her arguments on the previous century's developing welfare interests of the child, Mrs. De Manneville argued that the welfare of an infant of tender years, who was still of nursing age, necessitated custody with the mother. This

65. See Blackstone and Kent, note 29 above and accompanying text.

66. See *Blisset's Case,* 98 Eng. Rep. 899 (K.B. 1774) (granting custody to the mother and her parents based on the father's lack of financial stability); Creuze v. Hunter, 30 Eng. Rep. 113 (Ch. 1790) (denying custody of a child to a father who was in financial distress).

67. Wright, "Crisis of Child Custody," p. 186.

68. In re Agar-Ellis, 24 Ch.D. 317, 337-38 (1883) (summarizing In re Fynn, 2 DeG. & Sm. 457 [1848] and In re Curtis, 28 L.J. [n.s.] Ch. 458 [1859]).

69. R v. De Manneville, 5 East 221, 102 Eng. Rep. 1054 (K.B. 1804); De Manneville v. De Manneville, 32 Eng. Rep. 762, 1804 WL 1025 (Ch. 1804).

70. R v. De Manneville, 5 East 221, 102 Eng. Rep. at 1054.

early attempt to combine a child's welfare interests with the argument that young children particularly needed maternal care was not immediately accepted by the courts. Instead, the court declined to rule on the merits of which parent deserved custody or where the child would be better cared for and ruled that under the principles of couverture, the wife could not bring suit against her husband because she was not legally separated from him, and therefore they were one legal entity.[71] Although the court did not adopt Mrs. De Manneville's nascent best-interest and tender-years arguments, the court did concede that it had the power to terminate the father's custody rights and grant custody to the mother if the father's harmful actions required it, but the court did not specify what misdeeds would warrant judicial interference.[72] Nonetheless, the fact that the court theoretically agreed that the mother could be granted custody over the father opened the door to additional judicial discussion on custody, maternal care for children of tender years, and the welfare interests or best interests of the child.[73]

The *De Manneville* case demonstrates the prevailing legal issue at the very time that change was about to give way — as of that point children had no legal standing themselves and they remained chattel of their father. Because children were the property of their father, if a marriage were to dissolve, the father was automatically awarded legal and physical custody of the children. Such was the 1831 case of *Ex parte M'Clellan,*[74] in which the court declared the father had the right to decide the school for his children over his wife's preference for a different school and over the health interests of the child. The King's Bench refused to concern itself with the welfare of the child, who was in ill health, who had two siblings who had already died while attending the same school, and despite the fact that the school mistress handed the child in question to the mother because she believed the mother would be better able to provide the care and affection the sick child required.

Tender-Years Doctrine

In response to the common law that typically ignored the welfare interests and emotional attachments of children, women began campaigning in the

71. De Manneville v. De Manneville, 32 Eng. Rep. at 764.

72. R v. De Manneville, 5 East at 222, 102 Eng. Rep. at 1055.

73. For a discussion of the *De Manneville* case and its implications on family law in England, see Wright, "Crisis of Child Custody."

74. 33 Eng. Rep. 45 (1831).

early nineteenth century to reform custody laws. One of the most vocal supporters of custody law reform was an English socialite named Caroline Norton, who had lost custody of her children to her husband. Most reformers, like Mrs. Norton, focused on a mother's love and care as the reason that young children should remain in custody of their mothers. Mrs. Norton wrote that the "daily tenderness, the watchful care, the thousand offices of love, which infancy requires, cannot be supplied by *any* father, however vigilant or affectionate. . . . And it is in this very point that Nature speaks for the *mother.* It pronounces the protection of the father insufficient, . . . it pronounces the estrangement from the mother *dangerous and unnatural,* and such as must be immediately supplied by female guidance of some sort or other."[75]

As a result of this campaign and mounting public support, the English Parliament enacted the Custody of Infants Act of 1839, which gave some discretion to the judge in a child custody case and established a presumption of maternal custody for children under the age of seven years, thus establishing by statute the tender-years doctrine. This tender-years doctrine was eventually adopted by some British colonies. In 1873, the English Parliament extended the presumption of maternal custody until a child reached sixteen years of age. But courts made exceptions in cases in which the father established that the mother had committed adultery.

In the United States, a quarter of a century before the Custody of Infants Act, a Massachusetts state court opined that children of "tender age" would be best cared for by the mother.[76] This opinion illustrates that the premise of the tender-years doctrine was the consideration of what was best for the young child, not the needs or desires of either parent. This statement was unexpected, since the children of "tender age" in the case were 7- and 10-year-old girls. But more surprising was that the court concluded the best interest of the daughters was to stay with the mother, who had been found guilty of adultery, and the father had been granted a divorce on that basis.[77] Despite

75. Wright, "Crisis of Child Custody," p. 216, quoting Caroline Norton, *Observations on the Natural Claim of a Mother to the Custody of her Young Children as Affected by the Common Law Right of the Father* (1837), p. 52.

76. Commonwealth v. Addicks, 5 Binn. 520 (Pa. 1813).

77. Three years later, the father was awarded custody when the girls were 10 and 13 years of age. The reasoning of the court was that the two daughters were by then in less need of maternal nurturing, and, as two potential wives, the daughters should not be reared by an adulterous mother. See Michael Grossberg, *Governing the Hearth: Law and the Family in Nineteenth-Century America* (Chapel Hill: University of North Carolina Press, 1985).

finding no fault with the father and seriously disapproving of the mother's conduct, the court declared its obligation was to the welfare of the children. "It is to *them,* that our anxiety is principally directed."[78] This outcome was quite different from what would have been possible in English courts that had carved out an adultery exception in the tender-years doctrine.

Just two years later, the New York Supreme Court based its decision primarily on financial considerations when refusing a father's request for the return of his young daughter from his father-in-law.[79] The allegations laid at the father's feet were that he could not pay his debts and lived in his mother's house, which necessitated his wife to return to her father's house.[80] In contrast, the court noted that the maternal grandfather was affluent, "abundantly able to educate and maintain his granddaughter," and that this granddaughter would likely inherit substantially from the maternal grandparents upon their death, as her mother was then deceased.[81] Although much of the discussion focused on financial ability, the court was sensitive to the attachments the young girl must have formed in her grandparents' house and her complete lack of attachment to her biological father. The girl had been born in her grandfather's house and raised there since infancy. The court concluded that it was not "bound to deliver the child over to her father," despite the father's reliance on the English *De Manneville* case.[82]

A few decades later, but still five years before the English Custody of Infants Act, the tender-years doctrine evolved to the point where the court in *Commonwealth v. Briggs* considered the interests of the child vitally important, but the court's actions stymied its discretionary power to interfere with a father's natural right to custody.[83] The court stated, "[i]n the case of a child of tender years [the child in this case was 3 or 4 years old], the good of the child is to be regarded as the predominant consideration."[84] The language is important, though void of force in this case; the court did not consider the child when deciding the writ of habeas corpus to return this child to the father. Rather, it focused on the fact that the wife was living separately from her husband, without a divorce.[85] The court stated that in order

78. *Addicks,* 5 Binn. at 521.
79. *In re Waldron,* 13 Johns. 418 (N.Y. 1816).
80. *In re Waldron,* 13 Johns. 419 (N.Y. 1816).
81. *In re Waldron,* 13 Johns. 419 (N.Y. 1816).
82. *In re Waldron,* 13 Johns. 420 (N.Y. 1816).
83. 33 Mass. 203 (1834).
84. 33 Mass. 205 (1834).
85. 33 Mass. 204-05 (1834).

for it to interfere with a father's natural right of custody, the father would have to be a "vagabond and apparently wholly unable to provide for the safety and wants of the child."[86] The court's order that the child be returned to the father was based on the wife's unauthorized separation from her husband, not the child's welfare. "The unauthorized separation of the wife from her husband without any apparent justifiable cause, is a strong reason why the child should not be restored to her."[87] But, again, this case is important not only because the court stated that the welfare of the child is of "predominant consideration," but also because the court stated its power to grant custody to the mother in limited circumstances despite the father's natural right of custody.

Despite this case's limiting effect, the tender-years doctrine continued to develop strength and predominance in nineteenth-century American courts. A Maine state court, in *State vs. Smith,* articulated the strong preference of a mother to care for a daughter.[88] The husband and wife had previously entered into a contract that granted Mrs. Smith custody of the children and property to support them if her husband made her unhappy and unable to live with him. Although the court ignored the marital contract, it did grant the mother custody of the three children, Emeline, 10, and Solomon and Aaron, 4. The reason for granting custody to the mother was that "the eldest of these children is a daughter, requiring peculiarly the superintendence of a mother."[89] The judge opined that either parent could adequately care for the 4-year-old boys, but "parental feelings of the mother toward her children are naturally as strong, and generally stronger than those of the father."[90] The statement is given as fact with no evidentiary support. This is one of the earliest cases in which the judge seemed to inquire into the children's preferences for custody, as the opinion notes that the children wanted to stay with their mother.

These American cases from the early nineteenth century demonstrate "[t]he father's traditional common law claim to the custody of his legitimate child was being replaced by a vague but definite test for parenthood."[91] That test

86. 33 Mass. 205 (1834).

87. 33 Mass. 205 (1834).

88. 6 Me. 462 (1830).

89. 6 Me. 468 (1830).

90. 6 Me. 468-69 (1830).

91. Jamil S. Zainaldin, "The Emergence of a Modern American Family Law: Child Custody, Adoption, and the Courts, 1796-1851," *Northwestern University Law Review* 73 (1979): 1055.

included the age of the children, the sex of the parent (because mothers were considered inherently better nurturers for the young), and financial resources, but these components were not well defined or clearly weighted when applied.

In the United States, the tender-years doctrine flourished well into the twentieth century and incorporated love in addition to care. A New York court declared, "The child at tender age is entitled to have such care, love, and discipline as only a good and devoted mother can usually give."[92] And the Wisconsin Supreme Court opined, "[N]othing can be an adequate substitute for mother love — for that constant ministration required during the period of nurture that only a mother can give because in her alone is duty swallowed up in desire; in her alone is service expressed in terms of love."[93] Ultimately, this focus on a mother's love in the tender-years doctrine became a foundational aspect of the love and affection component later found during the development of the best-interests doctrine. Indeed, the two — love and best interests — coincided harmoniously during the development of the best-interests doctrine.

Best-Interests Doctrine

The Guardianship of Infants Act of 1886 put England squarely on the road to the best-interests-of-the-child standard. The Act abolished the absolute and virtually exclusive right of the father to the guardianship of his legitimate children by the introduction of the principles of the welfare of the child and the equal right between parents to child custody. This Act paved the way for the best-interests standard, as it was the first law to require the consideration of the child's welfare when deciding custody cases.

At about the same time, the best-interests-of-the-child standard was being solidified in American law.[94] The Kansas state court opinion *Chapsky v.*

92. Ullman v. Ullman, 135 N.Y.S. 1080, 1083 (New York App. Div. 1912).

93. Jenkins v. Jenkins, 181 N.W. 826, 827 (Wis. 1921).

94. While case law was incorporating the best-interests language in its decisions, state statutes were also incorporating this legal doctrine in family law. The Revised Codes of the Territory of Dakota referred, as early as 1877, to the "best interests of the child" as the first of three factors a court was to consider when determining the custody award of a minor or in appointing a guardian. Jane Ellis, "The Best Interests of the Child," in *Children's Rights in America: U.N. Convention on the Rights of the Child Compared with the United States Law*, ed. Cynthia Price Cohen and Howard A. Davidson (Washington, DC: American Bar Association Center for Children in the Law and Defense for Children International, 1990), p. 4.

Wood[95] is the American case most commonly cited for introducing the notion of the best-interests-of-the-child doctrine. In *Chapsky*, the court declared that when deciding the custody of a child, "the paramount consideration is, what will promote the welfare of the child?"[96] The court recognized that although the father is "prima facie entitled to the custody of his minor child," that custody would "depend mainly upon the question whether such custody will promote the welfare and interest of such child."[97] But what is frequently overlooked in this landmark case is the court's emphasis on love and affection when determining custody and the best interests of the child. Even before the best interest of the child is discussed, one of the two reasons the court states for the basis of a father's prima facie custody right is the "law of nature" that the love and affection a father possesses for his children derives from providing for a helpless child, and this love and affection "is stronger and more potent than any which springs from any other human relation."[98] However, the court recognized that love from other individuals, biological or not, could develop into this same love. This is an important recognition since this custody dispute was between the biological father and the maternal aunt who had been acting as foster mother to the child since its birth.

The court stressed several times that the child had received and would continue to receive from the foster mother/aunt "all that a mother's love and care can give."[99] This maternal love, the court stressed, was stronger than the potential affection that could be developed by the members of the father's family because such love is a byproduct of either mothering a child or caring for the child since infancy. The court concluded that the father's family would be unable to develop the type of love the foster mother (maternal aunt) had developed during the five and a half years since the child's birth. Thus, custody must be given to the foster family that had showered the girl with love and affection, under which the child would fully "ripen and develop."[100] Love was not the only factor. The court also considered the potential wealth from the father's family, educational opportunities, health, social position, and moral training. The father's family was financially more afflu-

95. 26 Kan. 650 (1881) (litigating a custody dispute between a foster mother who had cared for the girl from infancy for five and a half years and a father).

96. 26 Kan. 654 (1881).

97. 26 Kan. 652-53 (1881).

98. 26 Kan. 652 (1881).

99. 26 Kan. 657 (1881).

100. 26 Kan. 656-57 (1881).

ent than the foster family. Yet the "controlling consideration" in determining the best interests of the child was the love showered on the child, which the judges said would control a decision if one of their own children were in the same circumstances, notwithstanding the financial advantages of the opposing family.[101] The court clearly considered parental love and affection an important consideration, perhaps even the "controlling consideration," when determining the best interests of a child in a custody dispute.[102]

Nearly two hundred years later, U.S. courts continue to cite this case for the best-interests standard. "Without question, the paramount concern of courts in child custody proceedings is the welfare of the child. Beginning with the early cases written by Mr. Justice Brewer [including] . . . *Chapsky v. Wood* . . . this court has consistently adhered to the rule that when a controversy arises as to the custody of a minor child, the primary question to be determined by the court is what is for the best interest of the child."[103] And a child's best interests continue to include the love and affection of parents. The Wisconsin Supreme Court noted that "[m]inor children are entitled to the love and companionship of both parents in so far as this is possible and consistent with their welfare."[104]

Perhaps because the best-interests doctrine considers parental love, U.S. law recognizes a presumption that parents act in the best interests of their children. Justice Benjamin N. Cardozo explains that when a chancellor (or judge) acts as *parens patriae* "to do what is best for the interest of the child . . . [h]e is to put himself in the position of a 'wise, affectionate and careful parent.'"[105] Cardozo's comments illustrate the legal presumption that "a wise, affectionate and careful parent" decides or acts in the best interests of the child. Likewise, the U.S. Supreme Court interprets Blackstone and Kent's recognition of parental affection toward children as the cornerstone for the presumption that parents will act in the best interests of their children. "The law's concept of the family rests on a presumption that parents possess what a child lacks in maturity, experience, and capacity for judgment required for making life's difficult decisions. More important, historically it has recognized that natural bonds of affection lead parents to act in the best interests of their children."[106] A later U.S. Supreme Court case recognized this pre-

101. 26 Kan. 657-58 (1881).
102. 26 Kan. 657 (1881).
103. Perrenoud v. Perrenoud, 480 P.2d 749, 762 (Kan. 1971).
104. Patrick v. Patrick, 117 N.W.2d 256, 259 (Wis. 1962).
105. Finlay v. Finlay, 240 N.Y. 429, 433 (N.Y. 1925) (internal citation omitted).
106. Parham v. J.R., 442 U.S. 584, 602 (1979) (internal citations omitted).

sumption while slightly restricting the breadth of it. "[T]here is a presumption that *fit* parents act in the best interests of their children."[107] Fit is interpreted as "adequately cares for" the children,[108] and seems similar to Justice Cardozo's "wise, affectionate and careful parent."

Additionally, some courts and statutes follow a presumption that parental custody will be in the best interests of the child. "Studies indicate that the best interests of the child are usually served by keeping the child in the home with his or her parents. Virtually all experts, from many different professional disciplines, agree that children need and benefit from continuous, stable home environments. . . . Even where the parent-child relationship is 'marginal,' it is usually in the best interests of the child to remain at home and still benefit from a family environment."[109] It appears that these two presumptions — that parents act in the best interests of their children and that parental custody is in the best interests of their children — are founded on nineteenth-century comments on natural affection by Blackstone and Kent.

Following in the footsteps of Blackstone and Kent's natural affection ideology, and perhaps in the *Chapsky* court's primary consideration of love, many state statutes list several factors for judges to consider in determining a child's best interests, including the parents' ability to demonstrate love and affection to the child and the child's emotional ties of love to each party involved.[110] Some courts have specifically mentioned love in conjunction with a child's best interests. However, love is not the controlling consideration nor does it trump other best-interest factors. Many judges have stated in custody disputes and in parental termination cases that the love the parents have for their children is obvious and sincere, but it is not in the best interest of the children to stay with them for various reasons, including, *inter alia,* addiction to drugs and alcohol, returning to a partner that abuses the mother and/or children, lack of ability to control anger, and inability to provide a home of safety and security.

In one such case, the trial court stated that the grandfather, the legal guardian of his two grandchildren, loved his grandchildren very much, but his guardianship of them was severed when he could no longer care for and

107. Troxel v. Granville, 530 U.S. 57, 68 (2000) (emphasis added).

108. Troxel v. Granville, 530 U.S. 68 (2000).

109. In re Juvenile Appeal, 455 A.2d 1313, 1318-19 (Conn. 1983) (internal quotations and citations omitted).

110. Louisiana, Maine, Ohio, Tennessee, Arkansas, Michigan, and Minnesota are among the many states that list love as a factor to consider in the best-interests standard.

protect them following his wife's death, his heart surgery, and the death of his daughter who had come to help care for him and the children.[111] In another case, a state appeals court judge relied, in part, on the love the mother had for her children in preserving her position as joint-custodial parent.[112] In another, the court refused to terminate a mother's parental rights and grant a petition for adoption of the children without first considering the children's feelings. "It is not enough to examine the love and home environment provided by the petitioner/stepparent. The court must also examine the depth of closeness of the child's ties with the non-custodial natural parent, and the effect which the loss of this relationship would have on the child."[113]

In U.S. law, love is very much a part of the consideration of the best interests of the child. This emotional component, which played an important part in the development of the best-interests standard in U.S. jurisprudence, was not transferred to international norms when the best-interests language was first incorporated into the 1959 Declaration of the Rights of the Child. The drafting of this declaration occurred in the years following wars when the United States was perhaps at its peak in international influence and where the drafters personally had witnessed the suffering of children worldwide. It is reasonable to assume that when the standard was written into the 1959 Declaration, the drafters were familiar with the best-interests standard and knew of the love component. But as the concept was integrated into the 1959 Declaration and the Convention on the Rights of the Child, the factors that were historically considered in determining the best interests of the child, including love and affection, were ignored, as demonstrated in the following section.

Influence of Best-Interests Doctrine in International Documents

The 1959 United Nations Declaration of the Rights of the Child[114] contains the first reference to the terms "the best interests of the child" and "love" in an international human rights document. Principle 2 declares, "the best interests of the child shall be the paramount consideration" in the enactment

111. In re Jessica C., 59 Cal. Rptr. 3d 855, 858 (Cal. Ct. App. 2007) (describing the decision of the trial court).

112. Craig v. Craig, 956 So. 2d 819 (La. Ct. App. 2007).

113. In re D.D.D., 961 So. 2d 1216, 1222-23 (La. Ct. App. 2007) (internal citation omitted).

114. Nov. 20, 1959, U.N. res.no. 1386.

of laws to ensure that the child is protected and given opportunities to develop in a healthy manner. Principle 7 applies the best interests of the child as the "guiding principle" to "those responsible for his education and guidance; that responsibility lies in the first place with his parents." Nowhere is the best interests of the child defined, structured, or restricted; nor is the historical development of the concept mentioned.

Principle 6 mentions love, though not as a right, and states, "The child, for the full and harmonious development of his personality, needs love and understanding." It continues, that a child shall grow up "in an atmosphere of affection." The love, understanding, and affection here provided a template for the Convention on the Rights of the Child's treatment of love and affection, but these concepts were not directly tied to the best-interests doctrine. Neither were they connected to a right. Rather, they were associated with an understanding that these elements benefit a child.

Twenty years later, the rights of the child again were given prominence as they were placed on a path that eventually led to the drafting and ratification of the Convention of the Rights of the Child (CRC). During the International Year of the Child, 1979, Poland offered a proposal that the General Assembly write a convention on the rights of the child and put into treaty form (legally binding language) the values contained in the 1959 Declaration. After ten years of drafting and political compromises, the CRC was unanimously adopted by the General Assembly in 1989 and entered into force on September 2, 1990. The CRC does not embody all rights of the child, as the Convention was written with much political compromise, but the minimum rights that governments have committed themselves to guaranteeing to children.[115] Importantly, the CRC is a document written by and for governments, and would, therefore, be an unlikely source for finding a discussion of love and affection.

In the sixth preambular paragraph, the CRC recognizes that "for the full and harmonious development of his or her personality," the child "should grow up in a family environment, in an atmosphere of happiness, love and understanding."[116] There is no legally binding language associated with love, perhaps because it is an emotion impossible of enforcement. It is worth noting that there was no debate during the drafting sessions as recorded in the

115. Cynthia Price Cohen and Howard A. Davidson, eds., *Children's Rights in America: U.N. Convention on the Rights of the Child Compared with United States Law* (American Bar Association, 1990), p. iii.

116. Convention on the Rights of the Child, Nov. 20, 1989, 15 U.N.T.S. 3 (effective Sept. 2, 1990).

Hot topics that were passionately debated existed, but they did not include "best interests of the child" or "love."[121]

The lack of discussion on the meaning of the "best interests of the child" within the CRC could be attributed to a familiarity with the concept as an established decision-making tool regarding children's welfare, or an understanding among the drafters that vagueness was preferred to specificity, which could have stalled the consensus debates.[122] Perhaps states wanted the standard to remain indeterminate in order to allow each state to employ it as would be seen fit within its own cultural meaning.

Whatever the reason, the success and popularity of the CRC have catapulted the best-interests standard to cross-cultural heights. But the CRC is not the only international treaty focused on children's rights, and it is not alone in promulgating the best-interests standard. The CRC is merely the first and the most famous. There are other important international agreements, including regional conventions enforced by regional human rights committees and courts and numerous conventions dealing with the international protection of children drafted by the Hague Conference on Private International Law.[123] These documents generally defer to "the best interests of the child" when establishing a standard for resolving disputes where the legal interests of the child arise, though the norms typically defer to the responsibilities and choices of the child's parents. None of these documents mention love or affection. Likewise, many important international human rights conventions refer to the best interests of the child, but are silent regarding love.[124] Further, states generally have codified the best-interests standard but

121. See generally *Travaux Préparatoires.*

122. Breen, *Western Tradition,* p. 84.

123. The numerous Hague Conventions that deal with the international protection of children can be found on the Hague Conference's website at http://www.hcch.net/index_en.php. These conventions deal specifically with international adoption, abduction of minors, maintenance obligations toward minors, and the protection of children. The conventions date from 2007 back to 1956, some replete with references to the best interests of the child, and others only mentioning the child's interests in the preamble. Generally, more recent conventions use the phrase "best interests of the child" more often than the older conventions.

124. Convention on the Elimination of All Forms of Discrimination Against Women, art. 5(b) & art. 16(1)(d); African Charter on the Rights and Welfare of the Child, 1990, art. 4 (adopted by the Organization of African Unity as a complement to the Convention); Charter of Fundamental Rights of the European Union, Dec. 7, 2000, art. 24; American Convention on Human Rights, Nov. 17, 1969, art. 17(4). Arab Charter on Human Rights, League of Arab States, May 22, 2004, art. 33(3).

have not given legal recognition or protection to a child's right to give and receive love. Even most children's advocates and children's rights NGOs are silent regarding love, but prolific in their opinions and support of the best-interests standard.[125] Love is mostly an ignored concept by national and international law- and policy-makers and children's advocates.

Interests and Love in International Bodies of Law

The concept of love in legal issues involving children is not a useful concept for international lawmaking bodies. Because two of the three lawmaking bodies discussed below are regional courts of human rights, the concept of love seems to be pushed aside by the time the cases arrive at these regional courts, even if it had been an issue in the national courts. Additionally, conversations of parental and filial love in family law cases are better suited for courts of first instance where judges have the greatest interaction with the parties and can see personal interaction between them. International regional appeals courts are far removed from direct interaction with the parties and are therefore not in a position to decide issues of love and affection.

U.N. Committee on the Rights of the Child

The United Nations Committee on the Rights of the Child formally interprets the Convention on the Rights of the Child. The Committee issues comments on state reports, publishes interpretations on various major issues in its General Comments, and provides "Concluding Observations" of periodic sessions. It also publishes decisions, which are called "recommendations." The Committee does not directly discuss love in any of its many publications. It interprets nei-

125. Exceptions to this general statement include, but are not limited to: Janusz Korczak, one of the first children's advocates to declare that children were individuals who had the right to love; Betty Jean Lifton, Appendix: "Janusz Korczak's Declaration of Children's Rights," in *The King of Children: The Life and Death of Janusz Korczak* (New York: St. Martin's Griffin, 1997), pp. 355-56; S. Matthew Liao, "The Right of Children to Be Loved," *Journal of Political Philosophy* 14, no. 4 (2006): 420-40. See also Barbara P. Solheim, "The Possibility of a Duty to Love," *Journal of Social Philosophy* 30, no. 1 (1999): 1-17. Defence for Children International, which acted as secretariat to the Ad Hoc NGO Group on the Drafting of the Convention on the Rights of the Child, lists on its website that "children have the right to love and care" (http://child-abuse.com/childhouse//childrens_rights/dci_home.html).

ther the best interests of the child generally nor whether love is subsumed under best interests specifically. Nonetheless, the concept of love and affection surfaces on rare occasions in state reports and in general discussions.

During the General Discussion on the Rights of Children with Disabilities, a representative from United Nations Children's Fund (UNICEF) initiated a brief discussion on love (quoted in the epigraph at the beginning of this chapter) by stating what everyone should have known but no one had in fact mentioned:

> [A]lthough a pragmatic approach was needed [for] children's problems, an important point was being missed in the general human rights debate: the substantive provisions of the Convention made no reference to the emotion of love. . . . Disabled children needed love more than anything else, yet the Convention dealt only with rights and was addressed to Governments.[126]

A member of the Committee responded by saying that "[l]ove was synonymous with all that was implied by human dignity, a core concept of the Convention. The Convention required Governments to help parents and the general public understand the meaning of that concept."[127] Thus, according to the Committee, love is an integral part of the CRC, even though it is mentioned therein only once and even though state reports and committee publications are nearly void of any specific mention of love and affection. Additionally, according to the Committee response, governments are required by the CRC to educate parents and the public on the importance of love to a child's well-being. Importantly, the Committee did not assert that the government has an obligation to respond to children with love or to draft laws based on love of children. The government's sole obligation regarding love is to educate and encourage parents and the public to act in love toward children.

In another general discussion, the Committee encouraged parental love, or at least parental affection. The Committee stated that parents "are *expected* to provide appropriate direction and guidance to young children in the exercise of their rights, and provide an environment of reliable and affectionate relationships based on respect and understanding."[128] Because the

126. Committee on the Rights of the Child, General Discussion on the Rights of the Children with Disabilities, Oct. 7, 1997, CRC/C/SR.419, at ¶19.

127. CRC/C/SR.419 at ¶27.

128. Committee on the Rights of the Child, General Comment No. 7, Implementing Child Rights in Early Childhood, Sept. 20, 2006, CRC/C/GC/7/Rev.1, §29 (2006) (emphasis added, internal citations omitted). The Committee cited Article 5 of the CRC for authority.

CRC binds states and not individual parents, the Committee is restricted to simply "expecting" parents to love their children. But it did take an additional step toward facilitating love by admonishing states to create laws and policies that would help parents fulfill their obligations to provide affection, understanding, and love.[129]

Although the Committee has never defined love, it has refused to accept corporal punishment as a component of love. The Republic of Korea admitted that some parents engage in corporal punishment but asserted this was done out of love for their children in an effort to inculcate discipline and morality. The Committee asserted that corporal punishment is force, not love, and as such should be prohibited by law.[130]

Love and affection are mentioned by a few states in their reports to the Committee. The Youth's Charter of the Republic of Korea asserts that the nation "must" love its youth.[131] As such, "One of the most important tasks of the Government is to improve and encourage family functioning so that children have enough concern and love from their parents."[132] Trinidad and Tobago revealed their plans to amend their laws regarding custody to include parental love and affection as one of the factors to be considered in determining the best interests of the child.[133] Haiti's Constitution provides that "all children are entitled to love, affection, understanding and moral and material care from their father and mother."[134] Dominican Republic laws state that custody of a child or adolescent is granted to the parent who offers the best conditions for his training, emotional stability, love, and protection.[135] And in Finland, custodial awards are determined in part by where the child will be brought up in a "spirit of understanding, security and love."[136]

129. CRC/C/GC/7/Rev.1 (2006).

130. Committee on the Rights of the Child, Consideration of Reports of States Parties, Initial report of the Democratic People's Republic of Korea, Sept. 16, 1998. CRC/C/SR.459.

131. Committee on the Rights of the Child, Initial reports of States parties due in 1993, Republic of Korea, Nov. 30, 1994, CRC/C/8/Add.21.

132. CRC/C/8/Add.21 (30 November 1994), ¶77.

133. Committee on the Rights of the Child, Initial reports of States parties due in 1994, Trinidad and Tobago, June 17, 1996, CRC/C/11/Add.10.

134. Committee on the Rights of the Child, Initial reports of States Parties due in 1997, Haiti, June 21, 2002, CRC/C/51/Add.7, §57. No legislation has yet been adopted to implement this provision because of the lack of a parliament.

135. Committee on the Rights of the Child, Initial reports of States parties due in 1993, Dominican Republic, Aug. 26, 1999, CRC/C/8/Add.40, §60.

136. Committee on the Rights of the Child, Initial reports of States parties due in 1993, Finland, Jan. 31, 1995, CRC/C/8/Add.22, §131.

The Committee generally does not comment on each of these very brief references to love included by states in their reporting obligations under the CRC. Silence, however, in these cases, demonstrates that the Committee agreed with the inclusion of love in the reports as part of the best-interests principle. Although the Committee does not instruct states that are silent regarding love to report on laws and policies affecting parental love and affection, it has accepted the concept when brought up by states and has defended the CRC as embodying the concept of love within the larger concept of human dignity. Arguably, this creates a small niche for love in the CRC generally and as a component of the best interests of the child specifically.

European Court of Human Rights

The European Convention on Human Rights[137] established the European Court of Human Rights, which allows individuals to bring charges against a state to remedy violations of their rights under the Convention. The Convention does not provide for the rights of the child, and therefore has no mention of the best interests of the child or a child's need or right to love and affection.[138] Despite the lack of best interests and love or affection in the Convention, the European Court of Human Rights does encounter these issues with some frequency, specifically in cases alleging violations of article 8, the right to respect for family life. Most of these cases involve issues of child custody and access to children (visitation rights), and whether the state laws embodying these issues and their application violate the Convention's protection of family life. In determining these issues, the best-interests standard is almost always discussed because it is part of the state law applied to the initial conflict. The cases that mention love or affection generally do not engage in discussion of the issue, but only mention the lower court's finding that a parent did love the child or did seek access to the child based on sincere love for the child. But the fact that there are cases in the European Court of Human Rights that do mention love and affection in the family law context lends credibility to an assertion that love is an important component of promoting children's best interests.

137. Convention for the Protection of Human Rights and Fundamental Freedoms, Nov. 4, 1950, 213 U.N.T.S. 221 (commonly known as the European Convention on Human Rights).

138. The closest the Convention comes to including the best-interests standard is in Article 5 of Protocol No. 7, which provides for equality between spouses but limits their privacy in marriage and with their children, by state intervention in the *interests* of the children.

In one case against Germany, the ECHR reiterated the state court's finding that the father commenced his suit for access to his baby child because of his genuine bonds and true love for her.[139] Likewise, a dissenting judge based his opinion that Germany had violated the applicant's right to respect for family life, in part, on the applicant's love for his daughter.[140] In another case of access or visitation, the Court reiterated the German court's observation that the mother "educated and looked after her daughter in an atmosphere of love and understanding and took an intense interest in ensuring her well-being."[141] The issues of love and attachment are valid considerations under German law because the German Civil Code provides that in determining the best interests of the child, especially in child custody and access, emotional ties between the child and parents and siblings should be considered.[142]

In another case, the Greek courts initially granted the mother access to her daughter, in part, because of the mother's love for her.[143] In two separate judgments, the Greek courts recognized that the mother cared for the daughter and "undoubtedly love[d]" her prior to the divorce while living with the daughter, and that she still loved the daughter.[144] In a case of termination of parental rights by Germany, the European Court found a violation of article 8 and noted that the German courts would not hear the applicants' witnesses testify that they educated their children in an atmosphere of love and understanding.[145] In a somewhat similar case of removal of children from parental custody, dissenting judges criticized Swedish social welfare authorities for their failure to take into account the love the parents had for their children.[146]

Although the European Court of Human Rights does not engage in weighing love or gauging affection, it does ratify the inclusion of love and affection in these family law (personal law) matters where the best interests of the child are determined by mentioning when love and/or affection were discussed in the national courts and permitting those domestic court findings on love to stand.

139. Sahin v. Germany, no. 30943/96, ECHR (2003).

140. Sahin v. Germany, no. 30943/96, ECHR (partially dissenting opinion of Judge Rozakis).

141. Hoppe v. Germany, no. 28422/95, ECHR (2002).

142. BGB (German Civil Code) §§1671, 1685.

143. Kosmopoulou v. Greece, no. 60457/00, ECHR, ¶¶16-19 (2004).

144. Kosmopoulou v. Greece, no. 60457/00, ECHR, ¶¶16-19 (2004).

145. Haase v. Germany, no. 11057/02, ECHR, ¶19 (2004).

146. Olsson v. Sweden, no. 13441/87, ECHR (1992) (partly dissenting opinion of Judge Pettiti).

Inter-American Court of Human Rights

The Inter-American Court was established in 1979, for the purpose of enforcing and interpreting the provisions of the American Convention on Human Rights. Its two main functions are to interpret the Convention and to rule on specific cases of human rights violations. Article 17(4) of the Convention states that in case of dissolution of marriage, decisions regarding the child will be made solely in the child's best interests.

The Court incorporates the best-interests language in its decisions involving children, not just within a family setting, but also when state laws and policies affect children, as in the treatment of children in juvenile detention facilities.[147] The Court has not published decisions related to custody or visitation rights, where the concepts of love and affection are typically seen in the ECHR cases. As such, no decisions mention love as a component or even a consideration of the best-interests principle or of the actual decision.

Because the Inter-American Court has not decided a custody case, it is impossible to know whether it would consider love and affection as one of the factors in determining the best interests of the child. Certainly it would have to if the national law that was applied had such a component, as in the United States.

African Court on Human and Peoples' Rights

The African Court on Human and Peoples' Rights first convened in 2006.[148] It is a regional court that rules on African Union states' compliance with the African (Banjul) Charter on Human and Peoples' Rights. The Banjul Charter does not provide for children's rights specifically, nor does it contain best-interests language. This young court has only had the time to publish one decision, which did not deal with the best-interests doctrine, and it is

147. Juvenile Reeducation Institute v. Paraguay, no. 112, series C, IACHR (2004). The Spanish translation of the case name is *Instituto de Reeducación del Menor v. Paraguay.*

148. The members of the African Union voted in 2004 to consolidate the African Court on Human and Peoples' Rights with the African Court of Justice. It is unclear when and if this new court will convene since the treaty creating the African Court of Justice does not have the requisite number of ratifications for it to enter into force. The African Court on Human and Peoples' Rights has spent its first years drafting rules of procedure. For an update on this situation, visit http://www.africancourtcoalition.org.

not clear whether any future decisions will deal with family law and therefore best interests of the child and love and affection.

However, the African Charter on the Rights and Welfare of the Child does make provisions for children's rights.[149] Specifically, article 4 of the Charter states, "[I]n all actions concerning the child undertaken by any person or authority the best interests of the child shall be the primary consideration." The Charter was adopted by the Organisation of African Unity in 1990, and its advisory body, the Committee of Experts on the Rights and Welfare of the Child, was established in 2001. The Committee is charged with the responsibility of commenting on state reports and interpreting the Charter. None of the Committee's publications to date have dealt with family law, and specifically child custody and visitation, where discussions of love and affection are most likely to appear.

As has been shown, the emotions of love and affection are occasionally intertwined with the best interests of the child in international law, but most international bodies either ignore or quickly brush aside the emotive concepts, in part because love and affection issues are weeded out during the lengthy appeals process and because international tribunals and advisory bodies are too far removed from the parties. Additionally, these international tribunals and commissions do not concern themselves with parental love because their organizing instruments do not instruct them to do so.

Criticism of Best Interests of the Child

Despite its almost universal acceptance and usage in national laws and international instruments, the best-interests-of-the-child standard has received increasing criticism.[150] Some scholars, child advocates, and others search for

149. OAU Doc. CAB/LEG/24.9/49, July 11, 1990 (entered into force Nov. 29, 1999).

150. For criticism and solutions, see Stephen Parker, "The Best Interests of the Child — Principles and Problems," in Alston, ed., *The Best Interests of the Child,* pp. 26-41 (discussing the best-interests standard indeterminacy and how to reduce that indeterminacy); Breen, *Western Tradition.* Various jurisdictions have discussed and/or adopted joint custody presumptions, joint-parenting presumptions, or legislation mandating parenting plans. These presumptions and legislation are presumed to be in the best interests of the child and are enforced, unless harm to the child can be demonstrated. Canada, Australia, and several U.S. states are among those jurisdictions that considered or adopted such legislation. See Helen Rhoades and Susan B. Boyd, "Reforming Custody Laws: A Comparative Study," *International Journal of Law, Policy & the Family* 18 (2004): 119-46; Thomas J. Walsh, "In the Interest of a Child: A Compara-

ways to improve and modify the standard.[151] As Venezuela indicated during the drafting of the CRC, "the best interests of the child" is a phrase of "subjectivity."[152] It has been criticized as "a convenient cloak for bias, paternalism and capricious decision-making."[153] Because the best-interests standard was not defined or controlled at the international level with a list of factors, its application is indeterminate; anything can be said to be in the best interest of the child.

At the domestic level, the best-interests standard has been applied in an arbitrary and inconsistent manner. It has allowed national religious courts to adopt the language but continue applying religious law in the same manner as it has been applied for centuries.[154] It has allowed countries steeped in harmful tradition to modernize the language of their laws without modifying the meaning of the laws. At the international level, there are important differences in the social and cultural understanding of what is in the best interests of the child. Additionally, some policymakers, lawmakers, and scholars debate whether the best interests of the child are present interests, future interests, or a balance of the two.[155] As a result, the indeterminacy of

---

tive Look at the Treatment of Children Under Wisconsin and Minnesota Custody Statutes," *Marquette Law Review* 85 (2002): 929-74; Fla. Stat. § 61.13(2)(c)(2) (2004).

151. For modifications of the best-interests standard, see Marygold S. Melli, "The American Law Institute Principles of Family Dissolution, the Approximation Rule and Shared-parenting," *Northern Illinois University Law Review* 25 (2005): 347-62 (discussing the American Legal Institute's Proposal of replacing the best-interests standard in custody disputes where parents cannot agree to a parenting plan with the approximation rule, which establishes shared custody of children based on an approximate proportion of time each parent spent with the children prior to divorce proceedings). For discussion on the heightened harm standard being applied to children when grandparents or stepparents petition for visitation, see Margaret M. Mahoney, "Stepparents as Third Parties in Relation to Their Stepchildren," *Family Law Quarterly* 40 (2006): 81-108; Lauren F. Cowan, "There's No Place Like Home: Why the Harm Standard in Grandparent Visitation Disputes Is in the Child's Best Interests," *Fordham Law Review* 75 (2007): 3137-86.

152. *Travaux Préparatoires,* p. 137.

153. Parker, "Principles and Problems," p. 26.

154. Moussa Abou Ramadan, "The Transition from Tradition to Reform: The Shari'a Appeals Court Rulings on Child Custody (1992-2001)," *Fordham International Law Journal* 26 (2003): 595-655.

155. For two examples of present versus future interests of the child, consider female genital mutilation and forced feeding of young girls, in Alexia Lewnes, ed., "Changing a Harmful Social Convention: Female Genital Mutilation/Cutting," *Innocenti Digest* 12 (2005): 15-18; Pascale Harter, "Mauritanians Question the 'Fat' Look," *Crossing Continents,* BBC Radio 4, April 26, 2007, http://www.news.bbc.co.uk/2/hi/programmes/crossing_continents/6591835.stm.

the best-interests standard can be used to legitimize practices that are regarded by other societies as abusive, repressive, and all-around harmful to children.[156]

Apologists of the indeterminacy of the best-interests standard argue the standard lacks definition and guidelines because each child is different, each situation is different, each society is different, and so the standard to apply to so many changing variables needs to change also. The fluidity of the best-interests standard can be used in one society to recognize and take into account differences of peoples from other cultures living in that society.

France was one of the first countries to ratify the CRC. Its leading legal scholar of personal law, Jean Carbonnier, mocked the "magical notion" of the best-interests standard and cautioned against possible negative consequences of making the best-interests standard the highest principle in the children's rights deck of cards:

> Although "the interest of the child" might seem to convey a particular thought, it really is a meaningless ("magical") notion. Though it may be "the law," the issue that really is at issue is "abuse." Ultimately, the "interest of the child" will end up rendering superfluous all of the institutions of family law. There is nothing more fleeting, or more likely to lead to arbitrary judicial decisions.[157]

Such criticisms illustrate the weaknesses of the best-interests standard, but it nevertheless remains the governing standard for children and is the only viable standard at the international level. A simple way to improve the standard would be to secure it to a nonexhaustive list of factors to be considered by lawmakers when making decisions. One of these factors should be love and affection. It should also be found to be incongruous with specific harmful practices.

156. For cultural relativism problems in best interests of the child, consider "Genital Impairment of the Girl-Child: Female Genital Mutilation within the Framework of the Best Interests of the Western Child," in Breen, *Western Tradition*; Alston, ed., *The Best Interests of the Child.*

157. Rubellin-Devichi, *French Law and Practice,* p. 259 (quoting Jean Carbonnier's commentary on a decision rendered by the Paris Court of Appeal, Apr. 10, 1959: "L'intérêt de l'enfant, c'est la notion magique. Elle a beau être dans la loi, ce qui n'y est pas, c'est l'abus qu'on en fait aujourd'hui. A la limite, elle finirait par rendre superflues toutes les institutions de droit familial. Pourtant, rien de plus fuyant, de plus propre à favoriser l'arbitraire judiciaire").

Conclusion

The law intersects with children in several areas, but love applies with the greatest force only in the family law area. The best-interests standard developed from the Roman and English laws' notion that fathers possess total control over their children, to restricting parental authority, to concluding ultimately that children are possessors of rights whose best interests must be considered in the decision-making process. A review of cases and statutes illustrates that love was an important factor in the development of the best-interests standard. It remains a factor in the United States, where a significant portion of its development occurred. It also appears to be a factor in many other national laws, as evidenced by the cases cited from the European Court of Human Rights.

Love needs to be recognized in legal decisions regarding children in family law disputes to enable children to develop fully. But a standard based on love, such as best love of the child, is a legal impossibility. Rather, it would be better to tether the best-interests standard to a nonexhaustive list of factors to be considered by the lawmaker. And love (both a child's receipt of love and offering of love) must be a primary factor to be considered. This way, emotive love is weighed, but so are the important physical manifestations of a healthy parental love, such as basic care, protection, safe shelter, provision of necessities, and guidance. By including love as one factor, children, parents, and society at large could benefit.

CHAPTER 12

Can Law Shape the Development of Unconditional Love in Children?

MARGARET F. BRINIG AND STEVEN L. NOCK

Introduction: What Should Be "Maximized" in Families?

At first glance, deciding what values society should seek to maximize in families sounds like a silly question. Once we think about it, though, our disciplinary focus takes over our impulse as parents. As parents, we are apt to answer the question of what we want for our children by saying we want them to be happy.[1] Some parents will say they want their children to develop their

1. Happiness is not necessarily tied to wealth, as an interuniversity World Values Survey reported in 2003. Michael Bond, "The Pursuit of Happiness," *New Scientist* (UK) Oct. 4, 2003 (based on the sixty-five-nation World Values Survey 1999-2000, and reflecting attitudes since 1945). In this study, the happiest people lived in Nigeria, Mexico, Venezuela, El Salvador, and Puerto Rico, while the least happy resided in Russia, Armenia, and Romania. Jonathan Power, in "What Makes the Nigerians the Happiest of All People?" *Arab News* (Jan. 3, 2003), writes that it is because "we all have a great religious faith" and "We Nigerians look after each other. If I know you and you are hungry or ill I will try and help." Psychologists report that happiness is based on autonomy, competence, relatedness, and self-esteem. K. K. M. Sheldon, "What Is Satisfying about Satisfying Events? Testing 10 Candidate Psychological Needs," *Journal of Personality and Social Psychology* 80, no. 2 (2001): 325.

Professor Nock died on January 20, 2008, after this paper was essentially written. Professors Brinig and Nock acknowledge the support of both their institutions, the research assistance from the Foundation for Unlimited Love, and the very helpful assistance with the PSID from Greg Duncan of the Institute for Policy Research, Northwestern University. Law student Francis Budde has added his considerable research strengths to this project.

talents fully, or to have the advantages they never had, or at least not to make the same big mistakes.[2]

Once academics are asked the same question, they give different answers. Nobel Laureate Gary Becker writes that families seek to maximize utility, which he says is related to the production of "commodities" that cannot be purchased in the marketplace but are produced as well as consumed by households using things that are purchased, time, and environmental inputs: "children, prestige and esteem, health, altruism, envy and pleasure."[3] In other work he writes about the tradeoffs between the quantity and quality of children.[4]

In an important book, law professor Milton Regan argued that families were the best sites for the production of intimacy. Quoting various researchers,[5] he notes that the primary function of family is "caring, nurturing, and loving," and he prescribes a return to the legal concept of status to promote the intimacy people seek as an antidote to the alienation of the postmodern world.

Following Regan's train away from contract, Brinig argued in *From Contract to Covenant: Beyond the Law and Economics of the Family*[6] that successful families are characterized by three things: their relative permanence, their promotion of unconditional love, and the support and recognition given to them (because of these traits) of God and community. These, she writes, are the characteristics of covenant.

This project builds on the earlier work by showing empirically why unconditional love might be the critical value for society to maximize, as well as how it relates to the other covenant traits. Ultimately, we will argue for laws that support permanence and recognition of status rather than the *de facto* family because these promote "best love" in children. Although the exact prescriptions may vary with cultural groups, the ability to love others well and to give selflessly does not recognize cultural, socioeconomic, or physical boundaries.

2. J. R. Morse, *Love and Economics: Why the Laissez-Faire Family Doesn't Work* (New York: Spence Publishing, 2001).

3. Gary S. Becker, *A Treatise on the Family,* 2nd ed. (Cambridge, MA: Harvard University Press, 1991), pp. 23-24.

4. G. S. Becker and N. Tomes, "Child Endowments and the Quantity and Quality of Children," *Journal of Political Economy* 84, no. 4 (1976): S143-S162.

5. Mellman and Lazarus, Inc., *Mass Mutual American Family Values Study* 14 (Washington, DC, 1989).

6. M. F. Brinig, *From Contract to Covenant: Beyond the Law and Economics of the Family* (Cambridge, MA: Harvard University Press, 2000).

We hypothesize that children are not born loving unconditionally, but that this ability is learned over time, primarily through experiencing other models of love: their parents' love for each other, their parents' love for them, and God's love for people. We support our claims with a variety of empirical strategies: experimental, survey, diagnostic tests, and real-life behavior. We then conclude with some suggestions for future research as well as some legal strategies for promoting the permanence and formal recognition of families.

What We Mean by the "Best Love of the Child"

Psychologists are apt to call this project the creation of the child's prosocial[7] or altruistic behavior. Sociologists focus on altruistic volunteering or donating time or money to others and term its opposite exchange-based behavior.[8] Economists will call it altruistic, with its opposite tit-for-tat exchange.[9] They might even define children who "best love" as possessing interdependent utility functions with others:[10] they are made happier when someone else is happier.

Our plan is to examine what we call the creation of the ability to give unconditional love[11] (perhaps in tune with the theologians' definition of "best love," or *agape*[12]) and to discuss how laws might make it easier for children to

7. This is the term given in Nancy Eisenberg's *The Caring Child* (Cambridge, MA: Harvard University Press, 1992).

8. G. L. Hansen, "Moral Reasoning and the Marital Exchange Relationship," *Journal of Social Psychology* 131 (1991): 71-81. M. F. Brinig and S. L. Nock, "How Much Does Legal Status Matter? Adoptions by Kin Caregivers," *Family Law Quarterly* 36, no. 3 (2002): 449-74; John Wilson, "Volunteering," *Annual Review of Sociology* 26 (2000): 215-40.

9. For an engaging set of essays on altruism, see Jane Mansbridge, ed., *Beyond Self-Interest* (Chicago: University of Chicago Press, 1990). Tit-for-tat is discussed in Anatol Rapoport, *Fights, Games and Debates* (Ann Arbor: University of Michigan Press, 1960), and Robert Axelrod, *The Evolution of Cooperation* (New York: Basic Books, 1984).

10. Gary S. Becker, "Altruism in the Family and Selfishness in the Market Place," *Economica* 48, no. 189 (1981): 1-15. Some years ago, Brinig attended a talk given by Gillian Hadfield at the University of Toronto, at which she explained her frustration with a male economist trying to discuss family relationships in terms of symbolic representations of interdependent utility functions. The idea was something like $U_A=f(c_A + U_B(Hw_A - c_A))$!

11. In the parent-child context, see Brinig and Nock, "How Much Does Legal Status Matter? Adoptions by Kin Caregivers."

12. The reference is to C. S. Lewis's *Four Loves* (1960). A biblical reference is 1 Corinthians 13. The relationship between the loves is also explored in *Deus Caritas Est,* the encyclical of Benedict XVI (2006), especially par. 34.

acquire this most important capability. Given our past work, it is perhaps not surprising that we see this as requiring permanence in the relationship.[13] We hypothesize that children acquire this tendency (or longing, as Aristotle and Jennifer Roback-Morse[14] would term it) as they see it around them (though in a less superficial way than the Troggs' song "Love Is All Around").[15]

The most likely three relationships from which children can draw models of unconditional love are God's love for each of us, their parents' love for them, and their parents' love for each other.

This idea that we learn values through observation of others comes initially from learning theory.[16] For example, children pick up behavioral cues from their parents, particularly in ambiguous situations. The moral viewpoint learned primarily from parents will guide their learning throughout life.[17] They may also learn about intangible things, such as science concepts and about God.[18]

God's love is of course the model for all human unconditional love.[19] We might see parents' response to it in the frequency of their church attendance or how important they say religion is in their lives.[20] The ability of law (at

13. See the Introduction to M. F. Brinig, *From Contract to Covenant: Beyond the Law and Economics of the Family* (Cambridge, MA: Harvard University Press, 2000); and M. F. Brinig and S. L. Nock, "Covenant and Contract," *Regent University Law Review* 12, no. 1 (2000): 9-26.

14. See Jennifer Roback Morse, "Marriage, the Family and the State," in *Economics of Family Law,* ed. Margaret Brinig (Cheltenham, UK: Elgar, 2007).

15. Or even the slightly more nuanced understanding of love in *Love, Actually* (2003).

16. See, e.g., B. Rogoff, *Apprenticeship in Thinking: Cognitive Development in Social Context* (New York: Oxford University Press, 1990); T. A. Walden and T. A. Ogan, "The Development of Social Referencing," *Child Development* 59 (1988): 1230-40.

17. D. Narvaez and D. Lapsley, "The Psychological Foundations of Everyday Morality and Moral Expertise," in *Character Psychology and Character Education,* ed. D. Lapsley and C. Power (Notre Dame: University of Notre Dame Press, 2005), pp. 140-65; G. Kochanska, D. R. Forman, N. Aksan, and S. B. Dunbar, "Pathways to Conscience: Early Mother-Child Mutually Responsive Orientation and Children's Moral Emotion, Conduct, and Cognition," *Journal of Child Psychology and Psychiatry* 46 (2005): 19-34.

18. P. L. Harris and M. A. Koenig, "Trust in Testimony: How Children Learn about Science and Religion," *Child Development* 77, no. 3 (2006).

19. See *Deus Caritas Est.* One biblical source is 1 John 4:9-10. For those who do not believe, at least support (as opposed to modeling) can come from any mediating institution that helps generate what sociologists refer to as human capital. See, e.g., James S. Coleman, "Social Capital in the Creation of Human Capital," *American Journal of Sociology* 94 (1988, Supplement: Organizations and Institutions: Sociological and Economic Approaches to the Analysis of Social Structure): S95-S120. I thank Jeremy Gunn for his suggestion.

20. Sociological work on religion indicates that it is not denomination that is important, but religiosity. See, e.g., V. R. A. Call and T. B. Heaton, "Religious Influence on Marital Stability,"

least in the United States) to influence belief and the exercise of it is undoubtedly a delicate constitutional question.[21] The law can certainly continue to refrain from discriminating against religion and to allow such benefits as charitable tax deductions for religious contributions[22] and tax exemptions for religious properties.[23] Tuition vouchers are a help, too.[24] But the controversy in Massachusetts surrounding Catholic Charities' adoption policies (closing rather than consenting to place adopted children with homosexuals)[25] shows how politically and legally fragile this balance has become.

The parents' love for each other also can serve as a model for children. Other research,[26] including our own,[27] shows that unconditional love is most likely to flourish in marriage as opposed to cohabitation. Marriage is thus a powerful signal that the parents love each other.[28] It is associated with greater parental warmth as well.[29] It is also most evident in what Judith

---

Journal for the Scientific Study of Religion 36, no. 3 (1997): 382-92. Of course, as Jeremy Gunn helpfully suggested, the nonreligious (with an equal preference for no religion) can be happily married as well. The outside support needed to strengthen the marriage and promote trust probably stems from some other mediating institution, such as a charitable or social group. This is discussed in Coleman, "Social Capital," and Francis Fukuyama, *The Great Disruption* (New York: Simon & Schuster, 1999). Brinig discusses these topics at length in *Supporting the Covenant: Family and Community* (under review, but manuscript available from the author).

21. The First Amendment prohibits Congress from establishing religion. See, e.g., *Everson vs. Board of Education,* 330 U.S. 1, 15 (1947).

22. IRC §190 allows for deductions from taxable income for contributions to charitable corporations.

23. IRC §501(c)(3) allows these organizations to be tax exempt so long as they refrain from political lobbying activities and do not undertake profit-making ventures. For a discussion of this doctrine, see E. G. Stone, "Adhering to the Old Line: Uncovering the History and Political Function of the Unrelated Business Income Tax," *Emory Law Journal* 54, no. 4 (2005): 1478-1556.

24. These were upheld in *Zelman vs. Simmons-Harris,* 536 U.S. 639 (2002).

25. See Patricia Wen, "Catholic Charities Stuns State; Ends Adoption," *The Boston Globe,* March 11, 2006.

26. See, e.g., S. L. Nock, "A Comparison of Marriages and Cohabiting Relationships," *Journal of Family Issues* 16, no. 1 (1995): 53-77.

27. M. F. Brinig and S. L. Nock, "Marry Me Bill: Should Cohabitation Be the (Legal) Default Option?" *Louisiana Law Review* 64, no. 3 (2004): 403-42.

28. See, e.g., Robert Rowthorn, "Marriage as a Signal," in *The Law and Economics of Marriage and Divorce,* ed. Antony W. Dnes and Robert Rowthorn (Cambridge: Cambridge University Press, 2000), pp. 132-56. I thank Don Browning for making this suggestion.

29. In a very simple regression model, whether or not the mother ever married was associated significantly ($p = .02$) with parental warmth, while the family income from the preceding year adjusted for size of family and geographic region was associated significantly ($p = .001$). Although we will show that, in some sense, warmth conquers all, since marriage is associ-

Wallerstein calls "The Good Marriage,"[30] whose opposite is the "Separate Spheres" (or marriage reduced to its lowest common denominator) discussed by Lundberg and Pollak[31] or the "exchange relationship" detailed in Gary Hanson's "Marital Exchange Relationship" piece in the *Journal of Social Psychology*.[32] This love is threatened by any attempt to legally equate marriage and cohabitation (as with current Canadian law[33] and the American Law Institute's Domestic Partnership proposals[34]). It is strengthened by legal efforts to make marriages stronger, whether these are through requirements for premarital counseling[35] or through tax and other subsidies based upon marital status (listed in, for example, the Vermont same-sex marriage case of *Baker vs. State*[36]) and perhaps by laws that force couples to carefully think through the decision to divorce.[37] From a nonlegal perspective, marriage is strengthened by increased support from extended family and the community, secular and religious.[38]

---

ated with greater warmth as well as a tendency to marry and remain married when the child reaches adulthood, we concentrated on it here. I thank Annette Mahoney for this suggestion.

30. J. Wallerstein and S. Blakeslee, *The Good Marriage* (Boston: Houghton Mifflin, 1995).

31. S. Lundberg and R. A. Pollak, "Separate Spheres Bargaining and the Marriage Market," *Journal of Political Economy* 101 (1993): 988-1010.

32. G. L. Hanson, "Moral Reasoning and the Marital Exchange Relationship," *Journal of Social Psychology* 13, no. 1 (1990): 71-81.

33. Canadian C-23, the Modernization of benefits and obligations act (2000), RSC 4 (2d Supp.), SC 2000, c 12. For a still more drastic proposal, see *Beyond Conjugality: Recognizing and Supporting Close Personal Adult Relationships*, published in 2001 by the Law Commission of Canada.

34. These appear in the American Law Institute's *Principles of Family Dissolution* (2002), ch. 6. See Margaret F. Brinig, "Domestic Partnerships and Default Rules," in *Reconceiving the Family: Critique on the American Law Institute's Principles of the Law of Family Dissolution*, ed. Robin Wilson (Cambridge: Cambridge University Press, 2006), p. 269.

35. See, e.g., Ok. Code §43-5.1 (2005).

36. 744 A.2d 864 (Vt. 1999).

37. This would include the three "covenant marriage" regimes. Covenant marriage is authorized in Arizona, Arkansas, and Louisiana. Ariz. Rev. Stat. §§25-901 to 25-906 (West 2000); Covenant Marriage Act of 2001, Ark. Code Ann. §9-11-801 to 9-11-811 (Michie 2002); Covenant Marriage Act, La. Rev. Stat. Ann. §§9:272-9:284 (West 2000).

A *Washington Post* article suggests that a foundation will lobby for mutual-consent divorce laws in Virginia this term. Tim Craig, "Foundation Wants Stricter Rules for Splits," *Washington Post*, January 5, 2007, at B03. According to the news article, the same group successfully pushed through the state's constitutional amendment banning same-sex marriage.

38. Margaret F. Brinig, "Community Involvement and Its Limits in Marriage and Families," in *Revitalizing the Institution of Marriage for the Twenty-First Century*, ed. A. J. Hawkins, L. Wardle, and D. O. Coolidge (Westport, CT: Greenwood Press 2002), p. 15. See

The parents' love for him or her is perhaps the first unconditional love noticed by a child.[39] Outsiders can see it in what the parent says about the child, what kinds of activities he or she does with the child, how close the child feels to the parent, and perhaps by whether the child feels the parent stands up for him or her or acts as an advocate.[40] From an absent parent, we can still get some glimpse of this love through continued contact, attendance at the child's activities, and even faithful payment of child support. From a negative perspective, we see the absence of unconditional love in parents who say they are disappointed with their child, who neglect their child (when they have the means of support), perhaps when they engage in custody battles,[41] and certainly when they abuse the child. Law can strengthen parental relationships with children. On the extreme, children in foster care are unlikely to

---

also Steven L. Nock et al., "Intimate Equity: The Early Years of Standard and Covenant Marriages," Working Paper 03-04, Department of Sociology, Bowling Green State University.

39. See http://parenthood.library.wisc.edu/Berkowitz/Berkowitz.html. See also John Bowlby, *Attachment and Loss,* vol. 1 (New York: Basic Books, 1969); Mary D. S. Ainsworth et al., "Object Relations, Dependency, and Attachment: A Theoretical Review of the Infant-Mother Relationship," *Child Development* 40 (1968): 969-1025. Indeed, it has been argued that the attachment relationship is the template for most later relationships (Samuel Oliver and Pearl Oliver, *The Altruistic Personality: Rescuers of Jews in Nazi Europe* [New York: Free Press, 1988]; L. Allen Sroufe and June A. Fleeson, "Attachment and the Construction of Relationships," in *Relationships and Development,* ed. W. W. Hartup and Z. Rubin [Hillsdale, NJ: Erlbaun, 1986], pp. 51-71. This takes place over time. Grazyna Kochanska et al. ("Pathways to Conscience: Early Mother-child Mutually Responsive Orientation and Children's Moral Emotion, Conduct, and Cognition," *Journal of Child Psychology and Psychology* 46, no. 1 [2005]: 19-34) reported that mutual positive affectivity between mother and child and maternal avoidance of power assertion are related to the internalization of standards in preschool children. In a different report ("Multiple Pathways to Conscience for Children with Different Temperaments: From Toddlerhood to Age Five," *Developmental Psychology* 33 [1997]: 228-40) extended the notion of mutuality of affect to encompass a broader reciprocity between mother and child, and reported that conscience development is related to a sustained pattern of mother-child reciprocity including mutual affectivity, low power assertion, and maternal empathy. N. Eisenberg and P. H. Mussen (*The Roots of Prosocial Behavior in Children* [New York: Cambridge University Press, 1989]) conclude that parents of altruistic children are nurturant and supportive, model altruism, highlight the effects of actions on others, use induction, establish clear expectations for mature behavior, and create opportunities for their children to manifest responsibility for others.

40. For a study reflecting on the internal working model of relationships formed from parent-child interactions during childhood, see W. Furman, V. A. Simon, L. Shaffer, and H. A. Bouchey, "Adolescents' Working Models and Styles for Relationships with Parents, Friends, and Romantic Partners," *Child Development* 73 (2002): 241-55.

41. See, e.g., Margaret F. Brinig, "Does Parental Autonomy Require Equal Custody at Divorce?" *Louisiana Law Review* 65 (2005): 1345.

see this love,[42] and efforts should be made to either strengthen the family of origin or place the child in a permanent adoptive or kin-care[43] situation.[44] Child abuse is criminal and serious, and should be taken seriously by the law and prevented where possible (including abuse by non-parent adults living in the home).[45] For another example (of many), custody laws can be carefully drafted to minimize incentives for vindictive behavior and to promote relationships with non-custodial parents.[46] We can continue to promote family autonomy so that parents in less-stressed families can effectively allow their children to flourish.[47]

What we would like to do is to test these ideas to the extent we can. We already have data on altruism as it relates to age, gender, and marital status (including some original experimental research),[48] on which we will report here.

We can also get at least some rough measures of religiosity of parents, their own parents' marital status and closeness to them, how they contribute (in terms of time and money) to various kinds of charitable organizations and to their aging parents, how they interact with and feel about their children, and how the children are turning out — all through the PSID (the Panel Study of Income Dynamics from the University of Michigan) and its recent addition, the Child Development Supplement (now in its second round). The major contribution of this paper will be a presentation of the results we can obtain from the PSID and the suggestions for law and policy we can make from them.

42. Although some foster parents ultimately adopt the children in their care, at least until the goal for the child becomes permanent placement away from the birth parents foster parents are bound by contract with the agency to return the child for reunification or for placement elsewhere. Much research suggests that the combination of the circumstances that placed the children outside the home in the first place and the conditional nature of foster care itself creates poor outcomes for children. For one popular rendition, see R. Roche, M. August, et al., "The Crisis of Foster Care," *Time* 156 (2000): 74-82.

43. Brinig and Nock, "How Much Does Legal Status Matter? Adoptions by Kin Caregivers."

44. This is the goal of the Adoption and Safe Families Act of 1997, 42 U.S.C. §671(1)(15).

45. R. F. Wilson, "Fractured Families, Fragile Children — The Sexual Vulnerability of Girls in the Aftermath of Divorce," *Child and Family Law Quarterly* 14, no. 1 (2002): 1-23.

46. Margaret F. Brinig, "Feminism and Child Custody Under Chapter Two of the American Law Institute's Principles of the Law of Family Dissolution," *Duke Journal of Gender Law & Policy* 8 (2001): 301.

47. See M. Brinig, "Troxel and the Limits of Community," *Rutgers Law Journal* 38 (2002): 733-81.

48. Margaret F. Brinig, "Does Mediation Disadvantage Women?" *William and Mary Journal of Women and the Law* 2, no. 1 (1995).

Altruism (or Unconditional Love) Develops over Time: A Study by Brinig

Altruism in its simplest form is care for another. The altruist and the other, as defined by the economist, have interdependent utility functions, as economists Becker[49] and Posner[50] have noted, so that the altruist is willing to reduce his or her own consumption to increase the consumption of others.[51] The altruist takes the other's utility or happiness into account, so that the other's utility is an extension of the altruist's own.[52] As Paula England puts it,[53] neoclassical economists assume that A is altruistic toward B when whatever gives B utility contributes to A's utility.

Sometimes this connection provides the altruist with a kind of pleasure; at other times the altruist acts out of a sense of duty. Elster writes: "[H]elping or giving out of love is instrumental behavior, that is, concerned with outcomes. If I help my child, I seek the best means to make that child happy. . . . The concept of duty is more ambiguous: It can be instrumental or squarely noninstrumental."[54] Milton Regan, in one of his books, argues that the altruist perceives the self as part of a common humanity: as a relational self.[55]

Using the experiments of Robyn Dawes and others[56] as a model, Brinig devised a simple test originally to determine whether women are more willing to give than are men. A sample of 255 people ranging in age from 5 to 66 years was divided into groups of five. All members of each group were about the same age, with no member more than two years older or younger than any other in the group. Each participant indicated age, sex, and zip code (used as a proxy for income). The participants were given five Hershey's Kisses® each.

49. Gary Becker, "Altruism, Egoism and Genetic Fitness: Economics and Sociobiology," *Journal of Economic Literature* (1976): 817, 818.

50. Richard Posner, *Sex and Reason* (Cambridge, MA: Harvard University Press, 1992), p. 189.

51. Edward Wilson, *Sociobiology* (Cambridge, MA: Harvard University Press, 1975), p. 117.

52. John J. Seater, "Ricardian Equivalence," *Journal of Economic Literature* 31 (1993): 142, 147.

53. Paula England, "The Separative Self: Androcentric Bias in Neoclassical Assumptions," in *Beyond Economic Man: Feminist Theory and Economics,* ed. Marianne Ferber and Julie Nelson (Chicago: University of Chicago Press, 1993), p. 45.

54. Jon Elster, "Selfishness and Altruism," in Mansbridge, ed., *Beyond Self-Interest,* pp. 44-45.

55. Milton C. Regan Jr., *Family Law and the Pursuit of Intimacy* (New York: New York University Press, 1993), p. 114.

56. Robyn Dawes, Alphons von De Kragt, and John Orbrel, "Not Me or Thee but We: The Importance of Group Identity in Eliciting Cooperation in Dilemma Situations: Experimental Manipulations," *Acta Psychologica* 68 (1988): 83, reprinted in Mansbridge, ed., *Beyond Self-Interest,* pp. 101-3.

They were told that if three people in their group would contribute their five Kisses®, everyone in the group would receive ten more. Thus, if three contributed, they would receive ten Kisses®, and the others would receive fifteen. If less than a majority contributed, those who had contributed would lose their five Kisses while the others in the group would keep their original five. Those choosing to contribute were the altruists, since they could in no event do as well as those who more selfishly kept their own Hershey's Kisses®. However, their contribution increased the probability of a larger reward for the other members of the group. The results showed that age is significantly related to altruism: as the experimental subject's age increased, so did the probability of choosing to contribute to the group. However, gender does not predict altruism in this pure sense (although the results did show that women were slightly more willing to contribute, controlling for age).

Norms, Relationships, and Obligations: The Study of Nock et al.

In their piece "The Distribution of Obligations" (2007), Nock and his coauthors[57] explored the extent to which particular troubles are considered private — personal obligation, a legitimate concern for government, or some mixture of the two. They found that personal obligations appear to be conditioned by what people believe relatives, charities, and the government owe to a needy individual. In their study of 507 broadly representative people in Richmond, Virginia, they sought to establish whether social groups actually differ in how they allocate responsibility in a number of realms (e.g., healthcare and job training). They framed their questions only in terms of obligations that involved financial costs, reasoning that individuals who differ in how many dollars they are willing to give someone in need may be said to differ in their sense of obligation to that person.

The study was designed to assess respondents' allocation of financial responsibility in response to needs indicated in a set of hypothetical circumstances. The researchers asked them to indicate how much they personally would be willing to contribute to solving the problem, as well as the amount they think other relatives, churches and charities, and the government should contribute. The vignettes were randomly altered to reveal the effects of different relationships between the needy person and the respondent and the varying

57. S. L. Nock, P. W. Kingston, et al., "The Distribution of Obligations," in *Caring and Exchange Within and Across Generations,* ed. Alan Booth and Nan Crouter (Washington, DC: The Urban Institute Press, 2007).

culpability of the needy person in creating the problem.[58] The situations reflected various common kinds of need: unemployment with a need for job training, requiring nursing care uncovered by insurance, needing medical care uncompensated by insurance, and being evicted from home and needing somewhere to live. The relationships the authors varied included: Parent, Child, Brother or Sister, Grandparent, Grandchild, Aunt or Uncle, Niece or Nephew, Cousin, Son- or Daughter-in-law, Mother- or Father-in-law, Close Friend, Coworker, Close Neighbor, and A person in Richmond unknown to you.

Before undertaking the survey, a computer-based interview collected information on the respondents. The interview covered many background matters: family of origin, parental traits, recollections of home environment, marital, cohabitation, and fertility history, receipt of public assistance, social and political attitudes, scales of trust and empathy, questions about giving and receiving help, and demographic and household composition.

Basically, the researchers asked two sorts of questions in their survey. First, how do various aspects of the hypothetical situation affect personal obligations (as well as the perceived role of government, relatives, and churches or charities)? This involves, for example, how a person's relationship to the one in need influences the amount he or she feels should be contributed to help solve the problem. The second question is whether the respondents' personal traits, such as age or family background, affect the influence of the first set of results. For example, do older respondents react to culpability differently from younger respondents?

The results for the first question are summarized below:

Culpability. When problems are of the individual's own making, people feel less responsible for helping that other person — but only by a small amount. Even when the problem is completely the fault of the individual, personal obligations are reduced by less than $200 (while the average cost of solving the problems was about $1,500).

Thanks. The consequence of helping was described as possibly including various levels of thanks and praise. But respondents seemed notably unmoved by the prospect of thanks. Even if the norm of reciprocity is commonly invoked and seems to guide much social behavior, respondents profess little concern for thanks. However, they are notably responsive to the possibility of repayment. When that possibility was mentioned, people expressed much greater levels of obligation (generosity) than when it was not.

58. P. H. Rossi and S. L. Nock, *Measuring Social Judgments: The Factorial Survey Approach* (Beverly Hills: Sage Publications, 1982).

Relationship. The largest difference in personal obligations found by the authors is associated with the hypothetical relationship implied in the vignettes. Compared with an unknown stranger, a co-worker evinces only $58 more personal obligation. On the other hand, a child or parent produces vastly greater obligations — $2,536 and $1,778, respectively. For this reason, Nock and his co-authors focus primarily on the role played by relationship distance.

In so doing, they discover six "clusters" or types of individuals for whom personal obligations are ordered. First is a child for whom obligations are distinct and greater than for any other. Then come parents, and then grandchildren. A fourth level includes grandparents, children-in-law, parents-in-law, and siblings. Next are tertiary relations including cousins, aunts and uncles, nieces and nephews, and close friends. Least compelling are unrelated individuals, including an unknown stranger, a co-worker, and a close neighbor.

In other words, norms of personal obligations distinguish sharply among close relations (child, parent, grandchild), but less so as relationship distance increases. Parents-in-law, children-in-law, grandparents, and siblings occupy a similar position in the relationship dimension of personal obligations. All other relatives and close friends also constitute a cluster. Finally, tangential figures in most lives (co-workers, neighbors, and strangers) represent the least compelling object of personal responsibility. Not surprisingly, as personal obligations decline, the help expected from other relatives, churches and charities, as well as the state increases.

The second question focuses on how individual (respondent) traits influence personal obligations. Several patterns appear. First, respondents with higher incomes routinely assumed more personal responsibility for others' needs. That is hardly surprising. What is remarkable is the fact that other social factors are consequential *net* of the ability to absorb the cost of solving a problem, as well as the other variables. Older respondents assumed somewhat more responsibility than did younger respondents for several types of relatives: parents, siblings, grandparents, and in-laws. (Note the consistency with the altruism and age study discussed previously.) Males generally assumed more financial obligation than females for many close and distant relationships. Black respondents assumed more personal responsibility for parents, grandparents, nieces and nephews, cousins, and close friends than did their white counterparts, but also less for parents-in-law. Finally, whether a respondent was a parent or not had very little effect (assuming less responsibility for parents, siblings, and close friends). Personal responsibility, in sum, varies according to basic social addresses (sex, age, income, etc.)

However, personal and demographic factors do not explain (reduce to insignificance) the differences found for relationship categories. The authors' final analysis, therefore, focuses on a range of childhood experiences reported by respondents. Nock and co-authors' initial research plan proposed that obligations would be a result of (among other things) relationships and experiences in childhood. They reasoned that an adult's account of his or her childhood, for example, would help explain how needs were seen. Adults who recall their parents (or primary caretakers) as warm and trusting, for example, would differ from those who had different recollections.

The authors asked adults to report on whether they engaged in a number of prosocial experiences as well as specific circumstances that may affect senses of need. These included, for example, doing volunteer work as a young person, raising money for a cause, or belonging to a youth group. They also inquired about youthful experiences that might be expected to influence norms of obligation, including serious illnesses, poverty, or receiving significant help from someone other than a relative. Family structure at age 12 was also recorded (intact biological household, etc.).

The relationship between the respondent and his or her parents was measured by a scale of parent-child trust (e.g., my mother/father trusted me, I trusted my mother/father) and closeness (very distant to very close).

The regressions from the Nock et al. study immediately reveal some key results. First, for all relationships beyond grandchildren, the intercepts are not statistically significant. They were observed before childhood factors were introduced. This indicates that whatever variation there was in how respondents met the needs of these relations was eliminated by controlling the childhood characteristics. Childhood experiences or memories appear to play a significant role in how people respond to the needs of people who are not close relatives. The pattern of results is rather clear, even if not always statistically significant.

Second, to the extent that childhood experiences matter, they do so selectively. For example, adults who remember that a nonrelative gave them significant help respond more generously to a wide range of others, but are less generous with respect to their own parents.

The "prosocial" experiences the authors included (volunteered, raised money for charity, active in a religious organization) are generally shown to have small or *negative* effects. For example, having belonged to a youth group is associated with greater generosity toward one's child but less toward a parent-in-law. On the other hand, having worked as a volunteer is associated with lower contributions to parents and grandchildren. The authors concluded that their measures of such things are either too imprecise or they have more complex relationships with generosity than Nock et al. could discern with these data.

Those adults who were helped in a significant way as children by nonrelatives are notably distinct in their distribution of obligations. In particular, they respond less to the needs of parents and more to those of children, grandchildren, nieces, and nephews. They are even more responsive to the problems of co-workers. Presumably, the circumstances that led someone outside their family to provide significant help left a mark that makes such individuals particularly sensitive to the problems of children.

Neither having been religiously active as a youth nor living in a nonintact biological home as a child has much measurable consequence once all the other items in these equations are controlled.

Other results from the study refer to memories of intergenerational trust and closeness. All are uniformly positive in their effects, even if weak and inconsistent. Adults who recall their parents as having trusted them respond more generously to the problems of children, siblings, and friends. There is only one significant effect for having trusted parents, more generosity to nieces and nephews. Finally, those who reported their family as having been close assume more personal obligations for parents and grandchildren.

The authors concluded that norms of obligation are more strongly influenced by the relationships involved than by the circumstances of need implied. But there are some important variations in how people respond to the same type of relative. For example, males, African Americans, and higher-income individuals regularly assumed greater responsibility than females, other races, or those with lower incomes. And, as shown, childhood experiences influence personal obligations, as do trusting and warm relationships with parents.

The PSID: Intergenerational Influences on Unconditional Love

The Panel Study of Income Dynamics (PSID) is a nationally representative longitudinal study headquartered in the Institute for Social Research at the University of Michigan.[59] The PSID is based on a representative sample of

59. The Internet "home page" (http://psidonline.isr.umich.edu/) indicates that the PSID is a nationally representative longitudinal study of nearly 8,000 U.S. families. Following the same individuals since 1968, the PSID collects data on economics, health, and social behavior. The CDS focuses on the children and caregivers within PSID families, collecting information on education, health, cognitive and behavioral development, and time use.

American individuals (men, women, and children) and their families. It emphasizes the dynamic aspects of economic and demographic behavior, but its content is broad, including sociological and psychological measures. As a consequence of low attrition rates, the success in following young adults as they form their own families, and recontact efforts (for those declining an interview in prior years), the sample size has grown from 4,800 families in 1968 to more than 7,000 families in 2001. The PSID has collected information about more than 65,000 individuals spanning as much as thirty-six years of their lives. The PSID data from 1969 to 2003 are publicly available on the project's website. Between 1968 and 1997, data on PSID individuals were collected each year. Beginning in 1997, data have been collected every other year.

The Child Development Supplement (CDS) is one research component of the PSID. While the PSID has always collected some information about children, in 1997 the PSID supplemented its main data collection with additional information on 0- to 12-year-old children and their parents. The objective was to provide researchers with a comprehensive, nationally representative, and longitudinal database of children and their families from which to study the dynamic process of early human capital formation. The CDS-I successfully completed interviews with 2,394 families (88%), providing information on 3,563 children. In 2002-2003, the CDS recontacted families in CDS-I who remained active in the PSID panel as of 2001. CDS-II successfully reinterviewed 2,021 families (91%) who provided data on 2,907 children and adolescents aged 5-18 years.

Because the CDS is a supplement to the PSID, the study takes advantage of an extensive amount of family demographic and economic data about the CDS target child's family, providing more extensive family data than any other nationally representative longitudinal survey of children and youth in the U.S. In addition, the PSID-CDS data are "intergenerational" in structure, with information contained in several decades of data about multiple family members. This rich data structure allowed us a unique opportunity to fully link information on children, their parents, their grandparents, and other relatives to take advantage of the rich intergenerational and long-panel dimensions of the data.

Methods and Questions

As should be evident from the preceding paragraphs, the PSID presents a terrific free-of-charge source for intergenerational study. It also presents significant challenges to the researcher, who must learn to connect the files needed (in our case, going from child in the CDS to parent to grandparent over multiple years, with both individual and family files involved, with marriage and charitable histories in separate files). When we had accomplished this task, we formulated questions we thought we might be able to answer from the data. In particular, we were interested in the following questions:

RHS (Independent) Variables	LHS (Dependent) Variables
LOVE OF GOD:	RHS kids' religiosity, volunteer time and money, kids' marital stability (predicted), age at marriage (predicted)
parents' religiosity 119, 129	
CONTROLS (applicable to all equations):	
Family income/needs ratio, urban/rural, race (143), marital status of parents (GPs), age of parents at time of child's birth, education of parents, divorce of parents, legal and biological relationships with parents/caregivers	
LOVE OF PARENTS FOR CHILD:	ability to love own child (closeness) (measure from preceding generation? In PSID or predict), volunteer time and money, money given to parent and time given to parent (from PSID)
Parental attitudes re childrearing	
Closeness to child	
Time spent with child	
Absence of abuse, neglect, and abandonment	
Does parent act as advocate?	
LOVE BETWEEN PARENTS:	
Marital/relationship stability during relevant period	charitable activities and giving, marital stability (predicted) and marital quality in children (predicted or from PSID), love of kids for their own children (predicted)
Feelings of closeness	
Conflict or absence of conflict	
"good marriage" indicia from Nock paper	
Altruism of parents	

Hypotheses

Based upon our prior work, both the two studies reported previously in this paper and others we have done together and separately, we theorize that unconditional love will develop throughout childhood (and thus should be related positively to the child's age).[60] We see unconditional love as coming primarily from the three models to which children are exposed: love of God, love of parents for each other, and love of parents for the child. Again, based upon prior work, we believe that unconditional love is most likely to develop in a relationship that the participants (at least the adult participants) view as permanent and stable and that turns out to be stable.[61] Many studies, both in the United States and Western Europe, have shown that marriage is more stable than cohabitation. Many studies (ours included)[62] have shown that, at least in the National Survey of Families and Households in the early 1990s, parents' or one's own prior divorce predicts instability in one's own marriage. The more permanent the marriage (for example, choosing covenant versus standard marriage in Louisiana), the more the parties change during the first years of marriage to become committed, interdependent spouses.[63] We have also shown previously that adolescent children do better (at least in terms of depression) if their parents are living together and if their mother's last relationship did not end in divorce, and worse, for all groups of children, in foster care than in marriage, adoption, or kinship care. We also hypothesize, though, that the causality runs in both directions — that community recognition, or status, should encourage the kind of trust needed for unconditional love to develop.[64] Thus interracial marriages are less stable than

60. See Nock et al. on norms and age, Brinig on aging and altruism.

61. See especially M. F. Brinig, *From Contract to Covenant: Beyond the Law and Economics of the Family* (Cambridge, MA: Harvard University Press, 2000); Brinig and Nock, "Marry Me Bill: Should Cohabitation Be the (Legal) Default Option?"; Brinig and Nock, "Covenant and Contract"; and Brinig and Nock, "How Much Does Legal Status Matter? Adoptions by Kin Caregivers."

62. M. F. Brinig and S. L. Nock, "'I Only Want Trust': Norms, Trust, and Autonomy," *Journal of Socio-Economics* 32 (2003): 471-87.

63. S. L. Nock, L. Sanchez, et al., "Covenant Marriage Turns Five Years Old," *Michigan Journal of Gender & Law* 10 (2003): 169-88.

64. Nock, "A Comparison of Marriages and Cohabiting Relationships"; M. F. Brinig and S. L. Nock, "How Much Does Legal Status Matter? Adoptions by Kin Caregivers"; Brinig and Nock, "Marry Me Bill: Should Cohabitation Be the (Legal) Default Option?"; and Brinig and Nock, "'I Only Want Trust': Norms, Trust and Autonomy," 471; reprinted in *Family Life and Human Rights*, ed. Peter Lodrup and Eva Modvar (Oslo: Gyldendal 2004), p. 115.

intraracial marriages, perhaps because of lack of support.[65] Again, cohabitation, an informal relationship, provides fewer benefits and is less stable than marriage.[66]

Method

Because we saw that more than 95 percent of the children in the CDS lived mainly with their biological mothers, we excluded most other living arrangements (other than children living with two adoptive parents). First, the sample size in these groups was simply too small to draw valid conclusions. (The largest is for children living with biological fathers, and it is only eighty-three children.) Second, these families were likely to differ on a large number of other dimensions that we could not account for but which involved separation from biological mothers. Children are highly likely to live with their mothers, and if they do not, it is typically because of her death or because of her abuse, neglect, or abandonment of the child, all of which would undoubtedly have major influences on our dependent variables of interest.

What we have done in the case of each dependent variable is to begin with a very simple model in which the only independent (or predictive) variable is wealth (that is, total family wealth divided by the census needs index for that size family). That is, we begin with the older economists' assumption that wealth should be able to purchase the goods needed to meet emotional needs.

The next step is to add in family structure: With whom does the child live, and, for example, does it matter that she lives with her mother alone versus with both biological parents? This set of variables, which obviously interacts with wealth,[67] has certainly been the focus of policy debates for many years, from those of *King vs. Smith*[68] to those surrounding single-parent adoption and custody disputes following divorce.

In the third model, unique to our study, we add in the legal relationships

65. Margaret F. Brinig, book review, "The Child's Best Interests: A Neglected Perspective on Interracial Intimacies," *Harvard Law Review* 117 (2004): 2129.

66. Nock, "A Comparison of Marriages and Cohabiting Relationships"; Brinig and Nock, "Marry Me Bill: Should Cohabitation Be the (Legal) Default Option?"

67. See, for example, S. S. McLanahan and G. D. Sandefur, *Growing Up with a Single Parent: What Hurts, What Helps* (Cambridge, MA: Harvard University Press, 1994).

68. 392 U.S. 309 (1968), holding that the presence of a male cohabitant in the household couldn't keep the mother from receiving public assistance.

between the parties, looking for whether it matters that the mother never married or that a stepfather adopted a child. Again, we hold wealth and family structure constant to see whether it's the *de jure* or *de facto* situation that matters most.[69]

In the fourth model, we add only one, important, variable: parental warmth. Even in the worst of circumstances from a demographic point of view, does the child profit from the mother's demonstrated love? A positive response to this inquiry will show that our findings do not depend upon social class. If parental warmth matters despite a host of other variables, the findings would also be consistent with the great happiness found in relatively impoverished areas of the world.

In the fifth model, we add the mother's race and her age. It may be that some characteristics change when race is taken into account, particularly as "normal" family structure is associated with race.[70] Certainly children born to very young mothers tend not to fare as well as those born to older mothers,[71] in part for wealth, in part for lesser marital stability, and in part for purely biological reasons.

Finally, we look at the effect of the child's religious attendance, as always holding all the prior variables constant.

We do not anticipate that we will predict all, or even a very large part, of the differences in outcomes. Some of these differences are simply genetic and are not captured by wealth or marital status. For example, a disabled or autistic child can be born to any parent in any family structure. We have not yet accounted for the presence of siblings in the household (except in the wealth equation), nor whether these are older or younger. We have not necessarily accounted for domestic violence or substance abuse as long as these have not affected wealth or family structure or maternal warmth. We have not counted the critically important influence of fathers (except as these are captured in living structure). We have not accounted for the child's age, and know, for example, that depression increases as the child becomes older.

69. An early (successful) attempt to look at families' de jure relationships is *Butcher vs. Sup.* Ct., 139 Cal. App. 3d 58 (Cal. Ct. App. 1983), which allowed an unmarried cohabitant to recover from a tortfeasor in wrongful death.

70. Our earlier work (Brinig and Nock, "How Much Does Legal Status Matter?") suggests that outcomes for adolescents may be quite different for cultural groups with stronger traditions of extended families.

71. V. H. Hotz, S. W. McElroy, et al., "The Costs and Consequences of Teenage Childbearing for Mothers," in *Kids Having Kids: The Consequences and Costs of Teenage Childbearing in the United States* (Robin Hood Foundation, 1995).

Findings

Here's what we've found (as a very first cut), and using words instead of regression results. There are five sets of equations, with six models in each. The dependent variables (or effects we are trying to predict) are the Behavior Problems Scale (BPS, measured in 2002) and its separate Internal and External Scales,[72] the Pearlin Self-Efficacy Scale,[73] and the Rosenberg Self-Esteem Scale.[74] We begin with the usual economist's explanation: wealth. After controlling for it and a host of usual suspects (race, age, etc.), we find that any exposure to being married has more favorable outcomes than having a parent who never married, regardless of cohabitation experiences. In short, children pay a price on a very wide range of outcomes for having parents who never marry. It is even better to have divorced parents than never-married parents.

Further, we find that a very simple measure of parental warmth (saying

72. *Behavior Problems Index.* The behavior problem scale (G23, G32) was developed by James Peterson and Nicholas Zill to measure the incidence and severity of child behavior problems in a survey setting. J. L. Peterson and N. Zill, "Marital Disruption, Parent-Child Relationships, and Behavioral Problems in Children," *Journal of Marriage and the Family* 48, no. 2 (1986). Many of the items are from the Achenbach Behavior Problems Checklist. T. Achenbach and C. Edelbrock, "Behavioral Problems and Competencies Reported by Parents of Normal and Disturbed Children Aged Four Through Sixteen," *Monographs of the Society for Research in Child Development* 46, no. 1 (1981). Exactly the same set of items used in the NLSY was used in the PSID Child Development Supplement in order to maximize comparability between the two data sets, though the PSID-CDS asked the questions of children age 3 and older while the NLSY began the questions at age 4. The scale is based on responses by the primary caregiver as to whether a set of thirty problem behaviors is often, sometimes, or never true of the child. Behaviors include having sudden changes in mood or feeling, being fearful or anxious, bullies or is cruel or mean, demands a lot of attention. Behaviors are also divided into two subscales, a measure of externalizing or aggressive behavior and a measure of internalizing, withdrawn, or sad behavior. Scores provided are raw scores on the scales. Items G23aa, bb, cc, and dd were added by NLSY staff to provide additional measurement for the withdrawn-behavior scale. Finally, items G32 and b are part of the Behavior Problems Scale but are only applicable to school-age children. We created one behavior-problems scale by summing the scores on the raw items with direction of scoring reversed, using the thirty items for all children. We also created separate scores for two subscales, internal or withdrawn and external or aggressive. The analyst can either add the two items for school-age children to the thirty-item scale, or, as we did in *Healthy Environments, Healthy Children: Children in Families*, use the two items as a separate scale of school problems.

73. L. I. Pearlin, M. A. Lieberman, E. G. Menaghan, and J. T. Mullan, "The Stress Process," *Journal of Health and Social Behavior* 22 (1981): 337-56.

74. M. Rosenberg, *Conceiving the Self* (New York: Basic Books, 1986).

I love you, hugging the child, praising the child, telling the child nice things about himself or herself, telling others good things about the child) strongly predicts better outcomes on a wide range of child traits . . . even when everything else is controlled.

We find that a child's attendance at religious services is related to his or her lower problems (both depression and delinquency) but lower estimates of self-esteem and self-efficacy. (We may have more to say about Mom's religion, but a measure of strength of religious importance was not significant. We suspect that this is because of a high co-incidence of child attendance and maternal attendance at services. Since child variables are the outcomes, the child's attendance swamps the parent's.)

In every case, family structure matters *in addition* to marriage and/or marital history. So while kids are affected, for example, by having parents who were divorced before forming their current family, those kids are also affected by the arrangements in which they now live. Family structure is more than marital history, and vice-versa, and this holds true regardless of wealth.

Limitations on Use of the PSID for Conclusions about Unconditional Love

We cannot say for certain whether the adolescents included in the CDS will turn out to have greater or lesser capacity for unconditional love because they are simply too young to measure many of the outcomes, such as performance in marriage or parenting. If we rely upon their parents or grandparents, the independent variables are either too distant in time from the dependent variables of interest or simply weren't collected. We therefore have drawn and presented the conclusions we can know about, and our best guesses as to what the adolescent characteristics predict for adult behavior. The PSID and CDS are amazingly rich, broadly representative, and well-thought-out studies, and in ten or fifteen years we will be able to show whether our guesses were right.

What we can say for sure is that certain internal and external traits in adolescents are statistically and actually far more likely to be present under some conditions than others. If the other social scientists are correct, the group with what we think are characteristics of the ability to love unconditionally will do better as spouses, parents, and givers to community than the group without it.

Relationships between Adolescent Characteristics and Unconditional Love in Adults

Much of what we have to say here is not new: the differences are our large, nationally representative sample size and the longitudinal nature of our data, the introduction of religiousness in some of our equations, and the emphasis upon the mediation of legal (and otherwise stable) relationships.

Psychologists have long understood[75] the relationship between children's attachment to their parents and their own ability to form later relationships.[76] A recent study suggests that young adults' retrospective reports of parenting by their mothers and fathers are associated with their current romantic relationship quality.[77] However, most of these studies are small, and they typically do not move from adolescent characteristics to adult outcomes. However, there are a few exceptions, still, with limited samples in particular geographic areas. Some have also looked at the relationships between parents and with siblings in terms of young adults' own romances.[78] In earlier work, the authors found that such behavioral characteristics in parents promoted prosocial behavior and inhibited antisocial behavior in both boys and girls.[79]

75. The original reference is John Bowlby, *Attachment and Loss*, vol. 1 (New York: Basic Books, 1969).

76. See, e.g., M. Main and J. Cassidy, "Categories of Response to Reunion with the Parent at Age 6: Predictable from Infant Attachment Classifications and Stable over a 1-Month Period," *Developmental Psychology* 24 (1988): 415-26; E. Waters, N. S. Weinfeld, and C. E. Hamilton, "The Stability of Attachment Security from Infancy to Adolescence and Early Adulthood: General Discussion," *Child Development* 71 (2000): 703-6.

77. William T. Dalton III, Donna Frick-Horbury, and Katerine M. Kitzmann, "Young Adults' Retrospective Reports of Parenting by Mothers and Fathers: Associations with Current Relationship Quality," *Journal of General Psychology* 133, no. 1 (2006): 5. Sample size of seventy-five through volunteer pool from undergraduate psychology students; sample was 98 percent white, none were married, and all parents were in first marriages. The reported fathers' parenting behavior was most strongly related to the (primarily women's) relationships with romantic partners.

78. R. D. Conger, M. Cui, et al., "Competence in Early Adult Romantic Relationships: A Developmental Perspective on Family Influences," *Journal of Personality and Social Psychology* 79, no. 2 (2000): 224. The authors followed a cohort of 193 young people in rural Iowa from when they were in seventh grade until they were in their early 20s. The authors hypothesized that interactional processes (described as nurturant-involved parenting) in the family of origin would predict interpersonal skills in the romantic relationships of the target children, which in turn would be positively related to the early adult couple's relationship quality.

79. R. R. D. Conger, "Family Economic Stress and Adjustment of Early Adolescent Girls," *Developmental Psychology* 29, no. 2 (1993): 206.

The parents' marriage also has an effect on the child's later transition to parenthood in his or her own marriage.[80] If the couple honestly realized the adjustments their own parents faced in passing through the transition, they did better (meaning they were emotionally more attuned to each other) themselves than those who over-romanticized or understood the difficulties with low insight about them.

A longitudinal survey in New Zealand of 141 children found that even tendencies as young as age 3 (on scales of "undercontrolled, inhibited, or well-adjusted") could predict those in adolescence and even at age 21 when they were young adults. Though the ways in which the original traits manifested changed over time, the common patterns were revealed in a significant number of the subjects.

Similarly, sociologists have noted the relationship between parental divorce (or non-marriage) and various child behavior difficulties. In their pathbreaking book, *A Generation at Risk,*[81] Paul Amato and Alan Booth show the effects of divorce and separation on children's later success as young adults — measuring education, earnings, and relationship stability. Amato and Booth studied children born to married parents over approximately a twelve-year period, measuring variables supplied by parents in the 1980s and children in the 1990s. They found that support from mothers and fathers was positively associated with church involvement, community attachment, and the number of relatives and friends to whom the children feel close (p. 123). In keeping with other work, they noted that relationship quality tends to be transmitted across generations (p. 137), because children who are exposed to poor-quality marriages are deprived of appropriate models of relationship functioning.[82] In addition, marital conflict affects children's social competence because it leads parents to be less affectionate, less responsive, and more punitive toward their children, in turn leaving children feeling emotionally insecure.

What Amato and Booth found (p. 139) was that parents' marital conflict was associated with fewer relatives and with marginally lower religious involvement and community attachment. Parental divorce (p. 144), in con-

80. M. M. Curran, "How Representations of the Parental Marriage Predict Marital Emotional Attunement During the Transition to Parenthood," *Journal of Family Psychology* 20, no. 3 (2006): 477. This was a study of eighty-six couples in the Austin, Texas, area.

81. Paul R. Amato and Alan Booth, *Generation at Risk: Growing Up in an Era of Family Upheaval* (Cambridge, MA: Harvard University Press, 1997).

82. See, e.g., P. T. Davies and E. M. Cummings, "Marital Conflict and Child Adjustment: An Emotional Security Hypothesis," *Psychological Bulletin* 116 (1994): 387-411.

trast, by itself was not associated with children's levels of social integration. It relieves problems from children when it provides relief from high-conflict situations, but is problematic for children when it removes them from the more common and typical low-conflict household that divorces (p. 207). The authors suggest that "family characteristics measured when most children are preadolescents or adolescents have lingering consequences for the quality of offspring's social relationships, including aspects of both structural integration (church involvement and membership in clubs and organizations) and psychological integration (feeling close to others and attachment to one's community). Further, intraparental conflict has long-term negative consequences for children's psychological well-being (p. 204), while a stable, high-quality parental marriage maximizes offspring's mental health.

Amato and DeBoer[83] find that the transmission occurs primarily because the children, particularly of those following a low-conflict divorce, had a comparatively weak commitment to the norm of lifelong marriage. This difference in reaction based upon the context of divorce is also discussed in the literature review by Amato (2000).[84]

In more recent developments, Page and Bretherton reported that when parents of preschoolers divorce, girls and boys differ in their attachment to their non-custodial fathers. Boys who were more attached to their fathers had higher preschool teacher ratings for social behavior, while for girls the opposite was the case. With adolescents, attachment to non-custodial fathers doesn't seem to matter unless their mother remarries (or forms another residential adult relationship). At that point, lack of closeness is associated with psychological distress.[85]

Further, pre-labor market attitudes of high school graduates (admittedly slightly older than our sample children) predict real economic consequences for them later.[86] Glen R. Waddell found that poor attitude and self-

83. P. R. P. Amato and D. D. D. DeBoer, "The Transmission of Marital Instability Across Generations: Relationship Skills or Commitment to Marriage?" *Journal of Marriage and the Family* 63, no. 4 (2001): 1038.

84. P. R. Amato, "The Consequences of Divorce for Adults and Children," *Journal of Marriage and the Family* 62, no. 4 (2000): 1269.

85. C. Falci, "Family Structure, Closeness to Residential and Nonresidential Parents, and Psychological Distress in Early and Middle Adolescence," *Social Quarterly* 47, no. 1 (2006): 123-46.

86. G. R. Waddell, "Labor-Market Consequences of Poor Attitude and Low Self-Esteem in Youth," *Economic Inquiry* 44, no. 1 (2006): 69.

esteem (using the Rosenberg Self-Esteem Scale) corresponded later to fewer years of postsecondary education, less employment fourteen years after high school, and lower earnings. Waddell used the National Longitudinal Survey of Youth, where the respondents rated as very important to their life being successful in work (.850 of those surveyed) and finding the right person to marry and having a happy family life (.832). The third-highest rated was having strong friendships (.815). Friendships were also discussed by Engels, Dekovic, and Meeus,[87] who noted the continuing influence of parenting practices and family structures as well as adolescent social skills on the quality of the older children's peer relationships.

In pathbreaking work in psychology, Vaughn and Block[88] showed that parental agreement about values and in other psychological measures in early childhood was strongly related to their characteristics later. Parental intelligence showed up in harmony and moral development in boys, while ego control later appeared in girls' independence and harmony.

Children do, as we suggested earlier, pick up their models for loving behavior from their parents, according to Morman and Floyd (p. 123).[89] They look to the father for open expressions of love for the mother and wife and for spirituality (p. 118). Adolescents also model volunteer and other activities after their parents (although these work differently in boys and girls).[90] Boys were more likely to feel more connected to their community and more

87. R. C. M. E. Engels, M. Dekovic, et al., "Parenting Practices, Social Skills and Peer Relationships in Adolescence," *Social Behavior & Personality: An International Journal* 30, no. 1 (2002): 3.

88. B. E. Vaughn, J. H. Block, et al., "Parental Agreement on Child Rearing During Early Childhood and the Psychological Characteristics of Adolescents," *Child Development* 59, no. 4 (1998): 1020.

89. M. T. Morman and K. Floyd, "Good Fathering: Father and Son Perceptions of What It Means to Be a Good Father," *Fathering: A Journal of Theory, Research, & Practice about Men as Fathers* 4, no. 2 (2006): 113-36.

The present article details two exploratory studies on the nature of fatherhood and on the behavioral and psychological characteristics that define a good father. In the first study, 374 adult men who were fathers of at least one child responded to an open-ended question regarding the attributes of a good father. Inductive analyses of their responses yielded a twenty-item list of referents. The second study involved ninety-nine pairs of fathers and adolescent or young-adult sons who responded to the same question. Their responses were coded along the same dimensions and were compared within dyads and with the results from the first study. Implications for future study on father-child relationships are discussed.

90. A. C. Fletcher and R. A. Shaw, "Sex Differences in Associations Between Parental Behaviors and Characteristics and Adolescent Social Integration," *Social Development* 9, no. 2 (2000): 133-48.

likely to be involved with their community when their parents had been. For girls with more community-involved parents, the result was more likely to be more involvement in school- and community-based extracurricular activities.

Where families no longer live together, as we suspected, the quality of residential parent-adolescent relationships explained the most variation in adolescent psychological distress. In a study using the NSLY (National Longitudinal Survey of Youth), Christina Falci recently found that the quality of relationships with nonresidential fathers had a significant association with adolescent psychological distress only for adolescents in blended families.[91]

Of course, many of the characteristics of family structure are interrelated in complex ways. For example, both depression and conduct problems (similar to our internal and external BPI) are associated with lack of family cohesion and expressiveness and to a lack of exposure to intellectual and cultural activities or to family activities and recreation.[92] Depression in particular was associated with higher levels of family conflict and low cohesiveness (p. 173) and with family insularity. Conduct problems were uniquely associated with low cohesion, low intellectual/cultural orientation, and high conflict. However, ADHD (inattention and hyperactivity) did not contribute significantly to predictions of family environment characteristics.

As we predict what government ought to do for families, we need to be conscious of differences in race and sex (of the children involved) in our findings.[93]

What Do These Findings Suggest for Law?

We predicted that unconditional love (or at least the characteristics associated with its development in adults) is more likely to flourish in two interrelated conditions. First, it is strongly associated with relationship stability.

91. C. Falci, "Family Structure, Closeness to Residential and Nonresidential Parents, and Psychological Distress in Early and Middle Adolescence," *Sociological Quarterly* 47, no. 1 (2006): 123-46.

92. C. C. George, K. C. K. Herman, et al., "The Family Environment and Developmental Psychopathology: The Unique and Interactive Effects of Depression, Attention, and Conduct Problems," *Child Psychiatry and Human Development* 37, no. 2 (2006): 163.

93. K. J. Zullig, R. F. Valois, et al., "Associations among Family Structure, Demographics, and Adolescent Perceived Life Satisfaction," *Journal of Child & Family Studies* 14, no. 2 (2005): 195-206.

We argue that from an economic perspective people are more likely to trust each other and therefore specifically invest in their relationships when they are not acting in what is called the "last period," when it makes more sense to look out for one's self or at least expect an immediate reciprocal reward. Second, unconditional love ought to be more likely in relationships that are institutions, that is, when they are recognized and supported by society (and in law). In our other work we have called these covenant relationships. Of course, to the extent that law and society support the relationships, they are more likely to succeed, that is, be permanent. Similarly, to the extent that they are permanent, society and law will take the trouble to support them.

This in turn suggests that the capacity for unconditional love should develop more easily in recognized, legal, stable relationships. For the purposes of this study, this means marriage (as opposed to informal cohabitation), childbirth to married as opposed to single parents, and adoption as opposed to foster care or kin care (except in some ethnic subgroups with traditions of large roles played by extended families). Note that this does not mean that single parents can never transmit the ability to love unconditionally to their offspring or that unmarried couples cannot love unconditionally. As is typical with social science studies, we are showing tendencies and associations, "best practices," to use a term from healthcare.

From a public policy perspective, we suggest enacting laws (or keeping them in force) to strengthen marriage and adoption, and to keep these formal legal statuses privileged over less formal relationships. Again, we do not mean to suggest that no care be taken for children born to unmarried parents or for single parents trying to raise children. Both of us believe that keeping children (and their caretakers) from living in poverty is and should remain a vital concern for the community. However, our findings suggest that while unconditional love can be taught and flourish regardless of wealth, the best locus for it is in the formal, legally recognized family. As a first cut, therefore, we strongly oppose attempts to equate marriage with cohabitation. Couples who cohabit and never marry are less likely to be stable and less likely to love each other unconditionally. While this may be relatively unimportant (though breaking up is hard to do) for the adults involved, we show that the conditions of cohabitation hinder (or at least do not promote) the ability of the couples' children to form their own stable, loving relationships either with their adult partners or with their children. What is relatively unimportant for adults thus reaches critical proportions once children are involved.

We therefore support efforts to strengthen marriage. Many of these are already in place, as the list of benefits sought by same-sex couples seeking the rights of married persons attests. Better marriages are the goals of state premarriage education efforts as well as such nongovernment groups as Marriage[94] and Engaged Encounter[95] and the umbrella nonprofit Smart Marriages.[96] At the federal level, President Bush's Healthy Marriage Initiative embraces the goal of promoting and sustaining healthy unions through multiple public and private strategies.[97] More controversial, but seemingly warranted, are such legislative tools as covenant marriage (available in Louisiana, Arizona, and Arkansas).[98] Other two-tiered systems (simply making divorce more difficult without making the premarriage and postmarriage counseling regimes as in covenant marriage) are being considered by states like Virginia.[99] The point is that while couples may prefer for themselves to remain unmarried, a legal preference for marriage is warranted once children enter the picture.

Similarly, we support legally recognized parent-child relationships over less formal ones, however strong these may be. Again, we recognized that these may not always be possible, and that single parents and other informal caretakers may do a fine job in inculcating the ability to love unconditionally. Clearly, almost any option where children are loved is better than leaving children in abusive relationships. Most mothers are legally recognized as their children's parents. We encourage fathers who are not (in other words, fathers who are not the husbands of the children's mothers) or women who are in serious relationships with custodial fathers, to adopt the child (unless there is already a participating legal father or mother) or to marry the child's custodial parent, especially in places where being a stepparent gives significant rights and duties.[100] Our study is consistent with adoption being pre-

94. http://www.wwme.org/.

95. http://www.engagedencounter.org/ (for Catholics).

96. http://www.smartmarriages.com/.

97. http://www.acf.hhs.gov/healthymarriage/.

98. We discuss these at length in Margaret F. Brinig and Steven L. Nock, "What Does Covenant Mean for Relationships?" *Notre Dame Journal of Law, Ethics & Public Policy* 18, no. 1 (2004): 137-88.

99. See footnote 30 above. An organization long supporting mutual consent divorce can be found at http://www.divorcereform.org/nha.html.

100. In some states, a stepparent owes a duty of support to the children living with him or her. See, e.g., *Ruben vs. Ruben,* 123 N.H. 358, 461 A.2d 733 (1983). This duty will under most circumstances not continue if the parties divorce. See, e.g., *Miller vs. Miller,* 97 N.J. 154, 478 A.2d 351, 44 A.L.R.4th 499 (1984), holding that in an action for divorce, a stepfather should be required to pay child support during the divorce litigation where the natural biological mother

ferred over mere stepparenting, particularly when being a stepparent does not make the adult responsible for the child at least during the marriage. Guardianship or formal kinship care should be preferred to informal kinship care (with more financial benefits available even without more state intervention and intrusiveness into parenting), but in most cases (except for groups with significant care done by extended families), adoption will be still better if it is a choice. Again, adoption makes permanent parents; stepparenting or merely assuming care for kin does not. Foster care, by its nature transitory and not "real," is the least good option as a permanent solution.[101] Legal changes consistent with this emphasis are the Adoption and Safe Families Act[102] and related legislation, which privilege the rights of children to safe environments over the rights of biological parents to maintain relationships with them. Similarly, funding that promotes adoption for hard-to-place children (whether in foster care or in kinship care situations) should be continued and increased, if possible.[103]

Finally, we add our voices to those who have argued against any assumption that single parenting is as good as having two parents. Not only will children of single parents, largely mothers, be poorer and less successful educationally than children of married couples, but our results show that their very ability to form successful relationships themselves may be threatened.

Although laws that promote good parenting sound like a good idea, as opposed to the less direct status-promoting laws we suggest here, they would run afoul of the doctrine of parental autonomy that maintains that so long as parents are fit, their decisions should be given presumptive validity.[104] In other words, parents are presumed to be acting in their children's best inter-

---

demonstrates that she is not receiving support for the children from the biological father and establishes by affidavit that the stepfather's conduct actively interfered with the children's support by the father so that pendente lite support cannot be obtained from the father.

In the recent case of *O'Rourke vs. Vituro,* 638 S.E.2d 124 (Va. Ct. App. 2006), the Virginia Court of Appeals found that a husband had standing in a divorce to seek custody "as a father" even though he was not the biological father of the child.

101. See Brinig and Nock, "How Much Does Legal Status Matter? Adoptions by Kin Caregivers," p. 449.

102. 42 U.S.C. §671(a)(15)(1997).

103. An Iowa case that discusses the statutes but makes the decision to confine funding to adoptees coming from foster care is *Becker vs. Department of Social Services,* 661 N.W. 2d 125 (Ia. 2003).

104. See, e.g., *Troxel vs. Granville,* 530 U.S. 57 (2000). We acknowledge the suggestion of Annette Mahoney that we take on this issue.

ests.[105] A number of legal scholars suggest that such autonomy is necessary to enable parents to do their best parenting work.[106] We therefore suggest strengthening the legal statuses that promote good parenting as well as social policies providing assistance for those families who need it.

105. *Parham vs. J.R.*, 442 U.S. 554 (1979).

106. See, e.g., Margaret Brinig, "Troxel and the Limits of Community," *Rutgers Law Journal* 38 (2002): 733-81; David D. Meyer, "The Paradox of Family Privacy," *Vanderbilt Law Review* 53, no. 2 (2000): 527-94; Elizabeth S. Scott, "Parental Autonomy and Children's Welfare, *William and Mary Bill of Rights Journal* 11 (3003): 1071-2000.

CHAPTER 13

The Best Love of the Child? An Integrational View

Don S. Browning

Introduction

The "best love of the child" is a multidimensional social reality consisting of a variety of integrated factors. There is danger, however, that many aspects of Western society, including the sphere of family law, are narrowing this idea to a relatively one-dimensional psychological or affectional interpersonal and intersubjective relationship. The affective aspects of love are important, especially in early childhood. But there is more to love than this. The more classical integrational model of love may be in the process of being lost.

The phrase "best love of the child" brings to mind other concepts such as "best interest of the child" and "best care of the child." Although closely related terms, they do not have identical meanings and are often used in different social contexts. The best love is often used in familial situations. The idea of the best interests of the child has a distinctively legal meaning in our society today. Best care is likely to be used in both the home and institutional settings such as daycare, schools, or hospitals. Nonetheless, their various meanings interrelate. In this essay, I am particularly interested in the ways the phrases "best love" and "best care" influence the legal meaning of the child's "best interest." Increasingly, the concept of best interest is used in legal contexts on conflicting issues in family law, especially custody disputes in divorce, separation of cohabiting partners, or disputes over parental rights in the nontraditional family arrangements. Sometimes the overlapping concepts of best love, best care, or best interest are used to trump the rights of natural or legally married parents. In other cases, appeals to the best interest of children can be used to either marginalize or completely de-legalize the institution of marriage as the best context for childrearing. Depending upon how these concepts are interpreted, they can either affirm or deny the rights of biological parents to raise their offspring, the rights of children to be raised by the parents who conceived them, or subordinate the parental entitlements of formal marriage to the *de facto* involvements of informal but long-term caregivers. *With these issues in mind, I will argue for a multidimensional view of the best love, care, and interest of the child that communicates through affect and deeds respect for the emerging personhood of the child but also actively works to meet the child's developmental needs throughout the life cycle.*

It will be useful to expand our understanding of the social context of this inquiry. The legal belief that the best love, care, or interest of the child might not coincide with being raised by natural parents or legally married parents has emerged simultaneously with the multiple separations that now beset the sexual field in modern societies. I have in mind the increasing separations between marriage and sexual intercourse, marriage and childbirth, marriage and childrearing, childbirth and parenting, and — with the advent of Assisted Reproductive Technologies (ART) — childbirth from sexual intercourse and biological filiation.[1] These many separations are the result of how increased technical rationality (technical reason, *tekhnē*) in both the economic and reproductive spheres has been energized by the rise of cultural individualism — people's increased interest in using the tools of technical rationality to maximize their satisfactions in the economic, sexual, and reproductive fields of social life.[2] It is commonly believed by both sociologists and family-law scholars that these modernizing forces, for good or ill, are inevitable and cannot be stopped.[3] As childbirth and rearing are increasingly being separated from biological kinship and the regulations of marriage, law

1. For an excellent discussion of these multiple separations, see Brent Waters, *Reproductive Technology: Towards a Theology of Procreative Stewardship* (Cleveland: Pilgrim Press, 2001).

2. For the classic statement on the relation of technical reason and modernity, see Max Weber, *The Protestant Ethic and the Spirit of Capitalism* (New York: Charles Scribner's Sons, 1958), p. 182. For an important statement on the rise of cultural individualism in American society, see Robert Bellah, Richard Madsen, William Sullivan, Ann Swidler, and Steven Tipton, *Habits of the Heart* (Berkeley: University of California Press, 1985).

3. In sociology, see Frank Furstenberg and Andrew Cherlin, *Divided Families* (Cambridge, MA: Harvard University Press, 1991); William Goode, *World Revolution in Family Patterns* (London: The Free Press of Glencoe, 1964), p. 380. For family law, see Maria V. Antokolskaia, "The Development of Family Law in Western and Eastern Europe," *Journal of Family History* 28, no. 1 (January 2003): 52-69.

courts must determine in situations of conflict which persons, or combination of persons, should care for a child. More and more this decision is grounded on the trilogy of interacting concepts — best love, care, and interest of the child. *But interpretations of what these ideas mean vary significantly.*

As I noted above, in the context of disputes in family law, the concepts of best love and best care are generally absorbed into the requirements of the child's best interests. This idea functions as a psychosocial term that floats in meaning. Sometimes it means basic nurturance and physical care. At other times it refers to either economic capital or what sociologist James Coleman called "social capital."[4] In some custody disputes, the best interest of the child is used to give visitation rights to a long-term caregiver other than biological or married parents or even give legal parental recognition to a third-party caregiver, hence giving the child three and potentially more parents. This may be done to provide the child with psychological nurturance and continuity with meaningful persons amidst the transitions of family disruption. This possibility is being opened by the recommended custody provisions of chapter two of American Law Institute's (ALI) *Principles of the Law of Family Dissolution* (2002).[5] In a mild defense of this move, University of Illinois College of Law professor David Meyer acknowledges that a child having three or more parents might lead to more conflict, but it also might mean more love and social resources for the child.[6]

I will address the interrelated ideas of best love, care, and interest of the child by reviewing four commanding positions in contemporary family-law theory. These are the feminist legal perspectives of Professor Martha Fineman of the School of Law of Emory University and Professor June Carbone of the Santa Clara University School of Law, the proposals for family-law reform in the *Principles of the Law of Family Dissolution,* and finally the position of Professor Margaret Brinig of the University of Notre Dame Law School. Although the number of contemporary legal theorists with a more integrated view of the best love of the child is limited, I will advance Brinig as an illustration of that point of view.

4. James Coleman, "Social Capital and the Creation of Human Capital," *American Journal of Sociology* 94 (1988): 95-120.

5. *Principles of the Law of Family Dissolution: Analysis and Recommendations* (Newark, NJ: Matthew Bender & Co., 2002).

6. David Meyer, "Partners, Care Givers, and the Constitutional Substance of Parenthood," in *Reconceiving the Family: Critique of the American Law Institute's Principles of the Law of Family Dissolution,* ed. Robin Fretwell Wilson (Cambridge: Cambridge University Press, 2006), p. 66.

The Multidimensional Nature of Love and Care

I believe that law as it pertains to children should be guided by a multidimensional or integrational model of the best love, care, and interest of the child. I hold that to love a child is to simultaneously respect or honor the emerging personhood of the child and actively work to actualize the basic goods (sometimes called premoral goods) needed for the child's flourishing. This view is both Kantian in its emphasis on respect for the emerging personhood of the child and Aristotelian in its emphasis on the teleological goods required for the developing child. It is important to recognize that the needs of the child — as Erik Erikson, Robert Kegan, and many other psychologists have shown — emerge on a timetable in such a way that meeting early needs is foundational for the consolidation of later ones.[7] This is why nurture, both physical care and parental recognition and affirmation, are so important in early life. But the idea of a timetable for the child's emerging needs also points out why early nurture so defined is not enough. In view of this well-established principle in developmental psychology, the best love and care of a child requires the exercise of practical wisdom to determine which needs are crucial for a certain stage of the life cycle and which practices are required to meet them. Furthermore, as Erikson and the new hermeneutic approach to psychology have argued, the development of the child unfolds in the context of specific societies whose institutions are shaped by particular traditions with identifiable histories, cultures, and narratives.[8] The best love of the child provides ways to connect and critically appropriate these traditions, institutions, and their shaping narratives for what they contribute to the child's emerging capacity and identity.[9] Parents, immediate family, and custodians are important for the best love and interests of the child, but they are not omnipotent. At best they are key mediators of influ-

7. Erik Erikson, *Identity, Youth, and Crisis* (New York: W. W. Norton, 1968), p. 93; Robert Kegan, *The Evolving Self: Problem and Process in Human Development* (Cambridge, MA: Harvard University Press, 1982), pp. 43, 56-57.

8. Erik Erikson, *Young Man Luther* (New York: W. W. Norton, 1962), p. 41; Frank Richardson, Blaine Fowers, and Charles Guignon, *Re-envisioning Psychology* (San Francisco: Jossey-Bass, 1999), p. 257.

9. For a discussion of how traditions can be appropriated and yet critiqued, see Paul Ricoeur, *Hermeneutics and the Social Sciences* (Cambridge: Cambridge University Press, 1981), pp. 63-100. Also see his theory of how moral practices shaped by narrative traditions must pass the deontological test, his version of the Kantian categorical imperative in his *Oneself as Another* (Chicago: University of Chicago Press, 1992), pp. 207-9.

ences, logics, symbols, and narrative traditions that also make massive contributions to the growth and well-being of the child.

Hence, answering the question of what is the best love, care, or interest of the child is a complex multidimensional exercise in practical wisdom. In other words, the best love and interest of the child cannot be determined on either narrowly empirical or legal grounds. It requires wisdom — a philosophical, and perhaps even theological, critical retrieval of the history of our past efforts to define the best love, care, and interest of the child. It is *first* a question about *practices;* which parental, familial, and institutional practices will be the best for the child over the course of the human life cycle? But the best for what? This leads to the *second* feature of a practical wisdom of care; the best practices are those that meet the child's needs and actualize its potentials while also respecting the child's emerging selfhood.

But for what purposes are the child's needs and potentials met and personhood respected? This question points to the *third* dimension and requires a moral principle to guide care throughout the life cycle. Should needs be met and selves respected for the child's individual cost-benefit utility or personal self-realization and fulfillment? These are very popular answers in the social sciences and general culture, but they are inadequate. A more philosophically durable answer — and one consistent with the practical wisdom of both Judaism and Christianity and other great traditions — is that the best love of the child is to help him or her grow to live by the golden rule, properly interpreted. We should not simply tell the child "do to others as you would have them do to you" (Matt. 7:12); this can so easily be interpreted as a mere ethic of Kantian respect, which neglects the question of needs and potentials. We should follow the great French philosopher Paul Ricoeur and his agreement with Rabbi Hillel in interpreting the golden rule to mean the child should learn to do *good* to others as you would have them do *good* to you.[10] This brings together, Ricoeur contends, both the deontological Kantian respect for the other with a subordinate Aristotelian and teleological concern to actively do good and meet the concrete needs of the other. Maybe the Christian principle that "You shall love your neighbor as yourself" (Matt. 19:19) says it better. Love in this formulation includes both actively meeting the needs of the other as well as respectfully treating her as an end in herself — a child of God made in the image of God, as

10. Paul Ricoeur, "The Teleological and Deontological Structure of Action: Aristotle and/or Kant?" in *Contemporary French Philosophy*, ed. A. Phillips Griffiths (Cambridge: Cambridge University Press, 1987), pp. 109-10.

Christians would say. Hence, as love for the growing child should both respect her selfhood and meet her needs, the child should grow up to mediate this twofold love to others, especially the next generation. This formulation of the golden rule and neighbor love is a central dimension of care and points to the *moral principle* that should guide it throughout the life cycle. Of course, this principle will shift in concrete meaning and nuance as it guides parental and institutional love for the child at differing stages in the human life cycle.

But the best love of the child is thicker still. It must do more than be guided by the abstract principles of the golden rule or neighbor love, even as I have thickened them in my above formulations. A practical wisdom of love and care must always be surrounded by some kind of narrative that tells a story about the purpose of life and its beginning, middle, and end. As Robyn Fivush points out in this volume, shared history told in shared narratives have powerful effects on shaping a child's growth and maturity.[11] A practical wisdom of the best love of the child requires a narrative and supporting metaphors that give love this wider meaning and, as Erik Erikson and others have eloquently argued, give the child a deeper and historically grounded identity.[12] This is the *fourth* dimension of the best love of the child. And *fifth*, love and care always take place in specific social and environment contexts. How these contexts support, limit, threaten, channel, or fail to channel the best love, care, and interests of the child must be a concern of the practical judgment guiding parents, guardians, courts, or the state.

A summary formula about what goes into the best love, care, or interests of the child would go like this. *The best love of the child is a set of parental and institutional practices that (1) communicates respect for the child's emerging self while meeting needs and actualizing potentials, (2) guides the child to grow and live by a principle that respects the self and meets the needs of others, (3) enriches the child with a vision or narrative of life that both supports and justifies this ethic, and (4) does this in ways that realistically confront the opportunities and limits of various social and natural contexts.*

I will use this multidimensional and integrational model to analyze Fineman, Carbone, the *Principles of the Law of Family Dissolution,* and Brinig on their respective views of the best love, care, and interests of the child.

11. Robyn Fivush, "Parent-Child Reminiscing: Creating Best Love through Sharing Stories," this volume.

12. In addition to Erikson, *Young Man Luther,* p. 41, see the report *Hardwired to Connect: The New Scientific Case for Authoritative Communities* (New York: Institute for American Values, 2003).

Fineman, Carbone, and the *Principles* represent dominant trends of family law today. I will advance two criticisms of the direction of these three perspectives. First, in different ways they all think about the best love, care, or interest of the child from the back door of family life, i.e., from the perspective of family breakdown rather than family formation. Second, because of this, they split apart and overemphasize one or the other of the five dimensions of love and care. Fineman thinks of the child's best interest as nurturance. However, she views nurturance from the perspective of family breakdown and her advocacy of de-legalizing marriage and marriage-based parenting. Carbone wants law to preserve the link of parents to their children but believes marriage is no longer necessary to accomplish this. The *Principles* is the leading example of legal theory thinking almost entirely about the best care and interests of the child from the perspective of family dissolution. The continuity of care expressed as a psychosocial concept is the main value of the *Principles.* It also would shape law's influence on family formation from the perspective of the legal emergencies of family disruption and dissolution.

Brinig, however, is an exception to these trends. She exhibits how law can give the best love, care, and interest of the child balanced attention to both family formation and family disruption. She also has a more philosophically adequate, multidimensional, and integrational understanding of these concepts.

Fineman and the Omnipotence of Nurture

In three books and scores of articles, Martha Fineman has advanced a series of defining perspectives in family law that many scholars feel compelled to address and some to accept. In her books *The Illusions of Equality* (1991), *The Neutered Mother and the Sexual Family* (1995), and *The Autonomy Myth* (2004), Fineman has advanced telling criticisms of liberal feminism and its view of equality, especially at the moment of no-fault divorce.[13] She is known as a champion of "difference feminism" and is indeed considered as one of its earliest and most powerful proponents. This perspective contends that in divorce and family dissolution, superficial views of the equality of

13. Martha Fineman, *The Illusion of Equality: The Rhetoric and Reality of Divorce Reform* (Chicago: University of Chicago Press, 1991); *The Neutered Mother, the Sexual Family, and Other Twentieth Century Tragedies* (New York: Routledge, 1995); *The Autonomy Myth* (New York: The New Press, 2004).

men and women in property distribution and child custody have left many mothers financially impoverished and overburdened with the responsibility of child care.[14] When the wife or mother has the *de facto* major responsibility for the child, giving her even 50 percent of the family wealth at separation will generally not be enough because of the simultaneous demands of nurture and employment in the wage economy. Joint custody, although a favorite solution of most social workers and many courts, works to the great disadvantage of mothers. Fineman writes,

> Divorced women typically assume an unequal, more burdensome share of the postdivorce responsibilities for nurture and care of children. This is true even in cases of "joint custody," where mothers typically do the bulk of the day-to-day care. The fables we have created around "modern" fatherhood and our newly coined and much-applied legal label, *joint custody* obscure the fact that unequal material sacrifices are assumed, even mandated, by social and cultural factors in addition to the history of a particular family.[15]

This quote is a sample of the themes that run throughout Fineman's work. She defines best love and interest of the child primarily around a picture of the intimate nurture of highly dependent infants and young children. It is primarily a matter of holding, feeding, attaching, clothing, and cleaning human infants and children during a long period of dependency. Carol Gilligan's ethics of care is in the background of her writings.[16] In emphasizing the role that this long period of human childhood dependency plays in shaping the human family, she takes up a theme that goes back to Aristotle, Thomas Aquinas, and even the early liberal political theorist John Locke.[17] But whereas in these classic perspectives childhood dependency is used to emphasize the important role of the father in joining and supporting the mother-infant dyad, Fineman uses this naturalistic observation to de-emphasize the importance of fathers, both at the time of family dissolution and in the formation of families in the first place.

14. Fineman, *The Illusion of Equality*, pp. 175-76.

15. Fineman, *The Illusion of Equality*, p. 37.

16. Carol Gilligan, *In a Different Voice* (Cambridge, MA: Harvard University Press, 1982).

17. Aristotle, "The History of Animals," in *The Basic Works of Aristotle* (New York: Random House, 1941), Bk. 9; Thomas Aquinas, *Summa Theologica*, 3, "Supplement," q. 41.1; John Locke, "Second Treatise," in *Two Treatises of Government* (Cambridge: Cambridge University Press, 1991), ch. 7, para. 80.

Although the dependency situations that Fineman has in mind are not confined to the mother-child relation, that is chiefly what she has in mind. Government and public policy, she claims, should shift from supporting the "sexual family" in the institution of marriage to the support of actual caregivers to dependent persons.[18] Fineman believes that the institution of marriage is disappearing and needs now to be de-legalized — no longer given explicit recognition and support before the law.[19] Couples can marry within the contexts of their religious traditions if they wish, and they can regularize their unions with individually crafted and legally recognized contracts.[20] But they should no longer be supported by the institutional status of legalized marriage. Instead, law and public policy should give legal recognition, supports, and protections to caregivers and nurturers. This can include adults taking care of their elderly parents or close friends caring for each other, but Fineman mainly has in mind single mothers caring for their dependent children.[21]

Fineman tends to reduce the best care and interests of the child to nurturance. In *The Autonomy Myth* she writes,

> The obvious question is, how can we apply the "best interest" test without considering and heavily valuing those things that mothers overwhelmingly (even if stereotypically) do with and for children? Nurturing and caretaking — practices that are of primary importance to the rearing of children — are heavily identified in our society with the practice of responsible mothering.[22]

Fineman resents having either the economic contributions or biological connection of the father included in an understanding of the best interest of the child. She complains that in the idea of joint custody, "The rules reflect a preference for custody not in the most nurturing parent, but the most generous parent."[23] By the most "generous," she means the most economically affluent parent. And as for the father's biological contribution and what it might mean for his attachment with and care for the child, she writes, "A

18. Fineman, *The Autonomy Myth,* p. 47.

19. Fineman, *The Neutered Mother,* pp. 228-30; for her comments on the statistical decline of marriage, see *The Autonomy Myth,* pp. 110-11.

20. Fineman, *The Neutered Mother,* p. 229.

21. Fineman, *The Neutered Mother,* p. 9.

22. Fineman, *The Autonomy Myth,* p. 190.

23. Fineman, *The Autonomy Myth,* p. 191.

mere basic biological connection to the child justifies a claim for shared custody and control rights that equalize the postdivorce relationships between both parents and their child. Nurturing is devalued, ignored, and unrewarded in such a scheme."[24]

Even though she would de-legalize the institution of marriage, she does not eliminate the role of institutions for the best care of the child. Caregivers need financial resources and the burdens of care often prevent them from acquiring these material supports through employment. So, if marriage is to be de-legalized and the sexual family de-emphasized, to what institution do caregivers — especially single mothers — turn? The answer is this: they turn to the state. They require a new "social contract" that will provide them with subsidies from the government. Fineman writes, "Undertaking caretaking exacts a unique cost from an individual caretaker, who becomes derivatively dependent on society and its institutions for additional material and structural resources necessary to do care work well."[25] More specifically, this would mean, "The state would provide some subsidies directly, such as child-care allowances, but also oversee and facilitate the restructuring of the workplace so that market institutions accommodate caretaking and, in this way, assume some fair share of the burdens of dependency."[26]

Although Fineman nearly reduces the best love of the child to nurture, shadows of the other dimensions of a practical wisdom of love and care are detectible in her writings. But her vague and incomplete multidimensionality raises questions. *First,* at the level of *practices,* she emphasizes a consistent practice of nurture. But this brings up the issue as to whether raising a child to respect and care for others requires more than nurture? Lawrence Kohlberg's research shows that to learn to care for others, the child as it develops must confront, interact with, and take the role of others in their claims for selfhood.[27] The concept of nurture as such does not account for this developmental task. Nurture may be foundational, as attachment research indicates, but it is not everything.[28] The child must learn to confront difference and to deal constructively with it. *Second,* Fineman also has a the-

24. Fineman, *The Autonomy Myth,* p. 191.

25. Fineman, *The Autonomy Myth,* p. 285.

26. Fineman, *The Autonomy Myth,* p. 285.

27. Lawrence Kohlberg, *The Philosophy of Moral Development* (San Francisco: Harper & Row, 1981), pp. 141-42.

28. For research on attachment, see John Bowlby, *Attachment and Loss,* vols. 1-3 (New York: Basic Books, 1969, 1973, 1981); Allan Schore, *Affect Dysregulation and Disorders of the Self* (New York: W. W. Norton, 2003).

ory of human *needs,* but a thin one primarily identified with meeting needs for maternal warmth, sustenance, and bodily maintenance. This raises the question as to whether there are cognitive, moral, and spiritual needs as well that she disregards. *Third,* although Fineman ignores the role of moral obligations to institutions when it comes to her disestablishment of marriage, she does have an alternative moral principle. She would replace the vows, contracts, and covenants of marriage by a social contract with the state to support the private realm of mothers nurturing their children. Clearly, Fineman has an important point. There is a role for state institutions in providing subsidy for the best care of the child. But the question is this: Is Fineman's theory of what Roman Catholic social teaching calls the "subsidiarity" or *subsidum* of the state the best formulation needed to truly meet the best interests of the child? *Fourth,* on the *narrative and metaphoric* dimension of a practical wisdom of care, Fineman would remove from family law any vestige of the Christian metaphors of covenant or sacrament, or any secularized analogies such as the concept of marriage as a status. This raises the question: Has mother love or the "nurturant parent," as cognitive scientist and metaphor theorist George Lakoff argues, become the dominant metaphor in liberal political and legal discourse on the family?[29] Does Fineman neatly exemplify this trend? *Fifth,* Fineman clearly believes that the context of families today is dominated by the separation-producing rationalities of modernity, that there is no turning back from its onrush, and that there is no way to live with modernity and integrate the goods of marriage and childcare as happened in the past. In her view, the only love that can be integrated and legally protected in the future is the love and care of a mother with her dependent children.

Carbone and the De-Institutionalization of Care

June Carbone shares with Fineman a commitment to difference feminism; if women are to enjoy equality in family life and society, they must receive special considerations. She also agrees with Fineman in holding that marriage can no longer be at the center of family law. She is not as aggressive as Fineman in recommending that marriage be de-legalized, but she contends it can no longer be central to the law of families. Society and public policy

29. George Lakoff, *Moral Politics: What Conservatives Know That Liberals Don't* (Chicago: University of Chicago Press, 1996), pp. 108-10.

must shift from emphasizing married partners to making parents central, whether married or not. This all has implications for the best love, care, and interest of the child. Whereas Fineman marginalizes both marriage and the care provided by fathers — emphasizing solely the nurture of mothers and the supports of the state — Carbone values the care of both mothers and fathers although, for the most part, she is willing to relinquish the institution of marriage and replace it with the accountabilities of law enforcement and the subsidies of public welfare. For Carbone, moral obligations run primarily from the parent to the child and from the state to the parent-child relationship. There are few if any moral obligations between the parents as partners — married or not — that have implications for the best interests of the child.

Carbone agrees with sociologists such as William Goode, Frank Furstenberg, and Andrew Cherlin that the forces of modernization will increasingly and inevitably damage the child-centered marriage.[30] The decentering of married parenthood and childcare comes from what she and others call "the technological shock" of "married women's workforce participation."[31] As this advanced, women, wives, and mothers were no longer totally dependent financially on their husbands. This made both divorce and non-marriage increasing options for women, even when their intimacies with men left them with the challenges of childcare. This leads Carbone to assert the sociological generalization that no longer are sexual intercourse, childbirth, or childcare confined to marriage, even in respectable sectors of society.[32] For Carbone, the matter is settled at the level of both custom and official law. With the advent of no-fault divorce, the legalization of the use of contraception both inside and outside of marriage, the legalization of abortion in *Roe vs. Wade*, and the widespread legal use of ART in elective childbirth both inside and outside of wedlock, parenthood no longer depends on the institution of marriage. Carbone says it emphatically, "Today, the courts and legislatures have largely abolished the definitions of parenthood that depend on marriage, and the law — together with the rest of society — is struggling, one piece at a time, to rebuild the idea of obligation to children."[33]

Carbone proposes taking further steps to make parenthood, rather than marital partnerships, the center of American family law. Parents would be

30. June Carbone, *From Partners to Parents: The Second Revolution in Family Law* (New York: Columbia University Press, 2000), pp. 16-17, 199.

31. Carbone, *From Partners to Parents,* p. 99.

32. Carbone, *From Partners to Parents,* p. 162.

33. Carbone, *From Partners to Parents,* p. xiii.

required by law to remain responsible for their children, but not necessarily to their spouses or the other parent of their offspring. Here is Carbone's summary of the new legal regime that she would enact.

> Parents have no obligations to each other than those voluntarily assumed, and even those may be terminated at any time. Parent-child ties begin at birth and are the same for marital and non-marital children. They can be transferred (adoption) or terminated by the state, but not abandoned. Children's rights stand independently of the mother and father's relationship to each other. Thus, child support is independent of visitation, a parent cannot contractually forgo a child's right to support, and parental fault (e.g., adultery) is irrelevant.[34]

Carbone would include both the mother and the father in this new legal regime of parenthood. In this she varies from Fineman. But the difference may be less than meets the eye. She acknowledges the importance of the biological connection of both father and mother, whereas Fineman acknowledged it only for the mother. At one point, Carbone admits that law has "recognized it as a matter of natural law since Blackstone."[35] But, for Carbone, this connection means much less for the father than the mother since the mother has the added experience of gestation and delivery to reinforce her love and care. So, in situations of disputes over joint custody, Carbone holds that the father deserves to be included. But whether this would go beyond financial responsibilities, visitation, and some limited shared decision making to include equal residential custody would for her depend on the father's prior involvement in the daily care of the child.[36] Carbone is interested in the financial capital of the father far more than Fineman and is willing to compromise some of the autonomy, authority, and exclusive nurture of the mother in order to gain the financial support of the father. Nonetheless, like Fineman, she ends in de-emphasizing both the role of marriage and the father, turning to the state for institutional support for care. She says this about the centerpiece AFDC (Aid to Families with Dependent Children) welfare program of the U.S. government during the 1970s and 1980s; its "major failing was that it did not go far enough" in providing both resources and freedom for mothers and their children.[37]

34. Carbone, *From Partners to Parents,* p. 240.
35. Carbone, *From Partners to Parents,* p. 160.
36. Carbone, *From Partners to Parents,* p. 194.
37. Carbone, *From Partners to Parents,* p. 204.

In the last analysis, although Carbone retains a modest role for father care and joint custody after family dissolution, she differs only slightly from Fineman. In substituting the contractual supports of the state in place of the covenants of marriage, her position is still in substantial agreement with Fineman. With regard to the five dimensions of a practical wisdom of best love, Carbone would do the following. *First,* best *practices* are reduced to the ministrations of the mother with some financial capital from the father. *Second,* the *needs* of the child are expanded and now include not only nurturance from the mother but contact with and economic capital from the father as well as the state. *Third,* the *moral obligations* of care run primarily between parents and their offspring and secondarily between the state and the parent, with parents having few obligations to each other. *Fourth,* she replaces the *grand narrative* of family formation built around covenant and one-flesh union of mother-father-child with a narrative of contingency; men and women get together, have sex, have babies, and attempt to work out the best they can their asymmetrical one-flesh parental responsibilities to their children with no one-flesh obligations, however, to each other. *Fifth,* she recognizes that the "technological shock" of modernity places great stress on marriage as the context of the best love and care of the child, but feels powerless to do anything other than to strengthen the parenting bond with offspring while the ties between parenting partners in marriage continue to decline.

The *Principles:* Care as Continuity amidst Change

The Principles of the Law of Family Dissolution is a voluminous report issued in 2002 by the prestigious American Law Institute. It is customary for ALI to issue reports periodically that synthesize and update trends in various fields of American law. The *Principles* is its latest effort to do this for the field of family law and is the product of years of study and writing by leading legal minds in the country. It has, however, been the subject of intense review and critique, some of which occurred even before its official publication.[38]

The report is famous for two salient moves relevant to the best intercsts

38. See the Symposium on the ALI *Principles of the Law of Family Dissolution* held at Brigham Young University, J. Reuben Clark Law School, February 1, 2001, and published in *Brigham Young Law Review* 3 (2001); Robin F. Wilson, ed., *Reconceiving the Family: Critique on the American Law Institute's Principles of the Law of Family Dissolution* (Cambridge: Cambridge University Press, 2006).

of the child. At the moment of family dissolution, it renders legal marriage and a range of cohabiting relationships equivalent before the law. At the same time, it thinks about the best love, care, and interests of the child exclusively from the angle of family disruption. Because of this, it views love and care as continuity of the child's relationships with caregivers in order to minimize the stress of family change. It does this to the point of legalizing multiple parent figures with either decision-making authority or visitation rights. Yes, Heather can have two moms, but possibly three or four parents in all.

For those who might want the report to discuss how law can help channel couples toward optimal family formation and parenting, this massive 1,187-page tome will disappoint. The report concentrates principally on what lawyers do, i.e., help manage before the law the equitable dissolution of families who no longer wish to live a common life together. The report claims it is morally neutral.[39] At best, however, this means it is ostensibly neutral about the norms of family formation. This is what is meant when the report regularly announces that it supports "family diversity" without discussing what this actually means, especially for children.[40] On the other hand, at the point of family dissolution, the moral commitments of the *Principles* are clear. It is committed to the good of psychological continuity for children,[41] fairness for adults,[42] and nonviolence for all parties involved, especially women and children.[43]

Chapters two and six of the *Principles* are relevant to the best love, care, and interests of the child. Chapter two is titled "The Allocation of Custodial and Decision-Making Responsibility for Children."[44] To advance the best interests of the child at the time of family dissolution, the *Principles* says this means "predictability in the concrete, individual patterns of specific families."[45] Although the report gives passing acknowledgment of the importance to children of being raised by their married biological parents, it assumes this will happen less in the future. In situations of family dissolution, the continued participation in the life of the child of estoppel and *de facto* parents may be "critically important for the child's welfare."[46]

39. *Principles,* p. 12.
40. *Principles,* p. 3.
41. *Principles,* p. 7.
42. *Principles,* p. 12.
43. *Principles,* p. 7.
44. *Principles,* p. 91.
45. *Principles,* p. 3.
46. *Principles,* p. 5; see also p. 7.

This emphasis on the continuity of caretakers leads the report to formulate one of its strongest provisions. This is its requirement that dissolving families with children must file a "parenting plan," which should outline the role that parents and other caretakers will take in the life of the child. It should make proposals as to who would have legal rights and who only rights of visitation, who would make what decisions, and where the child will live and for how long if in more than one place. It proposes a plan for solving conflicts and a method for revising the plan when necessary.[47] Responsibilities and time allotments with the child of the various adults are to reflect the amount and depth of past involvement in care.[48]

This plan is highly contextual and reflects what moral philosophers would call a "situation ethics."[49] It is allegedly fine-tuned for the best interests of the child at the back door of family life — the point of family dissolution and reconfiguration. But even here the ambiguous borderline between what the report calls moral neutrality and at other times calls "fairness" injects the proviso that the plan must be enacted without regard to *"race, ethnicity, sex, religion, sexual orientation, sexual conduct, and economic circumstances of a parent."*[50] At this point, a moral or political philosopher might take notice of the tension that runs throughout the report between its situational ethic when considering children and its more Kantian or Rawlsian ethic of fairness when weighing the rights of adults. However this tension is resolved — even if it can be — the claims of moral neutrality that run throughout the *Principles* seem spurious.

This moral confusion, however, should not blind us to the strengths of the parenting plan. It is considered to be the "core concept" of the *Principles* and is intended to guide the court in making decisions as well as relieve it of the burden of inventing workable solutions to complex situations *de novo*.[51] Most of its provisions for the best interests of the child are context specific and designed to accomplish the maximum continuity, predictability, and security for the child in an otherwise chaotic situation. Seen from this perspective, the parenting plan is understandable and in some ways laudable. But it reflects a view of law that has relinquished responsibilities for helping to shape, in cooperation with other institutions, an average-expectable envi-

47. *Principles*, pp. 8, 332.

48. *Principles*, p. 193.

49. William Frankena, *Ethics* (Englewood Cliffs, NJ: Prentice-Hall, 1973); Joseph Fletcher, *Situation Ethics* (San Francisco: Harper & Row, 1966).

50. *Principles*, p. 12.

51. *Principles*, p. 145.

ronment that would meet the best love, care, and interests of the child in the formation of parenting institutions in the first place. In fact, the *Principles* as a whole reflects law actively contributing to, if not exacerbating, the fluidity and insecurity that it attempts to cure in its provisions for a parenting plan. This can be seen when we look at chapter six and its unwitting provisions that more directly shape the normative context of parenting — the front door of family formation.

Chapter six addresses the rise of domestic partnerships. In an effort to induce fairness between separating adult partners and responsibility of parents and caregivers to the children involved, it virtually imposes the same laws of dissolution applicable in legal marriage to cohabiting couples.[52] In effect, this makes domestic partners and married couples almost equivalent before the law. I say "almost," because the chapter stipulates that with regard to property distribution, its recommendations apply only to the *inter se* situation of the adult couple and not to third parties such as insurance companies, medical plans, and government programs.[53] However, as we saw in chapter two, third parties would definitely be affected by certain provisions applying to parenthood responsibilities.

Chapter six has important implications for the moral obligations of close relationships of the kind that become domestic partnerships. It fleetingly acknowledges, as I indicated above, that "society's interests in the orderly administration of justice and the stability of families are best served when the formalities of marriage are observed."[54] But the report also insists that the percentage of Americans forming domestic partnerships is rapidly increasing. Although the *Principles* is highly sympathetic to the reasons people give for not marrying, i.e., interest in avoiding the responsibilities of marriage, distaste for the formality of marriage, or simply finding it awkward after years of cohabitation, it openly acknowledges that it wants to "impose" rules on cohabitors that the couple has not requested. Indeed, the rules covering long-time cohabiting couples at dissolution would be default rules that would function without their consent and be indistinguishable from the rules applied to legally married couples.

> The default rules are, in effect, a contract imposed by law on parties who do not set forth their agreement to some different set of rules. The law of

52. *Principles*, p. 913.
53. *Principles*, p. 916.
54. *Principles*, p. 914.

> marriage and divorce can, of course, be similarly understood. For marital partners who do not make another agreement, entry into formal marriage subjects them to the law of marriage and divorce. For domestic partners who do not make another agreement, their course of conduct over a period of years subjects them to parallel rules set forth in this Chapter.[55]

It is interesting to notice how the *Principles* presents this parallel between domestic partnership and marriage without acknowledging that the difference is also huge. In marriage, couples *elect and consent* to the rules, make public promises to adhere to them, and in most cases treat marriage as a covenant of great seriousness to which they bind themselves before family, friends, community, and the state. The default rules that the *Principles* would impose on separating cohabiting couples have not been consented to before witnesses. The question this raises is this: *To what extent do the public contracts and covenants of marriage affect the best love, care, and interests of any children who might come forth from this union?* Does leveling the distinction between marriage and domestic partnerships and the construal of the best interests of the child from the perspective of family dissolution distort our fuller understanding of what is truly good for the most dependent and vulnerable among us — our children?

In summary, the *Principles'* practical wisdom of the best love, care, and interest of the child seems skewed. The *practices* it addresses are primarily the post-dissolution situation of parenting, yet its provisions would also affect the formation rules for all families. The *needs* of the child it considers, following closely in the trail of Fineman and Carbone, are primarily those of psychological continuity and nurture in the context of family disruption. Its *principles of moral obligation* swing back and forth between a situation ethic governing the lives of children and a Kantian ethic of adult rights and fairness with little regard for the consequential goods affecting either parents or their children. Although the report clearly relativizes if not dismantles the metaphors of covenant and one flesh once covering, even before the secular law, the rules of marriage and parenting, it has not left the metaphorical surround of the sexual field in a complete void. It has, instead, implicitly endowed it with the metaphor of what legal scholar Martha M. Ertman of the University of Utah calls the "implied contract" or implied "handshake."[56] This legal view injects into family formation and childrearing a world of

55. *Principles*, p. 915.

56. Martha Ertman, "Private Ordering under the ALI's *Principles: As Natural as Status*," in Wilson, ed., *Reconceiving the Family*, pp. 293-300.

contingency without conscious intentions, commitments, promises, and covenants witnessed publicly by friends and community and whatever wider metaphysical reality one might assume. It is a world in which persons must determine *ex post facto,* with the help and coercions of the law, the meaning of their decisions and actions in the sexual field. It is not only a world of the "handshake" but even more precariously a world of the *implied handshake.*

Margaret Brinig: Care, Covenant, and the One-Flesh Union

Margaret Brinig is unique among contemporary family-law theorists in addressing both the front door and the back door of the family, i.e., both family formation and marriage as well as family dissolution. This twofold concern also has implications for her understanding of the best love, care, and interest of the child. She believes that there are historical, theoretical, and empirical reasons for holding that children on average do better on a host of indices if they are raised by their own biological parents in a legal marriage based on a covenant commitment between husband and wife and between them and the community, the state, and perhaps even God. Brinig is the leading family-law scholar bringing together legal theory with empirical research. This gives her family-law scholarship a rich double language composed of the classical concepts of covenant and one-flesh union and empirical data interpreted by the new institutional economics.

On the basis of these three resources — the Western tradition of legal theory, the new institutional economics, and empirical facts — she opposes Fineman's desire to de-legalize marriage, Carbone's interest in replacing legal marriage with law's support of parenthood, and the *Principles*' concern to make domestic partnerships equivalent to legal marriage.[57] On the other hand, she is realistic about the need to make provisions for the back door of family law — the law of family dissolution. Once again, however, she affirms when possible the good of keeping natural and legal parents involved with their children after divorce through some system of joint custody.[58]

Brinig preserves in fresh terms the accomplishments of the older Christian jurisprudence without, however, becoming narrowly apologetic for

57. Margaret Brinig and Steven Nock, "Legal Status and Effects on Children," *Legal Studies Research Paper* no. 07-21 (Notre Dame: Notre Dame Law School, 2007).

58. Margaret Brinig, *From Contract to Covenant: Beyond the Law and Economics of the Family* (Cambridge, MA: Harvard University Press, 2000), pp. 193-94.

Christianity as such. She does not directly present theological arguments for her case. On the other hand, her position is theologically sensitive. For instance, it is consistent with the integrational model of care found in the classics on marriage and childcare in the writings of Augustine and Thomas Aquinas.[59] Her work, as would theirs, resists the emerging multiple separations in the sexual field sanctioned by much of legal theory, exposes the deception of law's alleged moral neutrality, and helps to restore its capacity to channel sexual intimacy into more durable one-flesh covenants.

She does this by first beginning with a phenomenology of covenant — a thick description of the cultural model of marriage that historically has dominated Western thinking in both law and religion. She then secondarily makes use of the new institutional economics and evolutionary psychology in ways analogous to how Thomas Aquinas used the psychobiology and institutional theory of Aristotle to shape Roman Catholic marriage theory and much of later Western legal tradition of marriage.[60] She does this to illustrate how covenant thinking can be translated into secular law's rightful concern with the hard procreative, economic, and health realities of marriage and family.

In contrast to most contemporary family law, Brinig begins her legal thinking something like the great sociologist Émile Durkheim, although she never discusses his thought. She does this by giving a phenomenological description of the idea of marriage as a covenant — the dominant normative understanding of marriage delivered to most Western societies by our religio-cultural heritage. She argues that the post-Enlightenment contractual model of marriage that sees it as a freely chosen agreement between husband and wife is inadequate to both our experience of marriage and our past legal understandings of the institution. Marriage, she insists, historically has been viewed as a solemn agreement to a union of "unconditional love and permanence" through which the "parties are bound not only to each other but also to some third party, to God or the community or both."[61] This phenomenological description of the inherited normative understanding of marriage is not presented by Brinig as a confessional religious statement. It is, rather, simply a description of the culturally received meaning of

59. Augustine, "The Good of Marriage," in *Treatises on Marriage and Other Subjects* (Washington, DC: Catholic University of America Press, 1955), pp. 9-54; Thomas Aquinas, *Summa Theologica 3, "The Supplement,"* qq. 41-44.

60. John Witte, *Law and Protestantism* (Cambridge: Cambridge University Press, 2002), pp. 210-14, 230-40.

61. Brinig, *From Contract to Covenant*, pp. 6-7.

covenant as the inherited dominant model. After she does this, she then gives a further economic account of its concrete institutional implications.

In order to understand the social implications of covenant, Brinig turns to what is today commonly called the "new institutional economics."[62] This perspective both builds on yet goes beyond the rational-choice view advocated by Nobel Prize–winning economist Gary Becker and law and economics theorist Judge Richard Posner. Marriage, she argues, is more like a firm than it is an individualistically negotiated contract. A firm is an association organized to perform a specific function, achieve economies of scale, capitalize on special talents of individual participants, and relate to external parties as a collective unit. A firm is based on a prior agreement — something like a covenant — between the parties involved and the surrounding community about the purpose of the corporate unit. Brinig says this about the analogy between firms and covenantal marriage: "This agreement does not purport to anticipate all future transactions among the firm members. In fact, one of the goals of the firm is the elimination of explicit interparty contracting and account keeping."[63] The new institutional economics helps us see things in the firm, and in marriages (especially marriages with children), that the older individualistic rational-choice economic model missed. It helps us see the "channeling," "signaling," and "reputational" aspects of firm-like marriages. The firm model enables us to grasp how marriages formed by settled public commitments (covenants) to each other, potential children, and society develop identifiable social patterns that convey trusted information, dependable access to known and valued goods, and valued reputations both within the marriage and between the marriage and the wider community.[64]

Marriages that result in children, however, are more like a particular type of firm called franchises. *This analogy between marriage with children and the franchise is especially important for the best love, care, and interest of the child.* A set of imposed responsibilities come from the child and from outside expectations that cannot be totally dissolved even with legal divorce. The inextricable one-flesh union and the shared family history do "not disappear" when the marriage ends or the child turns eighteen. Brinig points out something that the ancient "one-flesh" model of marriage profoundly understood but that scholars like Martha Fineman miss, i.e., that "divorcing

62. Brinig, *From Contract to Covenant,* p. 6.

63. Brinig, *From Contract to Covenant,* p. 5.

64. Brinig, *From Contract to Covenant,* p. 6.

couples never completely revert to a pre-marriage state. Nor do children leaving home entirely free themselves from their parents or siblings."[65] Brinig's twofold account of marriage conveyed through a phenomenology of covenant and an institutional-economics analysis of the goods that covenants organize leads her to say, "marriage persists to a certain degree in spite of divorce. To the extent that it persists, the family still lives on as what I call the franchise."[66]

Brinig's phenomenology of covenant and her institutional economics are supported by empirical research. Her empirical studies with Steven Nock lead her to assert that in contrast to much of contemporary legal theory, the status of parents in legal marriage is a leading positive asset for the well-being of children. Family form is a plus. Children on average do better on a host of indices when raised by their own two biological parents in legal marriage. As Carbone and the *Principles* seem to hold, income contributes to child well-being, especially in the child's early years, but in the long run, Brinig's empirical research shows it is not as important as either legal status of married parents or family form. Finally, her research shows that Fineman's emphasis on the mother's love and Carbone's and the *Principles*' advocacy of parental and caregiver continuity also count, but not as much as the marital status of parents and family form.[67]

Both covenant theory and institutional economics give Brinig and Nock an explanation for the importance of legal marriage in the best love, care, and interest of the child. They make their point against the background of the abundant number of studies from both the U.S. and Europe showing that cohabiting partnerships, even with children, are less stable. They write that when legally married couples "know they are in a long-term relationship ('until death do us part' or at least until the age of emancipation), they have incentive to 'specifically invest' in the relationship and in the other party to it." In addition, "legal recognition provides a signal for the provision of all kinds of outside support for the family, whether by government, by extended family, or by other affinity groups." These investments and subsequent benefits "should accrue to children as well as adults."[68]

Brinig and Nock arrived at these conclusions through an analysis of the University of Michigan Panel Survey of Income Dynamics and its Child De-

65. Brinig, *From Contract to Covenant,* pp. 8-9.

66. Brinig, *From Contract to Covenant,* p. 9.

67. Brinig and Nock, "Legal Status and Effects on Children," p. 11.

68. Brinig and Nock, "Legal Status and Effects on Children," p. 6.

velopment Supplement.[69] They analyzed the large longitudinal database of these surveys with standard social-science scales measuring child well-being.[70] Keeping children with natural mothers (both married and unmarried) constant, they measured child well-being from the perspective of the independent variables of income, family structure, legal relation of parents (unique to their study), parental warmth (close to Fineman's nurturance model), and mother's race and age.[71] As I indicated above, all of the factors counted in some way for child well-being, but in contrast to the major trend of contemporary family law theory as exhibited by Fineman, Carbone, and the *Principles, legal marriage and family structure count the most.*

Her position has many concrete implications, more than I can discuss in detail. For instance, she believes rendering cohabitation and marriage largely equivalent before the law, as the *Principles* proposes, would end in undermining the signaling and channeling functions of marriage — the front door of family formation. This would mean a significant loss for guiding men into aligning and integrating their sexuality, affection for sexual partner, and commitment to children. Brinig is fully aware — as was Aristotle,[72] Thomas Aquinas,[73] evolutionary psychology,[74] and other empirical studies — that men are more likely to attach and commit to children if they know the child is theirs, spend time with the child as it grows, get invested in the child through ongoing experience, and have a satisfying relation with the mother of the child.[75] Brinig and Nock accept the massive witness of tradition and the contemporary social sciences that on average children do much better on a host of measures of well-being when raised by their own married biological parents.[76]

69. Brinig and Nock, "Legal Status and Effects on Children," p. 7. The Panel Study of Income Dynamics has data on a large number of families, ranging from 4,810 in 1968 to 7,000 in 2001. The Child Development Supplement has data on 3,563 children between 0 and 12 in 2,934 families.

70. Brinig and Nock, "Legal Status and Effects on Children," p. 10. The scales used were the Behavior Problem Scale and its separate Internal and External Scales, the Pearlin Self-Efficacy Scale, and the Rosenberg Self-Esteem Scale.

71. Brinig and Nock, "Legal Status and Effects on Children," p. 11.

72. Aristotle, *Politics,* Bk. I, iv.

73. Aquinas, *Summa Theologica,* 3, "Supplement," q. 41, 1.

74. Robert Trivers, "Parental Investment and Sexual Selection," in *Sexual Selection and the Descent of Man,* ed. B. Campbell (Chicago: Aldine Publishing Co., 1972), pp. 139-41.

75. Brinig, *From Contract to Covenant,* p. 133.

76. For one of the most respected summaries, see Kristin Anderson Moore et al., "Marriage from a Child's Perspective: How Does Family Structure Affect Children?" 6 (2000), http://www.childtrends,org./Files//Child_Trends_2002_06=01_RB_Childs View Marriage.pdf.

In view of the witness of both tradition and the contemporary social sciences, she contends that law should not hesitate to do what it can, in cooperation with other sectors of society, to encourage the marital franchise with children as the defining center of family formation. Marriage can be encouraged through the law, she suggests, by not giving legal recognition or normalization to cohabitation, by not undermining the signaling power of the marital institution, and by greatly increasing the social and cultural rewards of marriage.[77] She holds it is worth taking seriously the Louisiana, Arizona, and Arkansas experiments in "covenant marriage." This is the provision these states have developed of offering couples both the no-fault marriage option ("marriage lite") or a marriage with higher standards of commitment (a covenant marriage) which demands more preparation as well as counseling and a waiting period before divorce.[78]

Brinig and Nock reject efforts by Martha Fineman to de-legalize marriage and place legal and social supports behind various caring relationships. They acknowledge, however, the importance of love and nurture. Fineman is right that it is an important factor for the best interests of the child and plays an especially important role in certain minority communities where legal marriage, income, and family structure are at risk.[79] Brinig also is skeptical of Fineman's proposal to eliminate joint custody in favor of a preference for custody by the mother. Brinig accepts social-science evidence showing that divorced fathers remain more involved with their children when awarded a role in custody.[80] Since Brinig's covenant or franchise view of marriage, especially when children are involved, holds that even in divorce there is no "clean break," joint custody provides a way for separated parents to deal with the one-flesh union that remains after the marriage officially ends.

Brinig, like Fineman, is a feminist legal scholar interested in the equal treatment of women in advanced modern societies. But she is a "difference feminist" who also holds that equality for women can be best achieved in a world where men relate to their children and sexual partners in marriage and where men and women in principle work out equal (not necessarily identical) privileges and responsibilities in the public world of paid work and the private world of domestic obligations and pleasures. Although she does not use the term, she is for a love ethic of "equal regard."[81] Brinig also

77. Brinig, *From Contract to Covenant*, pp. 28-29.

78. Brinig, *From Contract to Covenant*, p. 29.

79. Brinig and Nock, "Legal Status and Effects on Children," p. 13.

80. Brinig, *From Contract to Covenant*, p. 193.

81. The concept of the equal-regard marriage is a view I have developed in a variety of my

shows the implications of her views for several other issues in family law — same-sex marriage, surrogacy, divorce, care for the elderly, and the emancipation of children, but the illustrations above give a taste of the direction of her thinking.

As I indicated above, I make no claim that Brinig has a full theology of Christian marriage even though her phenomenology of covenant draws from this tradition. A richer Christian theology would develop a theology of marriage as willed by God in creation, a more explicit equal-regard ethic of marital love, an understanding of the role of self-sacrificial love in the wider view of love as equal regard, and a theology of forgiveness so crucial for the renewal of marital commitment. These latter elements would rightly be of more interest to the churches than to civil law. But in Brinig's perspective, we have a jurisprudence of marriage that meets the rationality test of legal theory yet is both influenced by and broadly compatible with the outlines of the integrational view of marriage, parenting, and the best love of the child so central to a Christian jurisprudence. Hence, it would help bridge the social space between secular law and the dominant models of love and marriage functioning in American culture.

Brinig has a superior grasp of a multidimensional practical wisdom of best love of the child in comparison to most of her colleagues in family law. She realizes that *practices* of love and care take different forms over the life cycle of the child. The *needs* of the child include nurture, but she understands that fathers and mothers may care, guide, and contribute in different ways at varying points in the child's growth. She does not believe that law can be morally neutral on *moral obligation.* Nor can it hold a flat Kantian fairness for adults and a context-specific situational ethic for children. Society and law should guide couples to organize their family life within the classic covenantal understanding of unconditioned love and the one-flesh franchise of mother-father-child. Brinig believes that the great *metaphors and narratives* of the Western marriage tradition can be retrieved, even if they must be cleansed of their patriarchal tendencies and fine-tuned for the limited tasks of secular law. And finally, she is fully aware of the dynamics of

---

writings, notably Don Browning, Bonnie Miller-McLemore, Pam Couture, Bernie Lyon, and Robert Franklin, *From Culture Wars to Common Ground* (Louisville: Westminster/John Knox Press, 1997, 2000); Don Browning and Gloria Rodriguez, *Reweaving the Social Tapestry* (New York: W. W. Norton, 2001); Don Browning, *Marriage and Modernization* (Grand Rapids: Eerdmans, 2003); Don Browning, *Equality and the Family* (Grand Rapids: Eerdmans, 2007). For a critique of this point of view, see John Witte, Christian Green, and Amy Wheeler, *The Equal Regard Family and Its Friendly Critics* (Grand Rapids: Eerdmans, 2007).

modernization that put pressure on the social *context* of modern families. She believes, however, in the possibility of a work of culture — one that would align law with education, government, and religion and together counter modernity's more destructive trends.

I feature the work of Brinig, and her associate Steven Nock, not to indicate that they are the only figures in contemporary family law moving toward a more adequate understanding of the best love, care, and interest of the child. There are others. But Brinig and Nock do merit our serious consideration and thoughtful analysis.[82]

82. For other perspectives that are close to Brinig in spirit if not in detail, see Carl Schneider, "Elite Principles: The ALI Proposals and the Politics of Law Reform," in Wilson, ed., *Reconceiving the Family,* pp. 489-506; Mary Ann Glendon, *The Transformation of Family Law: State, Law, and Family in the United States and Western Europe* (Chicago: University of Chicago Press, 1989), pp. 306-13; Milton Regan, *Family Law and the Pursuit of Intimacy* (New York: New York University Press, 1993).

Contributors

Peter L. Benson is president and CEO of Search Institute, a Minneapolis-based nonprofit organization that provides catalytic leadership, breakthrough knowledge, and innovative resources to advance the health of children, youth, families, and communities. He holds a doctorate and master's degree from the University of Denver as well as a master's degree from Yale University. Among his recent books are *Parent, Teacher, Mentor, Friend: How Every Adult Can Change Kids' Lives* (Search Institute, 2010) and *Sparks: How Parents Can Help Ignite the Hidden Strengths of Teenagers* (Jossey-Bass, 2008). Benson is a recipient of the William James Award for Career Contributions to Psychology of Religion from the American Psychological Association.

Margaret F. Brinig is the Fritz Duda Family Chair in Law and Associate Dean for Faculty Research at Notre Dame Law School. Her primary research and writing field is the law and economics of the family, and she is especially interested in empirical answers to questions addressed by law. Brinig has written more than 70 articles and book chapters and has worked with co-authors in law, economics, sociology, medicine, and public health from all over the United States and from Canada. Among her recent publications is *Family, Law, and Community: Supporting the Covenant* (University of Chicago, 2010), a sequel to her earlier book *From Contract to Covenant: Beyond the Law and Economics of the Family* (Harvard, 2000). She referees for numerous journals and presses including the *American Law and Economics Review, Journal of Legal Studies,* and Yale University Press.

Don S. Browning was the Alexander Campbell Professor Emeritus of Ethics and the Social Sciences at the Divinity School of the University of Chicago. He received his B.A. from Central Methodist College and his Ph.D. from the University of Chicago. A student of psychology, Browning had special interests in psychoanalysis, self-psychology, object-relations theory, and evolutionary psychology, and wrote on the cultural, theological, and ethical analysis of the modern psychologies. As Director of the Lilly Project on Religion, Culture, and the Family, he worked on issues pertaining to the shape and future of the postmodern family. He completed his final book, *Private Order to Public Covenant: Christian Marriage and Modern Marriage Law* (co-authored with John Witte, Jr.), just two weeks before his death. Professor Browning, an ordained minister of the Christian Church (Disciples of Christ), passed away in 2010.

Michael J. Broyde is a Professor of Law at Emory University School of Law and Projects Director at The Center for the Study of Law and Religion at Emory. Broyde received his B.A. in Biology from Yeshiva University and his J.D. from New York University where he wrote a note for the law review. He was twice ordained as a Rabbi by Yeshiva University as well, and serves as a member of the Beth Din of America, the largest Rabbinical Court in the United States. He is the author of five books and more than eighty articles.

Marcia J. Bunge is Professor of Humanities and Theology at Christ College, the Honors College of Valparaiso University (Valparaiso, Indiana); Director of the Child in Religion and Ethics Project; and the University's W.C. Dickmeyer Professor. Bunge received her B.A. in English and Music from St. Olaf College and her M.A. and Ph.D. from the University of Chicago. She is the translator and editor of a selection of writings by J. G. Herder entitled *Against Pure Reason: Writings on History, Language, and Religion* (Fortress, 1993). Her primary area of research is religious understandings of children and childhood, and she has edited and contributed to four volumes on the subject: *The Child in Christian Thought* (Eerdmans, 2001); *The Child in the Bible* (Eerdmans, 2008), co-edited with Terence Fretheim and Beverly Roberts Gaventa; *Children and Childhood in World Religions: Primary Sources and Texts* (Rutgers, 2009), co-edited with Don S. Browning; and *Children, Childhood, and Religious Ethics: Jewish, Christian, and Muslim Perspectives* (forthcoming, Cambridge University Press).

Robyn Fivush received her Ph.D. from the Graduate Center of The City University of New York in 1983 and was a Postdoctoral Fellow at the Center for

Human Information Processing, University of California at San Diego, from 1982 to 1984. She joined the Emory faculty in 1984 where she is also a core faculty member of the Emory Center for Myth and Ritual in American Life, associated faculty with the Department of Women's Studies and a Senior Fellow in the Center for the Study of Law and Religion. Her research focuses on early memory with an emphasis on the social construction of autobiographical memory and the relations among memory, narrative, identity, trauma, and coping. She has published over 100 books, book chapters, and articles.

T. Jeremy Gunn is an Associate Professor of International Studies at Al Akhawayn University in Morocco. He received his Ph.D. from Harvard University and his J.D. from Boston University (*magna cum laude*). He is the Senior Fellow for Religion and Human Rights at the Center for the Study of Law and Religion at Emory University and a member of the Advisory Council on Freedom of Religion and Belief of the Organization for Security and Cooperation in Europe (OSCE). His prior positions have included those of Director of the Program on Freedom of Religion and Belief at the American Civil Liberties Union, Director of Research for the U.S. Commission on International Religious Freedom, Senior Fellow at the U.S. Institute of Peace (seconded to the U.S. Department of State), and an attorney at Covington & Burling in Washington, DC. His dissertation was published as *A Standard for Repair: The Establishment Clause, Equality, and Natural Rights* (1992). Among his other works is *Spiritual Weapons: The Cold War and the Forging of an American National Religion* (Praeger, 2009).

Timothy P. Jackson is Professor of Christian Ethics at The Candler School of Theology at Emory University in Atlanta, Georgia, and a Senior Fellow at The Center for the Study of Law and Religion at Emory. A native of Louisville, Kentucky, Jackson received his B.A. in Philosophy from Princeton and his Ph.D. in Philosophy and Religious Studies from Yale. He is the author of *Love Disconsoled: Meditations on Christian Charity* (Cambridge, 1999) and *The Priority of Love: Christian Charity and Social Justice* (Princeton, 2003); he edited and contributed to *The Morality of Adoption: Social-Psychological, Theological, and Legal Perspectives* (Eerdmans, 2005). His current research and teaching interests are in biomedical ethics and political theory.

Heather M. Johnson is an Associate in the Antitrust practice of Cleary Gottlieb Steen & Hamilton LLP. Prior to joining Cleary, Ms. Johnson served as a law clerk to the Honorable Edward E. Carnes on the United States Court of Appeals for the Eleventh Circuit. She received a J.D. degree, with honors, Order of the Coif, from Emory University School of Law in 2005 and an M.T.S. degree from Candler School of Theology in the same year. She received an undergraduate degree, with highest honors, from Baldwin-Wallace College in 2001.

Rana R. Lehr-Lehnardt is Visiting Associate Professor of Law, University of Missouri — Kansas City School of Law. She teaches International Human Rights Law, Global Legal Systems, Introduction to American Law and Lawyering Processes, Multicultural Lawyering, and Spanish for Lawyers. She is the author of "Treat Your Women Well: Comparisons and Lessons from an Imperfect Example Across the Waters," 26 S. Ill. U.L.J. 403 (2002); and "Comment, One Small Step for Women: Female-Friendly Provisions in the International Criminal Court," 16 BYU J. Pub. L. 317 (2002).

Annette Mahoney is a Professor of Psychology at Bowling Green State University. She obtained a dual B.A. degree in Religious Studies and Psychology from Rice University and a Ph.D. in Clinical Psychology from the University of Houston. Her scientific work on roles that religion and spirituality play for marriage, parenting, and divorce has appeared in the *Journal of Marriage and Family, Journal of Family Psychology, Journal of Child Clinical Psychology, The International Journal of the Psychology of Religion,* and *Review of Religious Research,* among other outlets. She has received funding from the Templeton Foundation, Fetzer Foundation, and Ohio Department of Mental Health. She is also a licensed and practicing clinical psychologist.

Steven L. Nock was Commonwealth Professor, Professor of Sociology, and Director of the Marriage Matters project at the University of Virginia. He earned his B.A. from the University of Richmond and his Ph.D. from the University of Massachusetts-Amherst. He focused on the intersection of social science and public policy concerning households and families in America. Specifically, he investigated issues of privacy, unmarried fatherhood, cohabitation, commitment, divorce, and marriage. His book, *Marriage in Men's Lives,* won the William J. Good Book Award from the American Sociological Association for the most outstanding contribution to family scholarship in 1999. Professor Nock passed away in 2008.

Richard R. Osmer is the Thomas W. Synnott Professor of Christian Education at Princeton Theological Seminary. He holds a B.A. from the University of North Carolina, Chapel Hill, an M.Div. from Yale University Divinity School, and a Ph.D. from Emory University. An ordained minister in the Presbyterian Church (U.S.A.), Osmer is the author of several books, including *Practical Theology: An Introduction* (2008), *The Teaching Ministry of Congregations* (2007), *Confirmation: Presbyterian Practices in Ecumenical Perspective* (1996), *Teaching for Faith* (1992), and *A Teachable Spirit* (1990). A leading voice in practical theology and religious education, he is the former editor of the *International Journal of Practical Theology* and past president of the Association of Practical Theology.

Steven Ozment is McLean Professor of Ancient and Modern History at Harvard University. He has taught Western Civilization at Yale, Stanford, and Harvard. He is the author of thirteen books. *The Age of Reform, 1250-1550* (1980) won the Schaff History Prize and was nominated for the 1981 National Book Award. Five of his books have been selections of the History Book Club: *Magdalena and Balthasar: An Intimate Portrait of Life in Sixteenth Century Europe* (1986), *Three Behaim Boys: Growing Up in Early Modern Germany* (1900), *Protestants: The Birth of a Revolution* (1992), *The Bürgermeister's Daughter: Scandal in A Sixteenth Century German Town* (1996), and *Flesh and Spirit: Private Life in Early Modern Germany* (1999). His most recent book is *A Mighty Fortress: A New History of the German People* (2004). His biographical study of German artist Lucas Cranach, the Elder, and the Lutheran Reformation — *The Serpent and the Lamb: How a Painter and a Monk Changed the World* — is forthcoming from Yale University Press.

Kenneth I. Pargament is Professor of Psychology in the Department of Psychology at Bowling Green State University. He received his Ph.D. in clinical psychology from the University of Maryland and completed a post-doctoral fellowship in psychiatric epidemiology at Johns Hopkins School of Public Health. He has published over 175 articles. He is author of *The Psychology of Religion and Coping: Theory, Research, Practice* (Guilford, 1997) and *Spiritually Integrated Psychotherapy: Understanding and Addressing the Sacred* (Guilford, 2007). He is also Editor-in-Chief of the forthcoming two-volume *APA Handbook of Psychology, Religion, and Spirituality* (APA Press).

Stephen G. Post, Ph.D., is Professor of Preventive Medicine, Head of the Division of Medicine in Society, and Director of the Center for Medical Humanities, Compassionate Care and Bioethics at Stony Brook University School of Medicine. He received his Ph.D. from the University of Chicago

Divinity School and is Founder and President of the Institute for Research on Unlimited Love (www.unlimitedloveresearch.com). His most recent book is *The Hidden Gifts of Helping Others* (Jossey-Bass/Wiley, 2011).

Charles J. Reid Jr. is Professor of Law at the University of St. Thomas in Minnesota. He has degrees in civil and canon law from the Catholic University of America and a Ph.D. in medieval history from Cornell University. He is the author of *Power Over the Body, Equality in the Family: Rights and Domestic Relations in Medieval Canon Law* (Eerdmans, 2004). He is also the author of numerous articles and studies on the history of family and domestic relations.

Eugene C. Roehlkepartain is vice president of Search Institute, a Minneapolis-based nonprofit organization that provides catalytic leadership, breakthrough knowledge, and innovative resources to advance the health of children, youth, families, and communities. Among his recent books are *The Handbook of Spiritual Development in Childhood and Adolescence* (Sage, 2006; lead editor) and *Nurturing Child and Adolescent Spirituality: Perspectives from the World's Religious Traditions* (Rowman and Littlefield, 2006; co-editor). He is currently pursuing his doctorate in Education, Curriculum, and Instruction from the University of Minnesota, with a specialization in family, youth, and community.

Cynthia Willett, Ph.D. (Pennsylvania State University), is Professor of Philosophy at Emory University. Her publications include *Maternal Ethics and Other Slave Moralities* (Routledge, 1995); *The Soul of Justice: Racial Hubris and Social Bonds* (Cornell, 2001); and *Irony in the Age of Empire: Comic Perspectives on Freedom and Democracy* (Indiana University Press, 2008). She teaches courses in social and political ethics.

John Witte, Jr., J.D. (Harvard), is Jonas Robitscher Professor of Law, Alonzo L. McDonald Distinguished Professor, and Director of the Center for the Study of Law and Religion Center at Emory University. A specialist in legal history, marriage law, and religious liberty, he has published 180 articles, 11 journal symposia, and 24 books — including *Law and Protestantism: The Legal Teachings of the Lutheran Reformation* (Cambridge, 2002); *Sex, Marriage and Family Life in John Calvin's Geneva* (Eerdmans, 2005); *The Reformation of Rights: Law, Religion, and Human Rights in Early Modern Calvinism* (Cambridge, 2007); *The Sins of the Fathers: The Law and Theology of Illegitimacy Reconsidered* (Cambridge, 2009); *Religion and the American Constitutional Experiment* (3rd ed., Westview, 2010).

Index

Abortion, 1n., 142-75, 186, 229, 358
Abuse, x-xi, xvi, xx, xxii-xxiii, 9, 13, 19, 52, 64, 94, 119, 159, 198, 214-15, 221, 241, 279, 283-84, 289, 290n., 301, 307n., 315, 323-24, 332, 334-35
Adam, 142, 199-200, 208-13
Aderet (Rabbi Solomon ben Abraham Aderet), 265n., 267-69, 273-75
Adoption, xii, xviii, 2, 15, 146n., 179n., 193, 230n., 254, 258, 265n., 278n., 292, 297n., 302, 304, 306n., 319n., 321, 324, 333-35, 343-45, 359
Adult(s), xvi-xvii, xxi-xxii, xxiv, 2, 4, 6, 10, 13-14, 19-22, 25, 35-41
Agape, xviii, xx, 6, 8-14, 278n., 319
Alberti, Leon Batista, 128-29, 139
Alexander, Elizabeth, xix
Altruism, xiv, xxi, xxiv, 15, 42, 187-94, 226, 318-19, 323n., 325-26, 328, 332, 333n.
Amato, Paul, 339-40
Annan, Kofi, 168
Anxiety, xv-xvi, 61, 77, 81, 83, 127, 213, 278n., 296, 336n.
Aquinas, Thomas, 7, 210, 354, 366, 369
Aries, Philippe, 99-100, 282n.
Aristotle, 7, 11, 145n., 183-87, 191-92, 320, 350-51, 354, 366, 369
Arthur, Timothy Shay, 122-24, 141
Athenagoras, 147
Augustine, Charles, 148-49
Augustine, Saint, 149, 210-16, 220-21, 366
Autonomy, 4-5, 8, 13, 55, 82, 161n., 180, 183-85, 188, 190, 194-95, 282, 317, 323n., 324, 333n., 345-46, 353, 355, 356n., 359

Baby, babies, xiv-xvi, xxiii, 5, 39, 97, 101n., 167n., 216, 276, 311, 360
Barnard, John, 136, 141
Barth, Karl, xviii, 244-45
Batt, Barthelemy, 122, 130n., 131n., 139
Baxter, Richard, 116-18, 126n., 140
Becker, Gary, 318-19, 325, 367
Becon, Thomas, 116-23, 141
Behaim, Stephen Carl, 96-97
Benedict XVI, Pope, 142-75, 319n.
Benevolence, 11, 188
Benson, Joseph, 136, 141
Benson, Peter L., 12, 86, 200n., 278n.
Bernadette, Saint, 165
Berry, Wendell, 238
Bible, 58, 62-65, 114, 117, 128, 204-7, 212n., 227-47, 256n.

Blackstone, William, 113-14, 122, 284n., 286-87, 293, 300-301, 359
Block, J. H., 341
Blum, Lawrence, 7
Boff, Leonardo, 238
Bogle, April, xi
Booth, Alan, 326n., 339
Bradford, John, 127-28, 139
Brennan, Patrick M., xii, 113n., 231n.
Bretherton, Inge, 87, 89, 340
Brewer, David Josiah, Justice, 300
Brinig, Margaret, 14-15, 83, 349-52, 365-72
Brother(s), brotherly, 35, 103, 117-18, 141, 162, 166, 216, 245, 265n., 278, 327
Brown, William, 246
Browning, Don S., v, 15, 198n., 321n.
Broyde, Michael J., 14
Brunfels, Otto, 106
Bryan, Kathryn, xxv
Bullinger, Heinrich, 123, 130-32, 139, 141
Bunge, Marcia J., 1n., 14, 32, 42, 125n.
Bush, George W., President, 163n., 344
Bushnell, Horace, 141, 234-35

Calvin, John, 130n., 211-16, 220-21, 235
Calvinus, Arminius, 136, 141
Carbone, June, 349-69
Cardozo, Benjamin N., Justice, 300-301
Care, caring, xi, xiv-xxiv, 2, 4-5, 8, 13-15, 20-21, 25-28, 31, 35, 38-39, 41-45, 52, 60, 63, 69, 75, 79, 82-86, 103, 106n., 121-28, 138, 143, 150-57, 160, 165-72, 179n., 181-88, 191-96, 215, 222-23, 226, 231, 233n., 234-39, 242-46, 250, 254, 258, 260n., 271, 275-79, 283, 286, 289-90, 294-304, 307n., 309, 311, 316, 318, 319n., 323-36, 343-45, 347-72
Carlson, Cindy, 38
Cassirer, Ernst, 206
Channing, William Ellery, 117n., 119-23, 141
Charity, 3, 9, 11-12, 136-37, 157, 167n., 183, 187, 192, 329
Charles I of Spain, 104
Cherlin, Andrew, 348n., 358
Chikatilo, Andrei, 2
Christianity, Christians, xiii, xvii-xviii, xx, 1n., 3, 5, 9, 11, 13-14, 20, 42, 48, 62-63, 65-69, 98, 103, 106, 113-41, 146-47, 150-52, 163n., 184n., 197-225, 226-50, 255-56, 276n., 351-52, 357, 365-66, 371
Chrysostom, John, 236
Church(es), xviii, xx, 1, 3, 48-49, 53, 55, 63, 96, 98, 102, 108, 112-14, 117-20, 127, 130, 135-37, 140, 142-75, 188, 198-210, 221, 225-50, 320, 326-28, 339-40, 371, 374
Coleman, James, 200, 320n., 321n., 349
Common good, 3, 26, 135, 138, 228-33, 238, 246, 249
Compassion, xiii-xviii, xxiii, 3, 26, 49, 52, 60, 64-68, 129, 136, 162, 187-89, 196, 226, 231, 234-35, 242, 245, 249
Conscience, xvi, 84, 86, 89, 94, 117, 123, 126, 162, 170, 213, 241, 289, 320n., 323n.
Cook, Tennessee Celeste, 134-35, 141
Cooperation, xx, 180, 183-94, 319n., 325n., 362, 370
Cotton, Nathaniel, 131, 141
Courage, xiv, 131
Cover, Robert, 254-56
Cranach, Lucas the Elder, 104-5
Cranmer, Thomas, 116
Crime, criminal(s), xiv, 103n., 127, 129, 148-50, 164, 194-95, 279, 283-90, 324
Cross, the, 12, 119, 143
Cruelty, x, 2, 11, 14, 123, 147, 156, 283, 336n.
Csikszentmihalyi, M., 20, 30-31, 43, 45
Cyprian, 210

Damon, W., 23-24, 42-43
Dawes, Robyn, 325
Deane, Samuel, 136, 141
Death, 6n., 83, 97, 102, 118-19, 128, 143, 147n., 152, 201, 207-8, 213-14, 220, 226, 245, 253, 260n., 265, 271, 274-76, 281, 290, 296, 302, 307n., 334-35, 368
DeBoer, D. D. D., 340
Dekovic, M., 341

Delinquency, delinquent(s), xi-xvi, 50, 70, 262, 304, 337
De Manneville, Mrs., 293-96
Democracy, 11, 31, 160, 288, 309n.
Dependency, (in)dependence, 5, 8, 11, 13, 33, 77, 81, 103, 120, 122-24, 137-38, 151, 175, 180-95, 223, 243, 319, 323n., 325, 332-37, 341, 354-59, 364, 369
Devil, the, 95, 102, 213
de Vitoria, Francisco, 174
Dignity, 2-3, 5, 8, 143n., 155n., 164-67, 172-75, 232, 242, 308, 310
Dillon, Michele, xx-xxi, xxiv
Divorce, 14, 50, 253, 259n., 260n., 262-63, 271, 275, 295-96, 311, 314n., 321-24, 332-37, 340, 344-45, 347, 353-58, 364-71
Dixon, Henry, 118n., 137, 141
Dorff, Elliot, 239n., 243
Durkheim, Émile, 366
Duties, x-xi, 1-3, 13-15, 97, 113-41, 150, 173-74, 179, 186, 191, 193n., 231, 234, 239, 242-50, 254-58, 266-75, 286-88, 298, 307n., 325, 344
Dworkin, Ronald, 4
Dylan, Bob, xxiii

Edelman, Marian Wright, 35, 43
Edwards, Jonathan, 197, 202, 225
Eisenberg, Nancy, xix, xxiv, 319n., 323n.
Ellison, Eliza, xi
Elster, Jon, 325
Empathy, xi, xv-xvi, 2, 84, 323n., 327
Encouragement, xix, xxi, 20, 30, 40, 55, 64-65, 116-19, 125, 130-33, 159, 165n., 206, 217, 222-23, 236-39, 249, 291, 305, 308-9, 333, 344, 370
Engels, R. C. M. E., 341
England, Paula, 325
Equality, 2-3, 5-9, 13, 25, 124n., 134-35, 141, 147n., 150, 153, 169n., 180n., 181n., 184, 188, 194, 200n., 214, 223, 228, 260n., 272, 298, 310n., 321n., 323n., 353-59, 370-71
Erasmus, Desiderius, 99, 106, 108, 121, 139
Erikson, Erik, 350-52
Eros, 6-12, 14, 142, 278n.
Ertman, Martha M., 364
Ethics, xi-xii, xiv, 48, 61-62, 69, 111, 124, 133, 161, 175, 182-86, 189, 193-94, 218, 228-30, 233n., 239n., 254n., 258n., 344n., 348n., 351-54, 362-64, 370-71
Euthanasia, 151-52
Eve, 132, 208, 210-12
Evil, xviii, 3, 11, 14, 61, 103, 117, 120-21, 127-28, 148n., 159n., 161-63, 172, 206-25, 236
Ezekiel, 245

Faith, faithful, xiii, xvi-xxiii, 3, 6n., 26, 52-55, 59-60, 65-70, 98-99, 111, 118n., 126, 139-40, 143, 170n., 181, 197, 200-2011, 220-25, 226-50, 255, 275, 317, 323
Falci, Christina, 340n., 342
Father(s), xv-xviii, 2, 8, 11-15, 53-55, 72, 74, 82-84, 89-90, 93n., 95, 100n., 101-12, 113-14, 117-18, 122-38, 147, 150, 159, 163n., 165n., 168-73, 202, 220, 228, 232-33, 242, 245, 247n., 259-75, 281-90, 293, 301, 309-11, 316, 327-29, 334-45, 354-71
Fear, xvi, 21-22, 36, 65-66, 78-79, 95, 100, 106n., 107, 115-16, 120, 126-29, 131, 149, 153, 163, 169, 197, 223, 246, 250, 257, 336n.
Feminism, 9, 132, 134, 181, 184, 194, 217, 230, 276n., 324n., 325n., 349, 353, 357, 370
Fetus(es), 5, 95, 100-101, 144-50
Fineman, Martha, 180n., 349-70
Fivush, Robyn, 13, 278n., 352
Flanagan, Father, 2
Fleetwood, William, 117n., 119, 140
Floyd, K., 341
Francis of Assisi, Saint, 238
Francke, August Hermann, 233, 238-39
Frank, Sebastian, 99
Franklin, Aretha, 276
Frederick, John, 104
Frederick the Wise, 104-5
Free, freedom, x, xiv, xx, xxiii-xxiv, 2, 5, 8, 13, 19, 31, 97, 102, 104-6, 115, 120,

132-35, 143, 145n., 155n., 174, 180-83, 191, 207-8, 212-14, 216n., 220, 264, 310n., 331, 359, 366, 368
Friend, friendship, xv, xix-xx, 7-8, 11-12, 31, 35-36, 70, 71-72, 80, 93, 101, 110, 121, 136, 147, 169, 190-92, 240, 245, 247, 278, 323, 327-30, 339, 341, 355, 364-65, 371n.
Furstenberg, Frank, 21, 43, 348n., 358

Gardner, Howard, 224
Gender, 24, 28, 51, 72, 74, 81-84, 86-90, 100, 131-35, 182n., 227, 250, 282n., 324-26, 333n.
Gilligan, Carol, 82, 89, 354
God, xiii-xviii, 1, 5, 8-11, 15, 33, 47, 49, 52-64, 69, 95-96, 100, 107, 114-28, 131, 136-40, 142, 144, 150, 154-57, 165, 173-75, 197-225, 226-50, 254, 257, 275n., 276, 318-20, 332-33, 351, 365-66, 371
Goebbels, Joseph, 2
Goethe, Wolfgang von, 111
Golden Rule, xiv, xix, 351-52
Golding, William, 1
Goll, Richard, 38
Golombek, Silvia Blitzer, 35, 43
Goode, William, 348n., 358
Goodness, xv, xvii, xxiii, 3, 132, 152, 155, 211-12, 224, 238-39
Gouge, William, 114, 129, 139
Grace, xiv, xviii, 35, 60, 62, 96, 110, 126, 137, 140, 152, 197, 207, 220, 224n.
Gratian, 144
Gregory of Nazianzus, 210
Gregory of Nyssa, 210
Guilt, xiv, 145, 164, 194, 197, 214, 216-17, 220-22, 245, 283, 285, 290n., 295
Gunn, T. Jeremy, 14, 320n., 321n.

Hadaya, Ovadia, Rabbi, 262
Halevi, Mordecai ben Judah, Rabbi, 271
Hall, Douglas John, 201
Handicap, 153, 166-67
Hanson, Gary, 322
Happiness, happy, xv, xx, xxii-xxiii, 9, 12, 52, 59-60, 63-64, 104, 119, 121, 123, 128, 151, 158, 188, 219, 297, 303-4, 317, 319, 321n., 325, 335, 341
Hate, hatred, xvi, xviii, xx, xxiii, 41, 65, 138, 159, 207, 245
Health, healthcare, x, xvi, xix-xxiv, 2, 5, 19, 22-28, 31, 35, 39, 42-43, 51, 58-59, 63-64, 70, 77, 81, 95, 143, 147, 149-51, 162n., 165-72, 180, 249, 290, 293-94, 299, 303, 316, 318, 326, 330n., 336n., 340, 343-44, 366
Hedonism, xxiii, 11, 35
Henry of Ghent, 150
Henry of Navarre, 145
Hersch, Patricia, 22, 43
Hillel, Rabbi, 351
Hippolytus, 209
Hobbes, Thomas, 99, 151, 188
Holiness, holy, xviii, 5, 103-4, 132, 145n., 155-75, 202-3, 220-22, 234-35, 237, 288n.
Homosexuality, 186, 255n., 321
Hope, xvii-xviii, xxii-xxiii, 21, 28, 31, 35, 40-41, 48, 51-56, 106, 155, 158, 164n., 173-74, 202, 230n., 246-47, 305

Illegitimacy, xi, 4, 108
Ill, illness, xiii, 122, 165, 290, 294, 317n.
Imagination, xi, 100, 156, 198, 200, 230n.
Infanticide, xi, 5, 146n., 147n., 150
Innocence, innocent, xi, xiii, 1, 10, 97, 104, 119, 149-56, 159n., 161-64, 214-16, 219, 225, 314n.
Interest(s), x-xi, xiv, 3-7, 14-15, 27, 30-32, 37, 69, 82, 130, 171n., 189-90, 196, 222-23, 236, 254, 258-76, 277-316, 319n., 325n., 334, 337, 347-72
Isaac, 248
Islam, 63, 66, 69, 163n.

Jackson, Timothy P., xii, 230n., 254n.
Jacob ben Asher, Rabbi, 264, 256n., 260n., 264
James, William, xvii
Jefferson, Thomas, 151
Jesus Christ, xviii, xx, 1-2, 8-12, 57, 62, 119, 142-43, 152, 156, 169, 202-4, 207-9,

220-22, 226-27, 240-41, 245, 248, 255n., 278n., 288n.
Jews, Judaism, xiv, 3, 5, 14, 48, 63, 66, 69, 208-9, 239, 243, 253-76, 323n., 351
John XXIII, Pope, 151, 165
John Paul II, Pope, 143, 152-73
Johnson, Heather M., 13
Jolie, Angelina, 2
Jone, Heribert, 148
Joseph (Father of Jesus), 169
Joy, xiii, xvi-xxii, 8, 10n., 12, 30-32, 35, 61, 71, 96, 110n., 111, 121, 131, 133, 173, 247-48
Justice, xix, 3-9, 15, 25, 31, 35, 41, 60, 113-14, 117, 129, 154-56, 161-66, 171-75, 179-96, 214-15, 227, 236, 241, 245-46, 249, 255, 293, 312n., 363
Justification, 109, 209, 284n.
Justin Martyr, 209-10

Kant, Immanuel, 5, 188, 350-51, 362, 364, 371
Kaplan, Benjamin, 98-100
Karo, Joseph, Rabbi, 253n., 256n., 265n., 270
Kegan, Robert, 350
Kent, James, Chancellor, 284n., 286-87, 293, 300-301
Keifert, Patrick, 205
Kierkegaard, Søren, 11n.
King, Linda, xi
Kingdom of heaven/God, xviii, 1, 157, 240-41
Kohlberg, Lawrence, 356
Kolde, Dietrich, 118, 126n., 127, 139

La Rochefoucauld, Francois de, 1
Laible, D., 80, 89
Law, lawyer(s), xi-xii, xxv, 3, 8, 12-15, 103n., 108-9, 113-41, 142-75, 209, 215, 227-28, 245, 253-76, 277-316, 317-46, 347-72
Lehr-Lehnardt, Rana, 14
Lerner, R. M., 21, 31, 41-45
Lewis, C. S., 7-8, 319n.
Liberal, liberalism, 3-4, 66-68, 98, 180-96, 210, 235, 238, 353-54, 357
Liberty, 5, 44, 133, 135, 151, 164, 180-83, 287-88
Lima, Moses ben Isaac, Rabbi, 264-65n., 270
Locke, John, 125, 132-34, 140, 354
Loves, the six, 6-10
Lundberg, Shelly, 322
Luther, Martin, 105, 115-18, 121-27, 139, 228, 232-44, 350n., 352n.
Lynn, Robert, 198-200

Mabit (Rabbi Moses ben Joseph di Trani), 262-63, 272
Maharashdam (Rabbi Samuel ben Moses de Medina), 263, 265n.
Maimonides, 257-60
Manhoney, Annette, 12-13, 278n., 322n., 345n.
Mann, Anita, xi
Marriage, xiii-xiv, xvii, 7n., 15, 43, 69, 88, 103-4, 106n., 108, 116n., 119, 130-32, 137, 139, 142, 149-50, 239-42, 253-54, 260, 265-71, 275n., 277n., 294, 310n., 312, 317-46, 347-72
Martino, Renato, Cardinal, 157, 161-64
Marty, Martin E., xi, 32, 44
Marx, Karl, 184-87, 192
Mary (Mother of Jesus), 169, 288n.
Mary Ellen, case of, 283
Meeus, W., 341
Meilaender, Gilbert, 7
Menius, Justus, 105-6
Meyer, David, 346n., 349
Mill, John Stuart, 188
Moltmann, Jürgen, 230n., 246-47
Moody, Eleazer, 116, 120, 141
Moralistic Therapeutic Deism (MTD), 58-65
Morman, M. T., 341
Mother(s), xv-xvi, xxii, 8, 13-15, 51, 54-55, 66, 68, 71-90, 93-112, 113-41, 144-51, 157, 168-69, 216, 224, 228, 233, 242, 259-76, 277-316, 317-46, 353-72

Narcissism, xxi, 3
Needs, x-xi, 2, 5, 9, 19, 35-36, 41, 60, 84-86, 100, 108, 111, 122, 125, 166, 169-70, 180, 183, 187, 195-96, 213, 217, 222-23, 236, 243, 249, 278n., 280, 295, 317n., 326-34, 348-60, 364, 371
Newbigin, Lesslie, 203, 221
New Testament, xviii, 9, 11, 14, 114, 146, 209, 212n., 220, 240, 244-45
Niebuhr, H. Richard, 224-25
Niebuhr, Reinhold, 211-14
Nietzsche, Friedrich, xvii
Nock, Steven, 14-15, 365n., 368-72
Noonan, John, 144n., 146
Norton, Caroline, 295
Nussbaum, Martha, 181n., 183-91
Nygren, Anders, 10-11

Obama, Barack, President, xix
Old Testament, Hebrew Bible, 14, 212n., 256n.
Origen, 210
Orphan(s), 13, 179-96, 273-74, 278n.
Osmer, Richard R., 13-14
Ozment, Steven, 13, 71, 233n.

Page, Timothy, 340
Pain, 61-64, 122, 127-28, 157, 219, 248
Palmer, Parker, 36, 44
Pargament, Ken, 12-13, 278n.
Paterfamilias, x, 135, 281-82
Patience, xviii, 71, 119, 122, 131
Patriarchy, 97, 99, 102, 281, 371
Paul VI, Pope, 142-43, 154, 157, 166
Paul, Saint, 201-4, 208-9
Peace, peaceful, xviii, xxiii, 25, 31, 98, 110, 127, 154-66, 172-75, 248
Percy, Walker, 35
Peterson, Eugene, 204-5
Philia, 6-12, 278n.
Phillips, Samuel, 117, 129, 135, 141
Pius XII, Pope, 156-57, 169-70
Pittman, Karen, 19, 22-23, 42-44
Plato, Platonism, 6-7, 216
Platzeck, Mathias, 111
Pollak, Robert A., 322
Poor, poverty, xi, xiii, 19, 26, 41, 52, 118-23, 127, 137, 143, 154n., 156, 159, 166n., 169n., 191, 199, 230n., 236, 239, 329, 343, 345
Posner, Richard, 325, 367
Post, Stephen G., xi, xxv
Potential(s), 5, 9, 21, 23, 29-30, 40, 58, 60-61, 172, 189, 206, 219, 223, 351-52
Pratt, M. W., 86-87, 89
Pregnancy, xvi, xx, xxiv, 19, 95, 100-101, 109, 144n., 145-47, 214, 262
Primal sympathy, 6, 9, 11
Prodigal Son, xviii
Pufendorf, Samuel, 151

Race, racism, 19, 24, 28, 36, 51, 154, 181, 194, 207, 212, 219, 227, 248, 332, 335-36, 342, 362, 369
Radvaz (Rabbi David ben Solomon ibn Avi Zimra), 262, 265n., 271n.
Rama (Rabbi Moses Isserles), 264n., 270-73
Rape, xi
R. Asher (Rabbi Asher ben Yehiel), 266-75
Ratcliff, D., 68-69
Rauschenbusch, Walter, 210
Rawls, John, 4, 181n., 182-87, 362
Regan, Milton, 318, 325, 372n.
Reid, Charles J., Jr., 13, 124
Religion, xi-xii, xv, xix, xxv, 5, 32, 44, 47-70, 98-99, 111, 116n., 117, 141, 145, 152n., 175, 180, 199-212, 218n., 229n., 230n., 234-35, 255n., 276, 320-21, 337, 362, 366, 372
Reproduction, 87, 143, 145n., 174, 229, 348
Ricoeur, Paul, 212n., 213-14, 350n., 351
Right to life, 5, 13, 142-75, 254
Roback-Morse, Jennifer, 320
Rockwell, Norman, xix
Roehlkepartain, Eugene C., 12
Rousseau, Jean-Jacques, 125, 133-35, 141

Sacred, xvii, 1, 13, 32-33, 47-70, 94, 143,

150-52, 155n., 159n., 165, 168, 174, 200n., 228-36, 285
Sadness, xvi-xvii, 52, 132, 255-56, 336n.
Saiman, Chaim N., 255
Salvation, 60, 62, 145n., 221, 230
Sanctity, 3, 5, 9, 143, 217
Sarah, 247
Scheurl family, 101-4, 110n.
Schleiermacher, Friedrich, 210, 235, 240-41
School, schooling, xv-xxiii, 3, 11-12, 19-43, 47, 68, 72-90, 96-99, 108, 114-21, 130-41, 157-58, 166n., 167, 170, 179, 192, 197-206, 221-25, 236-39, 246-49, 254-55, 262-63, 269n., 287-88, 294, 323n., 336n., 340-42, 347
Self-love *(amor sui),* 6, 9, 11
Self-sacrifice, 3, 9, 60, 371
Seligman, M. E. P., 20, 30, 45
Sen, Amartya, 183
Sendler, Irena, 2
Severus, Alexander, Emperor, 281
Servetus, 99, 215
Sex, sexism, xi, 7, 11, 19, 21, 27, 36, 50, 52, 59, 64, 83, 87-89, 103, 130n., 170, 181, 198, 216-18, 229, 239-40, 254n., 255n., 260n., 283, 298, 321-26, 328, 341n., 342-44, 348, 353-72
Shakespeare, William, 7n.
Shame, 11, 96, 103, 127, 131-32
Sibling(s), 89, 103, 108, 116, 269, 294, 311, 328-38, 368
Sin, 13-14, 62, 96, 102-3, 107, 119, 127, 132, 143, 145n., 148n., 197-225 (original sin), 229-30, 241, 245
Singer, Peter, 5
Singer, Peter W., 157-58
Sister(s), 35, 106, 117, 134, 141, 162, 166, 288n., 327
Smith, A. M., 71, 90
Smith, C., 58-70
Smith, Susan, 2
Solomon, King, 275n., 276
Sorokin, Pitirim, xiii-xv, xxiii-xxiv
St. John-Stevas, Norman, 151-52
Storge, 6, 8, 14, 278n.
Suffering, xvii, 6, 11, 53, 55, 61-64, 99, 119, 123, 127, 131, 138, 143, 155-68, 215, 225, 238, 302
Suicide, xxiii, 9, 27, 50, 151-52
Sympathy, 6, 9, 11, 94, 129, 133, 147n., 185-96, 363

Talmud(s), talmudic, 253-76
Taylor, Charles, 67
Taylor, Jeremy, 125, 140
Tertullian, 146-47, 210
Theodore of Mopsuestia, 210
Tooley, Michael, 5
Torah, 255n., 260n., 266n., 274n., 275n.
Trujillo, Alfonso Lopez, Cardinal, 167
Trust, xvi-xvii, 15, 39, 84-86, 95, 115, 126, 150, 213, 244, 320n., 321n., 327-33, 343, 367
Turner, Tina, 253n., 276
Twenge, Jean, xxi, xxiv

United Nations, 2, 5, 14, 40, 157, 160-61, 164n., 167-74, 277, 291, 302-4, 307-10
Utility, utilitarianism, 190, 318-19, 325, 351

Vanier, Jean, xxii
Vaughn, B. E., 341
Violence, xi, xvii, xxi-xxiii, 19-21, 26, 120, 127, 148n., 154, 158-59, 164, 172, 180n., 335, 361
Virtue(s), xii, 3-11, 49, 66, 95, 107, 112, 115, 121n., 132-36, 139, 182-83, 197
Vives, Juan Luis, 132, 139

Waddell, Glen R., 340-41
Wadsworth, Benjamin, 118n., 123, 140
Walker, Rev. John, xx
Wallerstein, Judith, 321-22
War, 41, 99, 103-4, 143, 152-74, 192n., 214, 224-25
Washington, George, President, 136
Weed, Enos, 133-35, 141
Weinsberg, Hermann von, 108-10
Wesley, John, 135-36
Wheeler, Amy, xi

Wiley, Tatha, 210
Willett, Cynthia, 13
Williams, Wayne, 2
Wilson, James Q., 35, 46
Wink, Paul, xx-xxi, xxxiv
Winton, Sir Nicholas, 2
Wisdom, xi, xiv, xviii, 4, 37, 101, 112, 120, 132, 227n., 235, 240, 246-49, 350-71
Witte, John, Jr., xxv, 13, 97n., 254n., 275n., 366n., 371n.
Wordsworth, William, 1, 6, 10
Wyclif, John, 114, 127, 139

Young, Iris Marion, 195
Yust, K. M., 68, 70, 200n., 230n.

Zechariah, 247n., 248